T0350518

INVESTMENT-CENTRIC PROJECT MANAGEMENT

Advanced Strategies for Developing and
Executing Successful Capital Projects

STEVEN JAMES KEAYS

M.A.Sc., P.Eng.

Copyright © 2017 by Steven Keays

ISBN-13: 978-1-60427-142-3

Printed and bound in the U.S.A. Printed on acid-free paper.

10 9 8 7 6 5 4 3 2 1

Library of Congress Cataloging-in-Publication Data

Names: Keays, Steven, 1963– author.
Title: Investment-centric project management : advanced strategies for
  developing and executing successful capital projects / by Steven Keays.
Description: Plantation, FL : J. Ross Publishing, [2017] | Includes
  bibliographical references and index.
Identifiers: LCCN 2017023922 | ISBN 9781604271423 (hardcover : alk. paper)
Subjects: LCSH: Project management. | Project management—Finance. |
  Investments. | Capital investments.
Classification: LCC HD69.P75 K425 2017 | DDC 658.15/2—dc23 LC record
available at https://lccn.loc.gov/2017023922

Phone: (954) 727-9333
Fax: (561) 892-0700
Web: www.jrosspub.com

CONTENTS

PREFACE

"It is not even wrong." Wolfgang Pauli's
response to a student's research paper.

This book began in October 2014, nearly thirty years after I first became acquainted with the practice of project management. Back in 1985, I graduated from the Royal Military College of Canada (the equivalent of West Point in the U.S. and the Royal Military Academy at Sandhurst in the UK) and joined the Canadian Armed Forces as an aerospace engineering officer on the then-new CF-18 aircraft fleet implementation program. Within a week of starting my tour of duty, project management infiltrated a significant portion of my functions. Things like planning, execution strategies, budgets, schedules, change control, crisis resolution, work allocation, contractor oversight, and configuration management entered my vernacular under the auspices of military concepts. As I later joined the corporate world in 1989, managing projects became an organic extension of that first career in uniform. Decades later, project management continues to anchor my professional activities and those of NAIAD Company Ltd., the consulting firm that I founded in 2000. Over the years, I have managed several projects from the aerospace, defense, industrial, manufacturing, and oil and gas sectors. Some were small in scale and budget (less than $500K), while others breached the billion-dollar threshold. In one instance, the project concerned the design of a test furnace destined for the International Space Station. In another case, I managed the construction of an industrial pipe coating facility. My assignments have been tied to the energy sector, such as TransCanada's 650 km-long gas pipeline transporting five billion cubic feet of gas per day; Suncor's Fort Hills secondary extraction plant producing 166,000 barrels of oil per day; and Shell's LNG (liquefied natural gas) plant in Kitimat, British Columbia, rated at 26 million tons per year, to name a few salient examples. Each and every time, complexity became inevitable—spawned in part by the globalization of delivery strategies. In the process, I acquired an expertise in global execution strategies, construction and modularization, engineering delivery, and cross-cultural project management.

Over time, I also began to notice an unsettling disconnect between the expected outcomes promised by formal project management principles and the frequent occurrences of budget and schedule transgressions. I have managed projects that were structured by their owners in strict adherence to the practices prescribed by the Project Management Institute, yet failed utterly in terms of cost overruns, busted timelines, and crippled plant performance. This disconnect is not limited to the energy sector, but reverberates across industries and project scales alike. Global statistics, for example, record that over 65% of $500M projects fail, despite the professionalization of their execution. If professionalized project management is the right way of running expansive projects, why do so many still fail?

This book posits that the current interpretation of traditional project management in terms of plans, processes, and procedures, cannot, in fact, deliver its purported guarantee of success. The failure record simply overwhelms the proposition to the point of nullifying it. Many believe that the failure of projects is rooted in their teams' failure to execute according to plan. Granted, success will not ensue without cogent plans, proficient processes, and effective procedures. But these elements are only a means to an end, rather than being the end for which they are too often confused. The reality is that there is more, much more to project management than plans, processes, and procedures. A new paradigm is required, built on a new foundation that is itself erected upon a different perspective. What is that perspective? The true purpose of a project is to realize an asset that maximizes returns to its shareholders over its economic life. The project is merely the means to that end, and an investment vehicle to transform a concept into a physical operation that generates revenues and profits for its owners. This recasting also entails a dramatically different paradigm shift of the meaning of project management. It is no longer limited to the commonly accepted definition but broadened into three separate but intertwined mandates: it is an organization, it is a business, and it is a relationship nexus. The paradigm at the core of this book has a name: investment-centric project management.

CHAPTER SUMMARIES

PART 1—WHY

Part 1 addresses the reasons for redefining the practice of project management through the lenses of terminology, leadership, theory, interactions, and decision making.

Chapter 1 introduces the premise that the current state of the art in project management is adequate as a foundation to oversee the development of projects, but cannot be considered a complete theory considering the persistence of high failure rates seen worldwide in industrial initiatives large and small. The text also presents the reader with a new perspective on the objective of a project: to realize a revenue-generating asset that will deliver sustained investment returns to its shareholders over the economic life of the asset.

Chapter 2 establishes the foundational principles of project management, erected upon a new definition for projects and project management. It recasts project management as a corporate endeavor that is executed along three axes: organization, business, and relationship. It sets the underlying perspective of the discussion from the owners. The text also introduces the concept of *valunomy* as the metric from which economic decisions are made.

Chapter 3 highlights the importance of leadership to the success or failure of a project. Leadership is explored from the organizational and relationship viewpoints, across a spectrum of five leadership archetypes. It recommends what archetype is best suited to what project, and which ones should be shunned.

Chapter 4 sets down the theoretical foundation of project management, through the concept of the *unit transformation process*. The unit transformation process is both a technique and a methodology for mastering the complexities of a project, the sequencing of its execution, and the accountability for doing so. *Accountability* is no longer monolithic, but instead is comprised of three distinct functional roles of accountability, approval authority, and execution responsibility—forming the *directrix* principle.

Chapter 5 extends the *directrix* discussion by juxtaposition of its antithesis: the dabbler. Dabblers, meddlers, micromanagers, and superfluous team personnel are a direct consequence of a project management philosophy that insists on reviewing and approving everything, by everyone, from every other party.

The traditional *review and approve* approach is abandoned in favor of the more efficient *check-but-verify* approach, which slims down labor costs and schedule timelines. It introduces the idea that project management is performed at the *interface between dependent unit transformations*.

Chapter 6 takes on the sacred cow of project budgets and schedules, which are traditionally prioritized ahead of an asset's future performance during work execution. Project execution mindsets are explored. The text suggests a fundamental change in one's consideration of a project budget from the traditional obsession with immediate cost minimization *now*, to the budget as an investment vehicle for the asset's *future* performance. The idea of operating with the commonly-accepted *constraint trifecta* (cost-schedule-quality) is shown to run *counter* to the well-being of the asset. The new concept of a constraint diamond is advocated as the guiding axiom of cost management.

PART 2—WHERE

Part 2 concentrates on the realms of project management practice that actually matter to the outcome of a project.

Chapter 7 introduces the notion of the *project ecosystem* (i.e., PECO). The ecosystem comprises eight layers that must be traversed from the outside in, to achieve project success. The PECO encompasses all the sources of risk that are external to the project.

Chapter 8 deals with the issue of money, addressed from the *long-term investment* perspective. Can the owner afford the project? Should he afford the project? What should be spent on what? When? The text makes the case that *all spending decisions* on a project must serve the asset's future performance rather than myopically aiming at cutting costs during a project's development. If a project is worth the risk, which buttresses its very existence at this stage, then one should select a budget that is realistic and cognizant of the asset's *intrinsic value*.

Chapter 9 introduces the organizational principle of the *framework* as overseer of project managers and the PECO. The framework is a corporate function designed to marshal the resources of the project owner to fulfill the requirements of the project. The framework is *accountable* to the owner for the performance of the project management office. The latter is, in turn, *accountable* to the framework for the development of the profitably performing asset.

Chapter 10 tackles the topic of execution metrics by going beyond *key performance indicators* (KPIs). The text introduces a comprehensive system—*performance assessment metrics* (PAM)—to measure what matters across time, between players, and throughout execution phases.

PART 3—HOW

Part 3 explores the sequencing and planning of a project, starting with a set of rules and guidelines underlying the development of the execution strategy *per se*; then discusses the principal components of a project execution strategy, including the all-important issue of risk management.

Chapter 11 completes the discussion of project oversight—this time focused on management planning and orchestration. It delineates the roles of the framework and those of the project management organization, abandons the idea of project execution plans, and replaces it with an overall execution plan drafted by the framework team—also known as the *baseline asset execution framework* (BAEF). This chapter also offers guidelines for content development, based on the *what, why, when, where,* and *how* (W5H) technique.

Chapter 12 is the third salvo directed at the minutia of work execution. It develops the sequencing of the execution work into 80 *life-cycle phases,* defines the completion milestone of a project as the point in time when the asset has been proven to be profitably performing, and emphasizes the necessity of completing all deliverables associated with one phase before starting another phase.

PART 4—WHO

Part 4 takes up the matter of team formation, personnel selection, and recruitment strategies adapted to combat local inflationary pressures and exploit global labor markets.

Chapter 13 presents strategies and tactics for developing team hierarchies based on the physical configuration of the asset. It suggests the harmonization of the many tracking processes along that same basis, emphasizes the *directrix* in the functional reports, and provides guidelines for creating efficient and valunomic chains of commands with and without a project team. It introduces the concept of "A" organizations as a preference over "A" teams.

Chapter 14 addresses the issue of labor shortages, skill set atrophy, labor cost inflation, and outsourcing. It promotes the idea of miscegenation as a remedy for chronic labor shortages and turnover rates, highlights the link between project execution and team development, and develops further the concept of "A" organizations.

PART 5—WHEN

Part 5 delves into the practice of project management when things are under control and also when things go off the rails.

Chapter 15 explores various elements of routine project execution. It develops the mechanism of the *collection substrate* construct to integrate all tracking information and explores communication strategies, interface management, and risk management.

Chapter 16 explores situations when projects have gone off the rails. It uncovers their sources—along with the means to avoid them. It delves deeply into the built-in failure roots of various contract types, circles back on the ramifications of the project ecosystem on execution strategies relying on global sourcing, and discusses the effects of failed accountability assignments and how to fix them.

PART 6—WHAT

Part 6 highlights project management practices from the trenches of day-to-day project execution.

Chapter 17 consists of a selected overview of mechanics and mechanisms (M&M) that are applicable to the nuts and bolts of daily execution. It develops topics from the innovation perspective; contrasts the merits of database applications against spreadsheets; and introduces the concept of the *3-D model kernel* for anchoring all information that is developed during execution into a single-point-of-access repository.

Chapter 18 wraps up the M&M discussion with an in-depth analysis of project closeout—the forgotten child of project execution strategies.

Chapter 19 contains commentaries and conclusions.

PART 7—APPENDICES

Part 7 includes the appendices, the bibliography, and the lexicon (including mathematical symbols).

ACKNOWLEDGMENTS

I wouldn't be me, without you with me.

Several people were instrumental in the creation of this book. First among them is my wife, Margaret. Her patience, insights, honesty, and faith in the pertinence of my views fostered the creative environment that nurtured my efforts. Her expression *tight bibs* was a stroke of genius that simply had to be included in the book. Our children, Michael, Gabrielle, and James, in their own wonderful, uninhibited ways, also provided the kinds of insight that are foreign to so-called serious literature by asking innocent questions that forced me to work unexpectedly hard to come up with cohesive answers. I owe a debt of gratitude to my brother Glenn, himself a published author in both French and English, who provided the guidance, style check, grammar patrol, and hard anchoring of my writing inclinations, which initially bore the unmistakable volitions of a novice author. I admire his willingness, nay his courage, to bluntly point out the weaknesses that peppered the various drafts, regardless of the sensitivities of my ego. My gratitude extends to Jamie Baird, an ex-colleague of mine who answered the call to review the book *in extremis* before its final submission. I thank my childhood friend François Lavallée for the historical insight into the Chapter 9 quotation regarding the burning stables of France. Shantale Cyr, of Montréal, gracefully offered her Latin expertise in devising the expression "ego sum ergo possum" appearing in Chapter 7. I extend my thanks to my colleague and friend, Bryan Campbell (once engineering designer at NAIAD Company), who contributed the artwork for the artistic figures.

I was fortunate to benefit from the reviews of my brother Lloyd, my long-time friend Guy Dumais (management consultant at BDO), my work colleagues Nicholas Peggs (project manager at BP), Brian McCloskey (manager at WorleyParsons), Arno Wainikainen (management consultant at EY), Paul Hartzheim (regulatory affairs consultant), and Yongqiang (David) Song (project controls manager at Suncor) who volunteered their time to review the final draft. Finally, I wish to recognize the unique insights of several people who have shared my professional journey over the decades, which molded my own theoretical musings underpinning this book. These insights, gleaned from direct contacts or observations from a distance, seeded many of the strains of thoughts that colored my work over the decades in the trenches of project management. Thus, to Mike McSweene (SVP Suncor), Greg Kenney (VP Spectra Energy),

Robert Faulder (Director—IRAP, National Research Council of Canada), Peter Nickerson (CEO Excelsior Engineering), Bill Shepherd (retired), Marc Maeseele (Project Manager, LNG Canada Ltd), and Koichi Shirakawa (SVP, Chiyoda Corporation), I say thank you for the invaluable knowledge that came my way.

Last but not least, I salute the staff at Starbucks—Britannia Plaza (Calgary, Alberta)—who always brightened my writing sessions (by the corner near the bay window) as I sat almost daily over the better part of a year to complete this book. To Alphonso, Brad, Cailey, Cheyenne, Christoper, Daniel, Fraser, Greg, and Sam, I say: Dark always before Pike!

ABOUT THE AUTHOR

STEVEN JAMES KEAYS, M.A.SC., P.ENG., PMP

Steven Keays is a 30-year veteran of the aerospace, defense, manufacturing, and oil and gas industries. He is the founder and CEO of NAIAD Company, a project consulting firm specialized in the management of large and mega industrial projects. He is a graduate of the Royal Military College of Canada (B.Sc. Mechanical Engineering) and of the University of Ottawa (M.A.Sc., turbulent fluid mechanics). He is a specialist in large-scale project management, global execution strategies, construction, and modularization. Since 2008, he has been active on hydrocarbon projects with footprints in North and South America, China, Japan, Korea, and Russia. He is a registered professional engineer in the Canadian provinces of Alberta, British Columbia, Ontario, and Saskatchewan; an accomplished design engineer with several patents to his name; an expert in non-linear finite element analysis; and a member of the Project Management Institute. Mr. Keays resides in Calgary, Alberta, Canada, with his wife, Margaret, and their three children, Michael, Gabrielle, and James.

 Web
Added
Value™

This book has free material available for download from the
Web Added Value™ resource center at *www.jrosspub.com*

At J. Ross Publishing we are committed to providing today's professional with practical, hands-on tools that enhance the learning experience and give readers an opportunity to apply what they have learned. That is why we offer free ancillary materials available for download on this book and all participating Web Added Value™ publications. These online resources may include interactive versions of material that appears in the book or supplemental templates, worksheets, models, plans, case studies, proposals, spreadsheets and assessment tools, among other things. Whenever you see the WAV™ symbol in any of our publications, it means bonus materials accompany the book and are available from the Web Added Value Download Resource Center at www.jrosspub.com.

Downloads for *Investment-Centric Project Management: Advanced Strategies for Developing and Executing Successful Capital Projects* include numerous templates and materials to help ensure your successful deployment of large, complex, investment projects.

DEDICATION

This book is dedicated to my wife, Margaret, and my children, Michael, Gabrielle, and James.

PART 1—WHY

The subject of project management is introduced through an investigation of first principles. A foundation is laid down as to the meaning, direction, and mindsets of managing projects.

1

INTRODUCTION

"In theory, theory and practice are the same.
In practice, they are not." Yogi Berra

BETWEEN PROJECT SUCCESS AND FAILURE

The World of Projects

Humans have managed projects since the dawn of civilization. They built pyramids, warships, cities, irrigation systems, and the international space station. The language would have been different then, but not the challenges that we see today. Projects have forever faced constraints that will sound familiar to the modern reader: budgets, timelines, changes, labor, transportation logistics, construction techniques, quality assurance, and buy-in from rulers. What is perhaps different today is their complexity, arising as much from performance expectations as from regulatory and social demands.

It is no exaggeration to remark that our modern world creates wealth and advances the collective well-being on the strength of the project as an enabler of the creation process. The very idea of a project is so enmeshed into the reality of business that it is effectively invisible. If you are reading this book in a coffee shop right now, stop and take a look around, starting with the space itself. Everything that you see, touch, and hear was made by employees of a business, at some time, somewhere in the world. Their work was most likely executed within the confines of a project that was mandated by the owners of the business. Notice the shop, the table, the chair, the cup, the light fixtures, the electricity flowing through them, the cash register, the washrooms in the back, the painted parking lines on the pavement. If you are sitting at an airport awaiting the end of yet another delayed flight, pause for a few seconds and try to imagine the unfathomable complexity of the construction of this airport. Once you are seated in the airplane, remember that you are about to be transported safely by hundreds of thousands of parts working homogeneously, supplied by a myriad of vendors scattered across the globe. Then consider that each one of these parts came to life as an outcome of a project designed to birth it. Lest you are still not convinced, try to figure out exactly what's going on electronically when you pay for those peanuts, by credit card, 30,000 feet above an ocean. The magnitude of these invisible modern conveniences is simply staggering, yet effectively invisible to the casual observer. The technological underpinnings of our modern world are its very air supply: invisible, omnipresent, and a guarantor of death six minutes after it has been cut off.

A New Project Perspective

Projects are themselves underpinnings of technological underpinnings. People regard them (at least for those few of us who pay heed to such matters) as they would gravity: it's always there and therefore unnoticed (unless you need brakes), and it's always working in mysterious ways. Most people define gravity in terms of what it does: pull masses together. Far fewer will speak in terms of space-time warping predicted by general relativity. Rarer still are those who can dwell in its mathematics. The same goes with the management practices underlying project execution. Most project professionals will define a project in terms nurtured by traditional project management (TPM) orthodoxy. The Project Management Institute (PMI), for example, will define a project as *an agent of change, undertaken as a temporary endeavor to create a unique process, product, or services.* Few people would disagree with such a characterization. It is sufficiently generic to allow countless interpretations that remain true to its spirit. Nevertheless, this definition (along with its many variants) is also sufficiently amorphous as to be useless. It explains why 30% of $20M projects, 50% of $100M projects, and 70% of $1B projects will fail. A better definition is this:

A project is the development of a profitably performing asset (PPA).

The asset is the revenue-generating entity to be operated commercially for the benefits of its shareholders. An asset, for example, can be an industrial plant, a pipeline, an airport, a workers' camp, a cultural event, or a piece of equipment. *The asset exists to deliver sustained returns on investment (ROI) to shareholders throughout its economic life.* The causality is irreversible: the asset is wanted; therefore, the project is initiated to transform the initial concept into a revenue stream. However, it is not enough for the asset to generate revenues. It must do so profitably, such that its shareholders will maximize their ROI over the long run. That life spans the entire existence of the asset, from concept to development, from start-up to full operations, to modifications and decommissioning, or to its sale. *Once again, the causality must be grasped unequivocally: sharehold-ers will agree to foot the bill for the asset if and only if it is designed to maximize shareholder value over the long term*—nothing else matters. If the case can be made to invest in this asset, it follows that the sole, and indeed the ultimate purpose of the ensuing actions, will be to configure this asset in such a way that it will deliver the promised ROI.

The Return-on-Investment Imperative

The maximization of ROI rests on three vectors: the volume of revenues gener-ated by the asset, the cost incurred to generate them, and the profits resulting from the combined effects of revenues and costs. In this context, the project is never an end unto itself; it is merely the means to the end sought—the PPA. The project no longer ends when commissioning is completed, which otherwise completely misses the purpose of the asset since you have no clue whether the asset is profitably performing or not. On the other hand, if one agrees that the PPA is the purpose of the project, it stands to reason that the project should end when the profitability has been proven. This could be several months after operational start-up occurred. Defining the end in this manner has profound implications on the way budgets are managed, including the necessary aban-donment of the cherished constraint trifecta (budget-schedule-quality), which forces the project manager to choose to control two and accept the third to land where it will. *You cannot achieve a PPA if you manage by this constraint trifecta.* Otherwise, the only guarantee is that the budget will be spent, and the work may be finished on time. You will leave the entire matter of profitability undefined, unknown, and unpredictable.

Traditional Project Management

As recently as the early 1900s, projects were executed without any formal frame-work. The professionalization of the practice of project management really began in the 1950s. Today, project management is considered to be a full-fledged career vocation and is subject to professional accreditations from governing organiza-tions, such as PMI, to name but one. Project management principles underscore the execution of projects of any size, anywhere on the planet. These principles have evolved in tandem with the rise in project complexity. Control underscores their purpose—control over budgets, schedules, scope of work, labor, work sequencing, design, changes, construction, procurement, logistics, regulatory filing, communications, and risks. In many instances, they have been incorpo-rated in specialized software. In all instances, they provide project teams with the procedures to manage work execution. TPM principles generate certain expec-tations in the minds of the organizations footing the bill, such as completing projects *on budget and schedule* (OBaS), in compliance with performance targets, without undue upheavals, and with minimal bad publicity. Ultimately, organizations embrace TPM for its putative guarantee of success. We therefore pose a simple question: does the track record validate the premise?

The Reality of Failure

As we will see in Chapter 2, failure statistics across regions and industries cast a shadow on this TPM assertion. In fact, they point to a different conclusion: TPM practices do not guarantee project success to owners, or furnish sufficient probability of success to justify the initial investment. It is worth emphasizing once again the harsh reality of industrial projects far and wide: $20M projects will fail 30% of the time; above $100M, 50% will fail; and beyond $1B, a staggering 70% will suffer the same fate. This state of affairs was the impetus for this book. The evidence is inescapable: projects underscored by a TPM framework exhibit a high probability of failing to satisfy their starting expectations. There are several reasons why TPM fails, which will be investigated in this book. Some project professionals may be tempted to explain away the failure record with the widely held belief that *the fault is not with the accepted principles of project management, but with the failure to implement them*. Experience shows that this is too simplistic an explanation. For every problem, there is a solution that is simple, elegant, and wrong (H. L. Mencken). The fact of the matter is that *every single project involving your author* was executed within a formal TPM framework. Most of them adhered faithfully to the rigid plans, strategies, and procedures imposed by the owner at the outset. Almost none of them came in on budget and on schedule.

Project versus Program versus Function

What is a project? In this book, a project is an endeavor with a start and end date. Examples include building a house or a plant, taking a trip to Andalusia, and designing a new hire procedure. When the end date is missing, it is a program, such as developing a new drug or a team of aspiring Olympians. When both dates are missing, it is a function. Running the accounting department is a function. The PPA philosophy is applicable integrally to projects, and partially to programs; but projects will be the focus of the discussion from this point forward. Projects are further divided into *spend* and *investment* types. The spend project is not required to generate revenue upon completion. Otherwise, it is an investment project. The distinction is fundamental to the PPA philosophy. *Spend projects* are managed by the constraint trifecta shown in Figure 1.1. The overriding concern of the execution strategy is to minimize costs. *Investment projects* are managed by the constraint diamond of Figure 1.2, and strive to

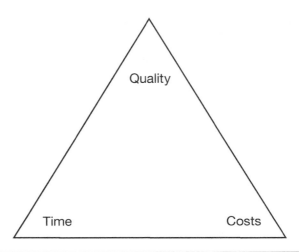

Figure 1.1   Constraint trifecta: classic management choices between costs, time, and quality

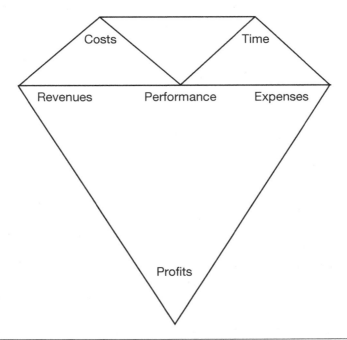

Figure 1.2   Constraint diamond: PPA objectives for project management. The budget drivers now include revenues, operating expenses, and profits. Note the inversion of the constraint diamond.

Table 1.1   Examples of spend and investment projects

Spend Projects	Investment Projects
Build a house	Build a rental property
Repair a car	Restore a collectible car ahead of an auction
Acquire an original Olenska painting	Buy the Olenska watercolor painting collection
Vacation travel to Emerald Lake Lodge	Client retreat at Emerald Lake Lodge
Buy a high-end racing bicycle	Buy a boat or plane
	Build a pipeline, an airport, or a mine
	Buy a petrochemical plant to modify it

maximize the asset's long-term ROI performance. Examples of the two project types are shown in Table 1.1.

Both types produce the same outcome: an asset. Both are justified from the outset on the assumption that this asset will be realized. For this reason, the PPA philosophy applies to both, equally. Nevertheless, the investment project will be the primary perspective of this book since its scale and costs are generally orders of magnitude higher than for a spend project. The most bang for the investment buck will accrue to large-scale projects with million or billion dollar budgets—things like civil infrastructures, airports, sea ports, city development, pipelines, plants, power generation, mining, technology development, and movies. As the reader will discover, *investment projects* fail when they are managed by the constraint trifecta.

THE JUSTIFICATION FOR THIS BOOK

One may very well ask, "why bother with yet another book on such a well-worn topic, given the plethora already offered on the market?" The reason is threefold: genuine project management is dramatically different than the TPM orthodoxy; project owners cannot afford the failure rates; and project success lies beyond the procedural horizon embraced by traditional practice. This book is not a *recipe book* on how to create a schedule, write a procurement plan, or develop a change management process. Readers who are simply interested in the tools of the trade are encouraged to consult information that is offered online or inside brick walls. The *raisons d'être* for this book are altogether different: (1) to address the shortcomings of TPM practices; (2) to redefine projects, project management, and their associated mechanics and mechanisms; (3) to alter the interpretation of project management away from tools and techniques, and toward the relationship aspects of projects; and (4) to equip the reader with a cohesive project delivery framework that will guarantee success, predictably, and repetition. The text will explore the underlying reasons for the disturbing failure statistics and offer practical, coherent solutions tested in the trenches of project execution. The methodologies, strategies, and techniques described herein will resonate with new and experienced project professionals alike, who struggle with the ever-present threat of budget overruns, schedule slippages, construction misfires, and plant deficiencies. Owners, operators, design firms, and constructors will discover the common threads that unite them in their shared and individual commercial objectives.

Few organizations can afford to deploy their project capital as inefficiently as history reveals. Fewer still can afford the status quo in an era of low commodity prices, complex global execution strategies, and regulatory minefields. This book offers project owners and developers alike a road map to predictable and repeatable success, and a guarantee of future investment returns from their assets.

The Status Quo Is Often Justified but Rarely Justifiable

There are no quick fixes or magic bullets to remedy the failure record. There is no way to tweak one's project delivery organization and painlessly change the prevailing *status quo*. The journey begins with four initial steps to be taken by the reader. The first step is an acknowledgment of the importance of the proven practices of TPM. The TPM processes and procedures are valid, solid, and understood broadly. For instance, the emphasis on developing pertinent plans and strategies before any project work is initiated remains unquestioned by the PPA philosophy. The next step asks the reader to admit to the imperfections of a TPM and to recognize that too many projects continue to fail in spite of their TPM implementation. Simply put, something must be amiss in TPM, otherwise success would be the norm. Third, the *status quo* must be challenged. Tweaks will not suffice; if they did, natural selection would long ago have embedded them into the DNA of the principles. The fourth and final step is to introduce a new, two-part management paradigm.

New Project Management Paradigm

Part 1 of the new paradigm recasts the definition of a project as *the development of a PPA*, as introduced earlier in the chapter. Let us emphasize once more that the point of a project is to bring to life a physical asset that will make money for its owner. The asset is acquired to generate revenues and yield profits to its owners. The asset is the justification for the project, not vice versa. *The asset exists to deliver sustained ROI to shareholders throughout its economic life.* The project is therefore a means to an end. It is the investment vehicle to conceive, develop, realize, activate, and operate the asset. All project activities, objectives, and decisions are resolved in favor of making the asset *profitably performing.*

Part 2 of the new paradigm redefines project management as the *controlled execution of a project.* This wording departs dramatically from the usual definition that, according to such authorities as PMI, is a set of skills, processes, procedures, and plans to execute a project in such a way that all stakeholders' needs are satisfied. In this interpretation, project management is reduced to allocating and managing resources to achieve a set of objectives. The definition takes on a pronounced procedural character which transpires, on a daily basis, into execution plans and strategies. Those are, in turn, constituted into management schemes for schedule, cost, quality, human resources, communications, risk, procurement, construction management, systems, and standards. The managing of a project is thus encapsulated in the aphorism: *if you fail to plan, you plan to fail.* However, although planning is a necessary condition to execution success, it is not a sufficient one. For example, your author was involved with a multi-billion dollar project whose execution strategy tallied 800 pages of plans, procedures, processes, and templates. Despite this depth of detail, the endeavor would eventually flounder. The fact of the matter is that a plan is akin to a music partition, one that is regarded as the end unto itself. But notes are only the starting point. The music that ensues is brought to life by executing this partition. The execution requires skilled players, aligned in synchronicity and led by one individual (and never, you will notice, a committee). The piece "*La valse des patineurs*" by Waldteufel can be played by a high school band and by a professional symphonic orchestra. The notes, the cadence, the phrasing, and the instruments are the same, yet listen to the difference!

On the Merits of a Plan

Any military commander will tell you that a battle plan is valid up until the battle commences. Afterward, the fog of war casts such a long shadow upon the intended theories of the battle plan as to render them ineffective. In battle, the victor keeps his eyes on the ultimate objective—be it to prevail in battle, take the hill, conquer the beach, or win the war; but never about how each combat unit recharges its weapons. A project, like an army, can win all the battles, yet still lose the war.

INVESTMENT-CENTRIC PROJECT MANAGEMENT (ICPM)

Striving to Thrive

In the new paradigm, profitability of the future asset sits at the top of management's priority. The management of the project, being circumscribed by the constraint diamond (see Figure 1.2), becomes investment-centric. The ICPM approach transforms the project organization into a full-fledged institutional structure. The structure is divided into three management functions: the organization, the business, and the relationship nexus—which will be refined in Chapter 2. In short, the *organization* deals with the application of knowledge, skill, tools, and techniques to project activities; the *business* deals with money; and the *relationship nexus* transcends the personal and functional relationships that make or break a project.

Anchors of ICPM Execution

The ramifications are profound. The tools and techniques of TPM are retained integrally in an ICPM schema, but not as execution anchors (anchors being, as a group, the foundation of the delivery strategy). The first ICPM execution anchor is the end of a project. Whereas in TPM, the end coincides with the end of commissioning (following construction), in ICPM the end occurs when the asset has been proven to be profitably performing. Practically, this means weeks or months later than commissioning.

The second ICPM anchor is the budget philosophy. In a TPM framework, all projects are of the *spend* type, subject to the constraint trifecta (see Figure 1.1). The work is always managed with a view to minimize costs. In the PPA paradigm, all projects are of the *investment* type, with the budget being the investment vehicle to realize the asset. *All project costs* are justified on the basis of maximizing the future investment returns, in accordance with Figure 1.2. Short-term cost savings are shunned if they run counter to this basis.

The third ICPM anchor concerns work sequencing. The traditional approach calls for dividing the scope of work into a series of phases (usually four to six), culminating in the commissioning of the asset. The design philosophy explicitly assumes that each output can be designed individually and linearly, while the design work spans two or more phases. These outputs are then explicitly assumed to accrue in perfect convergence over time to produce the final, integrated outcome. These various assumptions are rarely corroborated by reality for they ignore the effects of complexity. Any time multiple moving parts are in play (the quintessence of *investment* projects), complexity will arise. Complexity is, in fact, an emergent feature of such multi-part systems, and is manifested by the nonlinearity of coupled interactions between the components making up the system. The ICPM schema takes it for granted that complexity will arise. It seeks to corral that complexity by sequencing the work in such a way that outputs are produced once, at a specific phase of the execution. The nature of the outputs proceeds organically over time. It enables the gradual build up of the asset from requirements to specifications to individual systems, assembled into installations, networked together into the plant. Proceeding in this way allows the pursuit of maximized future investment returns (which will otherwise be compromised by pursuit of real-time cost savings).

The salient differences between TPM and PPA projects are highlighted by the three ICPM anchors. Others will be introduced throughout the text, such as the unit transformation processes (UTP), leadership, direct accountability, the *getting-to-no* mindset, team structures, framework, risks, collection substrate, asset configuration, and "A" organizations. Taken together, they amount to a comprehensive and cohesive execution infrastructure. Migrating from TPM to PPA necessitates a holistic transformation at both project and corporate levels.

TPM versus PPA Perspectives

We illustrate these ramifications with an example from the movie industry (a movie is, in a pure sense, an investment project). We wind back the clock to the 1970s, a time of revolutionary upheaval in cinema, with Hollywood seeking to redefine itself in contrast to its past. The industry was infused with fresh blood from such immortals as Spielberg, Lucas, and Coppola, whose names need only be spoken to turn admiration into inspiration. Back then, as now, the *movie project* was deemed completed when ready for theatrical release. In one instance, the project was espoused by a young, mildly successful moviemaker bent on trampling the conventions of storytelling. Not surprisingly, filming was plagued with production problems, technical failures, editing misfires, and painful budget and schedule overruns. When, at long last, the final version was ready for prescreening, studio executives were less than enthused, to the point where they feared an impending failure of the whole affair. The studio chose to limit the initial release to a mere dozen theaters across the U.S. By traditional project management standards, the movie project was a failure—budgets and schedules were busted; many technical processes went off the rails. The lack of faith in the project by the studio executives was so pronounced that they agreed to sign over the merchandising rights of the film back to its director (in an ultimate effort by said director to get the movie released). Against all odds, the movie made it to the screen. And so it was that, on May 25, 1977, the failed movie project *Star Wars Episode IV* hit theaters.

Evidently, had the definition of the movie project included the revenue phase, the assessment of its success would have varied ever so slightly from the studio's original stance. Had the studio executives focused more on the contents and magic of the film's cinematographic execution, rather than harp on the budget and schedule woes, they might have anticipated the magnitude of the film's impact and invested *more* money and *more* time on the special effects. Surely, they would then have retained the merchandising rights that would eventually make the director, George Lucas, a wealthy man.

ELEMENTS OF STYLE

Per force, the basis of this book is tied to the author's experience in the oil and gas sector, in the big leagues of gas and oil pipelines; processing facilities; SAGD and heavy oil extraction; oil sands; and liquefied natural gas. Many projects were on a massive scale ($300M and more) within execution frameworks spanning the globe, carried out in multiple phases that were spread over years. Its woes and tribulations are broadly common to other sectors and offer a treasure trove of examples from which to extract the necessary insights. The scope, size, duration, and nature of a project will affect the execution details, of course, but the execution *methodology* remains nearly universal, regardless of the nature of the project. The failure rates observed in large industrial projects—like building a plant, an airport, or an Olympic arena—are seen in other types of projects that don't even involve construction. Software development, app creation, summer festivals, and political campaigns are but a few examples. The theory, axioms, principles, and techniques discussed in this book will therefore apply to the individual experience of the readers, including the elements of the methodology that will pertain to fabrication, construction, and labor resources. The way to construct a plant, a pipeline, or an airplane is identically equivalent to developing voice-recognition software, deploying a marketing campaign, or organizing a peewee hockey tournament.

Readers from all walks of project life should find in these examples relevance to their own experiences. In places, readers will notice educated guesses to inform the thought process, which could take a variety of forms such as *in all likelihood*, *in many or most cases*, or *it would be reasonable to deduce*. However, frequent recurrence of these forms throughout the text would prove tedious. The reader is invited to infer them when the context leads to the suggestion of broad assumptions or conclusions. In other places, the topics are presented in accessible mathematical expressions. Fear not the math: it adds substance to concepts that would otherwise appear undeveloped or hard to describe. Elsewhere, the reader will notice a reliance on juxtaposition as a comparative device to highlight the range of embodiment of certain topics. This black-on-white juxtaposition simply serves to contrast more clearly the boundaries of the topic's range. It does not imply a corresponding black-and-white reality. Rather, the real range will normally span a continuum from one extreme to the other. Life is not so much a binary proposition as it is a canvas of 28 shades of penumbra i.e., shade or shadow).

2

THE POINT OF A PROJECT

"The great tragedy of science: the slaying of a beautiful hypothesis with an ugly fact." T. H. Huxley

EXQUISITELY EXECUTED MEDIOCRITY

Failure as an Option

Across the world, regardless of the industry, projects tend to fail by default and succeed by exception—the larger the project, the higher the probability of failure. Global statistics on industrial and government projects are sobering. Root causes run the gamut from disjointed expectations, misinterpretations of the scope of work, ignorance of the process, and absence of processes, to deficient management and inadequate funding. Edward Merrow, of *Independent Project Analysis*, points out that so-called mega-projects (valued at $1B or more) fail more than 65% of the time, the world over, without ever becoming profitable. An overwhelming volume of published statistics proves the point. In 2014, the Project Management Institute (PMI) published the results[1] of a poll of 1,100 members and credential holders. They showed that 54% of projects finished on time; 54% finished on budget; 38% finished on time and on budget; 13% of those polled finished 80% of their projects on time and on budget; and 27% of those polled finished 60% of their projects on time and on budget. Other published statistics corroborate these findings. For example, a simple search on Google will reveal that:

- 50% of project management offices close within three years.
- Since 2008, the correlated project management office implementation failure rate is over 50% (Gartner Project Manager 2014).

- 68% of stakeholders perceive their project management office to be bureaucratic (2013 Gartner PPM Summit).

The reasons for these depressing statistics are varied and tend to follow three principal arcs:

- The practice of project management is interpreted in terms of tools and processes to meet the expectations of the stakeholders. This mindset translates into a management approach that is focused exclusively on the execution of the work against budget, at the expense of the performance of the future asset. The pursuit of cost control at all costs creates the illusion of cost effectiveness. The minimization of front-end expenditures *now* is favored over the long-term investment return of the operating asset *later*. But cost containment for the sake of budget preservation frequently leads to technical and procedural trade offs with unforeseen ramifications that result in *cost increases* to the project and the future asset.
- Practitioners equate execution and deliverables at each phase. Each phase is carried out *independently* by contract, budget, and schedule. Yet, deliverables will require multiple phases to reach completion. The project presumes that progress stems from the cumulative impact of these deliverables. This assumption is flawed since asset performance is never assessed independently.
- Risk management is confused for risk registers and running checklists. Risks are regarded as external factors to be *managed*, instead of *emergent features* of the very process of execution. Multi-phase development is deemed sufficient to corral them. Unfortunately, not only does this approach fail to mitigate risks, it increases them through parallel work in the name of schedule efficiency. This is another assumption not borne out by facts. It is not possible to save execution time *economically* by trying to save time through concurrent efforts. Blown schedules are the inevitable outcome.

Our purpose from this point forward will be to uncover the insights and fixes that we can apply to traditional project management (TPM) to change the probability of failure into a probability of success—to make projects work and organizations succeed.

The State of the Status Quo

When confronted with these facts, the typical reaction of executives and senior managers will be to vehemently defend their own project delivery frameworks.

Such defensive posture is to be expected when confronted with the dichotomy between faith in orthodoxy and reality. Project organizations will take offense and turn to defend with ardor the large investments made to develop their gargantuan governance holdings of processes meant to corral, direct, govern, and prescribe all aspects of a project—things like policies, procedures, guidelines, templates, processes, regulations, codes, standards, go-bys, and ISO 9001, to name but a few—tallying thousands of pages of documentation. These organizations will definitely deploy some form of project life cycle schema, complete with decision gates and risk studies at each stage. They will demand the redaction of multitudinous plans such as the example list given in Table 2.1 (astonishingly, interface management, code compliance, and engineering authentication plans were left off this list). Despite these diligent procedural cares, the probability of failure will not have been nullified. For instance, the project that furnished Table 2.1 did eventually fail and required a complete redo of the engineering and design phase.

The Test

Executives not associated with this project will continue to object on the strength of their beliefs in their own organizational structures. Again, such a reaction is normal: dealing with cognitive dissonance is difficult in most circumstances and harder still when one is emotionally invested in the *status quo*. Therefore, set aside this example and consider these three projects. Consider the following questions in each case:[2]

- Did the asset yield by the project achieve the original return on investment (ROI) targets?
- If no, was it possible to modify it to get there?
- If yes, did the modifications deliver the ROI targets?

If the answer to any of these questions was *no*, the project delivery framework effectively left a whole lot of future earnings on the table—money that will never be recouped. The status quo is not an option for you.

The next set of questions asks:

- Was the project completed within budget and schedule (i.e., prior to turning over the plant to Operations)?
- If no, were you able to justify the actual execution performance (cost and time)?
- If yes, are you confident of executing the next project with at least a 90% probability of success?

Table 2.1   Examples of project documentation common to large projects

Activity List	Forms	Prime Contractor Agreement
Administration instructions and project controls	Health, safety, security, and environment (HSSE) policy	Program and resources
Assurance, audit, and review schedule	HSSE and social program	Project controls
Business travel policy	HSSE control framework assurance program	Project execution strategy
Certification of materials	HSSE control framework glossary	Prime contractor agreement
Clarification reply procedure	HSSE control framework manuals	Project management plan
Company directory	HSSE control framework specifications	Quality audit plan
Company-supplied materials	Implementation contracts	Quality management
Computer software list	Information management	Quality management system
Construction execution plan	Information management plan	RFID strategy
Construction services templates	Information technology	Request for standing offer checklist
Contract	Joint venture statement	Risk management plan
Contract—general conditions	Labor strategy	Risk management workflow
Construction execution plan	Limited agency appointment	Risk register
Contract bill of quantities (BOQ) estimation methodology	List of engineering reviews	Roles and responsibilities
Contracting and procurement plan	Logistics	Salary review policy
Contracting and procurement procedures	Logistics and infrastructure strategy	Schedule of prices
Contracting strategy	Lump sum conversion	Scope of work—concept
Contractor BOQ execution plan	Master schedule	Scope of work—construction
Contractor local implementation plan	Materials management procedures	Scope of work—construction management
Contractor open book estimate price breakdown structure	Methodology of 10% estimation work for major items	Scope of work—design basis

Criticality rating and inspection level—equipment and materials	Mobilization and demobilization plan	Scope of work—detailed design
Design engineering methods	Modularization strategy	Scope of work—front end engineering and design
Design practice list	Performance tests	Site material control
Design replication and expansion	Permit and consent strategy	Technical deviation requests and query procedure
Dispute resolution protocols	Permit register	Technical information
Engineering activity narratives	Permitting plan	Work hour policy
Execution plan	Personnel assessment	
Form of agreement		

Again, if any answer was *no*, the execution strategy failed the project. You are guaranteed to lose more money the next time around. Can you afford to get on this train again?

Why Project Management Fails

Modern project management is presumed by most people to be sound. Its theoretical underpinnings are assumed to be essentially complete, save for a few details (echoing, in a sense, the nineteenth-century views of physics before quantum mechanics and relativity obliterated the conceit). Project management theory predicts success for projects undertaken under its aegis. On the other hand, any theory, regardless of the field, is only as good as its ability to correctly predict outcomes. Theories must be grounded in facts, and facts only, lest faith-based dogma prevails (one is reminded of Goethe's remark that "there is nothing so frightening as ignorance in action"). A theory is acceptable when its pronouncements accord with the observed reality, preferably satisfying the *Ockham's razor* test.[3] Richard Feynman,[4] a Nobel prize winner in physics, suggested a very simple scenario to that effect. First, take a guess at what a physical law is, and write down its equation. From that equation, make a prediction for the outcome of a thought experiment. Run the experiment, and compare those results with the predictions. If the two diverge, the initial premise is wrong and the equation, invalid. That is all there is to it. It does not matter if the law was posited by a famous scientist, a Nobel laureate, or a religious imam. If the predictions don't match with reality, the theory is incorrect. End of story.

These words resonate with our discussion on the putative sufficiency of project management theory. Worldwide failure statistics show that it is incomplete and in need of advancement.

PREMISE OF THE PROFITABLY PERFORMING ASSET (PPA) PHILOSOPHY

The Point of Projects

Against the backdrop of the traditional definition quoted in Chapter 1, we posit that:

> *Project management is more than the sum of the processes, procedures, resources, and plans required to execute a project in accordance with the needs and expectations of stakeholders.*

How is it more? For starters, notice that the definition does *not* address the nature of the project; one is left to infer it from the *needs and expectations of the stakeholders*—a risky leap of faith. The same goes for its purpose and what it is supposed to do. Second, the standard definition assumes that the stakeholders are (or can be) aligned. That assumption is unrealistic. Numerous stakeholders such as landowners, environmental lobbies, political parties, special interest groups, and local kings have no interest in agreeing to a project. These stakeholders may never be aligned.[5] Third, the definition is silent on the end game. Is the project done when all tasks and processes are completed? What about the performance of the actual asset once it is taken over by its owner? Relying on needs and expectations to infer the answers is not a substitute for explicit prescriptions.

The definition of the *project* is equally generic and posited in terms of an endeavor with a start and end date that was undertaken to create a result, a service, or a product. Notice that the definition is silent as to whether the outcome is useful, productive, or even implemented (it is tacitly implied). The emphasis remains on the *creation* of that outcome. The immediate consequence of that emphasis is to infer that the end of the project corresponds to the completion of the creation phases. We can now see why the end of an industrial project is widely acknowledged to be the point in time when the physical asset has been commissioned and readied for transfer of ownership to the operators.

The Project's End Point Sets the Management Priorities

The importance of the assignment of the end is significant to the philosophy of management of the project, since it dictates the priorities of the project's owner and the management team. By the traditional definition, the priority will be to minimize project costs, in accordance with the constraint trifecta of Figure 1.1. The project, be it a capital expenditure (CAPEX) or operating expenditure (OPEX), is treated as a *spend project*, which demands the control of costs *now* rather than maximizing asset profitability *later. Total costs of ownership (TCO)* rarely, if ever, enters into consideration. *Better cheaper now than richer later* is the modus operandi of the project. Managing a spend project guarantees one outcome: the whole budget will be spent. As soon as costs or schedules are threatened, the obsession to finish the job intensifies, the expense of the outcome (i.e., the phase deliverables, rather than the profitably performing asset).

The ramifications of managing a project by either type of project (spend or investment) is illustrated in Figure 2.1. Figuratively, any project is akin to the proverbial iceberg. The execution works are the only ones visible above the water's surface. Visible implies controllable; hence the reflex of adopting a spend project approach to budget management. Nevertheless, what really matters is what lies beneath the surface, hidden from view (since profitability is in the future and measurable only when put into action). This is characteristic of an *investment project.* All that occurs above the surface must be done for the profit-generating capacity of the future asset to be realized. Figure 2.1 clearly shows the differences between TPM and PPA philosophies. TPM focuses on what happens above the surface; PPA keeps its eyes on the bottom tip, deep below the surface.

Valunomy versus Cost Effectiveness

Another salient difference between the two philosophies is the attitude toward budget spending. The pursuit of lowest costs, conveyed by the idea of cost

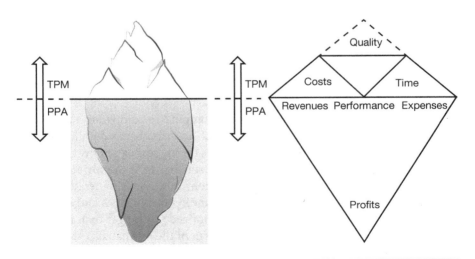

Figure 2.1   The project iceberg: Comparison between TPM and PPA—TPM focuses on what is visible above the surface, while PPM constantly probes the depths where what matters is hidden

effectiveness, is invoked by project professionals to premise the rationale for buying decisions. Cost efficiency prefers the least cost incurred *now* for an *immediate* outcome, over a higher cost designed to increase profitability *later*. In industrial projects with very large capital outlays, the dominance of the front-end price advantage is taken for granted (see *To Spend or to Buy, That Is the Question* in Chapter 8). The PPA approach takes an opposite stand, based on *valunomy* (a neologism coined by the author). Valunomy shifts the emphasis of a buying design toward the maximization of future investment returns, and always includes TCO in the analysis. The highest valunomy is the one that achieves the highest *sustained profitability* over an asset's economic life. Mathematically, valunomy is given by:

$$V = \frac{D^{wd} * O^{wo}}{\Sigma(I_c + e_c)} \tag{2.1}$$

where:

V = Valunomy
D = Time interval during which the outputs, O, must be produced
I_c = Accrued costs during time interval, D, to produce the outputs (the aim is to minimize I_c)
O = Number of outputs generated at the end of the D interval
e_c = Additional costs required by extra work to correct/complete the outputs. The ideal case is when $e_c = 0$.
wd = Importance factor for time.
   = +1 if D is meant to be maximized
   = −1 if D is meant to be minimized
wo = Importance factor for outputs
   = +1 if O is meant to be maximized
   = −1 if O is meant to be minimized

The units of V will vary as a function of the outputs. In comparative analyses, it is therefore essential that the same units of D, Ic, and O be used uniformly.

Among several options, the best one offers the highest valunomy of the asset. Let us examine three illustrative examples, starting with the hiring of a consulting firm to produce a system specification for a power generator. The incurred costs, Ic, may include the direct and indirect labor costs and specialized software licenses. The duration is to be minimized (no longer than necessary). The output, O, is to be minimized, in the form of the estimated cost to buy the system. Thus, both wd and wo would be set at −1.

In the second instance, we seek to obtain an industrial plant design. The incurred costs, Ic, include the contract value of the engineering and procurement works, along with the procurement costs (actuals). Duration is minimized, once again, with a corresponding $wd = -1$. The output, O, on the other hand, is defined as the number of drawings, specifications, and datasheets produced, thus maximized, with a $wo = +1$.

For our third example, we look at an entire operating asset. In this case, we may define the Ic in terms of operating, maintenance, and tax costs. The duration, D, is set as the operating life of the asset (i.e., $wd = +1$). Finally, the output, O, is defined as the accrued profits during the operating life ($wo = +1$).

The variable, e_c, plays a crucial role when comparing options. It represents the ability of the party doing the work to produce the outputs in a competed state. A value of $e_c = 0$ implies completeness: that is, no additional work is required on any of the outputs to either correct or finish them. If $e_c > 0$, more work (additional costs) will be needed to reach completion. If $e_c < 0$, less work is required to reach completeness, which implies a greater efficiency of the party doing the work. The classic case is the comparatively abnormal low price bid received in response to a competitive *request for proposal* from a bidder trying to buy the job or located in a low labor cost jurisdiction. When e_c corrections from past experiences are included in the evaluation of the bids, the cost advantage of the lowball proposal will, in fact, vanish entirely. *Invariably, the cheapest at the outset will cost the most in the long run.*

The Project Is a Development Process

The proper end point of an investment project occurs when the asset has been proven to be profitably performing. It also changes the philosophy of management, typically focused on spending control, over to investment maximization. This is what was meant in Chapter 1 by the statement that all *project activities, concerns, objectives, decisions, and financial priorities must be resolved in favor of making the asset profitably performing*. The project is the investment vehicle for developing the asset. We define *development* as the sum of the works and activities required to realize the profitably performing asset. In this context, *development* unfolds over time in two sequential stages: *conceptualization* and *realization*. The conceptualization stage encompasses all the activities leading to a theoretical definition of the asset, from which construction can take place. The realization stage begins with construction planning, continues with construction, and verifies the commercial performance of the operating asset (done during the initial period of revenue generation activities). The realization stage ends with the feedback process by which all the assumptions, predictions, estimates, and performance assessment metrics[6] are validated with operational data.

Terminology

The following definitions will be used throughout the book:

- *Asset*—The revenue-generating entity to be operated commercially for the benefits of its shareholders. An asset can be, for example, an industrial plant, a pipeline, an airport, a workers' camp, a cultural event, or a piece of equipment. The asset exists to deliver sustained ROI to shareholders, throughout its economic life.
- *Developer*—The organization retained by the owner to carry out the *development* of the asset. It can be a subset of the owner's organization, a single prime contractor, or a group of third-party entities. Within these definitions, the owner does not execute the work, but will approve the outcome of that work. This is the fundamental distinction between an owner and developer. Note that the taxonomy is recursive. That is, the corporate entity who is awarded the contract to develop the project, or a portion thereof, will also be internally divided into an owner (the executive team), a framework team (led by a department chief, a division manager, or a manager of projects, for example) and a project management owner (the assigned project management team).
- *Framework*—The organizational structure within the owner's hierarchy that oversees all projects. The framework is also the team, led by a leader, whose mandate is to protect the owner's interests. The framework counters the monopsony tendencies of the project management team. The framework leader manages the risks that are exogenous to the projects.
- *ICPM*—Investment-centric project management. The management philosophy associated with the constraint diamond (see Figure 1.2).
- *Owner*—The party that approves the project and operates the asset. It can be a company, a partnership, a joint venture, a government department, or any other legal entity that will own the asset.
- *PECO*—Project ecosystem designating the arena where the project action occurs; one that includes all of the variables that are external to the owner's organization.
- *Plan*—Generic term designating an ordered set of activities to execute a specified scope of work.
- *PMC*—Project management consultant. Typically, a third-party vendor hired by the owner to act as the PMO on a project.
- *PMO*—Project management office, vested with the mandate to execute the project. Unless otherwise stated, it is implied to be the owner's team. The PMO reports directly to the framework leader. Depending on context, the PMO will also designate the project manager (PM). The PMO manages the risks that are endogenous to the project.

- *PMT*—Generic term for project management team. The PMO is a PMT, but a vendor PMT is not a PMO. The term will be used to refer to a vendor or third-party entity employed on the project. A PMT reports either directly to the PMO, to the framework, or to another PMT.
- *Regulator*—Any government entity empowered by legislative fiat to impose conditions and constraints on a project that must be satisfied by the owner to obtain the permits or licenses required for regulatory compliance. ˙
- *SPT*—scope project team. The SPT, led by a scope project manager (SPM), is assigned a specific scope of work or function within a project. The SPT reports directly to the PMO.
- *SCP*—supply chain partner. The SCP includes all suppliers of goods and services to the project. All SPTs are SCPs, but not conversely.
- *Shareholder*—The entity who puts up the money to develop the asset. It can be a single person, a group of individuals, a department or division within a business, a business, a corporate partnership, a joint venture, or any other legally constituted body unto whom the financial ownership of the asset rests. The shareholder's interests are internal to the project, in opposition to stakeholders, whose interests are external to it (see *stakeholder*).
- *Stakeholder*—An entity *external* to the project and a source of risk to the project. Stakeholders are not shareholders. All project ecosystem (PECO) members are stakeholders.
- *Vendor*—A business supplying a service or a product to the project. All vendors are SCPs.

THE POINT OF PROJECT MANAGEMENT

What It Is

Project management is defined as a corollary of the project:

Project management is the controlled development of the project.

Notice the absence of references to the tools, techniques, and resources to get the project done and satisfy stakeholders. Project management is investment-centric rather than procedural; it is asset focused, not technique driven. The execution process gives rise to the triad structure noted in Chapter 1; that is, project management is simultaneously of an organization, a business, and relationship nexus.

Project Management Is an Organization

As an organization, project management mirrors the TPM definition. The organization owns the mechanics and mechanisms (M&Ms) to develop the asset. These M&Ms are essential to the execution of the work. *But they are not the end-all, be-all of the organization.* They are but one subset among a host of others that include:

- The marshalling of resources to do the work;
- The training and development of the personnel in parallel to the work done;
- The firm imposition of uniformity across the organization in the matter of rules and procedures;
- The close monitoring of the evolution and the metrics derived from it;
- The constant vigilance toward in-execution improvements and innovation; and
- Team building and owner nurturing.

The project management organization is akin to the field general tasked to march the troops across the landscape to secure the target. Planning is critical. The responsibility falls upon the organization to develop the *prescriptive* plans that will define, sequence, quantify, allocate, validate, verify, and measure the work to be undertaken. The work is complemented by the core skills and knowledge of the organization, through its people and its corporate parent. The organization has a duty to marshal the requisite expertise and organize the staff for the project team, in such a way that it will be *valunomic*—an economic concept related to cost effectiveness (will be presented in Chapter 4).

Project Management Is a Business

Projects are not carried out in a vacuum but are constrained by contracts, budgets, schedules, regulations, and expectations. Every single link in the supply chain must be profitable to minimize the risk of failure to the project. The business character relates to the commercial aspects of the work. The first obligation of this business is to develop, implement, and enforce an execution framework within which the organization works (more on this in Chapter 9). It sets the foundation underlying *how the work will be done* and establishes the hierarchy for decision making.

The second obligation rests with the contract. The work must carry on in accordance with the contract. The latter must be clear on its terms, conditions, requirements, and obligations. The business must adhere unconditionally to its full extent, *and must adopt the contract as a basis of interactions with the parties signatory to it*. One has leeway to inject informality and personality into those interactions; but contractual primacy must have hegemony.

The third and final obligation is tied to money. The business must get paid, and pay for the work done by its team, and pay for the work of others. The business must put in place the processes and systems to gather and track the metrics against which invoices and payments will be made. Finally, in addition to getting paid for the work done by its team, the business must do that work profitably. The profit motive pushes the business to continuously explore ways to improve process efficiencies, execution efficacy, and labor productivity. It must strive to acquire intellectual property (IP) assets which can satisfy the business' future endeavor.

Project Management Is a Relationship Nexus

People are led; all else is managed. Project management is about people. Ultimately, people make or break a project. They will be required to interact with complex computer systems to track, measure, quantify, and assess project metrics—and infer decisions thereafter. The inevitability of software yields an encouraging paradox: people will ultimately dictate the faith of a project, not machines. *People execute projects* (not companies or organizations). Even in a workplace already dominated by computers, the *human variable* remains at the heart of the practice of project management. This argument is superbly demonstrated by Geoff Colvin's *Humans Are Underrated*, in which he makes a convincing case for the future of employment against the backdrop of technology advances. Project management is a human endeavor powered by machines. The key is in finding ways to integrate the two.

THE BIG PICTURE OF A PPA SCHEMA

Orchestrating Principle

The PPA philosophy developed in this book takes a holistic approach to the management of projects. It emphasizes the organizational, procedural, and executive facets of a firm's corporate makeup. In PPA, project management is much more than plans, processes, and procedures, as illustrated in Figure 2.2. The success of a project requires a thorough integration of these facets—delivery, execution, people, M&Ms, development, and ROI—working in harmony to achieve the profitably performing asset. Failings from any one of these six facets are harbingers of a potential failure of the project.

Figure 2.2 Six facets of a profitably performing asset

The Schema's Pillars

The PPA schema transforms into a corporate management system that can be deployed within a firm as an operating principle for all project endeavors. The system is comprised of five pillars: (1) the primes, (2) risk management, (3) M&Ms, (4) framework, and (5) investment-centric project management (ICPM).

The Primes

These directives (collectively known as the group of seven) form the cadre of governance over the behaviors, interactions, and motivations of the people involved in a project, within an owner's firm. They apply universally within the firm, and equally to the owner, executives, managers, and project personnel. Each directive will be developed in detail throughout the text and will comprise:

1. Prime purpose—The project serves a singular purpose: to develop a profitably performing asset.
2. Prime directive—Do right by the project in all discussions, considerations, and decisions. Between egos and the project, the project must prevail. Execute against the constraint diamond (Figure 1.2).
3. Prime principle—Direct accountability, embodied in the *directrix*, governs the relationships between project participants (see Chapter 5).
4. Prime mindset—Manage by *getting-to-no* as the starting position, considering the budget as the investment vehicle to realize the asset. The budget is *invested*, not *spent* (see Chapter 6).
5. Prime execution—Advance all work *incrementally*, taking care to complete each task fully before moving on to the next one (see Chapter 12).
6. Prime tool—The unit transformation process (see Chapter 4).
7. Prime control—*Trust but check* rather than ubiquitous *review and approve*, in accordance with the Acceptance Maturity Model (see Chapter 6). Generate execution performance data in real time, using the *collection substrate* (see Chapter 15) and the *performance assessment metrics* (see Chapter 10) to measure progress.

Risk Management

In PPA, risks are classified in several groups which will be detailed throughout the text. Each type will be addressed in context and in relation to the individual or group deemed accountable for their control. Hence, some risks will fall under the purview of the owner; others to the framework and the project manager; and others still to vendors and suppliers. Regardless of oversight ownership, all personnel involved in a project must be aware of their existence and understand the ramifications of these risks roaming unfettered.

Mechanics and Mechanisms

We will describe M&Ms as the set of processes, procedures, templates, standards, directives, and other like-minded prescriptive tools and techniques that exist within an owner's organization and are available to the project team to execute its work. In most instances, the M&Ms are developed, controlled, and maintained by groups or departments that are independent of project execution (think engineering, procurement, accounting, and inventory control, for instance). In other cases, M&Ms may be developed specifically by a project team for its project. In all instances, they are directly associated with the *lessons-learned mechanics*, which will be discussed in Chapters 14 and 17.

Framework

The framework is a functional structure created by the owner to oversee a portfolio of projects and see to it that they are executed uniformly, consistently, and profitably. The framework oversees the all-important *PECO*, which is discussed in Chapter 7. Chapters 9, 11, and 12 discuss the framework at length.

Investment-Centric Project Management

The final pillar concerns the activation of the plans, strategies, and execution work required to develop the asset, embodied in ICPM. The ICPM approach can be applied to any project within an organization, as long as the first two pillars are already in place. One does not require the existence of a formal framework. Nevertheless, the highest probability of success materializes when the latter is in play *before* a project is initiated. Organically, the framework plans the project and sets its execution boundaries, while ICPM executes that plan within those boundaries.

NOTES

1. See: *Pulse of the Profession*® Highlighting Key Trends in the Project Management Profession.
2. See: http://stevenkeays.com/project-center/
3. William of Ockham (1287–1347) was an English philosopher and friar who posited that the best among many hypotheses is the one requiring the fewest assumptions.
4. Feynman was co-winner of the 1965 Nobel Prize in Physics jointly with Sinitiro Tomonaga and Julian Schwinger for a theory of quantum electrodynamics.
5. In the PPA schema, shareholders and stakeholders are distinct from each other. Shareholders are motivated by the success of a project and control the risks internal to it. Stakeholders are foreign to the project and generate the risks external to it.
6. Performance assessment metrics and key performance indicators are the subject of Chapter 10.

3

LEADERSHIP

A manager stands where he sits; the leader sits where he stands.

THE PRIMARY CAUSE OF PROJECT FAILURE

The Boss

The prominent cause of project failures is a failure of management. To paraphrase Ricky, in the classic movie Casablanca, all of the plans, strategies, and schemes can only amount to a hill of beans if your project manager (PM) can't cut it. Bosses make or break a project. We therefore begin our journey with the exploration of the causes, effects, and consequences of good, bad, and ugly leadership upon a project. First, we remark that, in business literature, the words *manager* and *leader* are used interchangeably. One reads about great managers of great companies leading their organizations through difficult times and about leadership teams going on management retreats to map out the future of their business. Whoever manages is also seen to lead, implicitly. Except, funny enough, in sports where one hears about a team's leaders, not managers, in the dressing room. In the world of projects, we need to distinguish between the two *because the person who leads can make or break a project.*

We define the term *boss* as the person vested with organizational authority. The boss runs things and makes final decisions. People will follow great bosses to another company but quit their own jobs if the boss is a buffoon or a tyrant. By extension, corporations exist on the strength of their values. Those values endure—or not—through their bosses. The truth of the matter is that bosses play an outsized role in the success or failure of their organizations. The fate of a project rests in the hands of the boss. We note, in passing, that all managers are necessarily bosses, pursuant to our definition, but a leader—not always.

Is the project better served by a leader or a manager? The simplicity of the question is misleading. For starters, the question is a false choice. In most instances, a project boss requires a combination of both. A project will always need a competent manager equipped with project, organization, and business skills. A project remains an ensemble of sequenced tasks that flourish within an ordered framework, which is the prerogative of the manager. A leader will be needed when the *people element* becomes an imperative of a project. This human factor manifests itself when emotions enter the fray against the backdrop of cold, rational work flows. The emotional currents that permeate project teams in such circumstances cannot and will not abide by the logic of a schedule, the demands of a contract, or the dictates of a boss. They require a leader who is able to deal with the emotional tensions at play. In extreme cases, a dictator may be the only remedy, as in instances of crisis, organizational upheaval, and personnel or contractual acrimony.

Authority Spectrum

Every boss is bookended the same way: subordinates reporting to him on one side and a higher-level boss to whom he must report, on the other. It is only at the highest level (CEO, president, prime minister) that one answers to constituents rather than another boss. The project boss oversees a team made of subordinates and reports to the framework lead (and likewise, to the owner for the framework lead). In all cases, the job of the boss is a *functional position* created by the organization that confers the boss' authority over subordinates. That authority is independent of the opinion of the subordinates, and liable to take on various forms along a spectrum between indifference and tyranny. Picking the right boss is of enormous importance to a project. Do you choose a manager who knows how things are run at the company? Or do you select a leader who can instill a desire to succeed in the team, beyond mere project metrics? Or must you appoint a tyrant because a project is already so far off the rails that it's do-or-die time? McGregor's classic division of managerial styles into Theory X and Theory Y (X believes in command and control; Y believes in participatory leadership) is one way to frame the question.

The Leadership Chromosomes

Douglas McGregor proposed his X and Y theories in the 1960s in an attempt to model human motivation in the workplace. In McGregor's view, one could divide workers according to two types—X and Y. The X type was unhappy with his job and tended to be lazy. The Y type characterized the opposite individual, one who is motivated, ambitious, and able to work autonomously. McGregor suggested that the X type would be managed best through a command-and-control, authoritarian manager, operating within a rigid hierarchy with tight controls and tight supervision at all operating levels. The Y type, on the other hand, would respond better to a manager who had faith in people's intrinsic desire to work well, be respected, and be accountable.

However, since very few people are pure X or Y, we need a more nuanced grada-tion. Organizational behavior theory approaches the question through the idea of *locus of control*. We wish to assess the impact of one's authority upon the fate of a project. For this, we define an *authority spectrum*, illustrated in Table 3.1. Note that the object of the spectrum is not a leadership model—that topic is amply covered in the literature—instead, the spectrum aims at differentiating the causes and effects of various kinds of authority immanent to an individual's emotional makeup.

Table 3.1 comprises six boss archetypes (*abdicrat, anager, misnager, manager, leader, tyrant*). The group *dangerous archetypes* is meant to be avoided on ac-count of their negative effects imparted to the state of the project appearing in the third row. The *recommended archetypes* trio is suggested as a function of the existing state of the project. The last row indicates the level of control exerted by the boss archetype over the progress and fate of a project. People are inherently inclined to operate preemptively, according to one of the six archetypes. In times of crisis, people will usually alter their behavior toward the archetype to their right. Conversely, when things are going smoothly, people may lapse toward the archetype to their left. For example, a leader will tend to turn tyrannical if things go off the rails, but may be in a relaxed managerial state when things are good. The extremities are paired in a circular fashion: tyrant—abdicrat—anager (for the abdicrat) and leader—tyrant—abdicrat (for the tyrant).

BOSS ARCHETYPES

Manager Archetype

The manager is a role within the organization. The role is externally created, externally justified, and externally controlled (by a higher boss). The manager exists to serve the needs of the organization rather than the subordinates. The authority flows from the organization, *imperviously from the expectations of the*

Table 3.1   Authority spectrum: boss archetypes and their effects on the state of a project

	Dangerous Archetypes			Recommended Archetypes		
Boss archetype	Abdicrat	Anager	Misnager	Manager	Leader	Tyrant
State of project	Condemned	Chaotic	Disordered	Ordered	Challenged	Threatened
Degree of control	Negative	None	Ad hoc	Explicit	Directed	Absolute

subordinates. The functions of the manager are oriented toward the orchestration of the work. The successful manager understands the purpose of the organization and its functional hierarchy, the roles of other managers, the capacity and limits of its immediate functional group, and the overall capabilities of the organization. A good manager focuses on the work to be done, the necessary mechanics and mechanisms, the human resources required, and the input/output needs of interdependent groups. The manager operates according to objectives defined by others. A good manager follows orders, rules, and regulations. He goes with the flow of his superiors and instinctively delegates upward when faced with difficult decisions.

Leader Archetype

The leader is altogether a different beast. His authority flows from the willingness of the subordinates to submit to his volition. Subordinates do this when they anticipate the leader's ability to fulfill their own needs. Consequently, the authority of a leader is granted by the subordinates, *imperviously from the expectations of the organization*. This is the crucial difference between leading and managing. The leader rules by consent of the ruled; the manager leads by consent of his ruler. A leader is moved by different motivations than the manager. The manager is motivated to do things right. The leader seeks to do the right thing. When in doubt, the leader's reflex is to seek counsel from within. The manager will consult his superiors. That is not to say that one reflex is better than the other. Each reflex has a place and time. In the wrong place or time, either reflex produces the wrong outcome, in the most wrong way possible.

Why should that be? The answer is found in their respective thymotic needs. The leader operates from personal conviction. His motivation, regardless of the purity of the intent, may not align with the expectations of the organization. It is this moral imperative that renders leaders so effective in times of emotional duress. The same imperative, in more benign circumstances, can lead to management discord. On the other hand, a manager who chooses to defer to a higher authority when the path seems uncertain or threatening may lose all ability to stir the group into action. The leader is less likely than the manager to play a zero-sum game tilted in favor of the organization at the expense of the team. Such instances will arise in business, demanding a certain level of gumption that may be lacking in the weak.

Tyrant Archetype

This archetype is self-evident. This is the individual whose reflex is to assume sole control and operate by the dictum *the means justify the end*. The tyrant is comfortable with power, and extremely obsessed. He is more likely to dictate than negotiate and expects unconditional obedience from subordinates. Their concerns are secondary to his objectives. They are, in his eyes, expendable as circumstances require. Tyrants are prone to micromanagement, vilify delegation, and refuse to yield. There are instances when a tyrant can be useful, preferably with a hint of benevolent character. When things have gone off the rails, the strong hand of a tyrant may be the only viable option to get things back on track.

Matching the Archetypes

The boss archetype should be the same for the PM and his immediate superior, pursuant to the principle of *sui generis*, which states that two or more people involved in a direct reporting structure will ideally work best when of the same archetype. The principle does not imply or endorse nepotism and sycophancy— coteries and cabals are nefarious to any organization. It is beneficial to recognize the fact that organizations function best when direct reports share the values and expectations of their superiors. Perennially argumentative relationships do not work in favor of the project. Unlike affairs of the heart, opposites do not attract in projects. Mismatches between a boss and a superior will often suffer from untuned values, divergent expectations, clashing *modus operandi*, and antagonistic conflict resolution. Fault lines will appear over time, under conditions of stress or strain. Nothing can come out of it unscathed. Worst of all is the case of the dynamic duo headed by a *manager* boss directing a *leader* PM. Under duress, each will instinctively revert to their characteristic selves, at the expense of the ultimate good of the project. One can never eliminate entirely the risk of *yesmanship*, which can be mitigated when professionals are trusted to act professionally. It is much better for a company boss, who is *at heart* a manager type, to hire a manager type as a project boss, and likewise, for a natural leader type to nominate a leader type as PM.

To Manage or to Lead, that Is the Question

The needs of the project must dominate the selection of its boss. Experience matters, but archetypes matter more. The manager archetype is best when:

- The owner-developer relationship is well established.
- The nature of the project is already familiar to the organization and modeled on the success of past projects with similar scope and size.
- The scope of the project is fixed at the outset, unlikely to be changed during execution, and matching past execution schemes.
- The project scale is small, relative to the organization's history.
- The work is to be executed recurrently over long periods of time in small-scope increments.

Conversely, the leader archetype is better suited when:

- The owner-developer relationship is new.
- The owner organization, or the developer organization, or both, will involve multiple partners.
- The nature of the project is new to the owner's organization, either in scope or scale compared to past experiences.
- The scope of the project is not yet fixed at the start and likely to be changed during execution.
- The project's complexity is high, compared to the organization's portfolio history.
- Project expectations for cost containment, schedule compliance, labor pool access, and supply chain logistics present material risk to the project's success.
- In doubt.

Finally, the tyrant archetype can be considered (carefully) when:

- The project has gone off the rails in a major way, is way behind schedule, or is grossly over budget.
- The client relationship is severely damaged and nearing the point of no return.
- Staffing upheavals and rampant discontent adversely impact the project's execution or progress.
- The strategic importance to the organization is such that its failure threatens its very survival.

More on the Principle of *Sui Generis*

The *sui generis* principle also applies to the hierarchy of a project and to the highest level of management (between owner and framework leader; framework leader and PM; and PM with key subordinates). At lower levels, the principle can be relaxed as follows.

The *manager archetype* is suited to areas of accountability characterized by predictability, repeatability, and the use of standard processes and procedures. Examples include administration, costing and scheduling, quality assurance, simulations and modeling, IT (information technology) support, drafting and drawings, time keeping, documentation management, and regulatory compliance.

The *leader archetype* is suited to areas of accountability where outcomes are prone to variations, redirection, change, perspective reconciliation, and conflicts—or, to put it simply, when activities are shaped by human interactions (recall the relationship nexus definition). Contracts and procurement, design evolution, innovation, change management, stakeholder containment, and construction oversight are typical examples. Crisis management, public relations, and operational readiness are especially well served by this archetype.

The *tyrant archetype* is not routine and applies to the special circumstances previously discussed.

Archetypes to Avoid

Three archetypes must be avoided at all times, or terminated once discovered. *There is no rational justification for employing any of these three types, unless the organization seeks self-destruction.* No project can succeed under the invertebrate management framework that they inspire. They include the *misnager*, the *anager*, and the *abdicrat* (three neologisms introduced by the author).

The misnager archetype describes an individual who is in a position of authority but is unsuited to the role, either out of incompetence, management whims, or career dissonance. The misnager is prone to making the wrong decision to solve an issue. He will tend to focus on the menial and the custodial matters at the expense of the big picture and material concerns (prone to *kyopia*, discussed later). Whatever the situation, the misnager is usually unable to discern what truly matters from the noise, and chooses to act on what is easy and benign, either out of cluelessness or cowardice about the potential consequences. The misnager shares one trait with the tyrant: the reflex of blaming others when things go wrong. He will even go so far as to select a fall guy *before* making a decision and include that person in his decision-making strategy. In the misnager's world, it's always someone else's fault.

The *anager* proactively seeks to *not* manage. He shares many of the misnager's traits but takes them to their logical extremes. The *anager* will *refuse* to make a decision or inject himself in the decision-making process. Fear of accountability, of responsibility, and of unemployment is the prime motivator of this individual. The anager readily delegates his authority to subordinates and assumes that he is off the hook if bad things occur. When forced to make a decision, he is paralyzed and prefers to flee rather than face the music. The anager archetype is not even interested in shifting the blame unto others; his ultimate objective is self-preservation.

The *abdicrat* is someone who will neither lead or be led. This is the individual who believes himself empowered to operate outside of the hierarchical structure of a project team. Most often, it is associated with people whose organizations are unwilling or unable to fire them. They develop a profound sense of entitlement and self-appreciation that is out of all proportion with their contribution to the team. The abdicrat will do as he pleases, when he pleases. When placed in a position of authority, he is wholly unreliable. One simply never knows what will ensue from his meanderings.

Archetype Selection

There does exist one ideal project boss: the manager who can lead. It is someone who knows the business, the features of the organization to succeed with the project, the right resources available, and the pertinent mechanics and associated mechanisms to get the job done. The PM can start from the mandate given by the boss and execute that mandate in an autonomous fashion, regardless of the vagaries of the evolving work. Great PMs do not need to be specialized in any of the accountability areas under their control. The real specialty is the ability to create and maintain a framework within which all functional areas work as one. Finally, great PMs succeed in developing profitably performing assets.

THE JOB OF A PROJECT MANAGER

Definition Redefined

The Project Management Institute (PMI) defines the job of a PM as the person designated to lead the project team, with the ultimate accountability for ensuring that the project delivers on its objectives. The reader is invited to ponder what this means on a daily basis. We once again face a definition that lacks definition. For one thing, to be *assigned* is utterly different than to be *mandated*. Nowhere is the matter of *authority* explicit. To *lead* in this naked manner presupposes a plan already in place. Who comes up with this plan? To *lead* is not the same as to *manage* or to *orchestrate*. To *lead the team* says nothing about the mechanics and mechanisms that are required, the training they imply, or the skill sets they demand. The *team* explicitly excludes all other parties privy to the project—such as the vendors, the regulators, and the external stakeholders. As for the *objectives*, they are nebulous. They are assumed to quantify, implicitly, the goal sought. This is a giant quantum leap of faith that may not survive scrutiny. One cannot quantify or measure metrically the performance of the team as posited in this definition. Finally, the *project* is equivocal. Is this the project in the owner's sense, or is the project associated with a specific scope of work assigned to the team? Consider instead the following definition of a PM:

> The project manager is the person granted overall authority to realize the mandate defined by the owner in accordance with the governing performance assessment metrics.

The mandate will be the asset, in the case of the asset owner, or a specific scope of work awarded to a vendor by the asset owner. The owner, correspondingly, is either for the asset, or of the vendor entity. Performance assessment metrics (PAMs) provide the quantifiable metrics by which the execution of the work is to be measured (discussed in Chapter 10). We can now deploy this definition to the daily life of the PM. We start from the triad definition of project management introduced in Chapter 2. The PM must wear three hats: *organizational manager, business manager,* and *relationship manager.*

Organizational Manager

The PM oversees the plans, strategies, sequencing, resources, and deployment of the standard operating environment (see Chapter 6). The bulk of the work occurs at the start of the project, when planning decisions are developed and mapped. The PM orchestrates this development across the delegated functional groups for each plan. Uniformity, consistency, and completeness guide the implementation of the work.

Once the project is launched, the PM switches to an oversight role split between information fluidity and anticipation of risks. The former targets the seamless transactions of information generated by all functional groups and vendors. The latter requires constant vigilance to head off any potential derailment; it is the more critical of the two. When a potential threat is identified, the PM must immediately assess its ramifications; provide advance warnings to the various parties potentially exposed to the deviation; quantify that impact and formally notify the holder of the purse strings of the consequence of the deviation; and finally, develop and implement the mitigation strategy that was approved previously by the purse holder. The key operating word here is *anticipate.* True project management acts *before* a problem materializes. Reporting on it after the fact, when costs and schedule delays have been irremediably incurred, isn't project management—it is journalism.

Business Manager

In this capacity, the buck literally stops at the PM's desk. The role is straightforward: deliver on budget and schedule (OBaS). The first job is to master the contract. The PM *owns* the implementation of the contract and the subsequent compliance to it. She must understand its nuts and bolts, especially the terms and conditions; PAMs; and conflict resolution mechanisms. The second job is to be the final arbiter of all contracts awarded to vendors, pursuant to the mandate's requirements. This implies, among other things, the selection of the right type of contract (discussed in Chapter 16) for the specific stage of development of the asset (discussed in Chapter 12). Job 3 is to get paid for the work done by the team, in accordance with the terms of the contract; while Job 4 is to pay for the work done by others. The fifth job is the obligation to verify that changes to the baseline mandate, approved in accordance with the pertinent contract, are incorporated into the new baseline, such that they are paid for on a timely basis. Finally, the PM must implement and operate a monitoring system able to capture, in real time, the entirety of the PAMs identified in the contract.

Relationship Manager

As team leader, the PM is required to deal with the human equation. Issues of personnel selection, deployment, training, termination, and conflicts fall under the direct purview of the PM, who is ultimately accountable for the performance of the team. She must remain vigilant about nascent relationship problems from within and without; assist the direct supervisors in their resolution or step in to sort things out (a role that is of the exclusive preserve of the PM, in matters of external relationships). Training is an integral part of the PM's strategic outlook (to be discussed in Chapters 14 and 15). Development of the team is part and parcel of this duty. The PM must not be content with letting the work unfold according to plan; she must also utilize that work as an opportunity to assess, in real time, the outcome of a particular piece of work (whether good or bad), by setting *ad hoc* debriefing sessions involving all individuals involved in that work. These sessions are inspired by the experience of the naval, air, and army services of the U.S. Armed Forces in the broadscale training of troops. *Learning by experience* is the best, most efficient method of imparting knowledge to people and teams alike.

In keeping with the principle of learning by experience, the PM and her team will gain great insights into the actual efficacy of the hierarchy by implementing recurrent *reverse performance assessments* of the team's chiefs. These assessments are provided, anonymously or not, by all direct reports of a given chief, on the latter's performance. The exercise is meritorious only if the questions are honest and the answers used as inputs to that chief's performance review by his own chief and the PM. Finally, it falls upon the PM to set the expectations, the lines in the sand, the consequences, and the decision framework (*perform or justify*, explored in Chapter 16) that will govern the work of everyone and the relationships that will ensue. Once they are enunciated, they are not up for debate or negotiation. She must roll them out and live by them from then on. Failure to do so will rupture any sheen of confidence that others held for the leader from the outset.

When to Get Involved

The PM will be busiest in planning the work. Once the planning is done, the team mobilized, and the work undertaken, the PM watches in order to gauge when to get involved:

- *Step out*—While things unfold according to plan, the PM should stay out of the team's way. As PM, you should trust in the abilities of your team's internal leadership, and trust that your people want to do a good job. When issues arise, allow those closest to the problem the freedom to find a solution. Most of the time, satisfactory outcomes will come out. Focus instead on the overall performance of the work through the PAMs gathered in real time. Keep your eyes on the big picture and its metrics.
- *Step in*—Not every issue will get resolved at the incipient level. That's when the PM gets involved directly. You provide guidance to the parties to arrive at a mutually acceptable solution. Remind yourself and everyone in the room that the desired solution is the one that best serves the interests of the future asset, not of any person or group. Abstain from taking sides.
- *Step on*—When issues fester, the PM must step on the scene to make the decision and get on with things. At this stage, which will inevitably come up, you must be prepared to assert your authority and dictate, in short, the terms of a resolution. This is never an ideal situation. However, the situation cannot be allowed to take on a life of its own. PMs get paid the medium high bucks for this very reason. The good ones will know how to shepherd the team through the unsettling times without disrupting the overall flow of the work. The bad ones won't.

The other instance when the PM must take full control is in times of crisis. Crisis management is a fundamental role of the PM, whose authority is also justified on that basis. Whether it is an external crisis, an internal incident, or simply a slowly unfolding train wreck, the PM must be prepared to take charge in unequivocal terms, impose order and discipline, control the message, and get everyone on the same marching orders.

Speak Softly

We come finally to the matter of a PM's voice. By virtue of her vested authority, the PM has no equal among the team. Hence, any comment, suggestion, pronouncement, or hint offered by the PM will be interpreted by everyone else through the lenses of that authority. An innocent comment made by the engineering manager will not be heard the same way when coming from the PM. This authority, tacitly understood by all, taints every word—and silence—of the PM. You, as PM, must never forget the veil draped over your authority. Speak sparsely; speak wisely; and never speak mindlessly.

Blind Spots

One of the hardest things for anyone, and for leaders in particular, is to exert a vigilant mental discipline against the dangers of *confirmation bias*. In psychology, the expression describes the propensity of a person or group of people to filter information in such a way that it strengthens or confirms a starting hypothesis or belief. The bias also tends to minimize or negate alternate interpretations. Every person possesses one or more such blind spots. Every group and organization is prone to them. The bias intensifies as a function of the emotional charge of an issue and acts as the default position when ambiguity or ambivalence surrounds a variety of options. It can be exceedingly difficult for a leader to discover one's own blind spots. It is always best to seek feedback from peers, subordinates, and spouses (especially). Let us heed the wisdom of the English physicist and chemist Michael Faraday who, on the occasion of a lecture entitled "Mental Discipline" delivered to the Royal Institution on May 6, 1854, explained why people have such a hard time changing their minds:

"Among those points of self-education which take up the form of mental discipline, there is one of great importance, and, moreover, difficult to deal with, because it involves an internal conflict, and equally touches our vanity and our ease. It consists in the tendency to deceive ourselves regarding all we wish for, and the necessity of resistance to these desires. It is impossible for anyone who has not been constrained, by the course of his occupation and thoughts, to a habit of continual self-correction, to be aware of the amount of error in relation to judgment arising from this tendency. The force of the temptation which urges us to seek for such evidence and appearances as are in favor of our desires, and to disregard those which oppose them, is wonderfully great. In this respect, we are all, more or less, active promoters of error. In place of practicing wholesome self-abnegation, we ever make the wish the father to the thought: we receive as friendly that which agrees with, we resist with dislike that which opposes us; whereas the very reverse is required by every dictate of common sense. The inclination we exhibit in respect of any report or opinion that harmonizes with our preconceived notions, can only be compared in degree with the incredulity we entertain towards everything that opposes them. It is my firm persuasion that no man can examine himself in the most common things, having any reference to him personally, or to any person, thought or matter related to him, without being soon made aware of the temptation and the difficulty of opposing it...That point of self-education which consists in teaching the mind to resist its desires and inclinations, until they are proved to be right, is the most important of

all, not only in things of natural philosophy, but in every department of daily life."

Origins of Confirmation Bias

A series of experiments in the 1960s suggested that people are biased toward confirming their existing beliefs. Later work reinterpreted these results as a tendency to test ideas in a one-sided way, focusing on one possibility and ignoring alternatives. In certain situations, this tendency can introduce bias in people's conclusions. Explanations for the observed biases include wishful thinking and the limited human capacity to process information. Another explanation is that people show confirmation bias because they are weighing up the costs of being wrong, rather than investigating in a neutral, scientific way. Confirmation biases contribute to overconfidence in personal beliefs and can maintain or strengthen beliefs in the face of contrary evidence. Biased search, interpretation, and memory have been invoked to explain attitude polarization (when a disagreement becomes more extreme even though the different parties are exposed to the same evidence), belief perseverance (when beliefs persist after the evidence for them is shown to be false), the irrational primacy effect (a greater reliance on information encountered early in a series), and illusory correlation (when people falsely perceive an association between two events or situations). Poor decisions due to these biases have been found in political and organizational contexts.

 Web Added Value™

4

THEORY

"One should not aim at being possible to understand, but at being impossible to misunderstand." Quintilian

THEORETICAL FOUNDATION

The Need for a Theory

This chapter lays down a theoretical foundation for project management. This idea of a theory is absent in the literature on the subject, save for niche academic papers. The Project Management Institute (PMI), for instance, makes no reference to it in its flagship handbook, *A Guide to the Project Management Body of Knowledge* (*PMBOK® Guide*). The allusions to such a theory, in the preceding chapters, proceeded from a tacit recognition that the practices espoused by project management orthodoxy constituted the theory proper. Nevertheless, a theory in the scientific sense is necessary. The act of management implies the need to predict an outcome. Actionable predictions require the correct understanding of the linkages among the elements of a project's execution. Such an understanding requires a coherent model of the inputs, processes, and outputs flowing through the linkages. Model creation requires a formal set of axioms to guide the dissection, synthesis, and quantification of the variables underlying the linkages.

Management is a proactive approach to future events, which requires the ability to predict, to anticipate, to gauge. To merely react after the fact is but journalism. Sound management is possible only through the construction of the right model for the project. To predict is to understand; to understand is to model; to model is to quantify; and to quantify is theory.

Projects as Information Networks

Conceptually, a project operates as a network of nodes connected by linkages through which information—inputs and outputs—flows. Inputs arrive at a node to be transformed into outputs. These outputs are, in turn, passed on to other nodes, sometimes cyclically. The creation and transmission of this information, in real time, constitutes the execution model of the project. This execution can only be managed efficaciously when the people shepherding it understand how information flows across the network. Each node is a process, a function, or a decision-gate representing every execution activity of the project, such as planning, sequencing, scheduling, cost control, risk management, vendor selection, scope redaction, progress measurements, quality control, social license audits, and the like. Within the network, these myriad of nodes give rise to even more numerous linkages, interdependencies, and couplings. To give but one simple example, a vendor drawing submitted for project management office (PMO) review involves two inputs: the transmittal form and the drawing proper. The node is the receiving function. The transformation process verifies the contents of the transmittal and the drawing's tracking data. The outputs are the confirmation of receipt; the receipt record; the notification of receipt to the PMO's accountable party; and the preparation of the drawing for internal circulation. On the input side, we have a single linkage between the vendor and the PMO. On the output side, we have several: send the receipt record back to the vendor; create the record into the document management system; e-mail the receipt status to the accountable party; prepare the requisite copies of the drawing; store the physical drawing in the master archive; and notify the contracts group of the status of the deliverable for this vendor. Each one of these linkages may, in turn, require additional inputs to accompany the transmission of the output.

Clearly, if this simplest of examples can generate this much transactional activity from just one event (the receipt), imagine the exponential growth experienced at the project level (akin to the *traveling salesman* problem in permutation analysis). The network model for any project will rapidly explode into a dense web of nodality beyond the reach of anyone's visual acuity, becoming, in effect, opaque and undecipherable. Forget trying to manage this network by hand with scheduling software or a database improvised on the fly; the only way out is in, through powerful software (which excludes the schedule, by the way, which is utterly incapable of mapping this network intelligently).

The Traveling Salesman Problem

A salesman wishes to visit "n" cities spread across the country during an extensive business trip. He wishes to minimize the total traveling distance that he will accrue during the trip. This Fermat-like problem, seemingly simple, is unfathomably difficult to solve for large "n" and is at the heart of an entire branch of mathematics called combinatorial optimization. It is known in the literature as the *NP-hard* problem, where NP stands for *nondeterministic polynomial time*. If "n" is small, say 3 or 4, the solution can be calculated by hand. But move up to 20, 50, or 100 (typical of the supply chain for an aircraft maker) and there is no hope of solving it by spreadsheet. Computing costs become a major line item driver in your budget.

The Rise of Complexity

Complexity provides the closing argument against the hands-on approach. The opacity of the project map is a direct consequence of the onset of complexity within the network, which is inevitable. Complexity, in turn, gives rise to dormant risks to the project's execution. Critically—and this cannot be overstated—*complexity is beyond the realm of direct, hands-on human control*. Once again, the only way out is in, through software. It follows, among other things, that the execution of a project must itself be programmable. This conclusion closes the circle on the need for a project management theory: coding requires a level of formalism which is possible only through an axiomatic theoretical foundation.

> *Risks are children of complexity. They cannot be managed without first mastering complexity.*

The Meaning of Complexity

Complexity is not limited to the project network, notwithstanding its seminal impact on it. This theme will emerge throughout the chapters, under various guises. A short digression is in order now to explore its meaning and implications. For starters, complexity is a field of study in physics, whose mathematics are beyond the scope of this book. We limit ourselves to a qualitative assessment of its character. In its simplest incarnation, complexity is a behavior whose outcome does not follow directly from cause to effect. That is, the sum of the parts interacting together does not equal the sum of the behavior of the individual parts. Furthermore, complexity is an emergent characteristic of a system. It appears only when its coupled elements begin to interact. It will lay dormant when things flow smoothly, and awaken when a coupling suddenly becomes nonlinear. The distinction between linear and nonlinear systems can be explained in several ways. One excellent perspective is captured by the *cynefin framework model* created by Dave Snowden of the consultancy *Cognitive Edge* (www.cognitive-edge.com). Snowden divides systems into four classes: simple, complicated, complex, and chaotic:

- Simple systems exhibit cause-and-effect relationships. They are predictable and repeatable. Simple systems are ideally suited to the use of so-called best practices to analyze a situation and select a course of action.
- Complicated systems also exhibit cause-and-effect relationships, but they are not self-evident. The relationships support the existence of several legitimate ways of doing things. The analysis of the situation does not lend itself to best practices but requires the input of an expert to determine the right course of action among the many options.
- Complex systems lack causality. Causes and effects are discerned in hindsight, but always with unpredictable, emergent outcomes. The decision process requires the conduct of safe-fail experiments to come up with fail-safe designs. Causality relationships can be determined through this iterative approach.
- Chaotic systems differ from complex systems in that the causes-and-effect relationships cannot be determined at all. The decision model in this case is to act first to stabilize the situation, sense how the situation reacted to the action, and respond to the reaction by adjusting the action. Chaotic systems cannot be modeled, predicted, or captured as heuristics for future applications. Every instance of a chaotic system is solved once.

The Three Domains of Management Action

Within the context of the theory, the act of managing a project occurs in three domains. The first domain, *mapping*, pertains to the creation of the project network by mapping the nodes, linkages, and inputs/outputs expected to occur in the execution of the project. This mapping is functional, in the sense that the nodes are associated with a task or activity. It is not, on the other hand, associated with a physical component of the plant. For example, a stress calculation on a steel column is a function. The second domain, *interface*, relates the management event proper, as discussed in the upcoming text. Once a project network is created, the management of the execution of the work takes place midway through the transmission of a node's output, before it arrives as an input to a subsequent node. The third domain is *control*, which occurs continuously over time. Control takes on the sense of monitoring by quantifying the progress of the execution in real time.

AXIOMS OF THE THEORY

The theory of project management comprises seven axioms. The axioms form a coherent design framework for breaking down a project into its constitutive elements; for defining the linkages between them to produce a comprehensive network of nodes through which the execution of a project will transit; for correlating the components of those nodes with organizational functions; and for permitting the translation of the components and elements into programmable objects suitable to an algorithmic foundation.

Axiom 1—Project Execution Is Managed at the Interfaces

Project execution boils down to this notion of an interface between relationships, shown in Figure 4.1. The transformation occurring inside the nodes (Processes 1 and 2) is carried out by the team accountable for the work. The management act takes place during the transmission of the output from Process 1 as input to Process 2. The act verifies that the output is wholly ready to be used as input to the next node. (Readiness is covered by Axiom 3.)

Axiom 2—A Project Is an Ordered Succession of Discrete Transformations

Everything that occurs during the execution of a project boils down to a series of discrete activities that transform a set of inputs into another set of outputs. The transformation is called a *mechanic* and the tasks, procedures, and tools

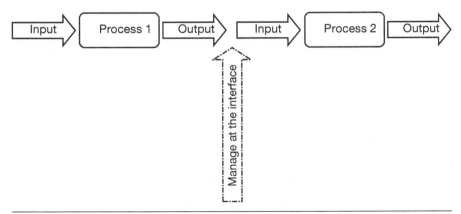

Figure 4.1 Managing at the interfaces: the act of management takes place when the output transitions into an input to the next node

involved, the *mechanisms*. An activity that produces no output or requires no input *is not an activity that belongs to the execution of the project*. The transformation itself is defined earlier and controlled henceforth as shown in Figure 4.2. As long as the inputs fall within the permissible range of the transformation, the outputs thus generated will be controllably produced and quantified. The transformation applies equally to the variations that may exist in the inputs: the resulting output variations are also controllably quantified. What goes on inside the box (the transformation) is where the execution occurs. The management of that execution takes place at the interfaces (the inputs and outputs).

Axiom 3—The Unit Transformation Process

This transformation schema of inputs into outputs forms the cornerstone of all execution plans. The transformation is discrete and called the unit transformation process (UTP).

A project can be modeled via a finite number of discrete transformation processes. Even when it is not necessarily possible to determine from the outset all the necessary processes, their effects can be quantified via input/output variations. Note, on the other hand, that it is not possible to achieve the end objective success if the transformation processes are incorrectly defined, missing, or erroneously sequenced. The elements of the UTP are illustrated in Figure 4.3. The term *activity* will henceforth represent the sum of the details, from input to process to output. The nature of the activity is discussed later in this chapter.

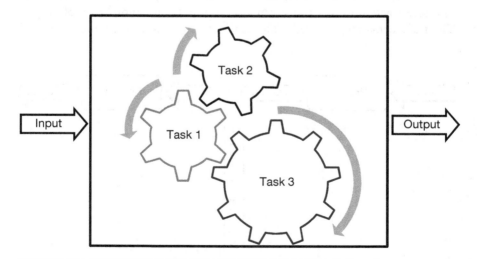

Figure 4.2 The activity as a black box: the mechanics and mechanisms involved in the transformation of the inputs into outputs reside inside the node—what goes · on inside is not accessible to the external manager

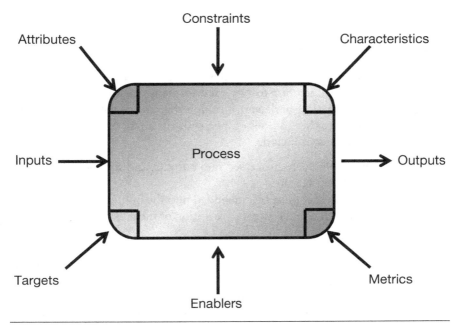

Figure 4.3 The components of an activity: the node is represented by the process—all other components are either supplied to the node or produced by it

Axiom 4—The Unit Transformation Process Is Fractal

The fourth axiom deals with scalability. The term *fractal* applies to an object whose shape is scale-invariant and self-replicating (i.e., it looks the same whether you zoom in or out). Fractals were discovered and popularized by the French mathematician Benoit Mandelbrot. This scalability is crucial from an algorithmic standpoint as an enabler of object linking and embedding and encapsulation. The fractal nature is uncovered quite readily. At the highest level, a project is a single UTP that transforms a set of inputs (cost, timelines, performance requirements, operating targets) into a single output—the profitably performing asset (PPA). This UTP is itself divisible into smaller processes; for example, an engineering process, a procurement process, a construction process, and a commissioning process. Each one can be viewed as a specialized UTP. Engineering is, in turn, divisible into design, modeling, analysis, calculations, etc. And on and on and on, until, in the limit, one has a comprehensive execution flow chart constructed from a multitude of specialized unit transformations. The nature of the transformations is immaterial from a theoretic standpoint. What matters are the junctions—the interfaces—that are created between sequences of unit transformations.

THE ACTIVITY STRUCTURE

Elements of the UTP

The structure illustrated in Figure 4.3 maps a set of inputs into a corresponding set of outputs (either one-to-one, one-to-many, many-to-one, or many-to-many, in mathematical parlance), through the encapsulation process. The activity is divided into three classes of mechanisms: input, process, and output.

The input mechanisms include:

- The *inputs*, which are processed into outputs, and supplied from one or more preceding activities
- The *attributes* that must be embedded into the output
- The *targets*, which quantify the execution of the *activity*

The output mechanisms include:

- The *outputs*, which are the outcome of the activity to be passed on to one or more subsequent activities
- The *characteristics* derived from the contents of the output
- The *metrics* achieved during execution (underwritten by the *targets*)

Finally, the process mechanisms include:

- The *process* that derives, transforms, or creates outputs from inputs
- The *enablers*, supplied by the organization to execute the activity
- The *constraints*, which create the closed boundary within which the activity is executed

Inputs and Outputs

The inputs are the independent variables to be transformed into outputs (the dependent variables). Some inputs flow through the process unchanged and emerge as identical outputs. Others will be converted into a different form. Others, still, will be created as new outputs.

The Process

We previously stated that the process is internal to the activity and is therefore defined ahead of time. The details of the process must already be fixed inside the activity. If any part of the process itself requires further definition, then that process becomes an activity unto itself. Additionally, the process is further defined or limited by the *constraints* and *enablers*. A calculation is an example of a process.

Attributes and Targets

These two input mechanisms differ from the inputs, in that they are *independent* of the process and essentially flow through the activity unchanged. The *attributes* pass through the process to end up as information embedded in the outputs. The *targets* go around the process to end up on the accounting ledger associated with the activity, as they are tied to the metrics obtained. Typical attributes include: a drawing number, a document title, a revision number, title block information, inspection requirements to appear in the notes of a drawing, a serial number, a part number, a price, weight and volume, owner of the activity, and reviewer of the outputs. Targets will typically be tied to time, money, and quality and will include things like: budget breakdown for each task of an activity, duration of the activity, schedule deadline, maximum number of errors, number of staff working on the activity, productivity, performance specifications on the output, and reliability rating of the output. Globally, the targets provide a baseline to quantify the actual execution of the activity (i.e., the metrics).

Characteristics and Metrics

These two output mechanisms are counterparts to the attributes and targets. The first, *characteristics*, are sets of countable features of the outputs that will be subject to future activities. For example, let the output be a single schematic drawing for a set of interconnected high pressure gas lines. The count would include the number of valves, regulators, indicators, switches, and I/O points (input/output control signals). If the output is a land survey report, the count could be the number of additional visits that will be required to complete the work. *Metrics* are linked to the *targets*. They are the actual, measured values of those targets obtained during the execution of the activity. *Metrics* provide a measure of the efficiency with which the activity has been performed. An example is given in Table 4.1 for the design of a concrete foundation for a machine. The *footprint* here specifies the maximum available space to install the foundation. Observe the implications of the metrics:

- The design work blew through the budget by $400.
- The design work is still not finished: $1,925 will be needed to cover the additional labor costs. This is seen in the *To Go* column.
- The schedule was exceeded by two days, while three additional days will be needed to finish the work.
- The size of the foundation, as designed, will fit inside the allocated footprint and will not require any more floor space.

Table 4.1 Example of project targets and metrics projects

Targets		Metrics	
Item	Aim	Actual	To Go
Cost	$2,000	$2,400	$1,925
Duration	6 days	8 days	3 days
Footprint	1200 m^2	1100 m^2	

Enablers

These are the tools, processes, people, systems, training, and task methodologies that the activity's parent organization must provide to execute the work. *Enablers* are artifacts of the execution framework underlying the project. Examples include an engineer who performs calculations; the calculation templates; the software to perform the calculations; the database of material properties; the training of personnel on the calculations; and the internal validation and verification mechanism to check the results.

Constraints

The last mechanism concerns the *constraints*. Constraints are imposed externally upon the project, usually by the owner or the regulator. The *constraints* establish the *acceptance space* within which the activity must take place. The boundaries of that space are deemed impenetrable from within. Some constraints are self-evident: budgets, timelines, physical location (such as land for example), tare weight (airplanes), and completion deadline (Olympic facilities). Some are legislated: building codes, electrical codes, occupational health and safety, union collective agreements, the practice of engineering, and foreign worker employment. Others are more subjective: community relationships, social development, environmental commitment, strategic positioning, and reputational. All of them are external in origin and subject to nonnegotiable enforcement.

No activity can be successfully completed if it cannot be executed within that space. Constraints are divided into four types: *compliance, standards, criteria,* and *allocation*:

- *Compliance* includes the regulatory requirements applicable to the execution of the work, to the individuals performing the work, to the tools used for the work, and the permits. Compliance implies an obligation created by regulators. Regardless of the origin of that obligation, once it is deemed to apply to the project or the task, it cannot be contravened (unless one wishes to test the goodwill of the pertinent regulator).

- *Standards* encompass the codes, standards, specifications, requirements definitions, templates, schemes, and other prescriptions upon the activity. Industry standards are usually adopted based on professional practice and acknowledged priority, or legislated. Standards are also specific to an owner's organization and imposed upon the project in equal force with the legislated ones. Standards differ from compliance acts and regulations in that they usually allow deviations, subject to thorough vetting procedures. Standards, ultimately, endow the project execution framework with a uniformity of expectations across the technical domains.
- *Criteria* are the externally defined constraints imposed on the inputs and outputs. *Criteria do not apply to the process.*
- *Allocation* represents the budget, time, and physical limits allocated to the activity or project.

The reader should observe that the four constraint types exist in a rigid hierarchy of precedence ruled by *compliance*, governed by *standards*, executed against the *criteria*, and produced by the *allocations*. A regulator will not care about the owner's cost to fix a leak in a high-pressure gas pipeline; the fix shall be made. The corollary of this hierarchy highlights the importance of aligning one's proposed budget and schedule with the mandatory *compliance, standard,* and *criterion* expectations. If the alignment is not possible, the project cannot succeed.

Examples

We consider two examples, beginning with a simple project to install a tankless, on-demand water heater in a house. The activity might be quantified as follows:

- Input: heater hardware, installation instructions, physical location, existing tie-ins to the existing electrical network
- Process: install the heater
- Output: working heater, successful test
- Constraints:
  - ▫ Allocation: $700 for parts and labor, one day for work
  - ▫ Compliance: electrical permit from city, journeyman certification, city inspector
  - ▫ Standards: CSA-approved material
- Enablers: Tool box, access to house
- Attributes: *heater* name on circuit breaker
- Targets: zero rework, work completed before 4:00 p.m., city inspector acceptance on initial visit

- Characteristics: installation checklist completed, city inspector label applied, water temperature verified at maximum flow rate
- Metrics: actual hours worked, final installation cost

For the second example, we contemplate the design of a vessel to store high pressure, sour natural gas. The activity in this case is more elaborate:

- Input: gas composition, pressure and temperature, moisture content, H_2S content, vessel sizing calculation report, flange connection sizing, vessel wall thickness, corrosion allowance, coating specifications, painting specifications
- Process: Create fabrication drawing
- Output: 3-D parametric model, 2-D fabrication drawing, schematic drawing, lifting lug calculations, material take-off listing
- Constraints:

  - Allocation: $4,000 budget, three weeks for completion
  - Compliance: Canadian Registration Number (CRN) through the Alberta Boiler Safety Authority (ABSA), drawings authenticated by a Professional Engineer registered with the Association of Professional Engineers and Geoscientists of Alberta, design guide imposed by the owner
  - Standards: Vessel design per the American Society of Mechanical Engineers' boiler pressure vessel code, drawing border template, drawing symbol template, color scheme, file naming convention, file extension convention, vessel material specification (from owner), instrument listing (from owner), construction specifications (from owner)

- Enablers: 3-D solid modeling software, associated computer hardware, past go-by, document management system, designer training program, designer certificate, access to online model database and client-supplied standards, library of technical codes and standards, cost control system
- Attributes: drawing name, number, revision number, nondestructive testing requirements, nameplate details, title block details
- Targets:

  - Costs: $2,500 (design), $600 (checking and quality assurance), $700 (ABSA registration), $350 (drawing stamp by professional engineer)
  - Time: five days (design), one day (client review), one day (final drawing), two days (ABSA submission), three weeks (ABSA registration)

□ Quality: one review cycle before final drawing, no error on the ABSA submission
- Characteristics: number of drawing sheets created, 3-D model file size, 2-D drawing file size, bill of materials obtained
- Metrics: actual labor costs, timelines and quality control, number of drawing errors found, hours and costs of rework, productivity comparison with historical averages

Evidently, the two examples could, and should, be broken down into additional subactivities to limit each process to a specific function or role. Take, for example, the pressure vessel scenario; the activity lends itself to a fractal division into the following sequence of UTPs:

- Vessel model creation
- Model verification—by engineer
- Drawing creation—by designer
- Drawing verification—by engineer
- Drawing review—by owner
- Model corrections from owner's feedback—by designer
- Final drawing creation—by designer
- Drawing stamping—by engineer
- Material take-off list—by designer
- ABSA submission preparation—by engineer
- ABSA registration—by ABSA, then engineer
- ABSA registration passed on to owner—by engineer
- File archiving—by designer and document control

THE ROLE OF RANDOMNESS

Axiom 5—Variability Is an Intrinsic Property of Networks

The fifth axiom takes its cue from Nassim Taleb's influential book *Fooled by Randomness*. Taleb informs us that randomness (in physics and in relationships) is always present and carries in its bowels the threat of rupture from predictability. The creation of a potent project network can easily fool its adherents into believing that they can exert complete control over a project's execution without surprises or deviations. Such a belief requires that everything that goes on between activities will do so in perfect unison. This is never the case since no transformable inputs can ever be quantified with absolute precision. They can only be stated with an approximate value, bookended by an error range. The result is immanent variability—unavoidable and impossible to eliminate from the execution of a project.

Error Propagation

The error range of an input is permanent. This variability will propagate throughout the network and result in error accretion to the extent that complexity and even chaos can ensue. Let us repeat the point: it is not possible to eliminate variations, uncertainties, and random effects. Taleb, for instance, states emphatically that any knowledge is imbued with limit beyond nothing is knowable, no matter what fancy and esoteric risk analysis model is used. The propagation of errors acts as a magnifying glass that amplifies the magnitude of these errors over time. The case is generically illustrated in Figures 4.4 and 4.5. In Figure 4.4, we note that the variability is always present at any point in time, but in varying degrees of ranges according to the project execution strategy. In Figure 4.5, the aggregate impact of the variations is indicative of the probability of failure of the project.

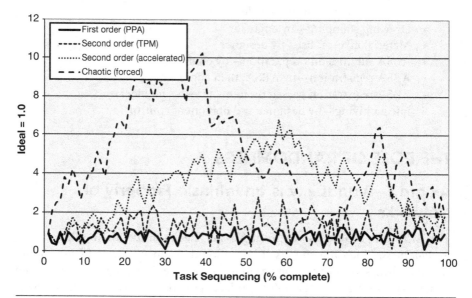

Figure 4.4 Effects of variability on execution across time: the PPA approach is best at minimizing variability by keeping it within the linear realm. Second-order nonlinear effects appear in a traditional project management (TPM) scheme. The nonlinear effects are accelerated when work is allowed to progress in parallel. Chaos ensues when parallel work is coupled with a broken change management process.

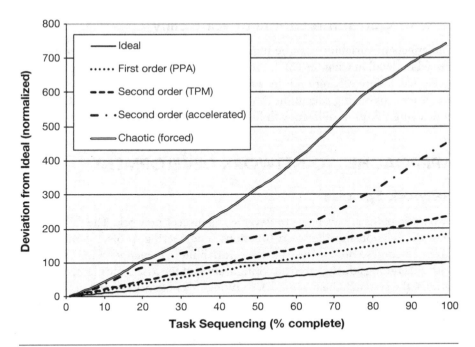

Figure 4.5 Cumulative effects of variability over time: variations will always widen over time as they pile up on each other.

In a world devoid of variability, all is known and reversibility ensues. Reversibility means that it is possible to invert a causation chain (from effect to cause) without any loss of information. Variability destroys reversibility. The causation chain is now irreversible, and cannot be inverted without information loss. This is the reason why audits of a project budget gone wild are so difficult. Irreversibility makes it difficult to infer the precise duration of a future activity. Ultimately, variability causes progress (i.e., work done) to deviate from the baseline. The baseline is reversible; the progress is not. Consequently, the order of a sequence of activities cannot be arbitrary.

Variability demands managing at the interfaces to contain its growth over time.

How to Corral the Effects of Variability

The effects of variability can be managed through *incremental execution* (discussed in detail in Chapter 12). Incrementalism insists on completing a deliverable once, before relying on it by subsequent tasks. It rejects calls to speed up the process by saving execution time through parallel work. It rejects the idea of delaying things until later, with the intent of *getting to it when we get there*.

APPROACHES TO NETWORK DEVELOPMENT

Network Spaces

Two basic paths are available to develop the project network. The first one follows the relationships between functions (engineering, project controls, procurement, and so on) and leads to a network built in the *labor space*. The second path rides alongside the physical configuration of the asset (the plant, the installations, the systems, the machines), resulting in a network erected in the *feature space*. When we speak of project execution, we are in fact implying the *labor space*, in which the nodal activities are defined in terms of human tasks. The inputs and outputs will be pieces of information generated as abstractions of the physical elements of the asset (the drawings, the calculations, the specifications, the permits, the contracts). The feature space is comprised of the physical elements of the asset to which labor must be applied to evolve from concept to reality. The network in this instance is represented by block diagrams of the physical features of the plant (the equipment, the distribution systems, the land, the buildings, the geography of the place).

At their inception, projects have historically been set up to be managed in the labor space, with their work divided functionally by engineering, procurement, logistics, construction, etc. Each function is then subdivided into disciplines (mechanical, electrical, civil for engineering), then into tasks (design, calculations, analysis). The master schedule and the work breakdown structure (WBS) pass for the project network. Therein lies a root cause of future failure. Why? This construct assumes that each function will capture autonomously the entire set of inputs, outputs, attributes, characteristics, and output-input interface exigencies. This assumption is most often wrong. The solution is to follow the physical features of the asset and its individual constituents.

Functions Follow Features

The work underlying the development of the asset is mapped in the feature space. For each component, UTPs are applied. Linkages between mutually dependent components are automatically identified through the output-input pairs. The labor associated with each transformation is then assigned in terms of *enablers* and *constraints*. Finally, the linkages between the various labor specialties are created from *characteristics-attributes* and *metrics-targets* pairings. For example, the capture of a given *attribute*, say the number of electrical connectors on a control panel, is then linked to the follow-on design UTP (create the drawing), to a procurement UTP (buy the connectors), to an accounting UTP (record the cost against the budget), and to a logistics UTP (expedite the delivery to meet schedule). This cascading set of labor activities derived from a single UTP constitutes the *fundamental difference* between the work scoping methodologies of the PPA and TPM. It will provide the impetus behind the sequencing of the work through the *esemplastic key*, described in Chapter 13.

The resulting network provides a governing work execution structure erected upon the physicality of the project. The resulting network of installations, systems, and components form the skeleton of the execution map. The plant configuration is mapped identically into an information network (the WBS); into the master schedule—and into the project's team hierarchy. The execution strategy inherits a single orchestrating principle—the plant configuration—from which all works, tasks, budgets, and timelines are organized. The work is no longer arranged by function or disciplines that are applied to sets of equipment and processes; it is sequenced by the reality of the plant's elements, which are then assigned the resources (personnel, enablers) and allocations for their complete definition.

> *In the feature space, the equipment justifies labor demands (skill, timing, numbers). In the labor space, labor demands justify the equipment.*

AXIOMS 6 AND 7

Dealing with Accountability

We have so far discussed five of the seven axioms of the theory. The remaining two axioms pertain to the issue of accountability. When we trace a diagonal across Figure 4.3, we obtain Figure 4.6. Below the diagonal lies the work and everything required to carry it out—in other words, the costs for the project. Above the diagonal sits the outputs generated by this work—or what the owner paid for. This duality is fractal, in that it is found at all scales of the project, from the simplest task to the entire plant realized by the project.

What is missing at this time is the determination of what component of an activity gets done by whom, when it gets done, and why. In other words, we need to sort out how to assign *accountability* to these components. In the next chapter, we will discuss Axioms 6 and 7 in more detail, which will clarify the matter.

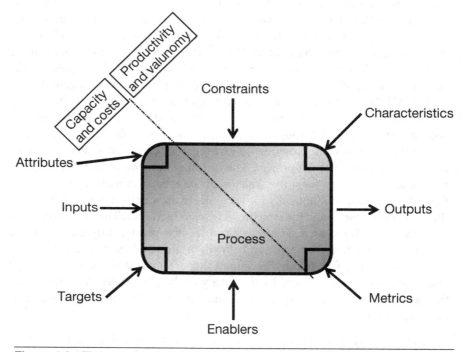

Figure 4.6   The activity drives both costs and resources: the owner pays for the asset—what this payment entails is encapsulated in the activity

5

ACCOUNTABILITY

The ancient Romans had a tradition for their engineers. Whoever built an arch, the engineer had to stand beneath it while the capstone was put in place. That is how Romans defined accountability.

THE MEANING OF ACCOUNTABILITY

Another Driver of Project Failures

When we speak of project execution, accountability and responsibility come to the fore. The issue isn't about management style, but mandates. This chapter will explore what happens when lines of authority are ill-defined, when the wrong people become involved in decision making, what the cost implications are to project budgets, and how an incorrect accountability framework can lead to project failures. The reader will be introduced to a new accountability paradigm that distinguishes between accountability, responsibility, and approval authority. Accountability is critical to the success of execution. Its absence, or dissipation, is a root cause of failure, and is manifested under the guise of *dabblers*—bit players who are intent on meddling into project affairs in the pursuit of justifying their existence. Dabblers, like bosses, can make or break a project.

Illusions of Accountability

Accountability is a term, like leadership, that is bandied about with reckless abandon in project circles. Its meaning is assumed to be understood to prevail and taken to be synonymous with responsibility. Lines of authority and reporting structures are erected upon that assumption. Detailed RACI (responsible, accountable, consulted, informed) charts are published at the project outset.

Progress and deliverables are subjected to onerous *review and approve* processes that involve large numbers of people who are indirectly impacted by those decisions. Decisions are considered under the ever-present shadow of the schedule, leading people to adopt a *"getting-to-yes"* philosophy, by which timelines trump decision inertia. The *review and approve* mindset imposes a communal approach anchored to an illusion of cooperation through management by committee. Decisions masquerade as optimal when derived from a compromise of disparate opinions. The scale of this oversight requires people—many, many people—leading to inflated head counts. Participants are afforded the luxury of plausible deniability. Since no single person decides, no single person is blamed when things go off the rails. Accountability effectively disappears at the price of higher execution costs.

Dabblers in the Midst

When accountability is diffused, dissipated, misappropriated, or absent, a project organization will fall back on the defensive reflex of doubling up on people involved in decisions. The net effect of this reflex is to foster an environment where dabblers thrive, first as individuals and, finally, as organizations. Dabbling is the bane of project execution, exemplified by the walking clipboard, armed with a checklist and marching toward the next *post-mortem* inspection. Dabblers feel compelled to offer unsolicited opinions on matters beyond their purview—believing their contributions useful. They meddle and prattle where analysis and acumen are called for. Dabblers are inclined to live by a trio of survival principles called FOE, JOE, and MOE—Finance One's Existence (find ways to be supported), Justify One's Existence (find ways to be involved), and Maintain One's Existence (find ways to continue to exist). Their credo might well be the hilarious wisdom of a motivational poster by www.despair.com, which highlights the fact that people who hold dear the belief that their lack of skill and knowledge can be compensated for by a doubling of their efforts, possess no limit to what they cannot accomplish.

Dabblers matter because they can wreak havoc on projects.[1] In the extreme, they become control freaks who are convinced of their indispensability. They can be fanatics in the Napoleonic sense: *there is no place in a fanatic's head where reason can enter.* When in charge, they will neither bear alternate perspectives nor tolerate others' deviations from their ukases. They neither trust nor delegate; they fear the unknown and crave control; and they give us a paradox: *in attempting to control all, none is.*

THE NATURE OF ACCOUNTABILITY

Axiom 6—Direct Accountability Is the Path of Attribution of Merit or Blame

The eradication of dabbling requires the unconditional imposition of accountability on people and groups alike. Accountability in our context takes on a very specific meaning. He who is made accountable is recognized and rewarded for successes—or blamed for failures. *Direct accountability* goes one step further by limiting the attribution of an accountability mandate to individuals. In the profitably performing asset (PPA) philosophy, groups, departments, and organizations *cannot be made accountable*. Projects will be successful when genuine accountability governs. It yields the most effective organizing principle for staffing a project with the smallest staff count.

To be accountable implies three conditions:

1. The decision of the accountable individual determines the success or failure of an outcome;
2. The individual can be singled out for reward or punishment for an outcome; and
3. The individual will directly live with the consequences of the decision.

All three conditions are necessary to guarantee that deciders will have skin in the game.

Direct accountability creates an organizing framework within which decisions are reached through clarity of intent and certainty of realization. Decision timelines will be shortened; cost certainty will be fortified; and associated labor costs will be minimized. Decisions may still be wrong in the end but the path underlying the decision will be transparent, lucid from within and without, and traceable. This fact highlights another benefit: the self-preservation of those empowered to decide. An audit could reveal the source of the error while concurrently demonstrating the rigor and reasonable care taken by the decision maker. Rigor leads to repeatability which leads to certainty. Being proven rigorous warrants continued employment. Perfection is never demanded, only sedulous reasonable care.

Axiom 7—Accountability, Responsibility, and Authority Are Distinct

The reader may have noticed that responsibility and authority have yet to enter the discussion. The seventh axiom is a corollary of Axioms 4 and 6, in that it assigns distinct meanings to both terms, separate from direct accountability. This distinction is rooted in the *unit transformation process* (UTP) introduced in Chapter 4. Within the UTP context, we establish the following delineations:

- *Accountability* is the power vested upon an individual to execute a UTP. The expression *accountable party* (AP) will apply to such an individual.
- *Responsibility* is the mandate assigned to an individual to marshal the resources required to execute the UTP. The expression *responsible party* (RP) will apply to such an individual.
- *Authority* is the power to approve the outputs of a UTP. The expression *probate party* (PP) will apply to such an individual.

Together, the three parties constitute the *directrix*. The *directrix* embodies functionally the principle of managing at the interfaces (see Axiom 1 in Chapter 4). It furnishes a vital check-and-balance structure that supplies the mechanics to validate and verify the execution of an activity. The roles of the AP, RP, and PP are illustrated in Figure 5.1:

- The AP owns what goes on inside the boundary of the activity. He defines what output must be generated, specifies the transformation mechanisms required to produce the outputs, specifies the inputs needed by the transformation, and identifies the enablers required to execute the activity.
- The RP lines up what is required to carry out the work. He supplies the attributes, the targets, and the enablers (project information, tools, processes, procedures, and appropriately trained personnel). The purpose of this role is in keeping with modern concepts of organizational behavior theory. This theory asserts that the role of managers is not to produce goods or services, but to supervise those who do the production, from which is derived their mandate as guarantors of operational effectiveness.
- Finally, the PP defines the limits, the constraints, and the output acceptance criteria. The PP certifies the correctness of the outputs and UTP characteristics before moving on to the next UTP. This work includes the verification of the compliance of the outcome against the constraints imposed upon the work.
- Once the PP has signaled approval, the RP accepts the metrics and imports them into the project control mechanisms for overall execution progress.
- Whenever a deficiency is noted, at least two of the three individuals confer to assess and solve the issue.

It is in this interplay that the check-and-balance principle comes into force. Even though the three parties are fairly equal, the AP is the first among them in one specific aspect: he is the one to take the lead to coordinate the timely participation of the PP and RP in the UTP.

The *directrix* runs counter to the widely held view in management circles that accountability is everybody's business. The consulting industry devotes an entire segment to behavior-centric organizational accountability. The topic isn't new either: *The Oz Principle*, for example, was originally published in 1994 and posits that a person is accountable for everything within her environment. It is but one instance of the message about accountability for all by all. However, when everyone is in charge, nobody is. That philosophy is incompatible with the 6th and 7th axioms.

Exclusion Principle

The idea of singularity is of paramount importance to the *directrix*. For any given UTP, there must correspond one—and only one—person assigned to each

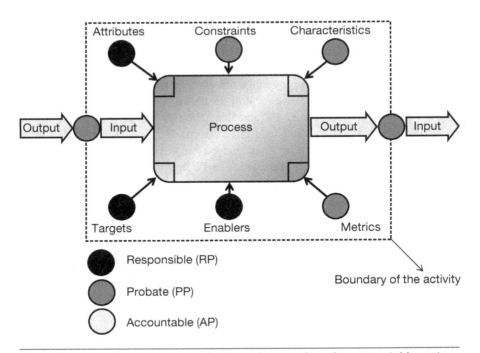

Figure 5.1 The directrix at work: the directrix comprises the accountable party (AP), the responsible party (RP), and the probate party (PP)—each one is assigned specific roles in the execution of a UPT, without overlap

one of the three roles. This is the exclusion principle underlying Axiom 7. *The assignment is never to groups or departments, nor can there be overlaps in kind between the AP and PP.* The principle is best illustrated by the following example by the engineering *squad check* mechanics found in the oil and gas industry. In its traditional project management incarnation, the mechanics works in the following way. The squad check is an ad hoc group gathered on-the-fly from representatives from all disciplines (electrical, mechanical, civil, automation, structural, process, quality, and operations—just to name a few). The squad is mobilized whenever a deliverable, say a schematic drawing, requires a review. The drawing is placed on a table. Over a period of days, a myriad of handwritten comments will be made by the squad members. These independent comments constitute the totality of the review process—no group discussion will be held. The comments are scanned and sent back to the drawing's originator. The drawing will be revised accordingly and recycled through the squad check mechanics. Several iterations of the cycle will take place before the final drawing version is approved. Note the complete absence of any direct accountability or differentiation between the AP, PP, and RP roles. Every member of the squad team is free to submit one, two, or three, as he so wishes.

In the PPA schema, things get done differently. First, one person within the project management office (PMO) is assigned the AP role for the drawing. Second, the AP designates one person from the PMO as PP for the drawing. Third, the PP determines what discipline expertise will be required for the review. The AP then assigns discipline representatives to the squad check team. Upon receipt of a drawing to be reviewed, the AP and PP perform a first check. The drawing is then either annotated by the PP, and the AP sends it back for updates, or the AP convenes a review by the squad check team. The review is attended by all members and may require more than one meeting. All comments, annotations, and changes are discussed by the team. The PP approves all annotations before they are placed on the drawing (the *markups*). At the end of the review, the AP transmits the drawing markups back to the originator. The revised drawing is received by the AP, who convenes a confirmation meeting with the PP only. Unless changes were missed, the drawing is then confirmed as acceptable. Otherwise, it is sent back to the originator for completion. New changes to the drawing should never be made unless a glaring mistake (made by the squad check team) is discovered. At all times, both the AP and PP maintain a *getting-to-no* attitude (discussed in Chapter 6) toward markups proposed by the squad check team.

The Directrix and Managing at the Interfaces

Managing at the interfaces is indicated by the junction circles in Figure 5.1. Neither the AP nor the RP is permitted to interfere in the verification actions by the PP. In turn, the AP does not get to decide what constraints apply (that's up to the PP), or control the message conveyed by the productivity metrics (owned by the RP). Figure 5.1 unambiguously delineates the applicable boundaries of each party. The direct control of one party ends where the other party's control begins. Interfaces occur at their shared junctions. The constraint and enabler junctions are intuitive. The input and output junctions, on the other hand, warrant a closer look. It is dangerous to take it for granted that the precedent output is compatible with the requirements of the subsequent input. *Compatibility* is the key word here and the very reason for the need to manage the interface. Compatibility makes or breaks the peerless execution of the work and comes in two modes:

- *Logistics*: the timing, quantity, and quality of the output
- *Configuration*: the form, fit, and function requirements of the input

Logistics in this context is simple to understand. The output must be available at the start of the subsequent activity. The output must come with all the bits and pieces needed by the activity's input. *Configuration* deals with the suitability of the output to *bolt-up* perfectly to the input. For example, let the activity be the sizing and selection of a water pump. One preceding output could be the calculated incoming flow conditions, characterized by flow rate, pressure, temperature, liquid composition, and density. Are they in correct units (metric versus imperial, for example)? Is the flow delivered by a pipe with an outlet flange that matches the rating of the pump's inlet flange? Is the physical orientation of that pipe aligned with that of the inlet flange? The physical *fit* could be indicated by whether the threaded pipe inlet on the pump is a tapped screw or a stud-and-nut assembly. The *function* aspect could be represented by whether the connection is meant to provide a shear-failure protection or a vibration-resistant assembly of the screwed part. Those are the kinds of issues that belong to the realm of *configuration* and which must not be assumed to be correct.

> The essence of managing at the interfaces is to verify that the compatibility requirements are comprehensively defined before and enforced after.

TEAM HIERARCHY VERSUS DIRECTRIX

The Reporting Structure Is Driven by the AP

The separation of the roles among the AP, PP, and RP is a characteristic of the *execution* of an activity. At the level of the project hierarchy, the project team is built based on the AP roles. In effect, the *organization chart* networks the AP roles as a decision hierarchy. The PP and RP will not, in general, appear as functional boxes in the organization chart; they are individual task assignments.

Paradoxically, each role will include elements of the other two in the daily execution of its mandate. For example, the AP for a given activity is *responsible* for orchestrating the enablers provided by the RP, and has the *authority* to deploy the enablers to execute the work within the defined constraints. The RP is *accountable* for the timely allocation of the enablers requested by the AP (as well as the suitability, adequacy, and sufficiency of those enablers). The RP has the *authority* to mobilize those enablers unto the activity. The PP is *accountable* for defining the applicable constraints for the activity, and for the verification of outputs accordingly.

Dabblers Be Gone

Projects fail when dabblers flourish at the expense of genuine accountability. It is best to measure the progress of the execution and its outputs by the *smallest possible number of competent people.* Conversely, a multitude of comments is no guarantor of an emergent consensus. The opposite is more likely to ensue: contradictions are revealed, conflicting agendas collide, egos clash, and decisions are delayed. Paralysis by analysis sets in. Amorphous phantom risks are given substance and take on airs of inevitability; these risks, in turn, foster the impression that larger teams are needed to oversee the work. Such a reality, to paraphrase Dorothy Parker, must not be set aside gently but cast away with virulence.

The curse of dabblers can only be lifted by institutionalizing direct accountability, operating on the basis of *trust but check* (discussed in Chapter 6). Never forget that if you ask someone's feedback on a drawing or a report, you *will* get comments, even after the document has been published! Accountability is to the individual what the *directrix* is to the team.

NOTE

1. Nassim Taleb, in his excellent book *Antifragile*, offers a nice variation on the theme, calling them *fragilistas*. The fragilista, in Taleb's mind, gets people engaged in all manners of artificial actions whose collateral effects can be unseen yet deleterious.

Web
Added
Value™

This book has free material available for download from the
Web Added Value™ resource center at *www.jrosspub.com*

6

GETTING TO NO

"It is the sort of bloody nonsense up with which I will not put."
Winston Churchill, to an aid pointing to a sentence ending in a preposition.

METHODS OF DECISION MAKING

Managing Mindsets

The direct accountability model equips the project manager with the tool to parse a project into an algorithm-ready, executable work sequence, managed at the activity interfaces. From the viewpoint of human relations, these interfaces are events where people interact and personal egos possibly collide. Motives, interests, self-preservation, and volitions greatly impact people's interactions in the pursuit of a consensus. Therefore, the direct accountability approach requires an *intent framework* to deal with clashing interests. It needs, in other words, an enforceable, global mindset to serve as a moral anchor to justify decisions.

The decision mindset rests ultimately with the project manager, who is under constant schedule pressures. These pressures are exacerbated by an insistence to *review and approve* everything. They induce the environment to become infused with a permanent sense of urgency to make decisions without retarding the progress of the work. Faced with competing vectors, the project manager must choose between *getting to yes* (get on with the work now and formalize later) and *getting to no* (no go until proven justified). The larger the team is, the stronger the bias toward *getting to yes*, an artifact of the psychology of groups characterized by Max Ringelmann early in the twentieth century.

Ringelmann's Rope

The truth of this management reality was uncovered by Max Ringelmann's famous study early in the twentieth century. Ringelmann (1861–1931) analyzed people alone and in groups as they pulled on a rope, and he measured the pull force. As he added more and more people to the rope, he discovered that the total force generated by the group rose, but the average force exerted by each person declined, thereby discrediting the theory that a group team effort results in proportionally increased effort. Ringelmann attributed this to what was then called *social loafing*—a condition where a group or team tends to *hide* the lack of individual effort (eerily resembling our dabbler concept). Hiding is easier than deciding, and it leads implicitly to a get-to-yes mindset.

The Three Poles of a Management Mindset

A management mindset has three poles: *progress, preserve,* and *protect.* The *progress mindset* seeks to protect the schedule above all else. The *preserve* mindset obsesses about the budget. The *protect* mindset strives toward the asset's future profitable performance. The first two are the inevitable consequence of the *constraint trifecta* (seen previously in Figure 1.1). The *protect* mindset stems from the *constraint diamond* (as illustrated in Figure 1.2).

Getting to Yes

Getting to yes is the hallmark of the *progress* and *preserve* mindsets. It is a culture that tends to justify continuing the work *now* to save time and schedule, leaving the formal approval until later. It is a defense mechanism against institutionalized inertia. It also justifies the strategy of empowering teams to progress their work in parallel with the decision-making process. The inertia in question is an intrinsic quality of large review and approve teams. Global project execution schemes exacerbate the problem. Twenty-first century projects are global affairs pursued by deep-pocketed organizations and governments. They heave upon their projects stringent expectations of speed to market, cost and risk containment, security of supply, and certainty of quality. These expectations add worrying levels of complexity to the execution strategy. Project teams respond by expanding their headcount in the hope of compartmentalizing risks. A vicious circle is set in motion: adding more people leads to more complexity and therefore, more risks. The end result is a condition by which competent people and organizations are booked solid and perpetually short of personnel. Under these circumstances, one can almost justify the reflex of getting to yes.

> *Getting to yes prevails where timeline imperatives are permitted to override slower, risk-driven decisional frameworks.*

Getting to yes leads project people to sacrifice execution discipline at the altar of schedule integrity. It establishes the precedent that *yes* can override the checks and balances of a disciplined decision-making process. It infuses the entire project execution with the deleterious effects of accountability dissipation and dabbler proliferation. Far from reducing execution, budget, and schedule risks—the opposite transpires.

The Worst Hole in All of the Gulf

BP's catastrophic explosion of its Deepwater Horizon drilling platform occurred in 2010 while drilling the Macondo well about 80 km from the Louisiana coast. The blast killed 11 crew members and spilled millions of gallons of crude oil into the water. The explosion came as a surprise, but not out of surprise. In fact, the cabin crew monitoring the well had botched a key safety test and had willfully ignored the abnormally high pressure readings that were pointing to obvious signs of trouble with the well. A *get-to-no* mindset would have required them to halt everything, but the crew acted in accord with the *getting-to-yes* mindset, which overrode the checks and balances of the operation.

Getting to No

The cure to the *getting-to-yes* culture is straightforward: *get to no* instead. That is, embrace an execution philosophy that stipulates that nothing occurs unless it can be formally justified first. The idea of defaulting all decisions to *no* originates in the necessity of accountability, which imposes checks and balances on the entire execution strategy. The principle applies to the project baseline itself; you should assume that all potential elements at the start are unnecessary until proven otherwise. From then on, all changes to the baseline are deemed rejected until proven necessary. *Getting to no* finds corroboration in, of all places, industries driven by innovation, and preached by the high priest of innovation himself, Steve Jobs. Jobs was unequivocal in his views on focus. In his eyes, focus is not agreeing to do all sorts of things, but saying no to most ideas quickly, in order to pick what is really worth working on. Jobs used to say that he was proudest about the things his team never pursued. Innovation, in Job's world, meant saying *no* to one thousand ideas.

Getting to no embodies the *protect* mindset. The latter comes equipped with five conditions:

1. The scope of work and its sequencing were produced from a thorough application of the parsing of the direct accountability model

2. The organizational structure incarnates the *directrix* requirements
3. The *acceptance basis* for each activity has been defined by the owner
4. The owner deems the integrity of the profitably performing asset the highest objective
5. The owner empowers the team to execute the work against this prime directive

When these five conditions are fulfilled, the principle of *getting to no* unfolds naturally. Note that the principle does not disavow schedule, scope, or budget changes; but it is obdurate in adhering to the decision-making process. The latter offers the owner the strongest hedge against execution failure. Project teams thus constituted will likely be optimally staffed; dabbling will be eliminated, and changes to the project will be realized valunomically.

Getting to Change

The contrast between the two approaches is greatest in change management. Projects can theoretically survive a progress or a preserve mindset—*except for changes. One must never manage changes on a preemptive basis, in anticipation of future approval.* All proposed changes must be considered within a *protect* mindset, with rejection as the default position. What if there is urgency to a proposed change? In that case, the onus is on the project manager to give it priority! If the schedule is that important, it follows that the change decision must be a priority.

ACCEPTANCE MATURITY MODEL

Trust Has No But

The management mindset is the moral anchor of the project's execution. The execution's attitude, on the other hand, dictates the intervention. This attitude concerns the decision-making mechanics. What gets reviewed by whom? Who approves what? When is a deliverable finally accepted? These questions fall under the aegis of the *acceptance basis*. We move away from *review and approve* and migrate instead toward the *trust-but-check* philosophy. *Trust but check*, as the name indicates, requires the existence of faith by the owner's project team in the work of others. The party executing the work (be it internal or external to the owner) is deemed competent to warrant trust in the validity of the outputs it produces.[1] The owner limits himself to verifying the compliance of the outputs to the standards, characteristics, and metrics imposed at the front end. The *trust-but-check* philosophy employs fewer personnel than *review and approve* while yielding faster execution speeds.

Vendor Maturity

Unfortunately, there can be no pure *trust but check* since not all vendors are created equal. In some instances, *review and approve* is inevitable. The pertinence of one over the other is a function of the vendor's execution maturity. Maturity is gauged from a deliverable's *contents* and *presentation*. The *contents* represent what is bought by the owner: a report, a calculation, a machine, or a plan, for example. *Contents* are the output in a unit transformation process's (UTP's) input-process-output mechanics. *Presentation* is the deliverable's physical embodiment of the owner's *standard operating environment* (SOE). The SOE is the complete set of standards, procedures, templates, document specifications (naming, numbering, style guide, color schemes), and administrative methodologies that apply ubiquitously over the project's life cycle. The mature vendor produces a complete deliverable in terms of contents and presentation such that the owner will approve it in the first review (with the least effort).

Acceptance Maturity Criteria

The vendor's maturity level is assigned by the owner using *acceptance maturity criteria*. These set out four categories of acceptance of an output, as a function of the level of effort required for its review:

- Category 1: Execute and accept
- Category 2: Execute, approve, and accept
- Category 3: Execute, verify, approve, and accept
- Category 4: Execute, validate, verify, approve, and accept

Execute means the work done to complete a UTP's *input-process-output* mechanics. The work includes the internal checks and quality assurance controls inherent to the organization performing the work. The *execute* role belongs to the *accountable party*.

Validate means repeating the *execute* work of an output by an independent third party. Achieving the same results as the original ones concludes the validation. The *validate* role belongs to the *accountable party*.

Verify means direct verification of the output's *contents*, either by the *accountable or probate party*.

Approve confirms the *presentation* compliance of an output. The contents are deemed accepted without further action. The *approve* role belongs to the *probate party*.

Accept declares the output can be formally relied upon by others. Acceptance is the event used to trigger, when applicable, the start of the warranty period. The *accept* role belongs to the *probate party*.

The level of effort varies considerably from Category 1 to 4. For the owner, the roles of *approve, verify*, and *validate* involve significant time and labor that must be factored into the execution strategy. The distribution of the roles within the project team must consider the organization's limitations (be it the vendor, the project management office [PMO], or the owner). These limitations include:

- The existence of the appropriate expertise within the owner's team to competently perform the step (beware the dabbler's curse)
- The timely availability of the competent staff to perform the step
- The availability of the tools for the effort, and the attendant training requirements of individuals on these tools
- A sufficient allocation of time and budget to perform the step
- The defined accountability, responsibility, and authority to the various team members
- A compatible duration and start of the step with the project schedule

The first five limitations must be totally satisfied for an organization to take on either a *verify* or *validate* role. When they are not satisfied, the intervention will turn into dabbling with inevitable damaging effects. In such a case, the superior option is to assign these roles to a trusted third party who does satisfy the five requirements. As to the last limitation, any negative impact should normally be thwarted by proper accounting in the baseline schedule.

The validation and verification roles transfer the accountability to the entity performing the role. If you edit it, you own it!

Can Must Not Mean *Must*

The selection of an acceptance basis enforces the principle of direct accountability on the owner and vendors alike. Just because an owner satisfies the five limitations does not mean that he should take on that role (directly or through a designate). For example, if a project requires a 5,000 kW electrical motor, the design accountability rests solely with the motor vendor. Any suggestion that the buyer should do anything beyond accepting this design as-is should be crushed with gleeful abandon. Remember that execution expertise can only be meaningfully verified or validated by another party with equal or superior expertise. Otherwise, dabbling will ensue.

The *acceptance maturity model* requires the PMO to assess the valunomy of getting involved in the acceptance process, regardless of the team's actual capabilities. The assessment is best made at the front end of the project definition, pursuant to cold rationalization rather than staffing justification.

Vendor Ratings

Vendors are rated in terms of *expertise* and *history*, in order to be assigned an overall maturity rating:

- *Expertise*, shown in Table 6.1, pertains to the vendor's relevant experience with the equipment or service to be supplied. It quantifies the vendor's level of knowledge, experience, and exposure to the type of equipment or process under consideration.
- *History*, shown in Table 6.2, relates to the vendor's relationship with the owner and characterizes the vendor's track record in the industry that is specific to the owner project's ecosystem.
- Each one is rated by the owner on a four-point-scale maturity level (low, medium, high, expert). The rating corresponds to one of five acceptance levels: avoid, validate, verify, approve, or accept.

Table 6.1   Acceptance maturity criteria for expertise

	Maturity	Definition	Level	Rating
SME[1]	Low	Little or no experience with the equipment or process	Validate	1
	Medium	Similar experience derived from other industrial sectors	Verify	2
	High	Sustained experience in the project ecosystem[2]	Approve	3
	Expert	Go-to solution trusted by the project ecosystem	Accept	4
Domain	Low	Little or no commercial activity in the industry[3]	Validate	1
	Medium	Active in the industry but not in the project ecosystem	Verify	2
	High	Successful player in the project ecosystem	Approve	3
	Expert	Go-to player trusted by the project ecosystem	Accept	4

[1]Subject matter expert.
[2]The project ecosystem is discussed in the next chapter.
[3]The industry encompasses all competitors to the owner, whether in the same ecosystem or not.

Table 6.2   Acceptance maturity criteria for history

	Maturity	Definition	Level	Rating
Owner	Low	Never worked for the owner	Verify	2
	Medium	Worked for the owner's competition, or with the owner in another project ecosystem	Verify	2
	High	Works regularly on owner's projects and familiar with the owner's SOE	Approve	3
	Expert	Awarded a Master Services Agreement by the owner	Accept	4
History	Low	Unknown or negative project performance track record	Avoid	0
	Medium	Positive project performance track record in the industry	Verify	2
	High	Positive project performance track record with the owner	Approve	3
	Expert	Provides benchmark to compare other bidders	Accept	4

The determination of a maturity level for a given vendor proceeds as follows:

1. Select the appropriate ratings for the four rows: SME (subject matter expert), Domain, Owner, and History
2. Calculate the maturity level by multiplying the four ratings together
3. Select the acceptance method (Column 2 of Table 6.3) by the maturity level shown in Column 1

The third column affects the execution strategy. It suggests the ratio of the probate team's headcount to that of the accountable team. The inverse proportionality follows from the implications of the maturity model: lower maturity ratings require greater oversight by the probate team. The inverse proportionality also goes for the complexity of the oversight structure, which in turn, goes hand in hand with execution risks.

Table 6.3   Selection table for assigning an acceptance maturity rating

Maturity Level	Selection	Head Count (Ratio to AP)
Equal to 0	Avoid	
Level < 25	Validate	80 : 100
26 < Level < 120	Verify	50 : 100
121 < Level < 240	Approve	20 : 100
Level > 241	Accept	10 : 100

SETTING THE STAGE FOR SUCCESS

We have reached the end of Part 1. We now possess the essential concepts to orchestrate the details of a project execution strategy. Part 2—WHERE—begins with setting the stage for success in executing the project. Projects are creatures of the space in which they unfold, and cannot exist imperviously to it. One should understand what that space is, before jumping off a cliff into execution darkness. The space is multidimensional and includes a physical component—the project ecosystem; a financial component—the budget; a planning component—the strategy; and the metric space—the performance assessment metrics. Our next stop is the project ecosystem, which encompasses the external constraints to the project.

NOTE

1. Who would, in any case, have already been vetted in this respect during the contract bidding phase.

PART 2—WHERE

A second act which surveys the practice of project management from the perspective of the externalities that ultimately govern a project's fate.

7

THE PROJECT ECOSYSTEM

"The past is a foreign country; they do things differently there." L. P. Hartley

THE NOTION OF LANDSCAPE

Internal Risks

The project network developed in Chapter 4 provides the reader with a map of the scope of work that will be required to realize the asset. The variability suffusing the lattice of nodes gives birth to execution risks. These endogenous risks are internal to the project and remain, as a result, under the purview of the project manager (PM). On the other hand, the network tells us nothing about the world in which the project will unfold or where the asset will be operated. This is the *arena*—a space both physical and relational that creates the constraints upon project execution and asset operations. The physical elements (location, geography, environment, operating conditions) and the relational components (supply chains, regulators, local chiefs) combine to form the *project ecosystem* (PECO).

External Risks

The arena is also the place where shareholders and stakeholders clash over the faith of the asset. These clashes are progenitors of the risks external to the project—the exogenous risks. The management of these risks lies outside the prerogative of the PM; the onus is on the framework leader to corral them (more on the framework in Chapter 9). This distinction between the two types of risks (endogenous and exogenous) is foundational to the application of the direct accountability principle at the corporate level. The framework manages the PECO; the PM manages the project within that PECO.

The Dangers of Ignoring the PECO

Among the two risk types, the exogenous risks present the greatest threat to the success of the asset because they are outside the direct control of the asset's owner. It follows that the execution strategy must be erected upon a stalwart understanding of the sources of risks emanating from the PECO. In the end, the matter boils down simply to asking the question: what could possibly go wrong? That which is not understood everywhere.

The perils that accrue from such misunderstandings or worse—regardless of the PECO—are a hallmark of history. Take this example, for the oil and gas industry, of an oil sands mega project pursued by one of the oil majors in Canada. The project had relied on a modularization strategy to fabricate equipment modules offshore and ship them to site as a means of reducing site construction costs. Contracts were issued to several shops in Asia. Sea shipments were to arrive in the U.S., and the final shipment would be by road. That was the theory. Then, reality happened. On the U.S. side, the producer was refused permission to transport the oversized packages by road, which flew in the face of the owner's initial—and unverified—assumption that road permits would be a breeze. Eventually, the producer was forced to cut up the packages into smaller, shippable cross sections. Cost overruns ran into the millions and the schedule—blown.

In another instance of corporate hubris gone wild, an oil and gas behemoth teamed up with foreign partners to develop liquefied natural gas (LNG) export capabilities on the North American continent. The partners had extensive experience in the Middle East and Eurasia, so everyone presumed to know better (keeping in mind that those regions are characterized by regulatory and environmental frameworks that are, shall we say, a tad less stringent). Construction labor was another matter. Compared to North America, labor in the Far East is cheaper, more plentiful, and more tolerant of physical discomfort. Labor estimates, informed by the Asian experience, proved significantly higher than estimates derived from local labor variables. So high, in fact, that the project did not go forward.

These two examples are illustrative of a persistent trend by big and powerful owners to be dismissive of local facts. Many projects suffer from downplaying or ignoring the ecosystem in which they will unfold. History's lessons, forged in the fires of battles and misery, never seem to percolate to the surface of the modern mind. And yet, the great Chinese philosopher, Sun tzu[1] had already captured these lessons in the fifth century BCE:

- It is not enough to know that an enemy can be attacked, or that your army can launch the attack. You must also know whether or not the terrain helps or hampers combat.
- Knowing oneself and one's enemy is necessary to survive many engagements. Knowing only oneself makes the risk of defeat a 50-50 proposition. Knowing neither oneself nor the enemy is a guarantee of defeat.

- The victor must first grasp the conditions for victory before launching the battle. The vanquished will fight first in the hope of securing victory, and then seek victory.

Sun tzu's perspective was, of course, forged from the blaze of war. The lessons, however, apply entirely to the prosaic world of project management. The success of a project rests upon an expansive understanding of the operational theater and the obstacles it presents. The bottom line: one should never jump into the unknown. Never assume that your self-appraised superiority is impervious to the vagaries of the PECO. Sadly, this conclusion is lost on managers of all stripes. History, once again, provides us with an example that every PM should heed. Back in the summer of 480 BCE, Xerxes I of Persia, self-proclaimed king of kings, took his huge army, believed to have numbered 500,000 men, to Thermopylae to launch the final leg of his conquest of Greece. The place, as described by Paul Cartledge,[2] was located in north central Greece and presented itself as a narrow passage. Thermopylae means *hot gates* in Greek, a moniker acquired from its reputation as the natural lynchpin of invasion campaigns by foreign armies. On this particular occasion, the passage was held for three days by the now-immortal group of 300 Spartan hoplites, led by King Leonidas, until treachery led to their deaths. Nevertheless, their sacrifice would prove seminal in the total defeat of Xerxes the following September. Having overcome this obstacle at a great human cost, the king of kings had learned nothing from this near catastrophe, choosing instead to believe in his invincibility. So, he repeated the same mistake at Salamis, where his numerically superior Navy was bottlenecked by a much smaller Athenian fleet. The Athenians proceeded to smash the Persian ships to achieve a stunning victory. The king of kings was ultimately defeated despite overwhelmingly favorable odds because his hubris dismissed the reality of the battle environment.

Here We Go Again

The same kind of degenerate hubris would afflict Napoleon two millennia later. His *Grande Armée*, totaling nearly 612,000 battle-hardened men, began its march across the Russian plains in 1812.[3] *La Grande Armée* had hitherto succeeded in all its battlefields by its ability to supply and feed itself from whatever land it traversed. What Napoleon failed to appreciate, unbelievably, was the sparsely populated land that lay on the Russian horizon. Even if Russia had existed in tropical climes, that population density could never have produced the resources needed by such a large army of soldiers. Of course, Russia's ultimate weapon of mass destruction, *winter*, cannot be overstated either. In the end, Napoleon's defeat was inevitable. Along the way, 400,000 conscripted men paid the ultimate price, with untold more collateral civilian casualties. It takes a rare kind of genius to inflict such carnage.

LOOKING THROUGH A GLASS ONION

The Seven Layers of the PECO

Battles and projects do not happen in a vacuum. Big or small, near or far, each one's reality is shaped by the *ecosystem* in which it unfolds. The *PECO* includes all the variables that are *external* to the owner's organization. We can imagine the PECO as a glass onion with the asset sitting at its core. The glass onion is comprised of seven layers that must be penetrated successfully by the project for the asset to come to life. The structure of this glass onion is reminiscent of the sun's internal structure.

Helios

Stellar astrophysics offers us an apt metaphor. Our sun encompasses six layers: the corona, the chromosphere, the photosphere, the convection zone, the radiation zone, and the core. Photons born in the core fight their way through the layers until the freedom of empty space unshackles their speed (of light, evidently). Such a trip will take thousands of years and gradually ease as the enlightened ones recede from their birthplace. The asset is the figurative photon, except that it travels in the opposite direction to shine its profitable light.

The seven layers are illustrated in Figure 7.1. Each layer is characterized by a density, representing its resistance to penetration, which increases inward. To answer the question *what could possibly go wrong* is to peer through these seven layers to understand the onion's chorography.

The Bulwark Layer (No. 7)

The physical realization of a project starts at the outer layer where resistance is least. This seventh layer acts as a sentry against incoming marauders. It is held in place by a network of competitors ready to defend their stakes. This competition takes on two forms: commercial and rooted. The *commercial* competition stems from corporate interests already invested in the ecosystem, or intent on entering or expanding their presence. These may already have proposed projects of their own and advanced their regulatory formalities far ahead of others. When an ecosystem is near project saturation, new proposals may face a moratorium. Multiple competing proposals vying for the same land or market opportunity may be straining the regulator's capacity to process new applications. A competitor may be entrenched in an area, benefiting from a deeply-rooted goodwill from the community. Projects already in construction may have effectively cornered the available capacity of the labor markets. Each

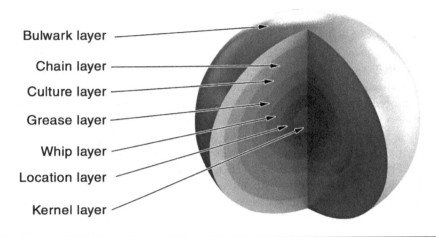

Bulwark layer

Chain layer

Culture layer

Grease layer

Whip layer

Location layer

Kernel layer

Figure 7.1 The glass onion: the project ecosystem is represented as a sequence of layers, defined by constraints and resistance to penetration specific to each one. Project success requires full penetration until the kernel is reached, where the asset physically exists and operates.

locality will be unique in this regard, the necessity for the project owner to conduct an expansive assessment of the competitive landscape before committing to the exploratory expenses of the proposed project.

The *rooted* competition mirrors the commercial type, but through local interests tied to the location. Communities, civic governments, and existing industrial concerns may be pursuing different priorities that are incompatible with the proposed project. Alternatively, the region may have suffered grievances in the past and soured the region's appetite for new attempts akin to the past. A central government may have unilaterally proscribed all competing concepts in favor of its own choice. Whatever the case, the project owner is once again advised to carry out a cold-eyes review of the rooted competitive landscape, to determine the risks and expectations that would shadow his own project proposal.

The Chain Layer (No. 6)

This is *supply-chain land*. In this orbit, we find logistics, vendors, *schlicked* paperwork,[4] and the questions: given the strictures of the previous five layers, what stuff can be bought from whom, from where, and when? What features of that stuff are subject to validation and verification prior to acceptance at the site? Who gets to validate, verify, and inspect this stuff prior to its arrival at the site? How does the stuff get there? Will it be permitted to enter the jurisdiction?

What paperwork is needed to get this permission? Will rail greasing be inevitable? Paperwork alone means friction, which implies that resistance will be greater than the previous layer.

A significant element of the chain layer pertains to logistics. One of the difficult challenges in buying anything is delivery. Delivery is tightly woven into the fabric of the preceding layers. The mere question of road quality, taken for granted in advanced economies, can derail any transportation plan. Road limitations represent a design constraint that must be folded into the front-end engineering of a project. They were, for example, a limiting factor in the design of the rocket components of the Apollo program. The PM must therefore exert diligence from the outset in identifying the limits and constraints of the chain layer. This imperative to understand the *physics of logistics* cannot be emphasized enough. Logistics are tied to a terrain to be traversed by the project caravan. This terrain is subject to laws, rules, and irreversibility akin to its own set of physical laws. You can't flow water uphill any more than you can truck a module through a tunnel too narrow for it. That's the essence of the physics of logistics.

The Culture Layer (No. 5)

At this orbital distance from the core, the focus is on the people who will get things get done (or not). It is a fractious layer, fraught with judgment, ignorance, and the one person who screams the loudest for local representation within the owner's project team. Resistance has again increased. Cultural specificities taint everything. In some parts of the world, large pools of low-skilled labor are happy just to be employed and will put up with all kinds of privations—as long as they get paid. In other places, the labor pool is highly qualified, in high demand, and expensive—and will not put up with any privation. Cultural biases also suffuse the business drivers of companies. For example, U.S. companies are driven by costs more than quality, safety, security, or reputation. In Canada, safety and interprovincial relations trump all. In China, nothing gets done unless the benefits accrue mostly to the domestic partner. In Russia, all is oligarchy; in Nigeria, patronage rules. Rosalie Tung,[5] for example, points out that the notion of corporate loyalty is deeply ingrained in the Japanese mind, but much less so for the Americans. The latter value their loyalty to friends and families much more intensely. One must understand the ramifications of culture to project execution. Such an understanding is especially critical to joint ventures and partnerships between global players. Frequently, their *modus operandi* clash with the reality of the asset's cultural backdrop, with predictable failures in the offing.

The Grease Layer (No. 4)

Despite its name, this layer is all about execution friction and its retarding effects on the project. Friction comes in three slicks. The first ties back to construction strategies. Some places are best suited to equipment modularization. Others will favor stick building. The key is the *in situ* productivity associated with the location, which is driven by skill pools, labor pools, weather, and season-limiting execution or local employment expectations. If any one of those goes against the grain, expect grinding friction all over the execution map. The second source of friction is found with the arms-length stakeholders who feel compelled to object and oppose. These special interest groups are usually vocal in their vociferations. Always ready to disrupt, but never inclined to construct, these groups can foment a sweat-inducing opposition that can derail a project. In third place comes the political sphere. The larger the project, the wider the attention it commands. Project owners must understand who's who in the zoo. Notwithstanding one's abhorrence to the veiled apprehensions of the actors' expectations, this is one instance where *greasing the rails* may be inevitable to advance the cause of the project, with graft being one insinuation away. One may be expected to bring in regional industrial benefits to the local community. The regulator may demand that local labor be trained and employed first, regardless of competencies. Design work may be barred from off-shoring. These are *legal* expectations. But flagrant kickbacks and bribery may also come to the fore, regardless of the moral principles of the project proponents.

Readers may take offence at this notion of graft in our discussion. Utopian professions notwithstanding, graft and bribery are a fact of life to anyone operating within a global setting. At the very least, a project that purports to have global features must appraise them without *eyes wide shut*. It's a risk that must be quantified, not wished away. Much of it is a question of interpretation. The values of a manager will be challenged by the reality of a foreign jurisdiction. In North America, what would be considered bribes and payoffs, and therefore frowned upon, may be regarded as business-as-usual elsewhere.

The world officially buys into the prosecutorial utopia, as evidenced by the number of countries with signatories to the United Nations Convention against corruption. Unfortunately, many such signatures speak lip service. Project organizations cannot but adapt—rue or not.

See No Evil, Hear No Evil

The December 2014 Organization for Economic Co-operation and Development (OECD) Foreign Bribery Report is telling. It analyzed 427 worldwide bribery cases by companies or individuals native to one of the 41 signatory countries to the OECD Anti-Bribery Convention. The report found that "most international bribes are paid by large companies, usually with the knowledge of senior management." These bribes went to grease the rails in procurement awards, paid mainly by companies from wealthy countries (rather than developing ones). Findings that are especially pertinent to our discussion highlight the worst offending sectors. Almost two-thirds of the cases occurred in just four sectors: extractive (19%); construction (15%); transportation and storage (15%); and information and communication (10%). Bribes were promised, offered, or given most frequently to employees of state-owned enterprises (27%), followed by customs officials (11%), health officials (7%), and defense officials (6%). Heads of state and ministers were bribed in 5% of the cases but received 11% of the total bribes. In most cases, bribes were paid to obtain public procurement contracts (57%), followed by clearance of customs procedures (12%). Six percent of bribes were to gain preferential tax treatment. In 41% of the cases, management-level employees paid or authorized the bribe, whereas the company CEO was involved in 12% of the cases.

The West may be sheltered from flagrant bribery and embrace the principle that defalcations (i.e., the misappropriation of money or funds held by an official or other fiduciary) will not be tolerated. In many western jurisdictions, however, the principle of graft morphed into the peddling of undue advantage abetted by veneers of legislated legitimacy. Article 18 of the UN Convention against corruption deals with this explicit matter under the heading *trading in influence*:

Each State Party (i.e., country) shall consider adopting such legislative and other measures as may be necessary to establish as criminal offences, when committed intentionally:

> (a) *the promise, offering, or giving to a public official or any other person, directly or indirectly, of an undue advantage in order that the public official or the person abuse his or her real or supposed influence with a view to obtaining from an administration or public authority of the State Party an undue advantage for the original instigator of the act or for any other person;*

> (b) *the solicitation or acceptance by a public official or any other person, directly or indirectly, of an undue advantage for himself or herself or for another person in order that the public official or the person abuse his or her real or supposed influence with a view to obtaining from an administration or public.*

The key words here are *undue advantage*. Now, consider this clause within the context of the extractive industry in Canada. The Canadian legal framework effectively grants to a class of stakeholders on the sole basis of race, the singular power to extort whatever economic benefits they can from proponents of large projects. The UN Convention is respected in the letter but not in the intent of the law. This is but one instance of legitimized illegitimacy. Project owners must grasp the nature of these special interests before reality comes extorting at their doors.

The Whip Layer (No. 3)

This layer belongs to regulators and exists to enforce from without the regulatory framework surrounding the construction and operation of the asset. It comprises all manners of permits, licenses, and permissions needed to design, validate, import, transport, construct, and operate the asset. The layer is impregnated with the codes and standards ordained by industry and government powers. For that reason, its density and resistance are increased once again, as we are dealing with *the government*. The whip layer is further constrained by labor standards, certification requirements, union rights, and equipment validation and verification compliance. Language, nomenclature, formatting, and even paper sizes can matter. Something as simple as a North American sheet size 8.5″ by 11″ may be frowned upon by an import inspection agency in, say, Germany. Or a project owner may wish to impose an Oxford version of the English language in its communications with the Environmental Protection Agency in the U.S. (which could object to spelling "colour" instead of "color"). As petty as it seems, such instances have more than once derailed applications.

The Location Layer (No. 2)

The location layer encompasses all possible bottlenecks to and from the site. First is access. What road, rail, sea, and air facilities exist in the neighborhood of the site? What are their shipping limits? Is local traffic an issue? Are roads in good conditions or traced in dirt? Are there donkeys and goat herders crossing every day? Are sacred cows roaming the countryside? Physical reality is cursed with a higher density from the simple fact that it cannot be wished or negotiated away. It must be shaped, chiseled, dynamited, or entirely rerouted. That's friction in a pure, gloriously stubborn physical sense. Then, the issue of utilities come up—such as electrical power, water, drainage and sewers, natural gas, and telecommunications. Can they be easily tapped? What restrictions on access or consumption are in place? Who owns them? How reliable is the supply? Local history comes next. What past projects have been built in the general area? Is the population accustomed to the rigors and inconveniences of industrial construction? Were social problems experienced by the town? Were the land and the river polluted or denied to the locals? Was there an impact to fishing and hunting? Is the population in tune with the politicians, or against them?

Finally, we have the local kings. These are the people and organizations who *own* the place by virtue of their influence in the locality. People like building inspectors, mayors, tribal chieftains, landowners, community activists, toll collectors, and union bosses. What language do they speak? What are their existential concerns? What financial affectations matter to them? These people may be otiose (i.e., inconsequential) in the grand scheme of things and bereft of institutional authority, but they can still mold the expectations of the community along their vested interests.

The Kernel Layer (No. 1)

We finally come to the innermost layer, buried deep inside the onion. This layer is all about the realized asset and its operations. The layer divides into two considerations: construction and people. The construction angle deals with the physical features of the site affecting construction activities. What are the features of the terrain? What are the limits of the land, where building will occur? Could neighbors impede construction? What is the climate like? How does weather affect construction productivity and operational readiness? Is the soil amenable to foundations, or is it water saturated and prone to liquefaction? Is the area afflicted by recurring natural disasters like cyclones, earthquakes, or avalanches? These are the kinds of questions that one must answer before anything else.

The people angle drives the profitability of the asset. During construction, labor availability dominates the execution strategy. Is the region capable of meeting the head count requirements across all skill sets? Are there training commitments for the community? Where will workers live? Will they commute daily; fly in and out; or ship in and out from foreign shores? How will health and safety mandates be enforced? What will be the impact of daily labor movements upon the community? Once the asset reaches operational readiness, how will the staffing requirements be met and sustained? Will there be recurring work/license permit renewals required? Ultimately, the project must demonstrate that the site can be made suitable for construction *and* to operate the asset to sufficient reliability that it will be sustainably profitable. Resistance is highest at this depth because if the place can't fit the project, the project can't be realized there. It is not even a question of physically altering the geography (unless at tremendous labor, time, and treasure) to make it amenable to the project. Pick the wrong spot and the project is doomed—think 2011 Fukushima nuclear reactors.

EGO SUM ERGO POSSUM

I Am Therefore I Can

The danger to an owner is to assume that his knowledge is sufficient to adduce the character of the PECO. A myriad of projects has been hammered into ruins on the altar of this reflex. Organizations with long project track records can delude themselves into thinking that they know enough to proceed with a new project of familiar scope and scale. The delusion is stronger when the project is in the same region, bulking up the project team's faith in its own interpretations. Or a company's gargantuan size may convince its project team that it has the wherewithal and influence to overcome *petty* local idiosyncrasies. Elsewhere, the company may already be active in the region, with a footprint that is assumed to carry influence with the local kings. These are but a few examples of corporate hubris manifested from the wells of good intentions. The project team's duty is to cast away all assumptions, whatever they may be, and seek out facts about the ecosystem. From a strategic risk standpoint, it is always preferable to humbly know what is not known than assume the unknown to be knowable. Pursuing this process of discovery is time-consuming but essential; to circumvent is to invite controversy. In the Facebook and Twitter age, no owner can survive the onslaught of digital dilettantes. The better policy is diligence to appease the owner's strategic agenda. In the wise words of British author Charles Caleb Colton:

> *"A man who knows the world will gain more credit by his adroit mode of hiding his ignorance, than the pedant by his awkward attempt to exhibit his erudition."*

The PECO Seen as Constraints

To understand the PECO is to comprehend the constraints that it imposes on the project. It is also to understand how those constraints flow through the seven layers. The layers are themselves liable to switch places in some instances. For example, a jurisdiction may be harder to reach than to get the permits to work (in a third-world country keen on attracting international investors to develop its resources, for example). The order of the layers matters less than the influence they bear on the flow of constraints through them. That knowledge is equally critical to the success of a project. The bottom line bears repeating: know the space before launching into it.

In his wonderful book, *Rising Ground: A Search for the Spirit of Place*, Philip Marsden alludes to space as an abstraction or template which can be dropped over any point on the surface of the earth. A place, on the other hand, is not transferable, but one to which it is possible to belong. The PECO is both space and place simultaneously. It is the space that contains the place where the asset will be built and operated. To know an ecosystem is to understand its zeitgeist (i.e., its spirit and attitudes). The project journey, however, cannot be undertaken yet; the next imperative is to grasp the potential costs. It is not enough to put together a budget based on past experiences, historical data, future trends, and possible sources of difficulties. One must also figure out the organization's resiliency against budget overruns. Is the organization fragile, resilient, or anti-fragile (in a Taleb sense)? Budget notwithstanding, can the traveler afford the cost of this danger without threatening the remainder of the journey? Can the owner buy his way out of a bad situation and still pursue the final destination? Or is the journey already looking too expensive with no leeway left to counter unforeseen expenses? Is the journey itself worth the price? Can the project, in other words, be undertaken without breaking the owner's bank in the end? The answers to these questions are the focus of our next destination.

NOTES

1. Famed military commander; born circa 544 BCE. His work, *Art of War*, is considered one of the most important military treatises in history. Its lessons are drawn for the battlefield, but apply to other fields as well.

2. See Paul Cartledge's book, *Thermopylae—The Battle That Changed the World*, page xi. Most historians count the battle at Thermopylae among the most important battles in the history of mankind. The 300, for their part, were immortalized by Simonides, son of Leoprepes, in a poem that translates into *Go tell the Spartans passerby, that here, obedient to their laws, we lie.*

3. See Alan Schom's book, *Napoleon Bonaparte*, p. 595.

4. The term "schlicked" refers to the sound of the stamping widget used by immigration officials to stamp a visitor's passport.

5. See Rosalie Tung's *Handshakes Across the Sea: Cross-cultural Negotiating for Business Success* for more details.

8

THE BUDGET

"An investment in knowledge pays the most interest." Benjamin Franklin

YOU CAN'T AFFORD TO BUILD A HOTEL WITHOUT WiFi

The Dark Art of Getting What You Paid For

The project ecosystem (PECO) challenges the mind to persist. With patience, resilience, commitment, and money, a project and its ecosystem can be aligned. The price of that alignment, on the other hand, goes beyond mere costs. Projects challenge *tresantas* (those who are ruled by their fears) to trust their fortitude. After all, a project is a gamble on the future but with great rewards to the savvy player. As the ancient poet Virgil wrote centuries ago, *fortune sides with him who dares*. To our discussion, the daring is in the spending. Every owner starts out hoping that he will get what he paid for: the profitably performing asset (PPA). This chapter examines the question of whether what's bought matches what's paid. We direct our attention to the cost reality that project proponents (owners, consultants, constructors) must confront when pondering the fate of an industrial endeavor. In the executive boardroom, projects are painted—and rightly so—as financial risks. The risks will linger for what seems like an eternity, until breakeven is reached. Even then, sustained profitability by the asset may remain mired in a fog of uncertainty. To management, a project is a disgusting ogre with a bottomless hunger for cash. This means that the owner will be expected to have faith in the competency of the project team. A faith that may span years to tame the beast before it is rewarded with the miracle of profits. Recall that a project is the investment vehicle to realize the asset, with costs justified based on maximizing future investment returns.

What the Budget Actually Buys

As a business investment, what is acquired through the project is not the set of tangibles—the asset, the equipment, the plant, the personnel. What is acquired is a set of corporate risks:

1. The risks to the actual revenue streams generated by the asset;
2. The expense risks incurred (whether the asset is active or not);
3. The risks to the profit stream that ensues (or not); and
4. The opportunity cost of those risks.

Until the asset has proven itself profitably performing, the asset remains a commercial risk far into the distant future.

This fact frames the cost picture of a project and bears further scrutiny. Everything that comes into existence while the asset is acquired or operated—such as the equipment, the controls, the plants, the permits, the operations—become enablers of those risks. *The project budget is spent on acquiring those enablers.* But what matters to the success of the project are the future risks manifested from those expenditures. Project decisions made to preserve schedule and budget may have seeded significant latent risks in the future (cue the Hubble telescope story here!). To wit:

- The project spends its budget on the risk enablers (the equipment, the controls, the plants, the permits, the construction labor, the bribes, the shipping, the operations);
- The asset inherits the risks arising from those enablers; and
- The owner owns the risks to the future revenues, expenses, and profits.

Hubble Telescope

The storied account of the Hubble space telescope makes the most impassioned plea in favor of a management philosophy anchored to the asset rather than the budget. In its day, the telescope presented its designers with a formidable technical challenge that was not appreciated from the outset when NASA awarded the contract for its design and fabrication to Perkin-Elmer, a U.S. optics manufacturer. After six difficult years strained by blown budgets and busted schedules, the final assembly was, at long last, completed. To save costs and time (in a pure instance of kyopia—discussed later in this chapter), NASA decided to skip the final test to verify the main mirror's curvature. That test would have revealed a dimensional flaw at the mirror's perimeter. No test, no flaw: the telescope was "go" for launch. The flaw reared its ugly head once the telescope reached orbit. It turned the Hubble into a colossal failure, which would require three more years of engineering, a second space shuttle flight, and a precarious extravehicular spacewalk by the shuttle's crew. The total cost of this repair mission was, predictably, monstrously higher than the skipped test.

THE MEANING OF SPEND VERSUS INVEST

The Treasure Hunt Analogy

Consider a hypothetical ocean expedition to recover the treasure of a sunken eighteenth-century ship laden with Peruvian gold. The sponsor considers two motivations: minimize the expedition costs or maximize the treasure recovery to boost the sponsor's return on investment (ROI). In the first instance, a small crew of divers is furnished with a large, fixed number of scuba tanks. The prime directive: retrieve as many artifacts as possible, given the scuba tanks on hand. In the second, the expedition is equipped with a robotic submarine. Its prime directive: retrieve them all. The first expedition will be shorter and cheaper to equip and carry out. Its managing attitude will adopt a *preserve mindset* (budget focused). The second expedition is likely to be longer. Its attitude will abide by the *protect mindset* (ROI focused). Both approaches underscore the importance of the sponsor's attitude toward execution.

This question of attitude is of fundamental importance to the practice of project management.

Budget Attitude

If the prime directive is to preserve the budget, what is bought with this budget is the execution of the project itself. It is the tip of the iceberg in Figure 2.1. *All* expenditures are regarded as credits against the project's general ledger. Spending is effectively viewed as a continual cash flow drain. Spending is the ultimate concern, impervious to the ramifications to the future asset. Naturally, it will fall under the spell of minimization: decide in favor of lowest capital costs *now* at the expense of higher operating margins *later*. As long as the budget is respected, the project will be deemed successful.

Asset Attitude

The budget is the investment vehicle to develop the PPA. What is bought are the future investment returns. Expenditures are regarded as investments in the future profitability of the asset. They land on the debit side of the general ledger. One speaks of *buying* rather than *spending*. One *buys* today a potential that will generate revenues tomorrow. The asset attitude hones in on what is submerged in Figure 2.1.

The two views are mutually exclusive: you either manage the budget or the asset. An expense is considered either a cost against a finite budget or an investment toward future profits. The time window is short for costs but very long for investments. And because there is no middle ground, the owner is forced to choose between these two attitudes from the outset to ground the execution framework. The *budget attitude* leads to an internecine war between the capital expenditure (CAPEX) and operating expenditure (OPEX) camps within the owner's organization. The tension is maintained by a belief held by both sides that their respective budgets are independent of each other. CAPEX people will strive to execute the project strictly within its allocation. Operating considerations for greater profitability are ignored if they cost more to the project. OPEX people are forced to make due with what they get from the CAPEX initiative. The *asset attitude* does not divide owner loyalties into CAPEX and OPEX camps. It recognizes the fact that CAPEX and OPEX money comes from the same place: the owner's pockets. There are no conflicts between project and operations because the expenditures of the former are solely justified by the needs of the latter. Within this context, the project budget exists on a financial continuum that leads to the operating asset at its other extremity.

The Real Purpose of a Budget

The budget exists to acquire the PPA. The expenditures are justified concurrently across three levels:

- At the revenue level—The asset exists to generate revenues. Those revenues, in turn, are a function of throughput capacity, installed configuration, built-in redundancies, response to varying demands, and the all-important reliability and maintainability.
- At the expense level—The asset incurs expenses to run such feedstock, power and utilities, maintenance, permits, taxes and remittances, and obsolescence.
- At the profit level—It's not enough for the asset to operate; it must turn a profit. Its profitability is driven by efficiency, productivity, performance, control optimization and resilience against failures, and off-design conditions of operation.

Thus framed, the purpose of the project budget must be to provide the funds to buy the products and services that will, *in the aggregate*, minimize the risks to the revenues, expenses, and profits of the asset in the long run. During *development*, the owner should be *less worried* about paying more than required, and more worried about *paying less than necessary* to get the PPA.

The better hedge against project failure is to choose foresight over hindsight and face reality rather than gamble on faith.

The reader is cautioned against drawing the conclusion that money is no object. The exact opposite is true: *money is a project's air supply*. The budget must be rationally allocated—commensurate with a realistic schedule. The onus is on the project management team to execute the project within those bounds, in accordance with the *getting-to-no* philosophy discussed in Chapter 5. Cost increases are never justifiable in the throes of inefficiency, incompetence, unproductivity, deficient planning, and the like. These failings mirror those of the project management team. The budget remains the most precious commodity to the manager. A valunomic execution of the project must be the obsession of the project team. Cost increases are justifiable when they improve or strengthen the profitability characteristics of the future asset. The key is to nail a budget that is rooted in reality.

THE NOTION OF INTRINSIC PRICE

The Competency Threshold

Nobody would deny the merits of paying no more than necessary for a good or service. Things go off the rails, however, when that decent pursuit is turned into a race for the bottom price. All *investment* projects (as defined in Chapter 1) share this truth: buying the cheapest of anything now will cost the most later. Owners and shareholders must recognize that industrial assets come with an intrinsic price that is inevitable to achieve the desired ROI. This intrinsic price has many counterparts in daily life. It explains why no self-respecting bride would risk a $5 hairdo on her wedding day, or why the price of a brake replacement job on your car is not worth saving 50% in a back alley. No amount of economic analysis could ever make the case for a cheap nuptial because women—willingly and justly—will pay more when the result warrants the expense. And therein lies a judicious aphorism:

Not paying enough guarantees failure, stylistically or otherwise.

The hair argument has nothing to do with vanity. There are no more $5 nuptial hairdos out there than there are $10 car brake jobs because inherent to any market is the supposition of a match between cost threshold and competency threshold. Someone once famously suggested that you could sell pizza so cheaply that nobody would buy it. People may balk at the cost of a haircut or a brake job but will still grudgingly admit that *they cannot afford the downside of a down rate*. That is why even if most people can't afford a new Ferrari, still fewer people can afford a $1,000 Ferrari. Who would risk paying $125 to fly from Montreal to Bangkok on a plane designed and constructed in Bangladesh? That's the essence of the cost-competency threshold.

Intrinsic Cost

This threshold leads to the concept of *intrinsic cost*, which is defined as the minimum valunomic price of a good or service that will warrant its purchase by someone. Any expense comes with an expectation of unlikely economic loss, i.e., nothing is bought to fail. Miss that expectation and something will inevitably hit the proverbial fan. In business, the act of selling is akin to the nuptial hairdo. Five dollar wedding specials are the fastest way to salon bankruptcy. There is no greater danger to the profitability of an asset than to pursue cost savings for the mere sake of preserving a budget.

Cost savings must be warranted on the basis of the risk they entail.

It is difficult to imagine a case where a company would willfully make a purchase knowing that it will result in a loss greater than the cash outlay. The risk may not be uttered, but it is unfettered.

In business, the cheapest is the costliest: whatever is saved at the front end will come back biting the bank account at the back end.

The case is thoroughly applicable to investment projects, especially those that can bankrupt a company. Would-be players cannot escape the fact that there is a price to pay to play the game. You can't get in for less; you can't ride for free; and you can't eke out higher margins by going cheap.

THE FIRST PASS TO GET TO A BUDGET

Intrinsic Risks

Projects collide with the will of their owners where targets and intrinsic costs meet. The target cost is the funding level that makes the business case for the investment. The intrinsic cost is the minimum price of the contemplated asset, imperviously from all other considerations. The project should go ahead when both agree. The execution of a project will fail if the target is arbitrarily set beneath the intrinsic cost *to make the numbers work*. You must be prepared to spend what's required to get the profitable performance of the asset. Landing on a rational project budget is the first instance of risk management. To that end, we introduce several risk drivers to shape a budget. The initial step deals not with the budget *per se* but with the existential question of surviving a failed project. Is the owner capable of withstanding the financial hit stemming from blown costs and schedules? This existential risk is the *intrinsic risk* driver.

The future profitability of the asset is driven by its *intrinsic cost*. Reality must trump accounting edicts or management whims. The project owner must accept the intrinsic cost, then set the target (the budget) accordingly.

> *No amount of faith, wishful thinking, management edicts, or corporate hubris can change the reality of a project's intrinsic cost. Either the project budget matches it or rushes headlong toward a financial quagmire.*

The Gambler's Risk

The intrinsic cost will be firmed up once *development* is completed, which is a long way into the future. At the consideration stage, it is but a shot in the dark, or at best an educated guess. To get beyond this uncertainty requires that some money be spent to solidify the concept. That money is called the *gambler's risk*. The name is apt, since money will be spent *just to find out if the project is worth pursuing*. It is not so much an initial investment, as an entry fee. Now comes the kicker: that entry fee is not cheap *if it must produce meaningful cost projections for the total installed cost* (TIC). The word *meaningful* implies a TIC estimate ranging between 80% and 200%.[1] A good rule of thumb pegs this entry fee at 1% of TIC. For a TIC of $100M, the fee is one million dollars. At $40B TIC, it is $400M. You can see where this is going: $400M *just* to find out if the project is worth pursuing is a lot of money to gamble away. You could spend less, of course, but at the price of a much wider estimate range. Spending 0.5% of TIC, for example, could only get you an upper estimate limit of 300% TIC. That is a huge range to carry in the project's financial model.

> *The gambler's risk is a necessity, not an option. If you can't afford it, you have no business playing: remember that the real financial risk is not that 1%, but the remaining 99%.*

Spin Cycle

The gambler's risk is an either/or game: either you spend it to firm up the estimate range or live with an entirely random range. The most bang for the gambling buck is to spend more, not less, to tighten the range. If the initial TIC projections are unpalatable, the owner has three options: (1) abandon the project; (2) scale back the project; or (3) investigate the concept further. Options 2 and 3 require more gambling money for the ensuing spin cycle. The solidity of the TIC estimate is a function of the number of iterations in this spin cycle (more iterations firm up the range limits). Sometimes, project proponents will consider a fourth option: the tantrum approach—which is to reject the estimate and launch the project on the arbitrary edict that cost savings will just have to be found during execution. This option does not warrant further discussion because the tantrum approach *never* works. It's a delusion, pure and simple—a substitution of project management principles by gambling based on blind faith.

> *The initial TIC estimate is* not *the project target. It is the owner's commercial risk that must be valued through a resilience risk analysis.*

The Resilience Risk

The end of the spin cycle yields the official TIC estimate. The owner is now able to assess his survivability risk should the project go off the rails in the future. This is the second risk driver, called the *resilience risk*. The exercise is straightforward. You begin by assuming that the worst-case scenario has occurred: the project is expected to cost twice as much as initially targeted (i.e., the upper limit of the estimate range). Can the owner incur this cost and remain financially viable? If the answer is no, whatever the reasons, the risk is materially severe to the owner. If the answer is yes, the financial risk is still present but not a show stopper. *It is important to understand that one does not assume that the project will cost that much.* The question is about one's ability to survive the worst-case scenario.

> *Commercially speaking, a project is safe to execute if the owner can afford the upper limit of the TIC estimate range, and be prepared to incur it—if push comes to shove.*

The resilience risk exists on a continuum bounded by unsafe and safe limits, as illustrated in Figure 8.1. The economic survivability of an owner will be high when the resilience risk is low. Conversely, the severity of the worst-case scenario follows the resilience risk. The degree of safety of the project is a function of the risk's position on the continuum:

- The project is economically safe if the owner can withstand a doubling of the original cost estimate (the upper bound of the TIC range) without suffering financial ruin. The resilience risk is lowest. Even if the project capsizes, the business will not drown.
- The project is economically unsafe if the owner can only afford the lower bound of the TIC range. The resilience risk here ranges from high to extreme and puts the business in the *junk bond* category if it goes forward with the project.
- The project is economically risky (medium to low resilience risk) if costs will lie inside the TIC range. Prudence dictates that the owner should seek partners or scale back the project to lower the risk.

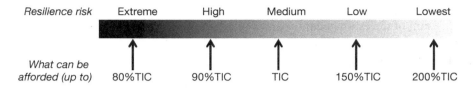

Figure 8.1   Resilience risk spectrum: the spectrum illustrates the consequences of a project's worst-case scenario. The severity of this scenario is in inverse relation to the owner's resilience risk. Conversely, the owner's financial safety is proportional to the risk. For instance, a *high* resilience risk means that the owner's worst-case scenario shows up quickly at the point where the project has accrued 90% of the TIC. A different owner blessed with the lowest resilience risk can afford going over budget (100%) while remaining financially viable.

Antifragile

A crisp parallel can be drawn between Figure 8.1 and the notion of *antifragility* developed by Nassim Taleb. Taleb describes risks in terms of randomness, assigning the expression *black swans* to the most severe. He proceeds to discuss systems as either fragile (permanently harmed under duress), robust (permanently unharmed under duress), or antifragile (improved under duress). Taleb subscribes to the idea of the unpredictability of randomness and the complete impossibility to forecast black swans (your author belongs to this school of thought as well). When setting up systems, the designer should be concerned—first and foremost—with endowing those systems with an inherent antifragility as a hedge against random events. In Figure 8.1, fragility lies at the extreme left, robustness in the middle, and antifragility at the extreme right.

LANDING THE PROJECT BUDGET

Target Budget

The reader should note that the resilience risk is predicated on an estimated project budget (the TIC in Figure 8.1) *for the purpose of assessing the owner's ability to survive the worst-case scenario of the project going off the rails.* We have not yet solidified the actual TIC to serve as a starting baseline for the development of the asset. This step occurs in the first phase of the development cycle from which the *Class V cost estimate* is obtained. Once designated as the budget baseline, the TIC becomes the *target budget* for the entire project. This is the value underlining the ROI analysis performed on the asset. The *target budget* is the sum of the estimated intrinsic cost and the *risk budget.*

The Risk Budget

The *risk budget* captures the cost uncertainty immanent to the development stage. This uncertainty is an aggregate of three types of risks:[2] the known *knowns* (*kk*), the known *unknowns* (*ku*) and the unknown *unknowns* (*uu*). The *kk* costs are germane to the physical configuration of the plant. They are finalized during the nucleation works of Phase 6.[3] The *ku* costs are informed by the owner's experience with the vagaries of the PECO and observed inefficiencies in the *development* of past projects. The *uu* drivers cannot be defined up front. All that can be said about them is that there will be surprises coming out of left field at some point in the future that will require containment. The *risk budget* is the sum of the intrinsic, *kk, ku,* and *uu* costs.

We divide the *risk budget* as follows:

- The *appropriation,* comprising the intrinsic cost and *kk* costs. The accountable party (AP), probate party (PP), and responsible party (RP) roles are assigned to the project management office (PMO) leads, the PMO manager, and the framework leader, respectively.[4]
- The *contingency* is made up of the *ku* costs, under the authority of the framework leader. The AP, PP, and RP roles are assigned to the PMO manager, the framework leader, and the owner, respectively.
- The *reserve* pertains to the *uu* costs, under the authority of the owner. The AP role is assigned to the framework leader, while the PP and RP roles are retained by the owner.

It should be clear by now that the owner's resilience risk will be manageable when the target budget is less than the upper limit of the initial TIC range.

Spending Priorities

With the *target budget* set, the project can proceed, which means that the time has come to spend. But on what? Once again, there is more to this than meets the eye. The expenditures incurred during *development* will be partitioned unequally. The *realization* stage will commandeer 50 to 60% of the target budget. Procurement will monopolize 30 to 40%. The remaining 10 to 20% will be taken up by the *conceptualization* stage. Critically, it is this last group of expenditures that bears the highest impact on the other two and, by extension, the asset's future profitable performance.

More, not less, money and time should be allocated to the conceptualiza-
tion stage to maximize the probability of achieving a PPA. It is the most
bang for the buck available to the owner.

Activities such as design, engineering, and manufacturing play vital roles in the procurement process. They yield a design that is producible or not. They form the basis upon which a production scheme can be devised. And they effectively guide the execution of this plan such that the resulting asset is a physical incarnation of the theoretical intent. How the asset is manufactured, refined over time, and improved in successive generations bears a direct impact over that asset's life cycle costs (LCCs). Surprisingly, 80% of those LCCs will have been locked in by the time a preliminary design review is conducted. Hence the immense influence of the early works on the future costs of the asset. Manufacturing, logistics, and operational concerns must be taken seriously early on, lest the asset development endeavor becomes uneconomical.

The outsized impact of the *conceptualization* stage is illustrated in Figure 8.2, which was developed originally for complex weapon systems but is pertinent to large industrial projects. The chart depicts the LCC of the asset over its economic life. The *conceptualization* phase spans the first 1% of the economic life. The

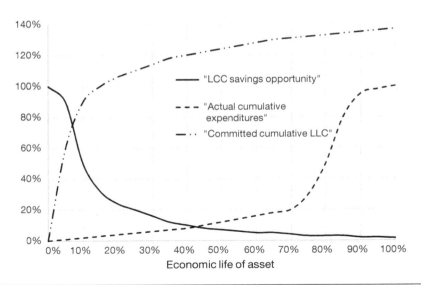

Figure 8.2 Impact of the spend profile over time: the greatest influence on the future profitability of the asset is at the front end when the conceptualization work takes places within the widest margin of design options. Conversely, projects will progressively go more off the rails when design changes occur in later stages. The impact is exponentially proportional to the time of occurrence. Last stage chances cost the most.

realization phase lasts until the 10% mark, approximately. The operation of the asset is assumed to take up the remaining 90%. Several aspects are noteworthy:

- The operating and support costs dominate the asset's LCC over time.
- Realization costs, which command the lion's share of the TIC budget, are themselves a minority in the asset's life budget.
- The most bang for the TIC buck is achieved at the front end, where savings in LCCs can be engineered into the design.

The Delusion of Savings Early On

The last two bullet points highlight a critical distinction between spend and investment projects. The greatest profitable performance of the future asset requires the maximum expense possible during the *conceptualization* phase. In a *spend* project, the object is usually the opposite. We find a corollary conclusion regarding the timing of a change to the asset's configuration: the cost of a change is inversely proportional to the LCC opportunity saving curve. This fact should be obvious to the experienced project practitioner, who will know that changes during conceptualization are orders of magnitude cheaper than during construction, and even more during operations. By extension, the level of front-end investment during *conceptualization* is inversely proportional to realization costs, namely:

- Low front-end investments tend to *increase* construction and operation costs.
- High front-end investments tend to *decrease* construction and operation costs.
- Low operational and support costs result from high reliability, performance, and maintainability characteristics of the equipment and installations.
- Conversely, high operational and support costs result from low reliability, performance, and maintainability characteristics of the equipment and installations.

Here is an example of an execution philosophy that draws the opposite conclusion. Lest the reader think it facetious, the language is borrowed from the contract written for an actual liquefied natural gas (LNG) project development in which I partook:

> *The long-term objectives of the company's LNG project shall be to minimizing both CAPEX and OPEX costs; minimizing maintenance; turnover of a plant with a high availability/reliability; minimizing with all*

appropriate efforts the "execute schedule" duration. Maximize value to investment ratio by maximizing plant availability.

The very first objective nullifies the subsequent ones! It creates the impossible expectation of achieving low operations and support costs (OPEX) by minimizing the front-end engineering, procurement, and construction costs (CAPEX). The company's edict results in an imaginary world that cannot be realized.

Maximized valunomy of future operations requires maximized development investment. Future ROIs are inversely proportional to front-end capital investments.

EXPENSE VERSUS INVESTMENT

The Primacy of the Appropriation Budget

Let us emphasize one more time how critical it is for the project management team to execute the project within the *appropriation*. The team must be ever vigilant with respect to the continuous outward flow of cash carried by the torrent of project expenditures. To the project manager (PM), the *appropriation* is akin to the air supply to a deep-sea diver. It behooves the PM to explore whatever opportunity presents itself to save costs, *as long as the future profitable performance of the asset is not compromised.* Cost increases during development are warranted when that objective is met. Spending on incompetence or nonproductivity, on the other hand, should be curtailed as soon as the case is observed. The obsessive drive to cut costs now, at the expense of asset profitability later, is behaviorally tainted by two common practices in the project world that not only fail to cut costs but actually increase them. The first, *kyopia*, deals with decimal management. The second one, *outsourcing*, addresses the pros and cons and dispels the perception that so-called offshore, high-value engineering and design centers actually offer high value in a valunomic sense.

Kyopia

Your author coined this neologism to describe the unfortunate reflex of certain PMs to obsess over changes that, in the grand scheme of things, amount to rounding errors in the overall budget. The term is a blending of the metric prefix K—for thousand—and myopia. Kyopia is a propensity to focus on the minuscule at the expense of the big picture; to dwell on decimals instead of whole numbers; to see the leaf but not the tree. The behavior is best explored through an example drawn from a multi-billion-dollar oil sands project. The issue concerned the procurement of several large process tanks at $3M each. A design change proposed to add rollers to each tank to facilitate positioning at the site. The proposed change came with a $6500 price tag per tank (two-tenths of a percentage point of the tank's price). The PM deliberated for three months on the merits of the change, given the combined $39,000 involved. It may sound like a big expense *now*, except that it is effectively a rounding error on the total order (actual: $18,039M versus rounded $18,000M). The PM failed to consider the cost savings at the site from the elimination of two cranes to move the tanks—with rollers, one would suffice. And, to add insult to injury, the three months of dithering affected the shop schedule, which delayed the arrival at the site. This is kyopia at work in all its glorious pedantry.

This proclivity to obsess over the decimals plagues all manners of projects. Kyopia possesses a universal quality that is intriguing. It seems to stem from the perception of cost as a function of time incurred. The difference between $1,000 and $1,000,000 is felt in the immediacy of the disbursement. $1,000 is easily spent now, without further ado, whereas a million dollars would be more likely to be paid in future installments. The impact of the former is perceived to be immediate to the bottom line, but not the latter—there is a much smaller sense of urgency to it. The same behavior is observed with a million dollars relative to a billion dollars. A million-dollar cost adder is deemed huge in the moment of decision; but it remains relatively insignificant to a billion-dollar budget when it comes across as a rounding error (to wit: $1.001B versus $1.000B). A billion dollars is spent over several years, and it loses any sense of immediacy.

Kyopia affects the perspective of the decision maker in another way. A million dollars is a large amount in absolute terms. A billion dollars is so much larger, as to become almost unfathomable. The correct perspective, however, is lost on the kyopian sufferer when viewed in terms of future revenues. Take the $40B LNG project example once again. Its throughput capacity is 25 million tons of LNG per year (about 48 tons per minute). In 2013, Japan paid an average of U.S. $800 per ton (corresponding to a revenue stream of *U.S. $38,400 per minute* for the owner). Say a design change during *conceptualization* costs $1M. Relative to the $40B price tag, the cost change represents 0.0025%. It also corresponds to 26 minutes of throughput production.[5] That is the proper perspective to combat kyopia.

Outsourcing

The second cost-cutting technique is known under various aliases: outsourcing, offshoring, high-value engineering. The tacit aim is always the same: save labor costs by getting the work done in a jurisdiction with lower wages. On the pure basis of hourly rate, the scheme is appealing to the accountant. In terms of valunomy to the project, it rarely pans out. Companies fare best when their core competencies are kept internally, with the rest farmed out. That is why car manufacturers buy their enterprise resource planning (ERP) software rather than code them in-house. Or why insurance companies buy toilet paper instead of pulp and paper mills.

There is no denying that outsourcing *can* be a potently effective execution strategy when chosen judiciously. But it can wreak havoc on budgets and schedules when embraced blindly. Since all functions of a business can theoretically be outsourced, the decision to keep or offload comes down to a simple question of value versus risk—reminiscent of our foray into nuptial hairdressing. The trick is to know when the risk warrants the cost. At this very moment, you can hire engineers at $5 an hour, on an outsourced basis, from several emerging markets. What looks like a no-brainer to the accountant may be *no brain* to the operations manager forced to deal with missed deliveries, opaque logistics, blown warranty costs, and quarterly bleeding. The outcome is predictable: focusing on the spending instead of the buying lulls the PM into a false sense of cost control. Never forget that:

Cheaper now is costliest later.

The proper outsourcing argument rests upon the following axioms:

- Risk explodes beneath a sufficient cost threshold.
- A unit of personal income in high cost regions has greater valunomy than a corresponding unit of income in cheaper cost regions.

The first point was already explored through hairdressing. The difference between value and cost lies in the notion that risk, not price, drives future profits. There is a valunomic threshold below which any cost saving is dwarfed by the extent of the magnitude of the size of the dimensions of the scale of the risks lying underneath. The second point speaks to the intrinsic value of labor, upon which outsourcing should be decided. It is dangerous to focus solely on the bottom line: one runs the risk of missing the fact that risk management goes far beyond simplistic hourly rates. It is fallacious to assume a valunomic dollar parity irrespective of location. The risk associated with a dollar's worth of labor is a function of where that labor takes place. That is why the $5 per hour engineer somewhere in Asia cannot match the valunomy of a $50 per hour engineer from an advanced economy. One dollar of labor yields a different output value as a function of location. A dollar here is not the same as a dollar there.

Outsourcing Risks

A project should always strive to beat costs down and enhance efficiencies. It cannot blindly assume that paying more automatically delivers higher valunomy.

Outsourcing can make valunomic sense if it is judged in terms of project and commercial risks. These risks are divided into six classes:

- *Dopey* risks—This first class of risk pertains to the pursuit of external expertise. There will be instances when a project requires assistance to resolve an issue that lies beyond its internal capabilities and resources. When a case cannot be valunomically made to acquire this expertise, whatever it may be, it then makes sense to contract for it in the marketplace.

- *Grumpy* risks—This second class of risk, also known as *insufficiency risks*, deals with resource limitations. Project teams are routinely booked (often booked solid) with little excess labor capacity. It makes valunomic sense, in this context, to seek out additional resources to complement, augment, or supplement one's own permanent pool. Taking the concept to its logical conclusion, a project can establish a back-up team (a.k.a. farm team) that can be mobilized and demobilized at will, as circumstances dictate.

- *Doc* risks—A host of competing emerging markets thrive because of this third class, better known as the race to the price bottom. The relentless demand of competitiveness is intolerant of non-valunomic activities. Cost is the great differentiator. All things being equal, cheaper always wins out. Note, however, that cheaper, within the present context, does not imply lower risk. Cheaper is justifiable when it yields better production performance without extra risk.

- *Sleepy* risks—Technology continuously evolves and advances. Enormous Darwinian pressures play on market players to keep up. What ensue are risks upon the laggards. It is a nearly insurmountable task to find from within the inspiration, wherewithal, and expertise to remain in the race, let alone join it. In such instances, and they are nearly ubiquitous, it is far simpler, faster, and more valunomic to seek external assistance. Often, merely getting a new perspective from an outsider will redefine the problem from the inside and set the path for meaningful advancements, rather than minor tweaks and modifications to create the appearance of change.

- *Sneezy* risks—The notion of *core competencies* underscores this fifth class of risk. A project must focus its energies and capital upon its core activities. What is and what is not considered *core*? It depends on whom you ask. One notional definition of a core activity is one with a strategic competitive advantage to the project or business *and* that possesses a proprietary nature. Everything else is potentially up for an outsourcing grab when warranted by valunomy. Going the outsourced route will ob-viate the potential of dissipation that always lurks around the owning and management of resources.

- *Bashful* risks—This last class deals with the idea of irrelevance and credibility. It is the only one, in fact, to explicitly seek a *higher unit cost structure* than one's own valunomic proposition. The pursuit of new markets may fail to overcome a credibility gap perceived by would-be clients. Out-of-reach clients, high barriers to entry, and inflated over-head expectations by those clients are examples of circumstances where low costs, unto themselves, are irrelevant to a client who believes that he must pay more to guarantee proper management, reliable results, and regulatory compliance. In such instances, a low-cost proposition kills the sale. In these cases, a business should seek to align itself with a recognized player to deliver the project. *When credibility trumps costs, success trumps costs.*

Outsourcing can be a prodigiously effective project execution strategy if it is selected on the basis of a risk-benefit analysis that places overall valunomy above short-term, up-front cost cutting. In all but rare cases, outsourcing awarded on the sole basis of price is a mistake that will cost more in the long run. One can-not get $100 of value out of $10 worth of cost, no matter where in the world that work is done. Forget the accountant; ask instead the manager responsible for future warranty claims!

INVESTING IS THE GAME

The overarching point of this chapter is to emphasize the importance of dealing with project costs from the perspective of buying a future asset instead of nar-rowly obsessing about execution spending. Management by the bottom line is achieved at the expense of the future economics of the asset. No owner is served by a budget obsession that can only yield mediocre future operating financials. Project costs occupy a rightful place in the pantheon of project priorities. Exe-cuting a project within its allocated budget and schedule is a hallmark of sound project execution. But achieving a PPA is the embodiment of outstanding proj-ect management. Getting there starts with a validated budget that is cemented in quantified facts rather than wishful thinking. The savvy PM will display the foresight to invest as much as necessary in conceptualization, where the majority of the future profits are seeded. The team will be guided by the asset's profitably performing character in deciding upon the merits of proposed changes.

The reader is once again cautioned against embracing the impression that money is no object. As air is to a scuba diver, so is money to a project. The prudent PM must be cognizant of this limitation and endeavor to maximize the valunomy of the *appropriation*, which is rooted in the successful control of costs. Such control is about organizational structures. That is the subject of our next chapter.

NOTES

1. This is what AACE considers a Class V estimate, see entries 1 and 2 in the Bibliography and Appendix 1.
2. Do not confuse these risk types with the endogenous and exogenous risk taxonomy discussed in Chapter 7. The *kk*, *ku*, and *uu* risks are found in both.
3. Refer to the section, ICPM Life-Cycle Phases, in Chapter 12.
4. These terms are defined in Chapter 10. The PMO manager is accountable for the *appropriation* budget. However, its management at the execution level is delegated to the various leads in accordance with their assigned scope of work. The PMO manager is invested with the authority to approve all spending within the appropriation.
5. This calculation is obviously simplistic to the extreme. However, say the full calculation yielded twenty times the number (i.e., 320 minutes), this corresponds to roughly 5½ hours of production. Even then, the relative perspective remains intact.

9

THE FRAMEWORK

"The greater the power, the more dangerous the abuse." Edmund Burke

FAILURE IS A MIRROR

Project Oversight

Chapter 7 gave us the taxonomy to categorize risks as endogenous or exogenous. The former falls under the purview of the project management office (PMO) team and the latter, to the framework. What is the framework? The framework is the organizational structure that reports to the owner, with the mandate to oversee the execution of all projects under its aegis. Some readers may interpret this in terms of a *management steering committee, portfolio management,* or *program oversight.* These common functional structures are well known in large organizations, and fulfill some of the functions that are assigned to the framework, in our profitably performing asset (PPA) context. In your author's experience, none of them have sufficed to properly guide and stir project teams toward success. The structure of the framework is, as we shall see, profoundly more involved and expansive.

Essence of the Framework

The framework tells the project how to move; the project tells the framework how to bend.[1] It is an organizational structure laid down by the owner to bridge the owner's organization, the project ecosystem (PECO), and the project team. By extension, the project team inherits the strengths and the failings of the framework. The strength, or weakness, of the framework can make or break a project. History once again serves up an ample supply of pertinent examples of symbiosis between execution and framework. First, we trek back to 1759 when

Nouvelle France faced an existential threat from the English general Wolfe, spoiling for a fight at Québec. New France's desperate plea for military help was summarily rebuffed by Louis XV's Minister of the Navy, Nicholas René Berryer, with his sardonic response, "*Quand la maison brûle, on ne s'occupe pas des écuries.*"[2] The improbable and romantic project of New France in a winter wonderland ended as probably the response foretold: New France burned on the pyre of England's battle supremacy.

We fast forward two hundred years to our second example, when we find an opposite outcome to an equally grim outlook from the travails of Apollo 13. Launched on April 13, 1970, the mission (i.e., the project in our parlance) suffered a dramatic setback 56 hours in, soon after the television transmission from the spacecraft was done. At that moment, the astronauts heard a loud bang and their capsule shook. Alarms went off, followed by a power failure. Then came the faithful message from the crew: "Houston, we have a problem." The rest also belongs to history. Flight director Gene Kranz took charge. He informed his team that failure was not an option. He proceeded to marshal NASA's wherewithal to successfully bring the men back home. In the face of extraordinary odds, a situation whose complete picture was sorely missing to the actors, the project team managed to extract victory from the jaws of ignominious failure.[3]

In the first example, the framework (i.e., King Louis XV's government) utterly failed the team charged with the survival of the colony. The second example, Apollo 13, in contrast, illustrates the usefulness of a cogent framework (i.e., NASA) to overcome a potential catastrophe. The two examples offer us two coruscating conclusions: (1) a project left to its own device has little chance of prevailing; or (2) when the project can count on the wherewithal of the entire organization, it can turn adversity into felicity.

The importance of the *framework* stems from the fact that a project's success or failure rests with the owner—yes, the owner. Granted, blame can spread to consultants and constructors, the PECO and regulators' idiosyncratic whims, and the project's supply chain. Nevertheless, it is the owner who chooses the scope, the expectations, the deadlines, the budgets, and the project players. The onus for the outcome rests with the owner. Consider a familiar scenario of an owner assigning a team to run a project and thereafter fading away from project execution. Project oversight is relegated to steering committee reviews or monthly progress meetings. The appearance of active oversight is thus created. In reality, these perfunctory gatherings are little more than news reports from team to management, with scant context at discrete moments in time interspersed by long periods of management quiescence. This isn't a framework at all: it's a 1-800 chat line, bereft of titillations.

In traditional project management, the PMO is the lynchpin of the entire operation, as seen in Figure 9.1. The project is managed by the *constraint trifecta* (see Figure 1.1). The team interacts directly with the PECO and the supply chain. The framework is merely incidental and emerges as a feature of the execution. The project succeeds or fails on the roll of the organizational dice.

Consider now the linkages in Figure 9.2 between the *framework*, the PMO, and the PECO. In this case, the project management team is shorn of its omnipotence and limited to an execution role. The project operates under the aegis of the *constraint diamond* (see Figure 1.2). The *framework* becomes an equal partner to the success of the project.

THE CONSTRUCT

Strategic Imperatives

The *framework* is a governing structure empowered to circumscribe the actions and decisions of the PMO—who would otherwise tend to behave as a hegemon (leader of leaders). A delinquent or missing *framework* condemns a project team to face an unforgiving execution desert, devoid of direction or resources. It is headed by a *leader* and comprises a small team of individuals who are expert in the various functions of the business. The framework team will oversee a portfolio of related projects. Recall from Chapter 8 that *the asset remains a*

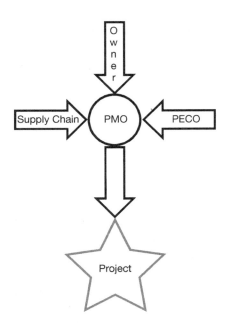
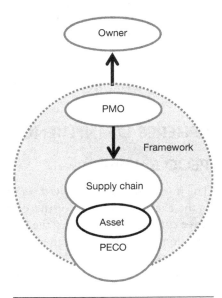

Figure 9.1   The traditional fulcrum of a project's execution strategy

Figure 9.2   The framework structure in a PPA

commercial risk far into the distant future, until it has proven itself profitably performing. This risk grounds the purpose of the framework, which exists to:

- Enable the project manager in delivering their PPA;
- Supply the checks and balance on the project by the project management team; and
- Protect the owner.

In this manner, the framework oversees the performance of all projects within its portfolio. The framework equips the project teams with the personnel, functional resources, corporate assets, and supply chain wherewithal necessary to deliver their respective PPAs. The framework actively *shelters* the project teams from the externalities of the PECO. At the same time, the framework plays the role of the owner's agent with regards to the owner's commercial imperatives to achieve speed to market, costs and risk containment, security of supply, certainty of quality, and respect of timelines. Finally, the framework is the primary line of defense against project teams going rogue or projects going off the rails.

Tactical Objectives

To these strategic imperatives we add three tactical objectives:

- To be the operational mechanism through which the owner manages the business's overall project portfolio with a focus on consistency, uniformity, quality, and repeatability of success across all projects.
- To impose and enforce the owner's standard operating environment (SOE).
- To achieve genuine alignment of commercial interests between the owner and the principal contractors.

SPHERES OF INFLUENCE

PECO Sphere

The framework *is not involved with the direct execution of the project.* Execution is the exclusive purview of the PMO. The framework operates instead across three coterminous domains: the PECO, the management sphere, and the execution dominion. It manages the expectations and interactions among them. In the first instance, the PECO layers coalesce into a complex web of heterogeneous demands, expectations, commitments, and objections that have nothing to do with project execution and everything to do with politics—as in the art of the possible. The framework, as agent of the owner, is specifically suited to a dual role of PECO gatekeeper. Success requires a significant amount of political deftness. Direct management of the PECO marshals the information flow, concentrates the message, and enables the efficient adaptation of a project's execution strategy in accord with the agreements reached with the PECO stakeholders.

Management Sphere

The framework sits squarely at the center of the background, framing a project's overall execution. It is in a unique position to gather the relevant information on the state of a project, at any point in time, and report to the owner its observations and recommendations. This information gathering is not limited to any specific project: the more salient benefit arises from the aggregation of information across an entire portfolio of projects. The framework takes on a strategic advisory role to inform the owner on the reality of the marketplace, in such areas as:

- Market intelligence and PECO analysis
- Competitive landscape analysis and project strategic planning
- Regulatory changes and geopolitical impact analysis (on portfolios)
- Global execution strategies and outlook
- Supply chain intelligence and trends
- Aggregate procurement
- Portfolio performance
- Global configuration management of assets
- Portfolio-wide continuous improvement
- Performance, compliance, risk, and fraud audits

Execution Sphere

The framework is both overseer and enabler of the project team. The team identifies its organizational requirements whereas the framework marshals what it must to satisfy them. The framework is the team's portal into the owner's capabilities. The framework is concerned with the effectiveness of resources deployed by the project team. It defines the rules and limits of a project team's execution latitude. This level of oversight includes:

- *Asset visibility*—Maintain a current account of the owner and the PECO's capabilities and capacities; head count and expertise; workloads and backlogs; and recruitment.
- *Asset allocation*—Identify jointly with a project manager (PM) the resource requirements of a project. Develop training plans for human

resources (internal and external). Assist with travel and immigration requirements, and develop travel and immigration toolkits.

- *Implementation*—Assist the PM in the mobilization, ramp-up, and ongoing management of the project's execution strategy. Develop, implement, and maintain the mechanics and mechanisms of execution. Advise project teams on cultural protocols specific to a global strategy.
- *Aggregate activities*—Explore opportunities to aggregate activities common to two or more projects within the framework's portfolio.
- *Portfolio management*—Monitor the progress of all projects under its aegis to enforce compliance with the owner's objectives, requirements, priorities, policies, procedures, standards, rules, regulations, and guidelines. These functions must include as a minimum:
  - Audits—performance, cost control, quality, risk, compliance
  - SOE—enforce SOE within the portfolio
  - Plans—review and approval of all project plans

MONOPSONY SLAYER

Keeping the Project Team Straight

One quintessential function of the framework is to counteract a project team's propensity toward monopsony. In economics, *monopsony* is a market in which several sellers face one buyer. It is the opposite of a monopoly. Projects often take on a monopsony character because the owner holds the purse strings. The power of the checkbook should never be underestimated. One could almost forgive the owner who believes herself entitled to have her demands satisfied unilaterally. One can equally commiserate with the unfortunate vendor who is reluctant to stand up for his contractual rights lest he loses the owner's business! The theoretical equipartition of the contract between owner and vendor does not always translate into a relationship between contract equals. More likely, the owner will tend to wield the contract unilaterally in the capacity of judge, jury, and executioner. In such circumstances, the short-term benefits to the owner come at the costly price of supply chain distrust, vituperations, and vendor intransigence. A strained commercial relationship may yet serve an owner in good times; but in bad times, the owner will struggle to find willing assistance from those who best possess the ability to assist.

Such is the importance of the framework to provide the much-needed checks and balances *against* the holder of the checkbook to protect the vendors (whose success is paramount to the project). It falls upon the framework to eviscerate this proclivity by the PMO toward monopsony. It behooves the framework to promote the contractual rights of vendors against the edicts of an unrealistic PM or owner. Quite simply, the framework's enforcement of vendors' contractual rights is a key factor to a project's success strategy.

Success Factors

The framework is the police that enforces the terms and conditions of the contract *upon the PMO* with the same alacrity as the latter in its dealing with vendors. The framework succeeds as an orchestrating principle when:

- *It enables the project team's functions.* As an organizational structure, the framework defines, manages, and deploys the complete set of mechanics and mechanisms of the execution of a project. The framework enforces those processes uniformly across all projects to achieve consistency, repeatability, and predictability of an outcome. The framework also provides any project team with a direct conduit to tap into the resources and capabilities of the owner organization.
- *It creates a straight line to the check holder.* Potent frameworks provide their PMs with direct access to senior management to consult, guide, bounce ideas off of, and elevate project issues that lie outside a project's immediate purview.
- *It shields the project team in times of turbulence and turmoil.* Think two words: black swans. From incidents to catastrophes, the framework manages the circumstances that are external but material to the project, and guides the PMO in navigating turbulent waters.
- *It assesses the performance of the project's management team.* This last characteristic correlates directly with the failure of projects. It is the framework's duty to monitor the performance of the project management team and counter its reflex to blame vendors and contractors. In the extreme, this could mean firing the PM, rather than replacing contractors.

TEAM STRUCTURE

The framework does as the project requires. Since no two projects are alike—even if only from differences in PECO circumstances—the same framework must be adept at tailoring itself to the needs of each project. The constitution of the framework team must therefore follow from this premise, which entails three levels of consideration: *strategic, tactical,* and *organizational.*

Strategic Considerations

The strategic standpoint focuses on the *agency* role that the framework plays on behalf of the owner. The framework leader must possess enough seniority within the owner's organization to deal directly with senior management. He must possess the positional authority to marshal whatever functional resources—from the overall organization—are required by any of the projects under its purview. And he must be vested with the power to command the effective collation of the outputs of those resources to achieve a real-time, big picture of the state of the portfolio.

Tactical Considerations

We discern three function categories: core, PECO, and aggregate. *Core functions* pertain to specific activities to be performed solely by the framework team (instead of project teams, executive management, or hired consultants). Core functions are by nature project-independent activities that are common to most or all projects of a portfolio. They generally include tasks that are:

- Strategically important to the owner (finance, accounting, legal, board oversight, investor liaison, external stakeholders, communications, marketing, sales, insurance, accounts payable/accounts receivable);
- Functions ubiquitous to the execution of all projects (auditing, quality assurance, cost control and reporting, health and safety, regulatory filing and reporting, regulatory compliance);
- Related to the verification of compliance by supply chain members
- Specific to personnel hiring and firing, training, development, and mobility;
- Specific to cost estimating;
- Specific to logistics, transportation, and expediting;
- Related to supply chain management;
- Related to the development of SOE elements; or
- Specific to quantitative risk analysis.

PECO functions are driven by the interaction requirements between the owner and the PECO layers pertinent to a given project. Generally, these functions will include:

- Community relations;
- Labor relations and jurisdictional compliance;
- Advocacy and lobbying;
- Regulatory permits and licenses;
- Jurisdictional codes and standards;

- Land acquisition and property access;
- Backroom dealers, middlemen, and influence enablers;
- Duties, taxes, levies, and fees;
- Import and export regulations; and
- Negotiations.

The *aggregate functions* arise when a portfolio of projects presents the owner with an opportunity to achieve economies of scale by aggregating the procurement requirements of multiple projects. Examples include:

- Qualifications and selection of supply chain members;
- Aggregate procurement of equipment, material, and consumables;
- Inventory procurement of long lead items;
- Logistics, transportation, and storage requirements;
- Expediting and vendor inspections;
- Trending analysis of supply chain limits and capabilities;
- Trending analysis of evolving rules and regulations;
- Standardized equipment design, facility layout, and configuration management of asset portfolios; and
- Evolution of the owner's SOE.

Organizational Considerations

The organizational standpoint deals with the operating principles of the framework team. In most instances, the framework team would be led by a full-time manager, who would be assisted on a full-time basis by a cost and schedule chief, a contract chief, and a procurement chief. Virtually all other functions (core, PECO, aggregate) will be supplied on a matrix basis from the various subject matter experts (SMEs) employed primarily by their functional departments. Eventually, the scope of a given portfolio may warrant the full-time assignment of any number of SMEs, as the case dictates.

The reader may be inclined to picture the framework as a variation on the theme of a functional matrix. The latter is common in the workplace and is especially dominant with multidisciplinary consulting houses. The matrix organization is distinctly different than a framework construct. In the latter, the framework leader and the PM share jointly the mandate of delivering a project, albeit with distinctive areas of accountability. Within a matrix environment, the framework is either token or nonexistent. Here, the PM negotiates requirements autonomously with the matrix-bound functional groups. The benefits of a dedicated framework over a matrix orchestration are juxtaposed in Table 9.1.

Table 9.1   Comparison between framework and matrix features

Feature	Framework	Matrix
Success probability	High as a minimum	Medium as a maximum
Delivery strategy	Direct, governed	Received, ad hoc
Project oversight	Direct, total	None
Accountability	Full	Assumed, function specific
Chain of command	Explicit, formal	Implicit, diffused, assumed
Project objectives	Internalized	Acquiesced
Project priorities	Explicit, managed	Implicit, negotiated
Owner visibility	Complete	Extrapolated, inferred
Project management	Shared, supervised	Autonomous, extensive
Organizational insight	Focused, centralized	Diffused, fragmentary
Risk management	Direct, complete	Parceled, limited
Responsiveness	Immediate	Bureaucratic, unformed
Resources	Dedicated, directed	Shared, negotiated
Reporting	Centralized, aggregated	Uncoordinated, self-limiting
Work sequencing	Proactive, managed	Acquiesced, submissive
Execution	Controlled, measured	Outsourced, submissive
Change management	Controlled and proactive	Passive, reactive
PECO management	Direct, complete	Incidental, non-extant
Performance metrics	Accountable, managed	Passive, absent
Aggregation	Planned, intentional	Accidental, incidental
Continuity of interest	Guaranteed, enforced	Assumed, random

JOINT VENTURES AND PARTNERSHIPS

Dangers of Asymmetry

The matter of joint ventures and partnerships is the last organizational variant that falls under the control of the framework. Either form results in a more complex management structure strained by greater alignment risks. The framework is the *de facto* leader of the partners. Note that the term *partners*, in this context, applies to any party signatory to the contractual agreement that forms the joint endeavor. From this point forward, the term *partnership* will be used to represent all forms of arrangements.

Partners join with the best of intentions to realize the PPA jointly. The reality of such compacts is fraught with dangers owing principally to a lack of symmetry between them. Dangers lurk everywhere underneath the veneer of uniformity:

- Partners may be direct competitors elsewhere in the marketplace—Naturally, openness about internal costs, processes, and resources will present a challenge.
- Valunomic philosophy—Different partners may exhibit a different focus or different culture regarding project costs. Some may be accustomed to fixed price contracts; others, to reimbursable time and materials; still others, to single sourcing. These differences extend to geographical features as well. Their cumulative ramifications on the management priorities of the framework can easily derail any decision-making efficiency.
- Cultural idiosyncrasies—Different cultures (social, business, and corporate) will value different, if not outright incompatible work ethics within a singular execution framework.
- Hubris—Size always matters, and more so to industrial projects. Partners of differing financial prowess come to the table with vastly different expectations of respect, of deference, and even of protocol. Large partners with extensive project experiences elsewhere may see themselves as immune to the whims of the PECO—which neither ends well, nor in their favor, incidentally. Corporate egos may need massaging beyond anyone's initial understanding of the partners' standing.
- Risk management—Partners may be accustomed to doing business in such a way as to assign their risks to their supply chain dealers, rather than take them on themselves. Some others may want to take on these risks, out of distrust of anybody else's ability to manage them. Within a singular framework, these diametrically opposed practices can create friction and dissent within the decision-making process.
- SOE—Each partner brings his own set of processes, procedures, protocols, execution strategy, decision making, and definition of accountability. Minutely simple matters like using Microsoft (MS) Outlook for meetings bog down into quagmires when one or more partners uses another system. Bigger issues like invoice submission and payment are the bane of many a partnership. Trying to foist one's SOE unto the other partners will not overcome this serious compatibility issue.

Primus Inter Pares[4]

It is extremely challenging to align partners along those lines. The way out of the problem is to go around it. The first step is in designating a framework leader for the partnership. Leadership, rather than management, is called for at this level because of the necessity to maintain all partners in full and willing alignment as to the objectives, interests, imperatives, execution, and decision making of the project. The management of the framework's activities, on the other hand, can be assigned to one or more individuals reporting to the leader. The second step is to quantify each partner's accountability, authority, and responsibility assignments. This parsing produces a successful *modus operandi* for the framework and eliminates role overlaps. For each assignment of authority, responsibility, and accountability, there is one, and only one, corresponding partner whose actions are then binding upon all partners. This is easier said than done. Achieving consensus among the partners requires them to be aligned and to acquiesce to the authority of the framework leader. Grandiose declarations of good faith, of working as one team, of sharing the same project objectives, will not do, as generalities and bland utterances leave too much wiggle room to appease the risk of internecine conflicts.

Shared Autonomy

Partners must not be forced to change their internal practices across-the-board to satisfy the operating requirements of the framework. Rather, partners must be free to operate autonomously; but they must agree to abide by common rules of interactions. Such interactions are essentially defined (and reluctantly agreed to ahead of time by each partner as governing) by the standard operating landscape (SOL), described below. One glaring example of a mechanics that is always contentious is the weekly reporting of work hours. Time reporting among globally distributed partners can be devilishly difficult to reconcile into a single structure without significantly altering their respective inner workings. Autonomy does not imply independence, however. The framework must equip itself with a decision hierarchy to resolve issues among the partners, up to and including an arbitration mechanism that is binding upon them all. Finally, the framework must take on the function of interface management to track and resolve all information conflicts between two or more partners. Examples of interface instances include inter-partner billing, engineered system integration, information flow blockages, work scope modifications, and accountability reassignment.

Standard Operating Landscape

The SOL can be a constant source of friction among partners. They must come to an agreement before any work is ever started on what the operating landscape will be. This landscape establishes the mechanics and mechanisms to be implemented ubiquitously on the partners, the framework, and the project execution ecosystem. Elements of the SOL include:

- Communications framework (commercial off-the-shelf only);
- Document management system;

- Presentation templates (style, format, structure, page sizes);
- Naming and numbering conventions (of documents, drawings, files);
- Accounting and invoice processing;
- Contracting and procurement strategies;
- Supply chain management;
- Contract terms and conditions;
- Engineering modeling and drafting standards;
- Engineering and design software infrastructure;
- Risk assignment and divestiture;
- Communication protocols and infrastructure (including web sites);
- Travel policies and teleconference plan;
- Work-sharing and subcontracting policies;
- Project execution plan (and associated functional plans);
- Change management; and
- Compliance enforcement mechanics.

The SOL should avoid the adoption of mechanics or mechanisms that are unique to one partner, especially in the realms of information flow, documentation management, reporting, and accounting.

Veto the Veto

The framework must be a powerful governance structure, with veto powers over the execution of the project. This is not the case, however, in relation to the partnership. The framework acts as an *agent* of the partners, whose authority derives from them. But being first among equals does not give it the power to veto or censure the partners. Such actions, when warranted, must take place among the partners directly. No partner should have veto powers over any other. This prohibition is especially true in matters of partner costs incurred from their respective roles on the project. These costs fall under the heading of partner autonomy; their merits stand outside of the other partners' purview, within the context of the framework. To act otherwise would foment dissent among the partners to the eternal detriment of the project.

Discovery Conferences

The final element of a successful execution strategy for the partnership is to achieve a shared understanding of the project execution's lay of the land. It is doubly important when the partners hail from across the globe and are unfamiliar with the particularities of the project's ultimate location. Understanding means discovery, starting with the PECO. The working partnership will typically form just before a project is activated, or just before the contract is awarded. Prior to that event, the partners will have invested significant labor and capital into the proposal submission. But they will postpone the resolution of issues related to partner asymmetries. This is a profound mistake, since there is usually little precious time available to address them after the project go-ahead is received.

It is imperative that partners figure things out before any work is started.

The path to discovery is to lay out a sequence of conferences focused on singular topics and interspersed with short gestation periods to enable all partners to gain a full understanding of what they are getting into. These conferences must occur prior to project launch, and after the framework leader has been nominated (who then takes over the execution of this sequence) in the following order:

- *Partner profiles*—Who's who in the zoo: who does what and what expertise is available. The conference should explore each partner's business systems (time sheets, invoicing, document management, information flow, scheduling, engineering systems, tele-presence).
- *PECO*—This conference introduces the partners to the idiosyncrasies of the project ecosystem.
- *Scope alignment*—This conference distills the partners' accountability allocations and shared autonomy characteristics.
- *SOL selection*—As previously discussed.
- *Framework alignment*—This last conference gathers all partners to review the findings and decisions reached in the previous conferences. The roles of each partner are delineated and quantified. A timetable for the implementation of the SOL is set.

Project Go

The go-ahead for the project triggers the launch of the following initiation activities:

- Formation and mobilization of the framework team;
- Implementation of the SOL and dry-run of the interaction linkages;
- Development of the project's scope, Level 1 milestone schedule, and Class V total installed cost estimate;
- Development of the project execution plan; and
- Systems roll out of the SOL across the partners' respective organizations. Train-the-trainers sessions are organized for all SOL systems.

STRATEGY IS FATE

The framework is the bulwark that stands erect between the project team and the vagaries of fate. It is one of the building blocks of the foundation of any project execution. It protects the owner in part by quantifying the performance of the project team, and measures the progress of the endeavor—which begs the question, "How do we do this?" *Key performance indicators* are one popular approach found in practice. However, as we will see in the next chapter, this basis of metrics is unable to explain the reasons driving the numbers. It is not enough to derive weekly or monthly journal entries that show, for example, that the schedule performance index is above one (implying milestone slippages). The more pertinent question is why? Why are activities taking longer to complete than planned? Why is labor intensity higher than expected to get the job done? And what will be the effects of these variations (negative or positive) upon the follow-on work? The answer requires a dramatically different methodology to quantify the execution of a project. *Performance assessment metrics*, the second brick in the foundation of execution, form the solution that is explored.

NOTES

1. This phrase is a play on words first uttered by John Wheeler in explaining general relativity: *spacetime tells matter how to move and matter tells spacetime how to curve.* Spacetime is to the framework as mass is to the project.
2. "When the house burns, no one bothers with the stables."
3. This story is all the more fascinating for the way it played out in full view of the public in an age when TV and radios ruled the airways. People forget that the crew spent three days to reach the moon for its slingshot back to earth. All the while, the *only* signal coming to earth was radio—no TV, no internet, nothing.
4. First among equals.

10

MEASURING SUCCESS

"You get what you measure. Measure the wrong thing and you get the wrong behaviors." John H. Lingle

QUANTIFYING SUCCESS

To Understand Is to Measure What Must Be Understood

Success means different things to different organizations. To the Montréal Canadiens of the National Hockey League, success is a Stanley Cup. To the Cleveland Browns of the National Football League, it could be three consecutive seasons with the same quarterback. The definition adopted by the team's owner, whichever it is, orients the execution strategy prior to the start of the season. The point, in our context, is the idea of defining success before any work is undertaken. The prime directive is to ultimately achieve a profitably performing asset (PPA). The success of the *execution* requires a different taxonomy. It is not enough, and it is specious, to strive mainly by budgets and schedules. Success requires a multidimensional set of metrics that are purposeful. As William Bruce Cameron remarked, *"Not everything that can be counted counts, and not everything that counts can be counted."*

Performance metrics must be able to reveal the underlying proficiencies and deficiencies in order to learn from them, adjust the delivery strategy, and plan the follow-on work.

Metrics are purposeful when they convey knowledge about their reported states.

Common Schemes

Common metrics such as the *manpower performance index* (MPI), the *schedule performance index* (SPI), and the *cost performance index* (CPI) may be easy to implement, but fail to inform the project team on the reasons behind their trending values. They convey no lesson or understanding beneath their numbers other than pass or fail. Key performance indicators (KPIs) are also universally adopted in practice. They too, however, fail the *knowledge* test. They are ill-suited to measure the genuine performance of an execution that spans long time periods and multiple phases. One would be well advised to heed the wisdom from Saint Isidore of Seville (circa 600 CE): "Take from all things their number and all shall perish."

When Success Is a Failure and Vice Versa

The assessment of *success* is a function of the definition of a project's end. To be on time and on budget may be deemed successful even in instances when its intended outcome is not. Consider the following examples:

Project success—outcome failure. The project is the design and construction of a well to produce fresh water for a remote village. The well is completed on time and on budget—a success. However, the geological formation subsequently proves unstable; the well dries up within twelve months—an unequivocal failed outcome.

Project success—outcome failure: Part 2. This is a variation on the above scheme, in which the project outperforms its cost and timeline targets. The project is the orchestration of a modern art exhibit in a city orbiting at the outer rim of the global art scene. The exhibition, marketing, catering, and logistic costs are aggressively controlled. The exhibit is ready four weeks ahead of schedule. The orchestration is deemed an unqualified success. However, skimping on marketing and floor arrangement costs cripples the ad campaign, which fails to generate the expected buzz. Attendance is disappointing. The project came in under budget and ahead of schedule but the outcome—the actual exhibition—is a commercial failure.

Project failure—outcome success. This situation is the reverse case of a failed project resulting in a positive outcome. The instance is a research and development project for a super-capacity lithium car battery. The research encounters severe engineering obstacles that necessitate a doubling of the project's budget and a tripling of the overall development schedule. The engineering solution, unexpectedly, leads to the discovery of a chemical process that doubles the storage capacity of the battery. The product leads to a cornering of the global car battery market. The project was a failure (blown budget and schedule) but its outcome—an unmitigated success.

Project success—outcome success—commercial failure. This example is a variant of the above scenario. The research and development effort yields a cell phone battery with a ten-year life, compared to two years offered by the competition. The phone's product life cycle is limited to sixteen months. Here, the superior battery life adds no differentiable value to the end product but increases costs (relative to the competition). The project was completed on time and on budget (success) and produced a successful outcome (the long-life battery). Together, however—they produce a commercial bust.

KEY PERFORMANCE INDICATORS

Insufficiency of Information

These examples highlight the difficulty inherent to the postmortem assessment of a project. How the project is defined at the start affects the definition of its success. They also point to the importance of factoring the couplings between execution, operation, and economics. The heart of the problem lies in devising a scheme to quantify a set of project metrics from which the assessment can be objectively derived. In traditional project management (TPM), the *constraint trifecta* is the default position, and KPIs, the preferred metrics.

Project management thought leader, Harold Kerzner, categorizes these KPIs into primary and secondary indicators as follows:

- Primary: within time, within cost, within quality limits, accepted by the customer
- Secondary: follow-on work from the customer, using the customer's name as a reference on your literature, commercializing a product within minimum or mutually agreed scope changes without disturbing the main flow of work, without changing the corporate culture, without violating safety requirements, providing efficiency and effectiveness of operations, satisfying OSHA/EPA requirements, maintaining ethical conduct, providing a strategic alignment, maintaining a corporate reputation, maintaining regulatory agency relations

Some of the secondary indicators are tantamount to not breaking the law, a dubious measure of success at best, and a statement of the obvious.

Faulty Foundation

The fundamental discordance between the intent and outcome of the primary KPIs is that they are handicapped by the estimating process that led to the budget and schedule targets in the first place. The discrepancy is immediately felt when the owner willfully selects a target budget that is known to be unrealistic with regards to the asset's intrinsic cost. All subsequent measures of progress will be crippled by the built-in impossibility of meeting the KPI, MPI, CPI, and SPI targets. Time and budgets will be perennially underfunded and hence, constantly busted.

The intent-outcome discordance is further aggravated by a disconnect between the project's conclusion and the future profitable performance of the operating asset (making or losing money). By focusing on a project's *constraint trifecta*, decisions will be made to uphold it, even at the expense of the asset's future performance. Compounding this misery is a lack of KPI continuity between successive phases of a project. The performance and success of a given phase is dependent on the inputs it receives from its predecessor and the outputs it produces to its successor. Significantly, meeting the KPI targets of each phase is no guarantee that the ultimate outcome—the PPA—will be profitable or performing. The sum of the parts does not automatically equal the whole. This fact is provable mathematically by the formalism of the so-called Cauchy-Schwarz inequality:[1]

$$\left(\sum_{i=1}^{n} a_i^2 \right) \left(\sum_{i=1}^{n} b_i^2 \right) \geq \left(\sum_{i=1}^{n} a_i b_i \right)^2 \qquad\qquad 10.1$$

where the a_i and b_i are pairs of KPIs.

Lack of Continuity of Accountability

The final nail in the trifecta's coffin is driven by the principle of *continuity of accountability*, which is discussed in more detail in Chapter 11. This principle posits that the *performance of the vendor is sustained and maximized by the prospect of assured future earnings*. This principle does *not* flow from a piecemeal execution of the project in separate phases. A vendor who hopes to extend his involvement throughout several phases of a project will be motivated to produce outputs that will not come back to hurt him later. His accountability at any stage of a project is projected into the future. TPM projects suffer from this lack of continuity.

PERFORMANCE ASSESSMENT METRICS

Quantifying the Meaningful and Actionable

The PPA methodology abandons KPIs in favor of *performance assessment metrics* (PAM). The assessment model utilizes quantifiable metrics gathered from real-time performance data. The metrics quantify the true performance of a project throughout its constituent phases. They provide a powerful project management process for real-time risk identification, execution management, and continuous improvements:

> *The model is predicated upon the measurement of execution outcomes inherent to a project's evolution throughout its life cycle. The model is prescriptive only in the tabulation of the success factors that enter into the assessment of the project; the types and number of those factors are left to the discretion of the project's participants. [...] The model applies to single and multiphase projects (continuously executed or not) and quantifies the impact of successive phases unto each other, and their influence upon the overall performance of the resulting outcome.*

Mathematical Formulation

The process begins with the selection of individual metrics, defined as variables that can be numerically quantified. They represent targets that are tracked over time. Each metric is assigned a value, R, given by:

$$R = \left(\frac{actual + min}{target + min} \right)^M \qquad \text{10.2}$$

where $M = 1$ if the intent is to maximize R, or -1 if R is to be minimized. Maximizing implies better cost performance (higher valunomy); minimizing implies lesser deficiencies (less re-work desired). For example, given a fixed budget and schedule, one wants to maximize the number of deliverables produced ($M = 1$) and minimize the number of errors found in those deliverables ($M = -1$). The term min is the minimum measurable increment for the target value. For example, if the target error rate is 2 per drawing, the minimum measurable increment is 1. If the target is a fuel emission rate per kW, e.g., 12 grams of CO_2 per kW, the minimum measurable increment could be set at 0.5 grams. The role of min is to allow null values for actual and target metrics to be recorded without causing a division error.

The second step is to group together sets of related metric-defined activities. Each such group of n activities is called a functional, and is expressed by:

$$F = \frac{1}{n} \sum_{i=1}^{n} R_i \qquad \text{10.3}$$

Next, each functional is assigned a weight, W, between 0 and 1, to express its relative impact upon the success of the project. That success is quantified by the K value given by:

$$K = \frac{1}{m}\sum_{j=1}^{m} W_j F_j \qquad\qquad 10.4$$

where m is the number of *functionals* and j is a *summation index*.

K generates a single number that can be less than, equal to, or greater than 1. The unitary value corresponds to a project that meets 100% of the performance targets established at the outset of the project. K values exceeding 1 also exceed the targets. Conversely, values lower than 1 highlight missed targets (or perhaps, unrealistic targets).

Multiphasic Extension

The K variable can be applied to multi-phase projects through three modifications. These modifications are needed to account for a phase's *allocation*,[2] A_p, a *completeness factor*, C_p, and a *phase weight factor*, Y_p, expressed respectively by:

$$A_p = (\text{Cost} * \text{Time})_p \qquad\qquad 10.5$$

$$C_p = \frac{A_p}{A_{extra} + A_p} \qquad\qquad 10.6$$

$$Y_p = \frac{A_p}{A_S} \qquad\qquad 10.7$$

In Equation 10.7, the term A_s represents the allocation for the entire project (across all phases). Equations 10.5 and 10.6 are combined to express the efficacy factor, SK, in Equation 10.8:

$$SK = \sum_{l=1}^{P} Y_l K_l C_{Pl} \qquad\qquad 10.8$$

In these formulae, the subscript p refers to a given phase; l is a summation index; and P is the number of phases in the project.

Operating Metrics

The K and SK metrics pertain to the *efficiency of execution* of a project, and not the actual performance of the asset. The latter requires that we quantify its operational success, based on parameters that include productivity, plant throughput, energy consumption, material rejection rates, plant reliability, daily number of visitors, orders from online marketing campaigns, market share, and revenue growth. The resulting factors R_o, F_o, and K_o are calculated from the same equations corresponding to R, F, and K, respectively.

Assessment of Performance

The overall assessment of the project will normally be derived from an economic analysis of the asset. Financial metrics are an intuitive choice for assessing the valunomy of the capital deployed to complete the project. However, the effects of the execution may not emerge explicitly from those tabulations. One may wish to understand how efficiently the project allocations were deployed to produce the asset performance. Such an understanding is critical to continuously improve the project execution process and improve the probability of success in delivering similar future assets. To that end, we define a coefficient, Q, which measures the efficiency of the allocation deployment:

$$Q = \frac{K_o}{SK} \qquad 10.9$$

A null value signifies a complete financial failure of the project, indicative of an asset that is inoperative. A value of 1.0 for Q validates the initial investment decision and the *development* strategy. Higher values mean greater bang for the investment buck, along with better financial returns for the owner.

TRUTHS, DARN TRUTHS, AND METRICS

Real-time Performance Improvements

The PAM method yields deep insights into the effectiveness of each of the execution elements of a project, be it stand-alone or multiphase, and the impact of each element upon the whole. The method provides real-time analysis of all targeted factors; enables the rectification of deficient elements in real time; produces actionable statistical data on execution elements for continuous improvement; and factors the couplings between execution, operation, and economics of a project. What gets measured is still selected by the owner or the framework. "Why measure what?" is rationalized based on real-time control and continuous improvement. The metrics are precious knowledge for the owner, the framework, and the project management team. Project metrics don't amount to a hill of beans in this crazy project world if nothing can be proactively done by them. The value of these metrics is realized through proactive feedback that is orchestrated jointly by the framework and the project management team.

Feedback Mechanics

The feedback mechanics involves four mechanisms: cash back, fix forward, improvement, and knowledge:

- The cash back mechanism is commonly used by owners as a financial incentive to enhance vendor performance. In their sinister form, these incentives take the form of claw-backs, withholdings, liquidated or consequential damages, liabilities, and penalties to punish sub-par performance. As auspicious incentives, owners reward performing vendors through bonuses, performance fees, and equity stakes. PAM play the evidentiary role in those deliberations.
- The fix-forward mechanism utilizes real-time performance metrics to inform the project manager (PM) on problematic and delinquent areas of project execution and corresponding potential remediation schemes. These metrics form the basis of all statistical analyses (including *Monte Carlo* simulations) that determine the probability of success in delivering the PPA.
- The improvement mechanism is the process through which the organization learns from the execution experience. This information can then be fed into a corporate continual improvement cycle. It can be used to refine the project's standing execution strategy or guide the evolution of the owner's project delivery framework over time.
- The knowledge mechanism enables the owner's organization to populate its knowledge databases with the data, information, and statistics derived from the PAM. Engineering, procurement, construction, and project ecosystem libraries can thus be constituted and maintained over time. This information set can afterwards be used to adapt the owner's standard operating environment or standard operating landscape; evolve the design, engineering, and equipment standards to keep up with an ever-changing technological landscape; and capture real-time costing data that are critical to the estimating process.

The Price of Estimating

The last point of the last bullet provides a second fundamental justification for the adoption of PAM. The reasons, to be discussed in Chapter 17, are rooted in the critical relevance of current costing information. That information forms the basis of authorization of any future project by the owner. Accurate and comprehensive historical data, economic and otherwise, are essential to the validity of the estimating process. Early phase estimates (Classes V and IV, specifically) are entirely dependent on these historical datum sources, whence the necessity to derive them in real time during a project's execution, via the performance assessment mechanism.

KPIs FOR A PPA APPROACH

Prescriptive Management

PAM coalesce into a potent management tool for the real-time execution of any phase of a project. They become effective KPIs in the hands of a competent PM. But this effectiveness only materializes within a *prescriptive* management framework. It is prescriptive when:

- It satisfies the what, why, when, where, who, and how (W5H) requirements as a KPI mechanics.
- It ascribes the KPI accountability to the assessed and the authority to the assessor. Both parties must be individuals and not groups or departments if the principle of accountability defined previously is to hold.
- It quantifies the KPI.
- It defines ahead of time the consequences of failing, meeting, and exceeding the KPI targets.
- It actualizes those consequences immediately as the KPIs are assessed.

All five conditions are essential to the effectiveness of a PPA KPI program.

Conditions 1 and 2

The first two conditions are self-explanatory—with the first derived from the second. To be held accountable requires the individual to know what that accountability entails and how it is measured.

Condition 3

The third condition creates four types of KPI:

- The first type, the *range KPI*: establishes a target *range* within which the KPI is met. The *range* KPI is typical of work that progresses over time. For example, in a given month, a specific number of drawings must be produced. If the actual production falls within the KPI range, the KPI is met. Measures that are meant to be maximized achieve superior KPIs when they exceed the upper limit of the range. Conversely, measures that are meant to be minimized (say, the number of errors in one drawing) are also deemed superior when they subceed[3] the range's lower bound.
- The second type, the *accuracy KPI*: is the inverse of the range KPI. Here, one aims to meet the target value, and fails increasingly as the measure departs from the target. The accuracy KPI is specific to comparisons between predicted/estimated and actual values. For example, a labor

man-hour prediction is met when the actual man-hours recorded equals the prediction. Alternatively, the target value may be given a tight tolerance band, expressed as target +/−% of deviation. Anything falling outside of the band is deemed a failure.

- The third type, the *limit KPI*: is typical of an externally mandated target, such as meeting a prescribed regulatory filing date; recording fewer incidents than the limit set by legislation; or achieving higher measures than set by a lower limit—such as achieving more total hours worked without one recordable accident, than a threshold previously established.
- The final type, the *set KPI*: is the pass/fail KPI. One either meets the set value (the Rio Summer Olympics shall open on August 5, 2016, or not). Set KPIs are pertinent to mission-critical aspects of the performance of project execution.

Condition 4

The fourth condition follows from the logic of the first two conditions. One must know from the outset what is guaranteed to happen when a KPI is measured—good or bad.

Condition 5

The last prescriptive condition, immediacy of the consequence, effectively creates a primordial feedback mechanism for keeping the project execution on track, and to remedy any propensity to go off the rails. Its importance is twice reinforced by the fact that KPIs are, by nature, reactive and lag in time from daily performance of execution. A KPI measured monthly, for example, is already one month late to effect remediation of a problem. Leaving that remediation to fester only aggravates the problem. It is imperative to act immediately upon the publication of KPI results.

PPA KPI AT WORK

Hail or Nail

The most effective consequence of a KPI assessment is monetary. Exceed a KPI target and earn a bonus. Fail a KPI at a cost or penalty. Meet the KPI and earn a token gain. Keep failing the KPI and risk losing the entire job, or one's own job. This three-tier system is clear-cut, unequivocal, and proaccountability. In contrast, the least effective consequence yields no immediate material impact. Warning letters, performance review berating, the threat of future work denial, and the lure of future work potential have a near-zero value in terms of rectifying an execution scheme that is handicapped by inferior KPI results. Talk is cheap, be it spoken or written—best to show me the money.

Analogy of the Equipartition Theorem

Chapter 9 alluded to the tendency of an owner to act in a hegemonic manner. The classic evidence is embedded in the imposition of KPIs upon a contractor but not reciprocally upon the owner's project team. The KPI program will be stalwart when both parties are held to the same KPI expectations—more so when the KPI is relationship-dependent. Take, for example, the review cycle of a document. Say the contract stipulates that the vendor has 20 days to produce it, then seven days to incorporate the owner's comments and reissue the final version. Correspondingly, the owner is given five days to review the first draft, then another five to approve the final version. The vendor would expect to be assigned KPIs for those two periods. But what about the owner? The turnaround time has a direct impact on the vendor's performance. Classically, this is where the KPI story would end, leaving the vendor alone to hold the bag. To the *project*, this failure to hold the owner accountable is also a failure of execution. Therefore, the owner's project management team should be assigned a KPI with attendant consequences on par with those of the vendor. And the vendor must have recourse against the owner for the latter's failure to meet her KPI. That is the idea behind dependent KPIs: the success of the project is a function of the performance of *all parties* involved in its execution, not just those contracted to do so.

Equipartition Theorem

In physics, the equipartition theorem is a general formula that relates the temperature of a system with its average energies. The original idea of equipartition was that the internal energy of a system in thermal equilibrium is shared equally among all its various forms; for example, the average kinetic energy per degree of freedom in the translational motion of a molecule should equal that of its rotational motions.

HOUSTON, LET'S NOT HAVE A PROBLEM

Project metrics conclude Part 2 of this book. We are now able to leave behind the elemental constructs of project management and set upon our next destination: that of getting a project off the ground. In this regard, projects are akin to rockets: their trajectories thrive or dive on the success of the launch sequence. Take off in the wrong direction and experience the true pull of gravity from the weight of expectations. How to launch correctly—that's the ticket to a successful journey, as we will see in Part 3.

NOTES

1. The role of inequalities in mathematics is very prominent in deciding maximum and minimum values of various functions. One such elementary, yet powerful, inequality is the Cauchy Schwarz inequality.
2. Allocation was defined previously in Chapter 5.
3. This term is a neologism coined by the author. It is defined as the antonym of the verb *exceed*.

PART 3—HOW

*Getting down to the business of planning
the execution of a project.*

11

THE EXECUTION STRATEGY

"There is nothing so useless as doing efficiently what should not be done at all." Peter Drucker

THE GENUINE MEANING OF A PLAN

Another Way to Make or Break a Project

The seeds of failure and success are sown together in the earliest stages of a project. This simultaneity may surprise the reader, who may have expected one or the other. The situation stems from the fact that the project delivery strategy must be engineered *before* any work is undertaken. A project needs a strategy, or more to the point, a series of strategies that must go beyond broad definitions, general plans, and generic expectations. The potential for project failure will lurk everywhere strategies lack. Maddeningly, these failings will tend to materialize at the worst of times, as any experienced project practitioner will attest. *The essence of strategy*, remarked Michael Porter, *is choosing what not to do*. And the first thing that one should not do is launch the project on the wrong path, at the wrong time, or for the wrong reasons. The launch analogy is apt, since we can regard a project (especially a large one) as a moon-shot rocket—a highly complex machine for which success depends on the liftoff. The imperative of defining the strategy from the outset cannot be emphasized enough; the probability of delivering a profitably performing asset (PPA) increases exponentially with the degree of its completeness.

Planning Is Complicated

The old adage "if you fail to plan, you plan to fail" is our starting point. It stands to reason that a project must be planned before any serious money is spent. On that point, the consensus is universal. It gets fuzzier in the matter of describing what the plan should be. It definitely fails when the plan is hatched from cutting and pasting from past experience, in the name of expediency. Project planners should heed the warning of Thomas Aquinas: "*Homo unius libri*" (beware a man of one book).

The process of defining a *project delivery strategy* is complex. The point of this chapter is to explore how to engineer such a strategy. A managing mindset that fixates on the dollar value faces the danger of attempting to manage everything to that one number. In reality, industrial projects are collections of smaller projects that interface with each other. A $500M project, for example, could be made up of 50 separate elements averaging $10M a piece. That number 50 could be 20 or 100, but it will not be one or two or five. Managing such a project isn't like eating the proverbial elephant (that would be one bite at a time), but more like eating an entire herd—it cannot be done in one sitting.

What Is a Viable Strategy

A *viable* strategy of execution breaks down a project into a large set of smaller pieces managed at their interfaces. This strategy is itself broken down into a set of smaller execution tactics. The overall strategy will be developed by the *framework team*, under the guise of the *baseline asset execution framework* (BAEF) plan. The BAEF governs the overall execution from the perspective of the owner's interests. The details of the execution work at each phase of the *development* will be captured in a *phase execution plan* (PEP) written by the project management office (PMO). These plans will involve several parties at various times as a function of their inputs into the process.

A strategy is not a generic statement of intent to do something. It is a precise road map to guide all the work and the participants on the journey toward the PPA. Its effectiveness is *not* measured by the number of pages and annexes and external references. Nor is it aided by regurgitating information that already exists within the owner's organization (a job description being a prime example). A strategy is effective when it is prescriptive, procedurally specific, action/consequence deterministic, continuously consulted, and adaptable. Above all, it must provide *any reader* with concise, complete, and unambiguous contents in terms of *what, why, when, where, who,* and *how* (W5H) (more on this technique later in this chapter). That is the differentiator between good and bad strategy documents. The good ones are prescriptive, which requires the writer to draft the text in direct, vapid-free form to get to the point of each question in the fewest words.

THE COVENANTS GUIDING THE PROCESS

The mapping of a strategy is critical yet will only be useful when it is documented efficiently. Before we launch into the nitty-gritty details of developing a *project execution strategy*, we first lay out markers to corral that process, which is subject to five covenants: *the owner drives; set then execute; define then plan then prescribe; enforce;* and *flex.*

The Owner Drives

We hold this truth to be self-evident. Whoever holds the purse has the last word. During the strategy definition, the owner works closely with the framework team to cement all aspects of the strategy. While the framework team handles daily duties, the owner remains final arbiter of the strategy's overall choreography.

Set Then Execute

We hold this second truth on par with the first. It is imperative that the entire strategy be established *prior* to the start of the project execution work. It is a grave—and often fatal—mistake to leave some aspects to later, when the issue arises. Never envision crossing the Rubicon sight unseen. The better approach is to tag what issues cannot be defined early on, and then assign them a hard-stop milestone on the master schedule with sufficient time built-in to decide.

Define Then Plan Then Prescribe

The division of a project into multiple scope subsets creates a chronological sequence for the work—the so-called life-cycle phases. Each subset of that sequence must be elaborated in terms of scope definition, work plan, and execution prescriptions. The scope definition quantifies what work is to be done and to what extent. This is what is meant by *definition*. The plan defines the sequencing of the tasks, the governing timelines and milestones, and the *performance assessment metrics* (PAM). It also defines the functional strategies for the framework (discussed later). Finally, a plan becomes useful when:

- It *prescribes* who will do what when;
- It defines the total staffing commitments commensurate with the acceptance maturity model chosen for each task of each work sequence;
- It specifies the standard operating environment (SOE) and the standard operating landscape (SOL); and
- It specifies the inputs and outputs of each task.

Enforce

Once a strategy is set, it must be enforced by the framework. What is obvious at the start may eventually fall prey to the vagaries of complacency as time goes by. On large, multiyear projects, the tendency is to allow the project execution to go about its merry way, which is when the prospect of an unfathomed rabbit hole will materialize. The onus is on the framework to maintain the strictures of the strategic edifice. The owner's role is to keep the pressure on the framework to maintain the strategic course.

Flex

The fifth and final rule manages the whims of the Fates. Over time, the original assumptions of the strategy may no longer apply. The framework leader must assess whether to maintain or alter those assumptions, and change the delivery strategy accordingly. At the very least, the owner, the framework leader, and the project manager should convene:

- Prior to the start of the work, to verify the shared understanding of all parties of the strategy;
- At around 30% (time-elapsed basis), to tweak the strategy with the reality of the work; and
- When a significant change to the work has occurred (scope, budget, timelines).

ELEMENTS OF THE STRATEGY

Where to Start

The owner begins the process of definition by stating the *contents* of a project:

- Asset specifications (throughput; reliability, availability, and maintainability; extents of automation; profitability; economic targets; financial targets; social targets; and budget tolerances discussed in Chapter 9)
- Ownership structure (sole proprietorship, partnership, joint venture, framework functions)
- Chain of command and oversight rules
- Project ecosystem (PECO) and timeline targets (including investment decision dates)
- Appointment of the framework leader

Once the contents are clear, the next step is the project delivery strategy by the framework:

- Define the project delivery hierarchy (PMO or project management consultant [PMC]) and the roles and overall accountability of each member of that hierarchy (i.e., owner, framework, PMO, PMC).
- Define the global core functions to be assigned to the framework team that will persist throughout the life cycle of the project.
- Prescribe the life-cycle phases of the project, from concept to execution to activation to operations. For each phase, identify the outcomes, expectations, and project decision criteria for moving on to subsequent phases.
- Define the global component strategies of the execution, which will remain invariant throughout the life of the project.
- Define the personnel development objectives.
- Select the SOE or SOL.
- Nominate the PMO manager or select the PMC.

Global Strategy Components

The rules of engagement between the PMO and the supply chain are established by the framework through *global component strategies*. Each component strategy is published in a stand-alone plan and should include, at a minimum:

- Engineering and design
- Contracts and procurement
- Supply chain management
- Logistics and transportation
- Fabrication
- Construction and construction management
- PECO management
- Records management
- Asset configuration management
- Design standardization
- Regulatory compliance and permitting
- Safety management

Alignment of Interests

The component strategies also serve to align the interests of the supply chain partner (SCP) with those of the project. Alignment is critical to the success of the project and cannot be overstated. The SCP may deem themselves limited only to their contractual obligations. Beyond legal threats and warranty claims, the owner most often struggles to impart a sense of shared interest upon vendors. True, bidirectional alignment of interests benefits from a contract philosophy anchored to the principle of *accountability of outcome*, explored in Chapters 5, 6, and 7. It is explicitly different from a warranty clause or liability, in that the SCP voluntarily recognizes her onus for the outcome without the threat of legal action. The SCP's commercial interests are tied to the PPA's success, rather than the completion of her contract work.

> *No project can succeed when suppliers fail. It behooves the owner to do what he must to make those suppliers succeed.*

Evidently, for such a principle to win, genuine incentives must be offered to SCPs. The promise of future work is ineffective in general, owing to the diversity of the overall supply chain and the commitment uncertainty embedded in multiphased, multiyear projects. Alliance-type work can work in principle, but not on a cost reimbursable basis. A different philosophy of incentives is needed. Viable options include:

- Continuity of work—Certainty of future work is a powerful incentive to any vendor. A vendor's interest will be maintained if he is assured of continuity of execution, whereby the vendor will be retained throughout the pertinent life-cycle phases of the project.
- Continuity of mandate—Focus instead on one of the more specific roles that a vendor undertakes across a series of projects.
- Continuity of exposure—Enable a vendor to be invited to partake in fields or initiatives that are beyond the vendor's bread and butter activities. This can appeal to vendors keen to expand their core competencies, service offers, or entry into dramatically different markets.
- Outcome performance reward—Albeit counterintuitive, this notion rewards a vendor for the quality of her output through the grant of a financial bonus on top of the payment for the work done. Conversely, the vendor will incur additional nonreimbursable costs as a penalty for inferior or deficient quality of outcome.
- Phase performance bonus—A variation on the outcome performance award, this financial incentive can be structured around the PAM of a given phase of the work. The amount of the bonus can also be tied to the metric measurement directly. This bonus becomes particularly attractive to those vendors who are involved in the work leading up to the completion of the actual asset. For the engineering vendors involved, the bonus can be tied to the asset's initial and steady-state operating capacity.
- Value improving returns—Split the cost savings incurred by the owner as a result of the action of a vendor. This is the innovation incentive that stimulates vendors to explore alternative ways of designing, procuring,

equipping, transporting, or constructing the asset. A vendor may, for example, uncover an alternate valve model that is cheaper and quicker in delivery than the standard one. Or, a vendor may achieve additional economies of scale by aggregating the procurement of a common instrument across several projects.

- Sustaining work award—So far, the approaches work on new projects. A *sustaining work* award opens vendors to the potential revenue stream from sustaining/brownfield type work associated with the maintenance, upkeep, or expansion of an existing asset. It is particularly appealing to engineering and procurement firms.

- Experience swaps—This is not a financial reward. It is instead a program to offer reliable key members of a vendor the opportunity to work within the owner's organization and experience projects first-hand from an owner's perspective. Contractually, the arrangement is readily implemented via a second agreement. Organically, it deepens the relationship with the vendor in a unique way. This program must, however, come with an ironclad ban upon the owner from poaching the vendor's personnel.

- Profit sharing—This is potentially the ultimate incentive for key vendors, whereby they are offered a percentage of the profits generated by the asset once it is operating. It is also the most politically explosive, admittedly.

The range of options available to the owner will per force be limited by business imperatives and may not jive with the interests of the SCPs. Why not simply ask the SCP what appeals to him the most? Indeed, that is perhaps the most effective way to achieve the deepest integration of interest. Just ask what will arouse them the most and watch where the conversation leads!

Personnel Objectives

Projects are fantastic opportunities for an organization to grow and learn. The same opportunity is afforded the people on the project. Making the most of it requires planning and foresight by the owner's organization. Every project execution strategy should include development objectives for key individuals assigned to the project (to strengthen the owner's long-term capabilities). Functional cross-pollination should be favored over skill specialization. Exposure to diverse business functions should be promoted far and wide, rather than retaining people in specific roles *sine die*. Teams of multidisciplinary people are more effective than invariant skill sets within multidisciplinary teams.

Baseline Asset Execution Framework

Once the foundation of the execution strategy is set, its details must be captured in the governing BAEF document, published by the framework leader. The reader should note that this document is different than a PEP, which is written by the PMO for a specific life-cycle phase. The BAEF acts as a prime directive for the entire project across all phases and establishes what remains constant over time, until the asset is operational. It also governs the interface requirements between successive life-cycle phases. Although subject to changes, in accordance with the fifth rule enunciated previously, the constancy of the contents is the primary criterion for inclusion into the plan. The structure of the BAEF is suggested in Appendix 2. Once the BAEF is published, the mobilization of the project management team can commence. Note that the execution work has not yet commenced. We are still in the planning phase of the strategy.

The Phase Execution Plans

The PEP is the blueprint of how a phase is to be done, by whom, when, with what tools, and in compliance with whatever contractual terms. It is written and published by the PMO *before* a phase is started. It is an exercise in futility to develop a single PEP spanning all phases, or to develop all PEPs concurrently from the outset. The key to writing an effective PEP is *tailoring*. Each PEP must be tailored to the specifics of a particular phase. The nature of the work, the scope of that work, the players, and even the constitution of the PMO will vary over time and must therefore be captured accordingly by the PEP. Before writing is initiated, the following features should be resolved:

- Prescriptions of the asset scope of work (resulting in asset deliverables).
- Prescriptions of the ancillary scope of work (enabling activities that do not result directly in asset deliverables).
- Core functions of the PMO and the nomination of individual leads accordingly.
- Sourced functions to be assigned to entities external to the owner's organization.
- Project delivery hierarchy and the roles and overall accountability of each member of that hierarchy (the framework, PMO or PMC, scope project team [SPT], SCP).
- Define the accountability matrix for the project delivery hierarchy.
- Define the accountability matrix for the change management process.

Once these features are affirmed, the development of the PEP can commence.

STRATEGY IS PRESCRIPTION

What It Is

The BAEF and the PEP are effective when they are *prescriptions*, meticulously written to satisfy the W5H requirements. Whatever the topic, the competent reader must come away with a working understanding of all W5H requirements applicable to it. The text must be prescriptive, or coercive in the limit. Vacuous, vapid, and bland pronouncements must be banished, such as "the project manager is responsible for satisfying all stakeholder interests"; "the quality assurance manager will ensure that the quality assurance policy is complied with"; "the engineering manager shall endeavor to ensure the delivery of a quality drawing set"; and the abhorrent form "as the work progresses, every effort must be made to comply with the health and safety targets." These statements are neither enforceable nor measurable. The passive form only creates the illusion of certainty. Consider the following alternate prescriptive forms:

- The project manager shall realize the PPA.
- The quality assurance manager shall enforce procedures X, Y, and Z at the intervals specified therein.
- The engineering manager shall, without exception, enforce the drawing verification and checking procedure XX, and maintain a record of the performance metrics derived from its application.
- The total recordable incident frequency (TRIF) limit for the work shall be 2.33. Higher TRIF values shall trigger penalties defined in Clause X.X-9(a) of the contract.

What It Cannot Be

The seasoned reader may have seen first-hand examples of bulky, ponderous PEPs tallying hundreds of pages of cut-and-paste text, written in breezily descriptive styles, with page after page of text extolling the roles and responsibilities of innumerable project positions, without tying them down to specific task mechanics and mechanisms. These types of plans are ineffective to the management of a project. They must be written in a compact, get-to-the-point style, bereft of prolixity (i.e., using too many words). A PEP and the BAEF can be none of these:

- Summaries of the work to be done, the nature of the asset to be constructed, or the various stops along the timeline.
- Profuse descriptions of the roles and responsibilities of the team members. A proper accountability matrix renders them redundant. The PEP

is not the place to explain what a project manager or a design lead does. Those belong in the organization's human resources (HR) handbook.

- Justifications of functions and processes. If you must explain why change management is essential to the success of the project, you are dealing with Training 101, not execution planning.
- Invitations to ensure and assure. One does not ensure that a procedure or a mechanism is followed; one prescribes its use for the pertinent task.
- Diffused responsibilities. It will not do to state that a given manager is responsible for meeting all stakeholder expectations, or to coordinate the review process with various departments within the owner's organization. One is responsible for carrying specific tasks in accordance with specific mechanics or mechanisms, with participation from specific individuals or named positions from explicit groups or organizations. This principle goes back to the accountability matrix.
- Purposeless actions. Any action, task, or process that is included in the PEP cannot be devoid of an output. For example, the PEP cannot merely establish the requirement for a weekly team meeting to review the progress of the work. The PEP must state the mandatory recurrence of said meeting; state the explicit purpose (ideally specifying the agenda); nominate the participants (by function or name); describe the inputs and documentation required for the purpose; and prescribe the outputs to be produced by the meeting (decision memos, meeting minutes, action item list, follow-up decision mechanics).
- Regurgitation of published contents. PEPs are like engineering drawings: they introduce new information once and reference all others. For example, a PEP that specifies the use of a procedural guide must not replicate the guide's contents into the body of the pertinent section, but refer the reader instead to the *specific* location of the pertinent text in the guide (say, *refer to Guide NSER1001, Rev 2, Section 2, paragraph 6.1.1, articles [a] and [d]*).
- A corollary of this prohibition is the specificity of a reference, which is a common practice across project professionals. For example, if a national code governs a certain task, then the specific sections of that code must be written out explicitly. For example, the PEP cannot simply state that a piping system will comply with ASME B31.3. Each feature of the system must be individually listed by compliance articles. The weld joint quality factor must comply with ASME B31.3-2004, article 302.3.4, while allowances for pressure and temperature variations must comply with article 302.2.4. This rule applies for any mandatory document specified by the owner, whether issued by a government body, a state regulation, or the owner's own specifications.

- Implied terminology. Never assume tacit commonality of language. The larger the project, the broader the potential audience. Technical terms, legal expressions, acronyms, abbreviations, and units of measurements must be defined explicitly, preferably in a stand-alone appendix (to make it portable and easily updated). For example, the term ASME mentioned earlier may not be known to all readers as the American Society of Mechanical Engineers. Neither would the expression *piping system*, for that matter. Legal expressions, in particular, are troublesome for most people. To wit, the expression *fit-for-purpose* is possessed of a very specific legal precedent definition that should frighten many an engineer.

W5H Example

From these elements, the contents formalism will follow from the W5H technique. An example of this formalism, for an activity, could take the following form:

What:	The activity
Why:	The specific list of deliverables
	The follow-on activities that require these deliverables
	The regulatory requirements
	The schedule requirement
When:	Specify when, during the phase timeline, the activity starts and ends and how much float is allowed
Where:	Specify the location of execution of the activity if material to the planning.
Who and How:	For each task required by the activity, provide: task description; discipline codes; essential skill set or certification; inputs required; procedure and process numbers; applicable SOE elements; tools and software required

The reader should note that each deliverable listed under the *why* banner should be accompanied by a specific accountability matrix that assigns the accountability, authority, and responsibility for the deliverable.

The clarity of any prescriptive text should be enforced through a comprehensive taxonomy of terms, abbreviations, and acronyms included in the SOE/ SOL. For instance, this book relies on the definitions listed in Tables 11.1, 11.2, and 11.3, which should be included in the work breakdown structure lexicon (discussed in Chapter 15).

Table 11.1 Labor taxonomy

Specialty	Specific expertise, by individual. Electrical engineer, architect, lawyer, and project manager are examples.
Discipline	Group of related specialties. Contracts, for example, could include the specialties of formation, administration, and billing.
Function	Group of related disciplines. Engineering, for example, could include mechanical, electrical, structural, civil, and chemical engineering disciplines.
Team	Group of functions.

Table 11.2 Work taxonomy

Output	The outcome of applied work and evidence of the work performed.
Deliverable	An output that is bought.
Task	Time-limited work performed by one specialty or discipline and producing at least one output. Examples include doing a calculation, preparing a letter, creating a drawing, etc.
Activity	Group of related tasks required to produce at least one deliverable.
Work Package	Group of activities resulting in a design.
Scope of Work	Set of all related work packages that form at least one system.
Phase	A life-cycle phase is a group of two or more scopes of work.
C&P	Contracts and Procurement (see Table 12.1).
DBM	Design Basis Memorandum (see Table 12.1). Conceptual design of the asset. Corresponds to the functional requirements.
EDS	Engineering Design Specification (see Table 12.1). Takes the outcome of the DBM phase to develop the plant's functional specifications.
FEED	Front-End Engineering and Design (see Table 12.3). Usually follows the DBM phase to develop the functional, design, and procurement specifications of the plant.
DD	Detailed Design (see Table 12.3). Takes the outcome of the FEED phase to develop the construction basis for the plant

Table 11.3 Physical taxonomy

Design	Set of related deliverables representing the theoretical features of the asset.
Component	Smallest, indivisible physical element of a design. For example, the components of a wheel include the tire, the rim, the bolts, the inner tube, the pressure sensor, and the hubcap.

Assembly	Group of components performing a physical behavior. The tire and inner tube, for example, form the tire assembly. The rim assembly includes the rim, bolts, and pressure sensor. The hubcap assembly includes the cap and the clips for securing it on the rim.
System	Two or more assemblies acting jointly to produce one or more physical unit transformations. Systems can be primary, secondary, or tertiary. The wheel system includes the above assemblies.
Installation	Two or more systems acting jointly to deliver at least one element of performance for the asset. Installations can be primary, secondary, or tertiary.
Plant	Set of all installations forming the physical asset.
Performance	The sum of the revenues generated, expenses incurred, and profits garnered by the asset.
Asset	The plant in operation producing the performance economics.
Project	The asset at a future point in time when its profitability and performance have been quantified.
Primary	A system or installation is said to be primary when its unit transformation directly contributes to the revenue stream. A gas compressor pushing natural gas down a pipeline is a primary system.
Secondary	A system or installation is said to be secondary when it acts as an enabler of a primary system or installation. The fuel gas supply to the engine driving the pipeline compressor is a secondary system.
Tertiary	A system or installation is said to be tertiary when it belongs to the operation of the system, installation, or plant. The access road to the station and the ground rainwater drainage network are examples.
BL[1]	Boundary Layer. The physical envelope of a system, installation, or plant. The envelope is a narrow band forming the perimeter (real or assigned) of the layer. The layer defines what lies inside and outside of it, and is used as an interface junction between what comes in and out of the envelope. The ins and outs include physical connections, control signals, geometric alignment between adjoining systems/installations. The layer also establishes the accountability of the parties involved inside and outside of the layer.
IBL	The Inside Boundary Layer delineates the scope assigned to the accountable party (AP).
OBL	The Outside Boundary Layer is that which *is not explicitly* comprised within the IBL.
Spacebox	The set of information comprising the spatial envelope of physical feature (height, width, length, elevation from ground) and the physical OBL interfaces associated with the feature. A feature can be a component, an assembly, a system, an installation, or the plant. Refer to Figures 12.7, 12.8, and 12.9.

[1]The allusion to a layer rather than a limit is intentional. It borrows from the notion of the boundary layer in fluid mechanics, which is a thin physical layer of a finite width inside a fluid adjacent to a physical boundary (such as a wall or another fluid). Within the PPA context, a good example of a layer rather than a limit is the area classification around a piece of equipment exposed to potentially explosive gases. For example, even inside a building, which forms a clear physical limit for physical connections, the extents of the area classification could extend from the wall outward by one meter.

The Contents

The value of a plan has nothing to do with its page count. As a rule, more pages mean less value. It is best to (1) capture into the main document the features of the work that are common to the phase and (2) append as many scope-specific annexes in order to render the written edifice portable within one's team. Appendix 3 provides an illustrative sample of the table of contents of a PEP. It is by no means comprehensive, but it suffices to highlight what should go in and what should be left out of it. Once again, the contents must be prescriptive rather than descriptive. Each article, each section of the PEP must be to the point, explicit, unequivocal, and uniquely assigned in terms of accountability. Accountability and authority lay with individuals rather than functions, departments, or organizations. Only the responsibility element is open to multiple individuals (but not functional entities), when the enablers come from different functional entities.

STRATEGY IS SEQUENCING

The BAEF and the PEPs require significant time and effort. The concision of the text will consume the most energy, a fact that must be factored in the schedule (recall Mark Twain's apology: "*I didn't have time to write a short letter, so I wrote a long one instead*"). This is the investment that is required to seed the success of the project execution before any work is carried out. What we need next is the mechanics of the work assignment. The journey from concept to asset is an exercise in risk containment fraught with riddles, mysteries, enigmas, perils, and derailments. We need tools to handle those risks and techniques for breaking down the odyssey into compact, manageable journeys dotted with fixed landmarks. We need, in other words, the next chapter.

12

WORK SEQUENCING

"Let our advance worrying become advance thinking and planning." Winston Churchill

CORRALLING EXECUTION RISKS

Readers old enough to recall the break-dancing phenomenon in the early 1980s will remember how difficult and painful it was to learn the moves. Lest younger readers feel left out, you'll be pleased to know that dubstep is monumentally more challenging (at least in your author's eyes) and exhilarating. Break dancing was a spectacular display of kinetic poetry, seemingly able to defy gravity. The *breaking* part was evident in the rhythms, the styles, and the bones caught in the line of practice fire—safety was anathema to artistry. One learned break dancing the same way that one learns dubstepping now—one tiny, itsy bitsy step at a time to keep the risk of injury at bay. Rare is the individual who could succeed in just a few sessions without breaking a bone, a ligament, or an ego ... Mind you, for the dancer, the risk never vanishes, whether adept or inept.

Risk is the threat that lurks at the edges of a project manager's sight. It must be corralled, controlled, and emasculated. Like dubstep, *project risks are most effectively minimized by maximizing development steps.* Conversely, the risks of failure increases exponentially when work is done in parallel, is accelerated, or the work on deliverables never seems to end across the phases. The fewest risks require the most steps—a sequence that implies completing an output before it is fed as input to others. Fewest risks also demand that the development sequence prioritizes the work on installations and systems as a function of their costs. If your objective is to build a road, the design of the ground preparations precedes traffic light concerns. If you build a race car, the engine is infinitely more important than body paint schemes. If you design a nuclear plant, the reactor chamber must be solved first before the outer building is sketched out.

The atomization advocated in Chapter 11 was the first step in this process of risk minimization. The second step is to devise a valunomic strategy for sequencing the development work incrementally. Such a strategy must enable the project manager to control six big-picture classes of risk that hover around the entire development.

SEQUENCING RISKS

President Kennedy's famous speech on September 2, 1962, included this inspiring call to aspiration:

> *"We choose to go to the moon in this decade and do the other things, not because they are easy, but because they are hard, because that goal will serve to organize and measure the best of our energies and skills, because that challenge is one that we are willing to accept, one we are unwilling to postpone, and one which we intend to win."* [1]

At the height of the program, Apollo commanded 12% of the entire U.S. budget, which should give pause to the reader and gauge the importance of doing the hard things right. Managing risks underscored everything that was going on. Lofty aspirations notwithstanding, projects today are perfectly reflected in this speech. Their budgets can rival or even exceed that of NASA, with financial risks commensurate with the magnitude of the gamble they represent. They are prone to a multitude of *developmental risks*, categorized in six classes: *control, cost, commitment, valunomic, nameplate,* and *machine.*

Control Risk

The first kind is the risk of control. Projects are complex and inordinately prone to vagaries, randomness, and bifurcations—the bigger the scope, the greater the unknowns. Ease of control is inversely proportional to complexity. Accordingly, one's ability to control is enhanced by the scale atomization of Chapter 11 and by the incremental progression of the scope of work.

Cost Risk

The second kind of risk is associated with the accretion of costs. The execution's tab begins to pile on from day one, then explodes in an inflationary blaze. The risk of costs running amok can be minimized. It requires that the development work be focused and free from inefficiencies, redundancies, and dabbling.

Complex cause-and-effect couplings are more easily corralled when done seri-ally. Therefore, do things sequentially by default and in parallel by exception. Avoid the temptation to save time by starting earlier than needed. Finish one task before launching another one that depends on it—get things done once and right, then progress. As Robert Faulder from the National Research Council (Canada) once quipped, "It's funny how projects never seem to give themselves the time to do things right, but always find more time to redo defective work."

Commitment Risk

The third kind of risk is committal. At each stage of an execution, an estimate of the total installed costs (TICs) is produced. Each one of these TIC versions binds the owner to pony up the money at some point in the future. How these estimates are engineered and refined over time is directly proportional to the development work behind it. The risk here is in the divergence between refine-ments. Ideally, it will be asymptotic to the asset's intrinsic cost. When it swings wildly as work progresses, it indicates serious deficiencies with the execution strategy. To obviate this risk, adopt the investment-centric project management (ICPM) sequencing (described later in this chapter).

Valunomic Risk

It is not enough to mobilize teams to launch the work. It is also necessary to make sure that the work is essential, singular, and predictive of the future reality of the asset. Otherwise, the valunomic risk will materialize. Too many projects are plagued by the belief that work can progress in parallel regardless of the state of completion of its different pieces. This assumption is regularly justified on the back of another assumption that time can be saved in this way. Reality is contrarian: nothing is actually saved by out-of-sequence attempts to save time. It is best to proceed based on atomizing the work in depth rather than execut-ing it in width. A low valunomic risk is obtained with smaller teams, employed efficiently and productively on highly focused mandates.

Nameplate Risk

The nameplate risk pertains to the plant. Right up to the moment preceding the turnover of the plant to operations—to become the asset—its profitability and performance are theoretical. The nameplate capacity has not been proven. While the proof will eventually be found in the pudding, the dough is best when each one of its ingredients is prepared and matched to the texture and taste sought. In ICPM parlance, this is done via the mechanics of nucleation per-formed in life-cycle Phase 5.

Machine Risk

Machine risks, our final frontier—emerges from the very nature of the equipment. Machines will wear, weaken, break, and fail—given enough time—whether they are in operation or not. Such physical degradation is inevitable and a consequence of the second law of thermodynamics. For the asset, degradation is code for the risk of failure, from the benign to the catastrophic. For the owner, therefore, machine risks never disappear. They can, however, be minimized with enough engineering fortitude, which will be addressed in the section called *Design on Stilts* near the end of this chapter.

More Reasons for Incrementalism

The insistence on sequential incrementalism deserves further analysis since it may leave the impression that longer development timelines will be required. The opposite is in fact the case. Incrementalism *reduces* development times by eliminating rework, design recycle, interdiscipline delays, and schedule slippages from missing or incomplete information. Incrementalism simplifies the master schedule and reduces the interdependencies between tasks. Finally, it keeps the entire strategy of execution focused on the actual objective of the project: the realization of the profitably performing asset (PPA). Owners and project managers will embrace the correct perspective when confronted with schedule slippages. That is, a slippage of weeks or even months that appears significant to a project schedule will seem insignificant when gauged against decades of profitable asset operation.

> One should never sacrifice the future profitable performance of the asset for the sake of immediate schedule preservation.

TRADITIONAL DEVELOPMENT SEQUENCE

All In, In Parallel

The division of a project's entire scope into discrete phases is a common feature of project execution. Invariably, minimizing the risks surrounding the evolution of the work drives the pace of that work through a multiphase route, carried out sequentially in time, with go/no-go decisions between phases, as to whether to continue or not. Surprisingly, what these phases should be is a point of contention among project professionals. As Harold Kerzner notes in *Project Management: A Systems Approach to Planning, Scheduling, and Controlling, 9th Edition*, there is no universally accepted taxonomy for project life cycles.

The entire development work leading to an asset can be divided into pre- and post-shovel works. The pre-shovel works include all the design, engineering, procurement, construction planning, and regulatory activities that must be completed before any ground is broken for construction. The post-shovel works include construction, commissioning, start-up, turnover, and operational proofing of the asset. The overarching priority of the pre-shovel groups is to incrementally refine the TIC estimates to inure the owner against potential liability. For the post-shovel group, the priority is on sedulous cost control to protect the owner's investment as the asset takes physical form. Both groups operate under the money imperative—as they should.

Three examples of a traditional life-cycle taxonomy are shown below (see Tables 12.1, 12.2, and 12.3). The first two tables are associated with an owner; the third, with an engineering, procurement, and construction management (EPCM) firm. Additionally, Appendix 4 provides a sample of the kind of deliverables that would be created during the pre-shovel work for a project typical of an oil and gas asset (associated with Table 12.2). The expressions C&P, DBM, EDS, FEED, and DD are defined in Table 11.2.

Table 12.1 A project implementation model

Idea	Front End Loading		Implementation		Evaluation
Scoping study	DBM	EDS	Execution	Start-up	Closeout
Business case	Business plan	Final plan	Set-up business	Start business	Operate business
Execution strategy	Develop execution plan	Final plan	Implement plan	Finalize turnover	Evaluate plan
Technical proposal	DBM	EDS	Detail engineering	Turnover and commissioning	Evaluate performance
Supply strategy	C&P strategy	C&P plan	Manage	Close contracts	Evaluate performance

Table 12.2 A project life-cycle model

Concept	Functionality	Specification	Execution	Construction	In-Service
Phase 1	Phase 2	Phase 3	Phase 4	Phase 5	Phase 6
Class V estimate	Class IV estimate	Class III	Class II	Class I	Close out and warranty

Table 12.3 An ECPM execution sequence

Identify	Evaluate	Define	Execute	Build	Close
Concept	DBM	FEED	Detailed Design	Fabricate, construct	Commission, start, as-build, warranty

What Is Spent, When

We can infer from these tables several general rules. The first phase of a project explores the concept of the asset: what it should produce, what the main systems would be, how big of a footprint it will require, and what kind of financial commitment must be contemplated. Subsequent phases proceed to refine the scope of the asset, its nature, and its physical attributes, until the equipment is bought (usually when the design is functionally set), the construction plans are engineered, and the construction itself begins. The cost of execution for each phase increases in step with the level of details produced. Historically, the pre-shovel works (up to Execution, Table 12.2) will consume 8 to 15% of the asset's final TIC. The cost of equipment, materiel, materials, and consumables will command 30 to 40%. The remaining 50 to 60% will be spent during construction.[2] As we saw previously in Chapter 8, the final costs of the asset are determined very early on by engineering. The 8 to 15% of the incurred execution costs directly determine the remaining 85 to 92%. This fact of project life often goes unheralded and bears emphasizing:

> *The profitability of the asset's performance is directly proportional to the investment into the engineering work during conceptualization.*

Again, historical statistics reported in the project literature inform us that the disbursements for engineering and procurement will typically accord with Table 12.4.

Appendix 2 also informs us that the majority of the deliverables transcend the phases before reaching their completion. The approach confers upon the multiphase philosophy a built-in mechanism for managing the first three *developmental risks*—control, cost, and commitment, but not the last three—valunomic, nameplate, and machine. Since all deliverables proceed concurrently, a permanent state of rework, recycle, and revision impregnates the execution strategy. In

Table 12.4 Allocations by phase: all figures are normalized against the concept phase, which is assigned a value of 1

Phase	Cost Range	Duration Range	Class of Estimate	Range of Estimate (%)
Concept	1	1	5	[−50, +100]
Design basis (DBM)	10 to 20	3 to 4	4	[−30, 50]
System specifications (FEED)	100 to 150	6 to 12	3	[−20, 30]
Construction specifications (detailed design)	300 to 500	15 to 30	2	[−15, 20]

fact, the pursuit of parallel work will cost more, not less, than a purely sequential approach. The scenario *inflates* risks.

ESEMPLASTIC KEY

Incremental Progression

The mechanics of allocation discussed in Chapter 10 serves to tightly control capital deployment during development. The key to gaining the upper hand over the six developmental risks is to work incrementally. Build from the ground up; progress the work step-by-step; complete each step before moving to the next one; add details in logical increments; and proceed sequentially (remember that no time can be meaningfully saved by trying to save time by working in parallel). Seen from a distance, the sequence resembles the pendulum in Figure 12.1. Its starting position is the big picture (the plant). As it swings down, the work steps appear (the work is differentiated). The plant is expanded into primary installations, which expand, in turn, into primary functions. At the bottom of the swing, the functions become primary systems. On the way back up, details emerge incrementally (i.e., integration). Systems are augmented with secondary

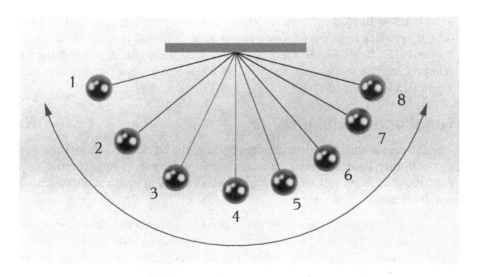

Figure 12.1 Incremental work progression: (1) plant; (2) primary installations; (3) functions for each installation; (4) primary systems for each function; (5) secondary and tertiary systems; (6) integration of systems into an installation; (7) secondary and tertiary installations; and (8) integration into plant

and tertiary functions. At midpoint, they combine into their respective instal-lations, from which ancillary installations take form (secondary and tertiary). These installations, in turn, combine into a unified plant configuration. At the top of the swing, the plant is fully delineated and ready for construction. At any time in this sequence, the appearance of problems may cause backtracking to rectify the issue. Otherwise, the normal flow of work progresses from one to eight incrementally.

The Design Sequence

We will use the term *constituent* to refer to the feature of interest in the work sequence, be it the plant, an installation, a function, or a system. From an over-sight standpoint, the installation is the major interface constituent falling under the purview of a designated manager. Within an installation, each system con-stituent is the province of a designated lead. Finally, the project's engineering manager looks after design integrity and uniformity between all constituents.

The pendulum has a name: *esemplastic key*.[3] The esemplastic key is the fundamental mechanics of work sequencing. It underlines the evolution of a proposal from concept to construction and establishes the information flow be-tween constituents. The key is a work sequence formulated as follows:

$$FR > FS > DS > PS > B > M$$

Where FR = functional requirements, FS = functional specifications; DS = design specifications; PS = procurement specifications; B = build; and M = monetize. Each step in the sequence is analyzed through the *unit transforma-tion process*. The sequence is further divided into milestone outputs, shown in Figures 12.2, 12.3, and 12.4.

Functional Requirements

The FR define what inputs and outputs are required, the transformation pro-cesses in each case, and the justifications for the outputs (why). The two steps A (throughput) and B (network) are carried in series to produce the functional requirements:

- Throughput (A) atomizes the initial feature (either the plant, an instal-lation, a function, or a system) into its *primary* constituents (the term "primary" is defined in Table 11.3). Therefore, the plant is atomized into primary installations; each installation is atomized into primary func-tions; and each function is atomized into primary systems. The constit-uents are assembled into a simple *throughput diagram* that illustrates

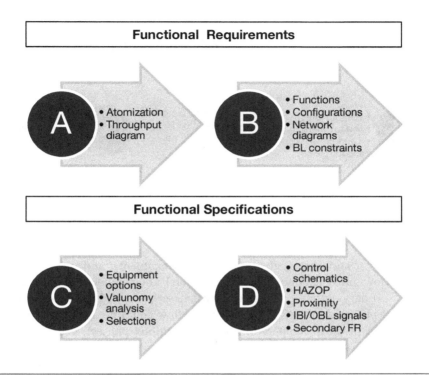

Figure 12.2   FR and FS steps

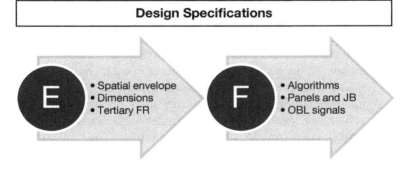

Figure 12.3   DS steps

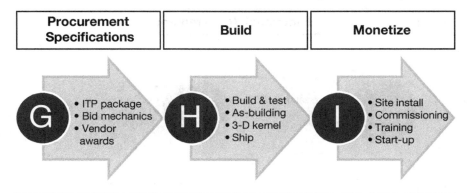

Figure 12.4   Realization steps: comprised of the PS, B, and M steps

the relationships between adjacent constituents, and quantifies what flows into each one (the primary inputs) along with what comes out (the primary outputs). The term *flow* is descriptive of the movement of the inputs and outputs. For example, a flow could be a gas stream (mass rate, pressure, temperature, gas compositions, phases), a stream of rock aggregates (via a conveyor belt) to be turned into concrete, or even a permit application (to construct a building). When dealing with fluid flows in particular, the *throughput diagram* will take the form of a *mass and heat balance* drawing. Next, the performance and operating targets of each constituent are established. Performance targets include design and off-design conditions, turndown ratios, variability of input sources, code prescriptions, emission and effluent limits, and total cost of owner-ship (TCO) prescriptions (reliability, maintainability). Operating targets include modes of operations (24/7, 18/5, 8/5, standby, backup, intermit-tent), level of automated control, staffing limits, future expansion, logis-tic infrastructure, and project ecosystem (PECO) constraints.

- Network (B) begins with an atomization of each constituent into a set of possible functions, arranged in one or more possible configurations. With each configuration, the relationships between inter-dependent functions are identified. Each configuration is assessed valunomically against the performance and operating targets. The final configuration of each function of each installation is selected. The exercise yields a series of network diagrams for each installation, often found in the liter-ature under the expression *process flow diagrams (PFDs)*. Finally, a phi-losophy of operations is written for each installation and each function within it.

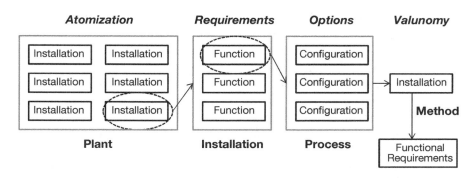

Figure 12.5   From plant to installation to functions

One FR document is published for each installation. It includes the targets, diagrams, and operating philosophies. It also includes an overall description of the governing constraints identifiable at that point in time (things like regulatory expectations, regulatory prescriptions (noise, emissions, water draws, illumination, traffic loads), and known PECO objectors. The entire process is illustrated in Figure 12.5. The reader should take note of the absence of schematic drawings at this stage of development. The various diagrams created in steps A and B do not contain any information regarding the sizing, placement, instrumentation and limit set points; control logic or physical layout; and plans. The project exists only at a conceptual level.

Functional Specifications (FS)

The FS proceed from the FR to answer *what and how* questions. That is, we progress from function to equipment, and from configurations to control schematics. The work, as with the previous case, requires two steps: C (selection) and D (control). The sequence is illustrated in Figure 12.6:

- Selection (C) is carried out for every function of each installation. One example of a function is the compression of a gaseous stream. Several methods are available to the designer: single-stage, multistage, booster-multistage, compression in series or in parallel. Each method, in turn, can be accomplished by a variety of equipment using reciprocating, axial screw, axial turbine, and centrifugal, to name but a few. Each potential solution is assessed for valunomy, against the performance and operating targets prescribed in the installation FR. A choice is made for each function as to what equipment is to be used. Then, for each chosen piece of equipment, specifications are stated in terms of sizing, performance, and operating targets, along with mandatory code/standard compliance.

- Control (D) is initiated once all the pieces of equipment required by a function have been chosen. In our compression example, the compressor could, for example, require an inlet separator, an inlet pulsation mitigation vessel, an outlet pulsation vessel, a compressed fluid cooling stage, and a pressure relief circuit. Each one of these items is engineered for size, physical interconnect, interconnect control instrumentation, inside boundary layer (IBL) signals, and displays. All instrumentation is sized and written up into instrument datasheets. The function is, at this time, transformed into a primary system (or installation) and engineered in the form of a *control schematic* (often called a process and instrumentation diagram, or P&ID for short).

From the control schematic, the secondary functions are identified. In our compression example, the compressor requires either an electrical motor or an engine (gas or diesel powered) as a driver. The driver is written up as an FR and is then subjected on its own to steps A, B, C, and D—yielding its own control schematic (this time called the utility and instrumentation diagram, or U&ID for short). The primary and secondary diagrams are integrated into a single package and subjected to a hazard and operability (HAZOP) analysis. Modifications are possible at this time according to the results of the analysis. The final schematics, datasheets, and calculations are revised accordingly.

Following the publication of the schematics, the entire system is subjected to a *proximity analysis* to determine what equipment must be located close to each other, and what equipment must be kept far apart. Another recommendation that emanates from the analysis is the assignment of the electrical area classification for the system, which will drive, in part, the spatial arrangement

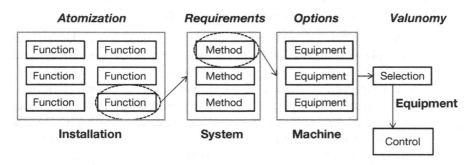

Figure 12.6 Picking the primary equipment: the objective of the functional specification is to finalize equipment selection

of the physical system. The final recommendation of the analysis deals with the secondary outside boundary layer (OBL) functions that must be supplied from external sources. These OBL functions are published in the form of FR documents, leading the B-C-D sequence in Figure 12.2 for those systems in the next phase (in our example, the choice of an electrical motor as the driver raises the requirement to bring an adequate power supply to the unit from the outside).

In parallel with the proximity analysis, a second analysis is carried out separately on the target compliance of the selected components. These are the performance and operating targets that were published at the FR stage. The analysis gathers reliability, maintainability, and failure data to develop an overall reliability profile for the system. This profile is validated against such targets as mean time between failures (MTBF), mean time to failure (MTTF) figures, uptime ratings, and turndown effects. The entire analysis is conducted in a manner that will answer the question: will the system be profitably performing? If the answer is yes, the FS can be written and the next stage—design specifications (DS)—can be initiated. Otherwise, the designer may have to go all the way back to step A and rework the sequence.

For each system, a single FS package is published. It will contain the engineered information (diagrams, datasheets, calculations) for the primary and secondary functions; the list of OBL signals that cross the system's boundary layer; the list of physical OBL interfaces at the boundary layer (primary and secondary piping connections for instance); the recommendations stemming from the proximity analysis; and the reliability specifications obtained from the target analysis.

Design Specifications

The DS transform the functional specifications into physical dimensions. The two steps involved, design (E) and command (F), are independent of each other and can be performed in parallel. The preference for (F), however, is to wait until the control schematics of the next higher constituent (the installation, when dealing with systems; and the plant, with installations) have been completed:

- Design (E) created the 3-D model of the unit (be it a system or an installation). All spatial dimensions, proximity distances, and instrument positions are obtained. The spatial envelope of the idealized system is fixed (height, width, length, elevation from ground). The position, in space, of the physical OBL interfaces are set (spatial envelope and OBL interfaces form the *spacebox*, defined in Table 11.3). Fabrication drawings are published along with prescribed and proscribed methods. Inertial and dynamic loads are quantified. Quality assurance and inspection requirements are specified. Testing and acceptance criteria are defined.

Shipping and transportation requirements are identified and built into the design. The unit's bill of materials, list of consumables, and bulk materials are tabulated. The specifications for the electrical area classification are published (often as a drawing). The (E) work yields two critical pieces of information that affect the development of the next higher constituent: the installation footprint of the unit and the tertiary FR for its site positioning (for example, foundation, underground piping, drainage, access, loading bays).

- Command (F) develops the control logic and the algorithm to operate the unit. Several deliverables are produced by the effort: the control philosophy, the shutdown key, the human-machine interfaces (HMI), the input/output count, and the signal specifications. Design specifications are also prescribed for the control panels, relay boxes, and junction boxes (IBL and OBL). OBL command signals are finalized.

The design will be subjected to three separate analyses prior to the release of the final drawings. The first one, *process safety analysis*, seeks to confirm the safety of the physical layout and the required warning and emergency devices. Safety is assessed in terms of spacing requirements, failure prevention, failure containment, unplanned emissions and releases, and fire and explosion containment. The second analysis, *constructability and maintainability*, is conducted jointly between the project team, the vendor team, the owner's operations team, and hired construction specialists. The point of the exercise is to make sure that the layout of the equipment is ergonomically suitable to human interactions and that the unit can be maintained, repaired, and upgraded with minimum access challenges.

The DS package is assembled for each system—in such a manner that it contains all of the information necessary to enable a third-party vendor to accurately estimate a price to build the unit autonomously. It will include all the drawings, the 3-D model, the 3-D kernel data acquired during design, and the specifications associated with fabrication, testing, quality assurance, and acceptance.

Procurement Specifications

The procurement specifications (PS) create the documentation necessary to purchase the components of the operating unit. The essential scope of work is captured by the DS. The scope must be complemented, nevertheless, with the following additional prescriptions:

- Contract terms and conditions
- Third-party terms and conditions (for procured items)
- Quality assurance (QA) records to be kept and delivered
- Materiel management

- Vendor data requirements (manuals, QA records, 3-D kernel data, budget and schedule updates, material inspections, material certifications, translations, training materials, as-built documents)
- Schedules (award, inspections, testing, audits, final acceptance, shipment)
- Design failure mitigation
- Equipment preservation and storage
- Shipping, transportation, and logistics specifications
- Delivery and site installation timelines
- Preferred and barred supplier lists
- Configuration management and recommended spares
- Maintenance program and cycles/data collection
- Installation support requirements (commissioning, start-up, ops training, initial operations)
- After-sale services (warranty, field maintenance, depot maintenance, data collection during operations, reliability and maintainability analysis)
- Publication life-cycle program
- Training program for plant personnel (operations, monitoring, emergency, maintenance, troubleshooting, and data transmission to the vendor)

Build

The build (B) step fabricates the unit from the DS datum set and the materials procured in accordance with the DS documentation. The logistics of shipping the unit to the site are resolved. The 3-D kernel documentation is produced (see information nucleation later in this chapter) and delivered. Planning around work crew support at the site is initiated. *As-building* (the process of updating the drawings to reflect the actual configuration obtained during construction) of documentation is carried out. Validation and verification activities are completed. The unit is either prepared for shipment or preserved and placed in storage to await future shipment.

The reader should note that fabrication and assembly activities that will take place at-site are part of the monetization step. Building activities are understood to take place. All of the documentation, vendor data, QA records, and other documents identified in the procurement specifications are compiled, digitized, and passed on to the buyer to trigger the final payment and hold back release.

Monetize

This final step, monetize (M), brings the unit to operational readiness toward revenue generation. Four steps are involved: installation, commissioning, training, and start-up:

- Installation, as the name implies, receives the shipped unit to site and carries out its integration into the plant. Building activities that could not be done at the shop are carried out here. Note that the unit's foundation, access, and other tertiary functions will have already been constructed in the B step of the installation comprising the unit. The same goes for the OBL secondary systems. The information data-set associated with the unit is also installed, but at the level of the plant's *3-D model kernel*, which is explained in Chapter 17. At the end of the installation step, the unit is physically and informationally embedded into the plant.
- Commissioning energizes the unit and runs it through its paces to verify its operational readiness. Controls and instrument signals are rung out. Control programs, HMI, and OBL interfaces are checked for continuity and integrity. During this step, support from the vendor may be required. Also, as-building of site documentation is carried out. Deficiency lists are drawn and warranty clauses invoked. At the end of commissioning, the unit has reached full operational status.
- Training is concerned with familiarizing the plant's operational staff with the operations, maintenance, troubleshooting, and digital records of the unit. Training will ideally occur before commissioning is initiated to provide plant personnel a platform to practice in real time. A critical element of this training concerns the transmission of data back to the vendor, in terms of performance, operation, reliability, and maintainability. Such data is required by a vendor mandated by the owner to manage the unit's reliability management program (which comprises the continual reliability and maintainability analysis described in the PS).
- Start-up brings the unit online operationally. Contractual turnover occurs at this time, from vendor to plant owner. The unit is subjected to an initial validation period, to verify its nameplate performance, as part of the project's last life cycle, Phase 8, *validation* (discussed in the next section). All documentation and data transmission channels are finalized, with communication channels activated.

Prioritization Within the Esemplastic Key

The *esemplastic key* is fractal. That is, it applies at every level of an atomization, from plant to system component. It applies as well to primary, secondary, and tertiary subdivisions, and to IBL/OBL segregation. This fractal nature imposes a built-in prioritization on what gets done when. The fractal pattern applies to all constituents (plant, installation, or system) in the manner shown by Map 1 in Figure 12.7. The pattern applies to the Set (1), a primary system for example. Sets (2) and (3) correspond to the secondary and tertiary systems, respectively, with each one developed in the sequence of Set (1).

The information flow within and without a constituent is indicated in Map 2, shown in Figure 12.8. The primary system (bottom of figure) is developed first and its secondary systems are integrated into an FS—the outcome of Step D. The interfaces at the system's boundary layer are passed on to the installation—the NLC—as OBL interfaces. The development of the installation is started (but, critically, not before). The system continues its development until the DS is obtained. The physical footprint of the system and the spatial location of the OBL interfaces are captured in the *spacebox*, which is fed to the installation for inclusion into its own model (Step E). The identical process applies to the command logic for the system, whereby its input/output OBL signal specifications are passed to the installation for inclusion into the installation's overall command algorithm.

Map 1

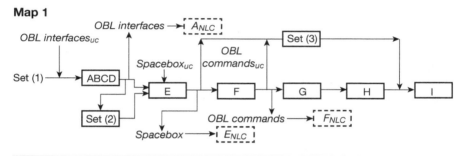

Figure 12.7 Fractal nature of the esemplastic key: next level constituent (NLC); lower level constituent (LLC)

Map 2

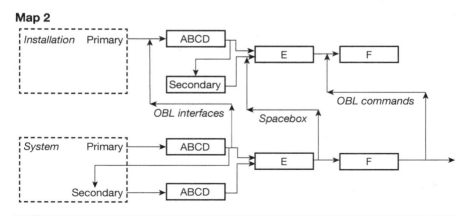

Figure 12.8 Linkages within and without constituents

Map 3

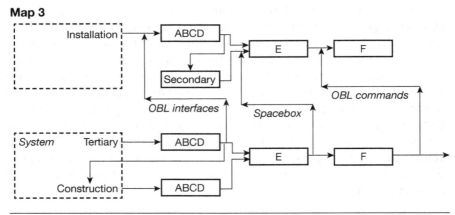

Figure 12.9   Treatment of tertiary features

The treatment of tertiary requirements—via Set (3)—follows the sequence of Map 1. They are integrated into the physical layout of the plant in accordance with Map 3, shown in Figure 12.9. Note the appearance of the construction features along the path of Set (2). At the system level, such features will include, for example, the dimensions of the hole to be dug out to permit the installation of the foundation and the deep underground connections. At the installation level, construction features will include temporary access roads, temporary water drainage for rain, and laydown areas. At the plant level, construction features will comprise the temporary facilities and buildings, material receiving, fabrication tents, perimeter fencing, and the like.

The IBL/OBL distinction is critical to the flow of work. The interfaces (both physical and command) are identified and categorized as IBL or OBL. IBL interfaces are treated on par with the other features contained within the boundary layer. OBL interfaces are treated as requirements that must be passed on to the NLC to be treated. There, they either become IBL features, and are treated accordingly, or are passed on again to the NLC. This approach to interface treatment borrows heavily from network theory to map out the functional and physical features of the plant. All the systems of a given installation are assembled into *physical networks* through which information flows back and forth. All the installations of the plant are likewise connected into a plant-level *physical network*.

Network Theory

The science of networks is the study of the relationships between discrete objects. These relationships can be causal (the predecessor uniquely determines the successor); coupled (the behavior of the successor reflects on the predecessor); or chaotic (either behavior can affect the other without predictable accuracy). In theory, relationships are either symmetric or asymmetric. As a matter of fact, our concept of the unit transformation process introduced in Chapter 4 is a subset of network theory. Managing at the interfaces is in essence the act of controlling the flow of information homogeneously between the discrete objects (systems/nodes).

Symbolic Shorthand

We are ready to apply the esemplastic key to the sequencing of the project via the life-cycle phase sequence. For this, we introduce special symbolism to communicate efficiently the inputs and outputs of each step of the *esemplastic key*. The corresponding shorthand is shown in Figure 12.10, illustrating a *functional specification* for a secondary (2) system (S), applicable inside its boundary layer (i).

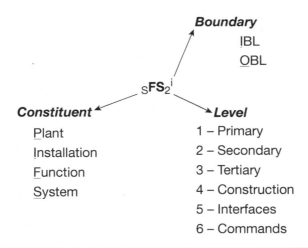

Figure 12.10   Symbolic representation

Linear Assets

The esemplastic key applies ubiquitously to all industrial projects, regardless of scale and includes, among other things, linear assets. This class of assets is so named because of their distributed nature. According to Yong Sun et al. in *Engineering Asset Management and Infrastructure Sustainability*, these assets are characterized by continuous infrastructure spanning long distances, such as roads, power lines, and pipelines.

ICPM LIFE-CYCLE PHASES

The Eight-Phase Development Sequence

We have seen that the development of an asset comprises two stages: *conceptualization* and *realization*. *Conceptualization* involves fives phases; *realization*, three. All phases share the same execution sequencing. The initiation, mobilization, and vendor on-boarding takes place in the manner described in the previous chapter. The scope of work is prescribed by the pertinent steps of the esemplastic key. The unit transformation process (UTP) mechanics is applied to each scope of work to delineate the required tasks and activities. The UTP is also used to identify the attributes and constraints, and assign the targets and enablers to carry out the work. Overall, the staggered distribution of the esemplastic work follows the layout of Table 12.5.

Tasks Common to All Phases

Once the esemplastic work is completed, the phase wraps up in a manner common to all phases (a.k.a. the *phase wrap-up tasks*):

- The TIC budget and project schedule estimates are compiled (to the class level specified for each phase)
- The owner conducts a *go/no-go* review to decide whether to proceed to the next phase, cycle back to modify the outcome of the current phase, or abandon the project
- A *go* decision leads to:
  - The development of the scope of work for the next esemplastic step for each applicable constituent (for example, for Phase 2, develop the scope of work of the design specifications to be developed in Phase 3)
  - The prescreening of potential vendors for each scope of work
  - The execution of the *bid mechanics* for each vendor scope
  - The recommendation for award for each scope of work
  - Awarding the contracts
  - Revising the class cost and schedule estimates based on the winning bids
  - Adjusting the project management office's (PMO's) staffing allocation for the next phase
  - Developing the next phase's execution plan, budget, and schedule
  - Initiating the next phase

Table 12.5   Evolution of primary, secondary, and tertiary elements throughout the development of the asset

Constituent	Conceptualization					Realization		
	Phase 1	Phase 2	Phase 3	Phase 4	Phase 5	Phase 6	Phase 7	Phase 8
System								
Primary	AB	CD	EF	G	H		...	...
Secondary		ABCD	EF	G	H		...	...
Tertiary			AB	CD	EF	G	H	...
Construction				AB	CD	EFG	H	...
Installation								
Primary	AB		CD	EF	EF	G	H	...
Secondary			ABCD	EF	EF	G	H	...
Tertiary			AB	CD	EF	G	H	...
Construction				AB	CD	EFG	H	...
Plant								
Boundary	A		B	CD	EF	G	H	...
Construction				AB	CD	EFG	H	...
Class estimates	V (initial)	V (final)	IV (initial)	IV (final)	III	II	I	Actual

Phase 1—Asset Mitosis[4]

Phase 1 defines the overall requirements of the asset. At the front end, the high-level targets are established by the owner, which includes the asset; nameplate performance; profitability and total costs of ownership (TCO) performance; development completion timeline; ownership structure; the technology priorities; PECO objectives; investment message; and a notional concept of operations. Afterward, the owner instructs the framework to initiate the project, nominate the PMO manager, and mobilize the core PMO leadership cadre (all managers reporting directly to the PMO manager). The initial set of deliverables includes the baseline asset execution framework (BAEF) (with the high-level targets), the Phase 1 scope of work, the Phase 1 execution plan, and version 1 of the asset's overall TIC and schedule.

Following the release of these deliverables, the pre-initiation work for Phase 1 commences via the *phase wrap-up tasks*. Once completed, the PMO initiates the core work of Phase 1. The order of the work proceeds as follows (refer to Figure 12.10 for the deliverable legend):

1. Step A (esemplastic key) for the plant (see Figure 12.5); release the $_pFR^i_1$
2. Steps A and B for the primary installations; release the $_1FR^i_1$
3. Steps A and B for the primary systems (Figure 12.6); release the $_sFR^i_1$
4. Develop the asset's initial Class V cost and schedule estimates

The selection process is valunomy-based, and is predicated on the TCO and its variables including operating expenditure (OPEX) and capital expenditure (CAPEX) costs; reliability and maintainability metrics, such as uptime ratings; operating cycles; reliability; availability; MTTF and MTBF; and their impact on the profitability of the systems *over their economic lives.* The best option yields the highest valunomy relative to the profitable performance of the asset over its economic life. This activity may require vendor inputs through consulting contracts. The go/no-go review by the owner calls up the resilience analysis to provide a decisions basis. A *go* decision activates the wrap-up tasks for Phase 2.

Examples of Valunomic Decision

New equipment. A new refinery project will produce diesel as one of its refined liquids and require a large pump (1,000 kW) with two options for a drive: an electric motor and a diesel engine. The electric motor has an annual 99.2% availability rating compared to 84% for the engine (MTTF and MTTB included). The motor's parts count is 32% lower than the engine. Power rates, equalized on the same $/kwH basis, are lower for the engine throughout the plant's operating life. The complexity of the installation and recurring maintenance activities are twice as high for the engine as the motor (on the basis of down-time × crew size). The electric motor is 40% more expensive than the engine to procure and install. The valunomic analysis predicts that their respective TCO will equalize after 21 months, and be lower for the electric motor, even when factoring the expected increases in future electric rates. The decision is unequivocal: from a PPA perspective, the electric motor is selected. Note that the CAPEX viewpoint, prevalent in traditional projects, would overwhelmingly favor the diesel engine.

Refurbished equipment. An airline considers the option of purchasing old but refurbished engines for its commercial fleet at a 42% discount from new engines (but with a 12% higher fuel consumption over new). Considering that fuel can consume upwards of 30% of an airline's operating budget, and that these engines will be in operation for two or more decades, is this 42% savings really worth the price to the long-term earnings?

Sales strategies. Although this example is not project-specific, the principle of the TCO decision is the same. Prior to 2009, insurer AIG routinely relied on short-term incentives to prop up sales numbers. Agents would get impressive results (thus commissions) selling underpriced products, which would adversely affect the long-term profits of the company. In 2009, CEO Bob Benmosche abandoned the practice and replaced it with a new incentive program that calculated rewards in terms of risk-adjusted returns, instead of mere growth. Commissions fell in some cases; overall, however, the new system proved financially healthy.

To illustrate the sequencing of Phase 1, consider a compressor station plant, shown in Table 12.6. The atomization of the plant (Step A) identifies a number of primary installations, appearing in the *installation* column of Table 12.6. The compression installation will, in turn, comprise several functions, listed in the second column. The pressure augmentation function is shown to be available in three configuration options, in the third column. We assume that the installation is subject to three high-level targets: a fourfold increase in throughput pressure, a 50% variation in design flow rates, and a 24/7 operating mode with 98% uptime availability. We observe that the second and third targets imply additional configuration options: two compressors operating in parallel, with a third one on standby; three smaller compressors with a fourth on standby; one compressor method to provide a step increase in pressure, and a second method to provide a second step increase (an axial compressor feeding a positive displacement compressor for example). The power supply (secondary system) for each compressor method also comes in options: electric motor, gas engine, gas turbine. The valunomy analysis will be complex and utterly nonintuitive but essential at this early stage to satisfy the economic return on investment (ROI) targets of the asset once in operation.

Table 12.6   Example of the outcome of a phase for an installation

Installations	Functions for Compression	Options for Pressure Augmentation
Compression	Pressure augmentation	Single-stage compression
		Multi-stage compression
	....	Booster and prime compression
	Liquid separation and drains	
	Pulsation mitigation	
....	Inlet flow control	
	Flow bypass	
	Flow re-circulation	
	Throughput modulation	
	Over-pressure protection	
	Gas cooling	
Discharge cooling		
Discharge gas chilling		
Inlet separation		
Pipeline pig sender/receiver		
Pipeline blowdown		
Plant blowdown		
Interconnecting piping		

The reader should note the appearance of vendors at this early stage. Their involvement stems from the four-step procurement mechanics that will be described in Chapter 15. It requires, among other things, that the functionality of a system or installation be completely defined before soliciting bids for its fabrication. The contract awards made in Phase 1 cover only the scope of work to define the functional specifications of the primary systems. Note also that the installations have not been networked together within the plant; likewise, for the set of functions within an installation. At this stage, the plant exists solely as a collection of discrete black boxes representing the installations—a fundamental departure from traditional project management (TPM). All the work done in Phase 1 (and most of Phase 2) pertains to IBL requirements. Note that *dimensions* have yet to enter the picture. Fabrication is still two phases away.

Phase 2—System Definition

The second phase is focused on the primary and associated secondary systems of the primary installations. All IBL and OBL requirements (physical and signals) are identified. The secondary systems are atomized in the same manner seen for the plant. Geo-spatial works will usually commence in Phase 2. This work encompasses all the studies, surveys, and site condition analyses required to quantify the physical environment in which the plant will be built and the asset will be operated. Most of these elements belong to the PECO—such as site locations, existing transportation infrastructure, soil and ground studies, botanical and zoological inventories, archeological investigations, fish audits, water systems, environmental studies, land records, and population consultations. Some of these activities are covered by the esemplastic key (geotechnical investigations, site surveys); others are single-task activities that may extend across several phases (consultations, local king negotiations). The deliverables specific to Phase 2 will be:

1. Steps C and D for the primary systems; release the $_sFS^i_1$ and $_sFR^o_1$
2. Steps A and B for the associated secondary systems; release the $_sFR^i_2$
3. Steps C and D for the secondary systems; release the $_sFS^i_2$ and $_sFR^o_2$
4. Release the $_sFR^o_5$ (primary and secondary) and $_sFR^o_6$ (primary and secondary) to the installation
5. Develop the asset's final Class V cost and schedule estimates based on the feedback from the FR and FS vendors

The secondary extraction echoes the scheme adopted for the plant in Phase 1. Continuing with the compressor example, we can imagine various options for the power plant for the compressors—such as electric motors, diesel engines, natural gas engines, and turbines. Additional configurations also exist, whereby one power plant drives two or more units via gearboxes and transmission splitters; or alternatively, one power plant is shared between a prime unit and a standby, via another kind of gearbox. The selection logic follows the path taken for the systems. Finally, note the absence of installation and plant work in Phase 2. The entire focus is on the systems, which form the backbone of the throughput performance of the primary installations.

Phase 3—Installation Integration

Phase 3 integrates the primary and secondary systems of a given installation into a functional network. The primary installation itself begins to take shape functionally, and the associated secondary installations are designated. At the project level, the permit and license plan is compiled. The deliverables specific to this phase will be:

For primary and secondary systems:

1. Steps E and F, either separately or jointly
2. Release the $_sDS^i_1$ and $_sDS^i_2$ (include *spacebox* and commands)
3. Release the physical interfaces via $_sFS^o_5$ to the installation
4. Release the command interfaces via $_sFR^o_6$ to the installation

For tertiary systems:

5. Steps A and B; release the $_sFR^i_3$

For primary and secondary installations:

1. Steps C and D for the primary installations; release the $_iFS^i_1$ and $_iFR^o_1$
2. Steps A and B for the associated secondary installations; release the $_iFR^i_2$
3. Steps C and D for the secondary installations; release the $_iFS^i_2$ and $_iFR^o_2$
4. Release the $_iFR^o_5$ (primary and secondary) and $_iFR^o_6$ (primary and secondary)

For tertiary installations:

5. Steps A and B; release the $_iFR^i_3$

For the plant:

1. Step B to network the installations; release the $_pFR^i_1$
2. Develop the asset's initial Class IV cost and schedule estimates

Table 12.7 lists examples of secondary and tertiary installations.

Table 12.7   Example of ancillary (secondary and tertiary) systems

Secondary Installations	Tertiary Installations
Motor control center	Administration building
Utility fuel gas conditioning	Plant control room
Power generation building	Utility and maintenance building
Satellite tower	Warehouse
Refrigeration compression	Laydown areas
Refrigeration condenser	Parking
Flare system	Site roads
Fuel gas distribution	Site drainage
Instrument air distribution	Perimeter control
Deep underground piping	Temporary buildings (construction)
Utility water distribution	Site-wide lighting

Phase 4—Plant Integration

Phase 4 replicates the work of Phase 3, but at the installation level. The various deliverables will be:

For primary and secondary systems:

1. Possible changes and updates to the DS because of issues uncovered during the installation work
2. Step G; release the $_sPS^i_1$ and $_sPS^i_2$

For tertiary systems:

3. Steps C and D; release the $_sFS^i_3$ and $_sFR^o_3$
4. Release the $_sFR^o_5$ (tertiary) to the installation

For construction systems:

5. Steps A and B; release the $_sFR^i_4$

For primary and secondary installations:

1. Steps E and F, either separately or jointly
2. Release the $_1DS^i_1$ and $_1DS^i_2$ (include *spacebox* and commands)
3. Release the physical interfaces via $_1FR^o_5$ to the plant
4. Release the command interfaces via $_1FR^o_6$ to the plant

For tertiary installations:

1. Steps C and D; release the $_1FS^i_3$ and $_1FR^o_3$.

For construction installations:

2. Steps A and B; release the $_1FR^i_4$
3. Release the $_1FR^o_5$ (construction) and $_1FR^o_6$ (construction)

For the plant:

1. Steps C and D; release the $_pFS^i_1$ and $_pFR^o_1$
2. Steps A and B for the construction requirements; release the $_pFR^i_4$
3. Develop the asset's final Class IV cost and schedule estimates

Phase 5—Plant Design

Phase 5 completes the design of the entire plant through which the physical configuration of the asset is finalized. Construction requirements are included into the physical layout. All command and control details for the operation of the plant are finalized. Finally, the design is submitted to a *nucleation mechanic* to validate, in theory, the PPA targets of the future asset (nucleation is discussed later in the chapter). Phase 5 completes the conceptualization phase of development, and serves as a basis for the follow-on *realization* phase.

For primary systems:

1. Step H

For tertiary systems:

2. Steps E and F; release the $_sDS^i_3$ (includes *spacebox* and commands)
3. Release the physical interfaces via $_sFR^o_5$ to the installation
4. Release the command interfaces via $_sFR^o_6$ to the installation

For construction systems:

5. Steps C and D; release the $_sFS^i_4$ and $_sFR^o_4$
6. Release the $_sFR^o_5$ (construction) to the installation

For primary and secondary installations:

1. Continuation of E and F

For tertiary installations:

2. Steps E and F; release the $_ıDS^i_3$ (includes *spacebox* and commands)
3. Release the physical interfaces via $_ıFR^o_5$ to the plant
4. Release the tertiary command interfaces via $_ıFR^o_6$ to the plant

For construction installations:

5. Steps C and D; release the $_ıFS^i_4$ and $_sFR^o_4$
6. Release the $_ıFR^o_5$ (construction) to the plant

For the plant:

1. Steps E and F; release the $_pDS^i_1$ (includes *spacebox* and commands)
2. Release the physical interfaces via $_pFR^o_5$
3. Release the command interfaces via $_pFR^o_6$
4. Develop the asset's Class III cost and schedule estimates

For construction of the plant:

5. Steps C and D; release the $_pFS^i_4$ and $_pFR^o_4$
6. Release the $_pFR^o_5$ (construction) to the installation

The outcome of Phase 5 is the physical configuration of the plant, shown in Figure 12.11. The physical features of the construction requirements continue to be worked on, and will be completed in Phase 6. Notice the distinction between the plant and the asset, rooted in the *Services* branch, in keeping with the taxonomy

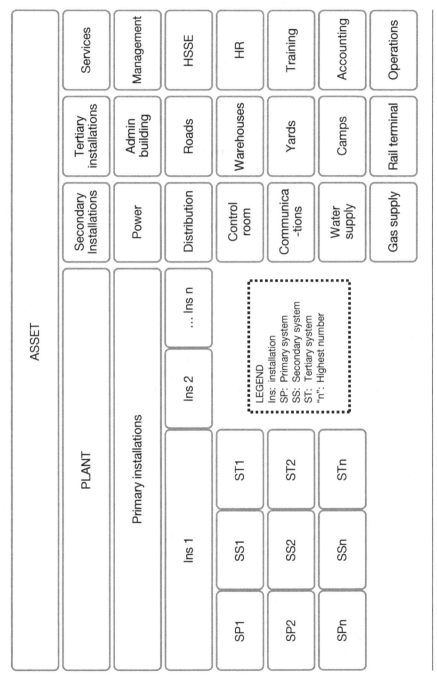

Figure 12.11 Physical configuration of the asset

of Table 11.3. The establishment of the physical configuration automatically creates the work breakdown structure (WBS) for the entire project, as well as the hierarchy of the execution teams (see Chapter 13) and the *collection substrate* explored in Chapter 17. The plant design forms the *construction basis*. The basis comprises the entirety of the drawings, specifications, material lists, manuals, and other deliverables produced hitherto. It is, in effect, the theoretical incarnation of the asset that must be transformed into physical reality.

Phase 6—Realization Planning

Phase 6 completes the physical configuration of the plant, as well as the site requirements to enable construction. The *construction basis* is finalized at this stage, after which changes *are no longer allowed*. Phase 6 is critical to the management of the financial risks carried by the *post-shovel* works. The level of effort required should be of the same order of magnitude as that of Phase 3.

> *Money saved on the cost of Phase 6 will be incurred several times over during construction. Never go cheap with Phase 6.*

In this phase, the project enters the post-shovel stage, by which the sequencing and scoping of the entire construction phase is cycled through the esemplastic key. Planning is predicated upon the *construction basis*. What gets built is the construction basis, nothing more or nothing less. The construction basis sequencing will usually involve the development of additional drawings, specifications, datasheets, and other planning documents to convert the contents of the construction basis into executable actions. The management plan for the construction activities is published. Manpower and labor strategies are developed for the duration of the works. All associated contracted work not already awarded in the previous phases are prepared and awarded. Logistics, transportation, and warehousing solutions are devised and rolled out. The permit and license plan from Phase 3 is deployed at maximum berth to secure the entirety of the remaining approvals and to be certificated in time for construction to start.

The *construction basis* also serves as a baseline from which construction planning will be carried out in Phase 6. Once the basis is published, the conceptualization works are complete, the configuration of the plant is fixed, and the contents are existing in their final, *issued for construction (IFC)* state. Needless to say, but restated anyway, changes are no longer acceptable at this point in time. Phase 6 also covers the development of the plans that will govern the transition from construction to operations. Major transition milestones include commissioning, start-up, as-building, turnover, operational training and maintenance, and asset validation. Once the work is completed, the PMO compiles the final Class II cost and schedule estimates.

For primary and secondary systems:

1. Continuation of Step H

For tertiary systems:

2. Possible changes and updates to the DS on account of issues uncovered during the installation work
3. Step G; release the $_sPS^i_3$

For construction systems:

4. Steps E and F; release the $_sDS^i_4$ (includes *spacebox* and commands)
5. Release the physical interfaces via $_sFR^o_5$ to the installation construction
6. Release the command interfaces via $_sFR^o_6$ to the installation construction
7. Possible changes and updates to the DS on account of issues uncovered during the installation work
8. Step G for each system; release the $_sPS^i_4$

For primary and secondary installations:

1. Possible changes and updates to the DS on account of issues uncovered during the plant work
2. Step G; release the $_IPS^i_1$ and $_IPS^i_2$

For tertiary installations:

3. Possible changes and updates to the DS on account of issues uncovered during the installation work
4. Step G; release the $_IPS^i_3$

For construction installations:

5. Steps E and F; release the $_IDS^i_4$ (includes *spacebox* and commands)
6. Release the physical interfaces via $_IFR^o_5$ to the plant construction
7. Release the command interfaces via $_IFR^o_6$ to the plant construction
8. Possible changes and updates to the DS on account of issues uncovered during the installation work
9. Step G; release the $_IPS^i_4$

For the plant:

1. Finalization of the DS
2. Step G; release the $_pPS^i_1$
3. Develop the asset's Class II cost and schedule estimates

For construction installations:

4. Steps E and F; release the $_pDS^i_4$ (includes *spacebox* and commands)

5. Release the physical interfaces via $_pFR^o_5$
6. Release the command interfaces via $_pFR^o_6$
7. Possible changes and updates to the DS on account of issues uncovered during the installation work
8. Step G; release the $_IPS^i_4$

Phase 7—Construction

Phase 7 breaks ground and starts to consume the remaining 50–60% of the budget. Project management transforms into construction management starting with the early works, site development, and temporary facilities to get the ball rolling. Construction management utilizes the same mechanics of project management expounded in this book. The nature of the risks is now driven by four new imperatives: safety risks to personnel, equipment, and milieu; labor risks arising from fluctuating manpower demands; schedule risks stemming from the exigencies of the work sequencing; and cost risks inherited from materialized safety, labor, or schedule risks. Given the budget importance of Phase 7, these risks are magnified in real time and place enormous pressures on the construction management team to execute the work diligently. The techniques described in Chapters 5 through 8 will go a long way to help the team execute thus. The efficiency of that execution, on the other hand, will find its source in the strength of the plans developed in Phase 6.

Phase 7 becomes a fulsome project on its own. The sequencing of the work is intimately connected with the physical configuration of the asset; it is not possible to define them in some universal manner in this book. The PPA principles apply verbatim to the execution of the construction project.

Constructive Reading

The reader interested in the study of construction management is invited to consult *Construction Management for Industrial Projects* by Mohamed El-Reedy; *Professional Construction Management, 3rd Edition*, by Boyd Paulson and Donald Barrie; and *Construction Management, 4th Edition*, by Bolivar Senior and Daniel Halpin as starting points of an investigation into the mechanics and mechanisms of the trade. It is an art unto itself and a specialty all its own that has been developed extensively and successfully in the literature and by the marketplace.

Phase 8—Asset Validation

The end of construction marks the start of Phase 8. The project migrates to operational readiness, starting with commissioning, personnel training, and turnover to operations. Start-up is commenced, followed by in-service activation. Over the subsequent months, the plant is run through its paces to verify its actual nameplate capacity, and to have its profitable performance quantified. While the plant is checked out and ramped up, the project management team initiates the close-out process for the project. The performance assessment metrics (PAM) of all phases are gathered and integrated into one final PAM. Warranty claims and hold-backs are resolved. All project documentation is archived (physically and digitally) and the project itself is contractually closed.

ACCOUNTABILITY DISTORTIONS

At Which Point Accountability Returns

Multiple parties will interact at various times across the phases. The question of accountability arises forcibly in the context of construction. After all, stuff will get built by parties that are forced to rely on drawings created by others. When things don't line up during construction, who will be blamed? This risk is one reason why owners prefer to deal with construction contractors who can execute all phases under one roof. If we proceed with the logic developed in Chapter 11 for the alignment of interests, we can readily untie this Gordian knot. The development of any element of the construction basis, prior to reaching IFC status, resides with whichever supply chain partner (SCP) was selected by the PMO. The SCP is thus the accountable party. This accountability *must at some point* be transferred to the construction/fabrication SCP. This transfer implies that the SCP accepts the contents of the element at the IFC stage. Consequently, the latter must be directly involved in the IFC development process of the element, such that the release of the IFC element is approved jointly by the two SCPs. For example, a foundation drawing developed by a civil engineering firm must involve the foundation contractor directly through design and constructability reviews before the civil firm is permitted to issue the IFC drawing. This permission is controlled by the probate party, which could be the PMO, for instance. The foundation contractor is henceforth obligated to accept the accountability for realizing the foundation in accordance with the IFC drawing.

Temporal Distortions

Major projects command thousands of tasks that must be performed over time by many parties linked together by schedule dependencies. It is extraordinarily difficult to orchestrate a schedule that optimizes these relationships. It is far easier to accept that some activities will slip and build into the schedule sufficient elasticity to buffer the impact of resulting delays. Of course, the activities on the *critical path* may not be as lenient. Some projects have zero margins: the Olympics shall start on a set date, for example. Some projects are contractually obligated to start on a fixed date or risk liquidated damages. The challenge of the PMO manager can be immense: turn the project team upside down to get back on schedule, accept the prime milestone to slip, or find a middle ground to reduce the delay. The right decision requires the right perspective. That perspective is drawn from the point of the project: to realize a PPA. Preserving the prime milestone (typically the plant start-up) may very well entail project decisions that will affect the future profitability of the asset. Recall the liquified natural gas (LNG) plant example in Chapter 8, which produced 25 million tons of LNG per annum at a 2013 price of U.S. $800. That's $380M of revenues per week, over three to five decades. Imagine a project manager faced with a project delay and an added capital cost (6 months and $50M) dictated by a design change required to maintain the revenue stream, or degrade it to $379.5M if nothing is done (a minuscule 0.13% revenue loss). That minuscule loss, compounded over the life of the asset, will cost the owner $750M in lost revenues. In terms of schedule, the six-month slippage represents 1.67% of the plant's economic life. On what basis can one justify not incurring the 1.67% schedule slippage?

Another nefarious practice perpetrated in the name of schedule efficiency is the ubiquitous reliance on *free-issue* materials by or on behalf of the PMO to a fabricator/constructor. The act is invoked most often for materials *that are deemed long lead by the purchasing party*. These materials are ordered without consultation with the receiving party, who will nevertheless be left holding the bag when deliveries are late. In such instances, there is genuinely no way to assign accountability to any one party. What is true of IFC deliverables is equally true for procured items: the party accountable for the construction/fabrication must by extension be accountable for the materials needed for that construction. In other words, *stop the practice of free issue materials*. If an item exhibits signs of stretched delivery times, the intended fabricator must be brought into the procurement cycle to acknowledge the requirement and execute the purchase himself. Not only will this practice strengthen the integrity of the schedule, it will cost *less* to the project because of the elimination of middlemen who would otherwise go through the motions on behalf of the owner.

ABOUT THIS BUSINESS OF NUCLEATION

In physics, *nucleation* refers to the thermodynamic process of forming either a new thermodynamic phase or a new structure within a self-organizing behavior. Snowflakes are the poster children of nucleation mechanics. Analogously, project nucleation is the mechanics of modeling numerically the theoretical state of the asset. The model simulates the plant's operational and financial behavior, from which are inferred the design limits, the risk profiles, the operation details, and the profitability performance. Material risks—immanent and tacit—lurk at the interface between knowledge and ignorance. Those risks are corralled, if not emasculated, from a thorough understanding of the physics underlying the entire behavior of the plant, and its impact on the asset's revenue generation potential. The work is carried out in three dependent domains: engineering nucleation, information nucleation, and operational nucleation. *Engineering nucleation* models the full-field physics of the plant. *Information nucleation* models the entirety of the data associated with the asset and integrates it into a virtual asset kernel database. *Operational nucleation* models the activities of the asset throughout its economic life. All three abide by the maxim:

Physics rules; engineering governs; risks constrain; economics ensue.

Engineering Nucleation

This is a hard-core engineering endeavor that goes beyond canned code-checking software. Its aim is to model numerically the physical behavior of the *plant*. The objective is to understand the limits of this behavior up to black swan scenarios. The outcome is a comprehensive set of models, simulations, behavioral limit tables, and fail-safe criteria that quantify the operations of the plant under normal, abnormal, and extraordinary conditions. The results may also result in changes to the design of the plant—changes that could send the project execution back to Phases 1 to 6 for rework and redress. These numerical models will include:

- *System level full-field physics modeling*—The term *field* takes on a mathematical sense, whereby the spatial, temporal, and compositional variables at play in the behavior of a given system are quantified.
- *Installation-level nonlinear behavior modeling*—Nonlinear is once again mathematical and includes the operating conditions of an installation that is within and without the design range of its input and output variables; operations at the margins of safety; transient, unsteady, and degraded states of either the equipment or the input and output variables; and externally-driven fluctuations in inputs and outputs.
- *Quantitative risk assessments*—These are the assessments of large-scale installations that may be subject to explosions, losses of containment, pressure and temperature spikes, earthquakes and climate vagaries, fires, and power losses.

- *Failure-containment studies*—In tandem with the quantitative risk assessments, failure containment studies seek to quantify the ability of a system or an installation to continue to operate safely when subject to a partial or severe failure of one or more components; to what extent can the equipment contain the results of a failure; and the cascading risks of a propagating failure throughout an installation or plant.
- *Life-cycle cost* (LCC) *modeling*—This is the final analytical model to be created. This is the model that initiates the quantification of the variables that will determine the profitable performance characteristics of the asset. One of these sets of variables concerns the reliability of each system and of each installation under the operating regimes defined above (the so-called installation-level nonlinear behavior model). MTTF, MTBF, failure modes, probability density functions, maintainability vectors, recurring maintenance requirements, and plant-wide reliability management specifications are some of the principal quantities derived. Concurrently, these LCC model parameters serve as inputs to the operating cost models developed to predict the cash flow requirements of the operating plant. Finally, plant-wide maintenance and upgrade plans are elaborated from these datum sets for the duration of the asset's useful operating life.

Information Nucleation

Phases 1 through 6 produce a gargantuan volume of data, documents, information, and numeric records, across a bevy of formats and media. The objective of information nucleation is to orchestrate this mass of information into a singular framework tied to the *internet of things*. The latter is a concept best captured by Caterpillar's CEO, Doug Oberhelman, who was speaking about his company's intention to manage in real-time the performance of its equipment worldwide for the benefit of their owners. Oberhelman remarked that the company had three million machines in operation at any time somewhere on the planet, but had no visibility into their real-time performance and failure occurrences.

The internet of things is no longer a question of *if*, but *now*. This next disruptive wave of digital connectivity promises a cornucopia of efficient processes for managing and operating industrial assets. This is the trust behind information nucleation, which occurs along three interwoven threads: model-centric architecture, access, and integrated maintenance management.

- *Model-centric architecture*—The concept: orchestrate the entire set of data and information associated with the asset through a datum architecture that is centered on the 3-D model kernel of the asset (more on this in Chapter 17). The model is a computer rendering of the physical features of every component, machine, system, and installation making up the plant. To each one of these plant features corresponds a set of technical data, drawings, manuals, and other documentation (i.e., the complete information set) that can be accessed immediately by computer, by clicking on that feature. The 3-D model is stored in the plant *vault*.

- *Access*—The vault must be accessible by any authorized person—from anywhere, at any time. It can be locally hosted or deployed on the cloud. It goes without saying that this access should be through a web browser with an emphasis on an intuitive user-graphic interface.

- *Integrated maintenance management*—The operating plant will generate a steady stream of dynamic data from the machines and systems in operations in real time. Reliability and availability data will also be derived, over time, on these machines and systems. It is critically important to enable the vault to automatically gather these datum streams to compare them with the life-cycle maintenance and operations data obtained from the engineering nucleation phase. Thus, designing the plant's information and communication infrastructure in accordance with this operational imperative is a necessity.

Operational Nucleation

This nucleation closes the loop on the modeling of the asset. Whereas engineering and information nucleations are specific to the physical plant, operational nucleation seeks to simulate the *resources involved in the operation of the asset* (note here the switch from plant). Staffing requirements are established; training needs are specified; regular maintenance plans and schedule derivatives are created; sparing, consumable, and inventory levels are set; personnel and materiel movements are quantified; emergency responses are designed; and economic performance estimates are compiled to gauge the theoretical profitable metrics of the asset and assess the corresponding nameplate risk. The outcome of this nucleation is a large dataset from which the commercial business plan for the asset is drafted.

DESIGN ON STILTS

Managing Risk, by Any Other Name

Why bother with nucleation? The answer is because the business of technology is risky and characterized by *machine risks*—the bigger the plant, the more complex its behavior, the riskier its character. Notwithstanding the widespread practice of risk management in the project world, real-world equipment failures will keep on occurring, processes will routinely go awry, black swans will appear, and liability costs will accrue. There is an inherent dichotomy here that puzzles. Is risk management beholden to the usefulness of its purported purpose? Dogmatically, it is; realistically, it is not. Risk management requires front-end results which are then applied to various *what-if* scenarios to uncover causes, effects, ramifications, and probabilities of occurrence. The entire edifice is predicated upon three tacit assumptions that the results are: (1) adequate, qualified, understood, measurable, and sufficient; (2) the people, tools, and processes involved in their creation are equally adequate, qualified, knowledgeable, available, and sufficient; and (3) the integration of these results yields a controlled, controllable, and predictable overall system. The ubiquitous presumption leads to the perception that risk can be effectively corralled. And therein lies the fallacy. Absent a comprehensive nucleation phase, results stemming from risk management practices are not even wrong.

> *Without nucleation, the existence of risk analysis results is riskier than their absence because of the false sense of security that they foster.*

There is no such thing as a simple system lending itself to sequential build up *without consideration of coupling effects*. Engineered projects are inherently and inescapably complex, imperviously of scale. A food processor, a cordless drill, a car muffler, an iPad, a jet engine, a submarine, or an offshore drilling platform is a direct example of complexity whose *safe and profitable life cycle* will not ensue from simplified, sequential design execution. Complexity theory demonstrates that such systems cannot be designed in isolation. Their design is dependent on the interplay of potentially multifarious coupled variables whereby everything affects everything else. The quintessence of system risks finds its origins in the fact that insular, isolated silo work cannot uncover the interwoven factors.

> *Risk is an emergent property of any physical or algorithmic system.*

Complexity theory teaches us that emergent properties can form pockets of stability in the phase space of an otherwise unstable or chaotic system. The nature of a complex system tends to evolve to counter external attempts to change those pockets. In nonmathematical terms, stability pockets cannot be externally forced out. Once a risk appears, it stays. How is risk to be corralled then? The first thing to do is change its definition. The word *risk* is too vague, almost benign. One cannot quantify a risk the way a system specification can. Consider instead, risk as a *failure in waiting*. Not merely a potential, which only implies a probabilistic eventuality, but a *loss* that can be modeled, initiated, and analyzed before it actually occurs. Second, this definition makes the failure calculable *because it is ruled by physics and governed by design*. One can calculate the threshold above which a widget or a process will degrade, loosen, or fail catastrophically. The failure is quantified and its liability, understood. Liability here is key—whereas the loss (in production, in profits) is the effect of risk; liability is the consequence. The objective is met—to produce a true picture of the effective overall liability embedded into the system. Granted, this is a vast oversimplification of what is by itself a complex process prone to more risks, but the principle remains. Risk is transformed into a *system variable* on an equal footing with all other motive variables, mathematically formulated by equations. It can, therefore, be modeled and simulated within a set of controlled analytical experiments to explore and set the boundaries of safety of that system.

Results Are Not Answers

Machine risks can be divided into two classes: labile and Taleb. The labile class includes all types of potential failures over which the owner can exert some level of *preventive* control. Labile risks exist within the asset (equipment, personnel, operations) and outside (regulations, taxations, labor pools) and are inherently predictable. The Taleb class—named after author Nassim Nicholas Taleb—are inherently unpredictable or random; control can only be reactive. Examples include massive system leakages, installation explosions, plant fires, earthquakes, egregious regulations, and wars. The Taleb class is embedded into the fabric of the asset and its PECO under the guise of randomness. Randomness defines the system's overall failure potential. Labile risks drive the owner's warranty and TCO costs. Taleb risks drive the owner's liability and survivability—they are more critical.

To assess the asset's labile risks, one must understand its behavior under normal and abnormal conditions. The asset's Taleb risks require an understanding of that behavior under extraordinary conditions (random external constraints, operating extremes, worst-case scenarios, geopolitical catastrophes). Taleb risks also require an understanding of human-machine interactions. In both cases, the behavior is assessed from results obtained by the human-software tandem involved in their generation. *Everything that matters to risk assessment is anchored to this tandem.* No matter who is running what software, the outcome always produces results. The WYSIN (*what-you-see-is-not*) principle flares up because *results are not answers*. Results hint at the existence of a risk; answers quantify that risk. Often, results are not even wrong! Turning results into answers is what makes risk assessment profitable. Getting answers out of results demands a deeply proficient human-software tandem.

Cheaper Is Costlier than Better

Knowledge is not software. Software is not expertise. Expertise is not experience. Too many people don't know that they don't know. Work gets done with computers and applications that are ill-suited or not understood by *menu drivers*, unaware of their limits. Playing a violin concerto on a Stradivarius does not guarantee a sublime performance. In the end, machine risks can only be corralled, understood, and managed by experts orchestrating expert systems to do their work. An expert with spreadsheets or a novice with expensive software will produce the same thing: unknowable uncertainty. As the adage goes, *if all you have is a hammer, pretty soon everything looks like a nail*. Risk is a child of engineering and a kin of liability. Real engineering is hard, and harder than commonly imagined. But real engineering is also the greatest bulwark available to mitigate risk. Liability's costs increase exponentially with *going cheap at the front end of assessment*. Low-cost *menu drivers* coupled with canned software only spreads risk across the entire design process because they focus on producing results to create the illusion of understanding. The accompanying illusion of economy will last until the day reality comes crashing down. The choice lies not in paying more than required, but in paying no less than necessary. It is, in the end, a choice that owners must make between foresight and hindsight, between facing reality and gambling on faith—that is why nucleation matters.

THE BENEFITS OF EIGHT PHASES

More Is Less

Readers who are accustomed to fewer phases in TPM may recoil at the perspective of two more, let alone the novel nucleation works. Fortuitously, the ICPM method will incur *less cost* in *less time* than its TPM counterpart. The salient difference lies with the fact that ICPM solves the valunomic and asset risks, whereas TPM magnifies them. The key benefit is an execution philosophy that builds incrementally over time without dragging the same deliverables across phases in a never-ending state of developmental flux. The scheme also imposes a structural discipline on the owner's project team, through the obligation to complete a phase before starting another, with no rework attending the bridging between successive phases. This approach further obligates the project team and its hired consultants to think things through more broadly right from the get-go, instead of stumbling upon new requirements as time goes by. Phase simultaneity is nevertheless possible in discrete cases. For example, if the owner decides on a specific engine to drive a compressor from the outset, then the activities related to that engine in Phases 1 and 2 could be pursued concurrently. Similarly, self-contained installations (a parking lot for example) could be developed jointly between Phases 5 and 6. Nucleation of self-contained systems or installations can be started earlier. Ultimately, the details of these overlaps must be worked out by the PMO and captured in the pertinent *phase execution plans.*

The extent of staffing mobilization is another key difference between TPM and ICPM. We observe in Appendix 4 that all engineering disciplines are mobilized early in a TPM project and carry on till the bitter end. In ICPM, expertise is mobilized in lock step with the nature of the work, and limits the number of disciplines at each phase as a result. The staffing requirements of ICPM will be significantly lower than a TPM scheme.

The R&D Project Class

The research and development (R&D) initiative form a subset of investment projects and are, as such, implicitly covered by the foregoing discussion. Nevertheless, their nature endows them with unique features that distinguish them from industrial projects. The salient difference is this: R&D projects seek to marshal physics unto an economic path, whereas industrial projects seek to marshal systems unto a similar path. In this respect, R&D initiatives can be viewed as physics projects, while industrial plants can be viewed as system engineering projects. From an execution standpoint, the R&D project life cycle is best described by the *technological readiness level* model, developed by the U.S. Department of Defense and NASA. This model is summarized in Table 12.8, which also indicates the correlation with the PPA phases. The nature of the work at each readiness level is far more iterative than what we find in a PPA scheme. Nevertheless, the more important point to make is that the management structure of an R&D project is readily embodied by the PPA philosophy advocated in this book.

Peeking at the PECO

The reader may have noticed that the ICPM sequence has dealt mainly with the physical characteristics of the asset. Elements of the PECO were addressed in the geospatial works that were initiated in Phase 2, but not all of them. The full characterization of the PECO is pursued by the framework because it does not lend itself to the linear sequencing of ICPM. Intimate and constant exchanges between the PMO and the framework will mitigate the randomness injected by the PECO, arising from the whims and vagaries of stakeholder interactions. Phase information requirements will dictate the timeline imperatives of the PECO interrogations. Conversely, regulatory deadlines mandated by the PECO will drive the scheduling of the phase work. The PECO-project symbiosis is thus woven tightly into the execution strategy of the entire project. When the latter is scoped, defined, sequenced, and de-risked, the owner is able to launch

Table 12.8 Correspondence between the ICPM life-cycle phases and the technology readiness level system

Technology Readiness		Description	PPA Phases
Level	Stage		
1	Basic principles observed and reported	Scientific research begins to be translated into applied research and development.	None
2	Technology concept and/or application formulated	Applications are speculative, and there may be no proof or detailed analysis to support assumptions.	1
3	Analytical and experimental critical function and/or characteristic proof of concept	Includes analytical and laboratory studies to physically validate the analytical predictions of separate elements of the technology.	2
4	Component and/or breadboard validation in laboratory environment	Basic technological components are integrated to establish that they will work together.	3
5	Component and/or breadboard validation in relevant environment	The basic technological components are integrated with reasonably realistic supporting elements so they can be tested in a simulated environment.	4
6	System/subsystem model or prototype demonstration in a relevant environment	Representative model or prototype system is tested in a relevant environment. Examples include testing in a high-fidelity laboratory environment or in a simulated operational environment.	5
7	System prototype demonstration in an operational environment	Prototype near or at planned operational system. Demonstration of an actual system prototype in an operational environment.	6
8	Actual system completed and qualified through test and demonstration	Technology has been proven to work in its final form and under expected conditions. In almost all cases, this technology readiness level represents the end of true system development. Determine if system meets design specifications.	7
9	Actual system proven through successful mission operations	Actual application of the technology in its final form and under mission conditions.	8

the execution of the works. To launch is to populate; therefore, our next area of focus will be the selection of the personnel and the project teams that will execute the work.

NOTES

1. See Piers Bizany's *The Man Who Ran the Moon* in the Bibliography for more details.
2. These ranges are notional only and will obviously vary between projects and between industries.
3. *Esemplastic* is defined as having the ability to shape diverse elements or concepts into a unified whole.
4. In biology, mitosis refers to the serial division of cells.

PART 4—WHO

People, projects, and profits through
teams, labor pools, and strategies.

13

TEAMS

"It is not enough that we do our best; sometimes we have to do what's required." Winston Churchill

PERSONNEL IS POLICY

Teams Are Designed, Not Copied

The next step of the execution strategy is personnel assignment. In the profitably performing asset (PPA) schema, teams are assigned once the strategy is affirmed, which sounds reasonable enough until you realize that the opposite occurs in traditional schemes, through the reflex of cut-and-pasting the organization chart (a.k.a. org. chart) from the last project. The fact of the matter is that project teams warrant the same level of deconstructive analysis applied hitherto.

An execution strategy, by itself, is useless unless it is carried out by performing teams capable of metamorphosing its plans into actionable actions. The makeup of a team must be engineered in accordance with the *directrix* principle. At the organizational level, this principle dictates that different teams are required at different times for different tasks. For example, if the owner's project management office (PMO) structure mirrors that of the prime contractor, the principle is negated explicitly. Teams will change over time; the people who start and finish a project are rarely the same. Teams are also cultures that are, in turn, teams. *Talent wins games; teamwork wins championships*, as basketball great Michael Jordan once remarked; hence, the importance of choosing the right people, at the right time, in the right numbers.

The Fallacy of *One-Teams*

The purpose of project teams is to execute the work that will deliver the PPA. We must first address, however, the comforting fallacy of the idea of *one-teams*. This is a popular principle embraced by owners to bend the interests of all parties about the event horizon of the project. Owners host elaborate and costly charter sessions to align everyone on the expectations. Signatures are etched upon poster-size charters. Everyone willingly signs up in the belief (hope?) that their respective motives will be satisfied. The project will launch on a wave of composite harmony, until reality shows up. Inevitably, the grandiose promises of yore are cast aside in the defense of a signatory's profits. To paraphrase an old management saying: *The conditions behind a promise vanish in time, until only the original promise remains.*

The term "one-team" is code for placing an owner's interests ahead of all others. Without a stalwart alignment of interests—as discussed in Chapter 9—*one-teams* rarely manifest themselves. How could they? From the get-go, the owners, the scope project team (SPT), and the supply chain partners (SCPs) are driven by different commercial imperatives. Each participant is in it to make money, without *any* willingness to sacrifice oneself for the greater good of the owner or the project. But a project really needs a collective embrace if it is to have any hope of developing the PPA. To echo a famous line from Start Trek: *the needs of the many outweigh the needs of the one.* The one-team idea is flawed from a managerial standpoint. Within a genuine PPA team, communication and information flow is a two-way affair. Transparency is not optional. The team's hierarchy itself is open to checks and balances. However, these features vanish in a composite *one-team* setting where transparency is sacrificed first. For instance, the owner sees the commercial terms of all contractors; they, on the other hand, see none from anyone. The hierarchy of a *one-way* structure results in one-way enforcement from owner to vendors—effectively transforming the owner's position into a monopsony. That is why we never see an owner's project manager (PM) get fired in response to a serious complaint from a vendor. Vendors have no say on the overall execution strategy or the performance of that execution by the owner's personnel. They are at the beck and call of the owner who effectively rules as a hegemony.

It all comes down to this: *one-teams* never are, and never can be. Better to accept this aphorism and manage the hierarchy with eyes wide open. The better policy is for the owner to actively promote the commercial success of all SPTs and SCPs involved.

AS THE PLANT, SO THE TEAM

The PPA Team Is *Sine Qua Non* to Risk Management

Often, owners will combat the six types of execution risks (see Chapter 11) by overstaffing their PMO teams. This is a deeply rooted reflex borne out of a deeply rooted fear of the unknowns and unknowables associated with SCPs. Strength in numbers is believed to provide greater assurance of project success—sacrificing, by the same token, the *directrix*. The outcome, unfortunately, will be widespread dabbling. This staffing reflex reverberates beyond the owner's organization and ripples through labor pools. Rabid competition among owners, the SPT, and the SCPs lead to labor cost inflation. Redundant job titles that propagate throughout the execution hierarchy—from framework to the PMO to the SPT and the SCP—compound the tightening of labor markets. Recruiting in far flung, low-cost labor regions soon loses the sheen of affordability. Going far and wide is plagued by higher management complexity, higher communication risks, and lower quality. Jostling to cherry-pick teams from shared labor pools turns into a zero-sum game: one's gain is another's loss, with zero benefit accruing to the project.

The Team Is an Investment

By way of contrast, the investment-centric project management (ICPM) approach considers human resources as an investment into the project, to be tuned to the demands of the work. The investment perspective lengthens the time horizon beyond the end of the project. The recruitment strategy seeks to achieve repeatability and capability growth *within* the organization. Staffing is entirely engineered around the requirements of each life-cycle phase, such that the makeup of a project management team will evolve and change over time.

Staffing up is subject to two universal constraints: (1) qualified labor pools are always limited; and (2) they are slow to grow. In an ideal world, the project team would feature the smallest number of personnel with the highest expertise, charging the highest hourly rates to produce the highest valunomy for a given scope of work (an idea explored in Chapter 15). This ideal is achievable, but under conditions of perfect timing—otherwise, different staffing approaches are needed.

HIERARCHY CONSTRUCTION

The Wrong Way to Build a Team

Consider Figure 13.1, which shows an organizational chart taken from your author's experience. Can the reader determine if this is a PMO or vendor

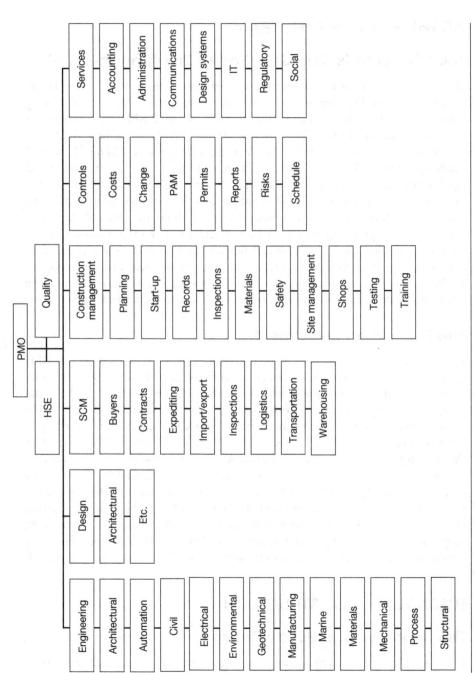

Figure 13.1 Undifferentiated project organizational chart

hierarchy? The answer is both. The structure was first chosen and subsequently adopted by the vendor. The vendor's team head count was a mere 20% greater than the owner's. The structure remained unchanged through the entire project life cycle. This example is representative of the *mirroring technique* that is so common in large-scale projects. The owner selects the team structure before the execution strategy is set. The vendor adopts it *before* the contract is awarded, evidenced by its inclusion into his commercial proposal. In both cases, the structure will have been lifted *verbatim* from a previous project. Aided after the fact by a generic execution strategy, people with titles will be motivated to justify their own existence (see the FOE, JOE, and MOE effects in Chapter 5). Features like the accountability matrix, continuity of interests, functional differentiation, and span of control are ill-defined or not defined at all. The owner will tend to overstaff the PMO team as a hedge against management risk. The valunomy of the edifice is weak. What the owner gets out of this Faustian bargain is a dabbler *modus operandi* bereft of execution efficiency.

Finally, when project personnel are drawn from the same labor pools by owners and vendors, the PMO staffing strategy will oversubscribe the supply of competent people. Labor costs will rise while expertise is dissipated. Poaching may accelerate. In the end, project costs and schedule will inflate to the detriment of all players. The case isn't theoretical: the Canadian hydrocarbon industry has suffered from it for decades.

The Right Way to Build a Project Team

Project teams *must* be *fit-for-purpose*. Teams are, functionally, another design variable to an execution strategy. They must be engineered in accordance with the differing roles of the framework, the PMO, the SPT, and the SCP. The PMO team, for example, cannot adopt a structure that replicates that of its vendors *because its mandate is entirely different than theirs*. The design of the team must furnish the lattice upon which the *directrix* schema operates. Labor constraints enter the design equation: team sizes cannot be arbitrarily set as a means of reducing execution risks. The same team will also undergo changes to its hierarchy over time as the work progresses throughout the life-cycle phases.

The hierarchical structure of a team will evolve and change over time.

From an organizational standpoint, the hierarchy of a team reflects the accountability structure of the team. The corresponding organizational chart shows the accountability (AP) relationships at play between superiors and subordinates. Pursuant to the individual principle of the *directrix*, each box appearing in the organizational chart is assigned to an individual, never to a group. We speak of the individual's *role* as an organizational function within the team. To this role corresponds a set of *duties* which are the tasks and activities carried out daily by the individual.

The reader may wonder why the hierarchy excludes the *responsible* and *probate* parties. Organizationally speaking, the RP (responsible party) and AP are *directrix duties* assigned to individuals *in relation to their duties vis-à-vis other accountable roles*. For example, the supply chain manager (AP for procurement) may be vested with an RP duty towards the discipline managers (AP) of the engineering group in matters of vendor liaisons and tender process. This same individual may be assigned the PP (probate party) duty for the contract terms and conditions related to bid evaluations and contract award (both conducted under the aegis of the designated discipline manager acting as the AP for the tender process). There may be instances when a role is purely supportive to the team (IT support, for example) but that role still exists organizationally as an accountable mandate within the hierarchy.

STAFFING STRATEGIES

A potent team design philosophy will rest upon five *staffing strategies*.

Strategy 1—Divide and Conquer

Start from the big picture of execution illustrated in Figure 5.1. Where do the owner, the framework, the PMO, the SPT, and the SCP fit?

- The owner is the *probate party*: he approves, stops, or cancels the project; he has the final say on allocation decisions; he defines the asset; and he bankrolls the entire project endeavor.
- The framework is the *responsible party* to define the overall execution strategy; it imposes the standard operating environment (SOE)/standard operating landscape (SOL); and enables the PMO team to execute the project. The framework reports to the owner.
- The PMO is the *accountable party* for realizing the PPA. It reports to the framework. The PMO quantifies the scope of work; hires the SCP, and manages their interfaces; and acts as *probate party* for all project deliverables and decisions.
- The SPT reports to the PMO and is the *accountable party* for its contracted scope of work. The SPT will also act as *probate party* over its hired SCP.

- The SCP reports either to the PMO or to an SPT. It is the *accountable party* for its contracted scope of work and *probate party* over its own supply chain partners.

Strategy 2—Organizing Principles

Two organizing principles are available to the PM for creating an organizational chart: *labor* and *physical*, as we saw previously in Chapter 4 under the heading *Network Spaces*.

The *labor basis*, exemplified in Figure 13.1, follows the labor taxonomy of Table 11.1. For example, the engineering function is divided into discipline groups (architecture, civil), which are, in turn, divided into specialties (engineer, designer, analyst). The labor structure is resource-specific but matrix distributed in terms of the work to be done. The same engineering group, for example, works on all installations, mostly simultaneously. The labor basis assumes that all of the installation work gets parsed comprehensively for each system.

The *physical basis* acts in reverse. The team hierarchy mirrors that of the physical configuration of the plant. Each system and each installation is parsed in terms of requirements, specifications, and deliverables (i.e., the outputs). Then, the tasks required by these outputs are defined and the labor resources assigned. Labor assignments proceed from the physical reality of each element of the plant.

From a theoretical standpoint, the physical basis is a unit transformation process; the labor basis is not.

The physical configuration of the plant encapsulates the development work required. Thus, it automatically defines the accountability matrix for the project and for the participating teams.

Strategy 3—DoDoDab

To repress dabbling within the hierarchy requires a clear and definite delineation of the mandates of all parties involved, *without functional or redundant overlaps between them*. This is done via a *DoDoDab* analysis: figure out who DOes what and who DOesn't, to avoid DABbling. DoDoDab analysis yields a differentiation of the functions in terms of direct accountability. The functional differentiation sets up an accountability matrix between the teams by approval maturity level. What if the expertise of the PP subceeds that of the AP? Consider this real-life example of the acutely specialized expertise of manufacturing high-strength steel plates. If the PMO decides to audit the mill's fabrication process, it better not send some generalist quality assurance person armed with an ISO 9000 certification and a checklist strapped to a clipboard. The audit will be meaningful *only* if the auditor has prior experience with the actual steel-making process. Deploying such a lethal *weapon of meddlesome destruction* (WMD) for the sake of going through the motions can only result in wasted time, treasury, and the supplier's goodwill.

The probate function demands from its practitioner: (1) a depth of subject matter expertise that is at least equal to the party accountable for the work reviewed; and (2) to be attuned to the project ecosystem idiosyncrasies underscoring that work. This twin requirement presents the probate team with three valunomic options on how to perform its functions: (1) employ a subject matter expert (SME); (2) hire an SME consultant; or (3) accept the contents of the deliverable at face value, which implies a vendor's acceptance maturity rating of 121 or more, pursuant to Table 6.3.

Strategy 4—Uniformity of Execution

Consistency dictates that the mechanics and mechanisms (M&M) of the probate and responsible functions be carried out uniformly across the project hierarchy (from PMO to SCP). Consistency implies oversight. Oversight implies a lead group, function, or role. Consequently, a project team should have one lead for responsible activities and one lead for probate activities—separate from each other. On large projects, the multiplicity of functional disciplines may also warrant the delegation of a lead's oversight duties by specific areas of expertise, thereby creating an intermediate management level.

Strategy 5—Head Count Control

This last strategy is driven by the importance of tying the accountability matrix to the *acceptance maturity ratings* in Table 6.3.

The head count of a probate team is inversely proportional to the acceptance maturity rating of the subordinated accountable teams.

An AP with a maturity rating greater than 121 requires the least amount of oversight from the probate team. Probate personnel are not required to be co-located with the AP. The opportunity exists, in fact, for representatives of the AP to operate from the probate team's offices. A maturity rating between 80 and 120, on the other hand, will require more personnel by the PP to interact more frequently with the AP. Site visits will be mandatory, with corresponding cost increases to the project. Finally, a rating below 80 causes the head count of the probate team to approach that of the AP. In this instance, probate personnel should be operating principally from the AP's offices. Obviously, working with high maturity SCPs should be the objective of any project execution strategy. The objective is achievable through the adoption of the remedies advocated in the subsequent text. Absent rating mechanics, probate teams often respond by compensating with a surfeit of overlapping functional roles trending toward the low rating scenario.

TEAM STRUCTURES

The Owner

The owner's team is comprised of senior managers, at arms length with the PMO and operating in a stewardship role. The team will be part-time in nature and embody a matrix structure. It will not mirror the hierarchy of either the framework or the PMO.

The Framework

The framework team will be labor-based and operate in hybrid matrix/assigned modes (shown in Figure 13.2). The matrix mode applies to the functions associated with the global component strategies and the PECO. The assigned functions are associated with the core competencies and the team's leadership cadre.

The PMO

The structure of the PMO team is based on the idea of high-end expertise producing minimal head count. The leadership comprises the PM and his six immediate reports: Deputy PM, Execution Chief, Metrics Chief, Technical Chief, Construction Chief, and Asset Chief:

- The Deputy PM for commercial accountability (supply chain management; health, safety, and environmental management; contracts; external compliance)
- The Execution Chief for relational accountability (interface management, resource management, convergence management, organizational relationships, project systems)
- The Metrics Chief for performance accountability (performance assessment metrics, audits, close-out)
- The Technical Chief for conceptualization accountability (for the asset)
- The Construction Chief for realization accountability (for the asset)
- The Asset Chief for operational accountability

Functionally, the first three exert oversight over the *delivery* of the project. The last three look after the *development* of the asset. In this manner, the delivery

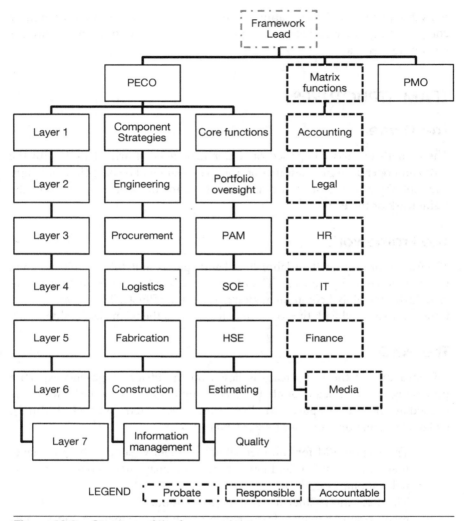

Figure 13.2.   Structure of the framework team

leaders are concerned with the efficient deployment of the project's allocations while the development leaders are focused on the creation of the physical features of the asset. The arrangement is shown in Figure 13.3, which also delineates the accountability mandate for each role.

The resulting organizational chart is shown in Figure 13.4. The reader will see that the Metrics Chief is shown reporting to the PM and also to the Deputy PM (the last box shown in a dash line contour). The latter indicates an alternate

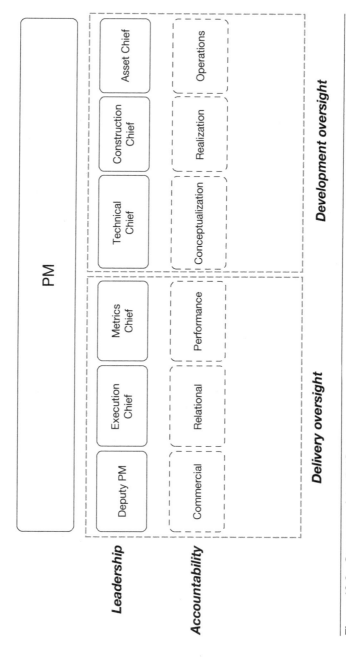

Figure 13.3   Structure of the PMO team

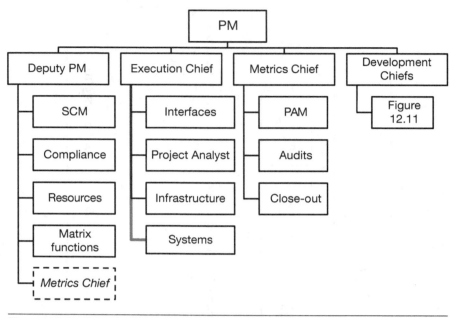

Figure 13.4 Organizational chart corresponding to the PMO hierarchy

structure when metrics are to be overseen by the Deputy PM. Another salient feature is the grouping of the three development chiefs into a single role with the underlying details already included in Figure 12.11 (shown schematically to simplify the presentation).

The evolving nature of the team mandate is embodied by this aggregate role, as shown in Figure 13.5. During the *conceptualization stage*, the Technical Chief carries the AP mandate. The other two operate as RPs until life-cycle Phase 6. At that time, the Construction Chief takes on PP duties. At the start of the *realization stage* (life-cycle Phase 7), the AP role is transferred to the Construction Chief; the PP is assigned to the Asset Chief; and the Technical Chief becomes the RP to both. A final round of assignments occurs at life-cycle Phase 8: The Asset Chief becomes the AP; the Framework Lead becomes the PP; and the remaining chiefs fall back to an RP role.

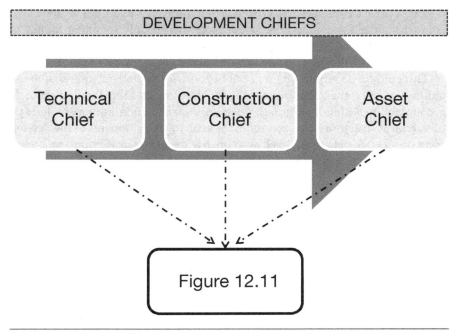

Figure 13.5 Evolution of the development accountability over time among the Chiefs. During conceptualization, the Technical Chief is the AP. During realization, the Construction Chief takes on the AP role. From asset validation onward, the Asset Chief is the AP.

STAFFING TACTICS

"A" Organizations versus "A" Teams

Figure 13.3 embodies the reporting structure but says nothing about head count. How many chiefs must there be? Who has the final say over what? The answer depends in part on who's who in the delivery zoo. We want a team that is finely tuned to its mandate and limits its head count. Such a team will be inherently high performance. We must nonetheless keep in mind the require-ments for consistency of execution, resilience to labor scarcity and personnel growth. Whereas a traditional project management (TPM)-minded owner will ask for the "A" team, the PPA-motivated owner will cultivate an "A" organization. The "A" organization is characterized by a stalwart commitment of its people, defined as strength of devotion toward the employer. This is an objective that belongs more to the owner's organization than the project team. The reader who is familiar with *organizational behavior theory* will recognize in this the concept of competitive advantage. The existence of a motivated and trained labor force is much harder for competitors to duplicate than simply spending money on capital improvements (see Robert Dailey's MBA course *Organizational Behavior* for more information).

This cultivation requires patience. It begins with an understanding of the relationship between a team's organizational hierarchy and the distribution of the accountability within its *directrix*. Such an understanding intimately links the hierarchical structure of the project to the evolving requirements of the *development* process. To get there as well as to finalize the team's head count, we require four staffing tactics: *skeletal, span of control, stratification,* and *radial*.

Skeletal Tactic

A team is as performing as its leaders. The structure of the team is a lattice network that maps directly unto the labor space network (see Chapter 4). The *skeletal tactic* requires that *a node be assigned to an individual qualified to fulfil the primary function of that node*, in accordance with the DoDoDab principle. Furthermore, the DoDoDab qualifications extend to the exigencies carried by the remaining three tactics. The ideal node leader will exhibit an ability to manifest the objectives of the control, stratification, and radial strategies. If the qualified individual cannot do so, the solution is to fall back on the following corollary.

Each strategy deficiency by a node leader is compensated by a strategy-qualified deputy. The ideal candidate will exhibit no deficiency. By contrast, several deficiencies would point to the addition of several deputies, which becomes a selection criterion for the position. As we will see in the *stratification tactic*, even an ideal leader should not operate alone, but be supported by at least one deputy.

Span of Control

Ours is a world of instant connectivity and smartphones. Technology enables collaboration across time and space. People are expected to manage more people—from anywhere, at any time. This is an illusion perpetrated by the pervasive power of software, one that ignores a basic fact of life: people are not computers. Direct supervision requires presence, not Ethernet bit rates. Computers are sublime multitaskers, people are not (contrary to another received notion). From an evolutionary standpoint, we are no different from our Neolithic ancestors: our ability to juggle relationships and mental facts is severely limited—to about seven, as it turns out. This is what is called *span of control*.[1] A manager will be most effective when direct reports do not exceed seven. Of course, five, six, or nine would not be nefarious, but more than 10 will attract complexity and chaos. *Nobody* can manage 20 people effectively. Forget cell phones and e-mails and video-conferencing; even with globally distributed cross-functional teams, the homeostatic[2] tendency favors single-digit head counts as a hedge against complexity. The concept of *span of control* is intrinsic to the PPA methodology.[3] Management is communication, but communication is not management. E-mails alone produce a perverse effect: *the maximum number of direct reports is inversely proportional to the number of daily e-mails/texts received.*

The number seven has deep historical roots. It formed the organizing principle of Roman armies of the classical period.[4] Roman armies did have potent communication methods, collaboration tools, and messaging infrastructure. Yet, those features were incidental to the issue of *span of control*. They succeeded because of their innate grasp of the limits of control on the battlefield. Whether at the highest level (legion) or down in the trenches (contubernium), leaders held sway over a very small number of direct reports.

The Roman Legion

The makeup of the legion evolved over the centuries but reached a standardized configuration through the reforms of Gaius Marius in 107 BCE as follows:

- The smallest unit, the *contubernium*, was composed of eight legionaries led by a *decanus*.
- Ten contubernia made up a *centuria* led by a *centurion*, who was assisted by one or two *options* (80 legionaries, 2 options, 1 centurion).
- Six centuria constituted a *cohort*, which was headed by the most senior-ranking centurion among the six centuria (480 legionaries, 12 options, 6 centurions). The first cohort was the first among equals and led by the *primus pilus*, the highest-ranking centurion in the legion. The first cohort included five centuria staffed with 160 legionaries (instead of 80) each. The first cohort numbered 800 legionaries.
- The imperial *Legio* included nine cohorts and one first cohort. The legion was commanded by a *legatus legionis*, aided by one *praefectus castrorum* and other senior officers. A Legion would contain about 5,000 men in total.

The legionaries within a legion were themselves divided into four categories of infantry and one cavalry. The first infantry category included the youngest, the *velites*, who were teenagers numbering 1,200. Next came the *hastate*, young adults in their twenties also numbering about 1,200. The third category, the *principes*, was made up of 1,200 or so men in their thirties. The fourth category applied to the oldest legionaries, the *triaii*, who numbered only 600. Finally, the cavalry numbered 300 horses.

The *legion* would typically number 5,000 men. Remarkably, only four hierarchical layers formed the reporting structure. Think about this: a mere four levels sufficed to control the chaos of the battlefield, bathed in the fog of war. Obviously it worked, which offers the modern reader a precious lesson in organizational management. The choice of seven as ideal is also guided by modern findings.[5] It appears to be the inherent limit of the human brain. Yet this low number hides the mathematical power of exponential progression to generate large organizations. Imagine an organization built from it. The head count will progress as follows:

- The first level, headed by a lead, supervises 7 workers (7 workers, 1 lead, 8 total)
- The second level, headed by a group lead, supervises 7 leads (49 workers, 7 leads, 1 group lead, 57 total)
- The third level, headed by a manager, supervises 7 group leads (343 workers, 49 leads, 7 group leads, 1 manager, 400 total)
- The fourth level, headed by a director, supervises 7 managers (2,401 workers, 343 leads, 49 group leads, 7 managers, 1 director, 2,801 total)

Stratification

The third tactic is to skills distribution as the second is to staff distribution. It is driven by the objective of nurturing "A" organizations. The "A" team would comprise individuals with the most expertise—a rare instance at the best of times. The "A" organization, on the other hand, relies on its aggregate expertise and heuristics to assemble, at will, performing teams. Achieving an "A" organization requires: (1) stratifying each nodal layer into sublayers of increasing experience; and (2) propagating all individual subject matter expertise throughout the team.

Node stratification—Node stratification produces an expertise and experience pyramid matching the structure of the team. In other words, increasingly more people as it moves down through the levels of the hierarchy. A project team will be *repeatedly* successful over the long run with a labor force that is bulging at the low end of the expertise spectrum; one that is given to horizontal growth within the ranks and vertical growth within the hierarchy. The diffusion of skill sets among a broad pool of resources counters the nefarious effects of poaching and staff turnover in tight labor markets. It also inures the organization against an unhealthy dependency on scarce individuals imbued with broad knowledge residing in their heads.[6]

Roman Pyramids

The pyramidal construct of the Roman legion has been perpetuated into modern, combat-ready armed forces. An army is made up overwhelmingly of lower rank soldiers (privates, corporals, master corporals, and sergeants in the Canadian case) who are managed by decreasing numbers of higher rank personnel. No army was ever successful with battalions of senior officers marshalled unto the battlefield. Great armies succeed in training their massive resources at the low end of the expertise spectrum and deploying them under the savvy leadership of mid-level leaders. The acumen and experience of an army's senior leadership is critical to its success, as long as it is complemented with potent ground troops who will dominate the trenches.

SME propagation—The propagation of SMEs takes its cue from organizational behavior theory. The concept is, in fact, a well-honed application of the *job characteristic model* (JCM) studied extensively in business management literature.[7] We see it in action at large corporations—they will often rotate high-potential individuals across several functional areas of the company. Consider the story of Mary Barra, who was named CEO of General Motors in 2014. Prior to her nomination, she was successively VP of global manufacturing engineering (2008); VP of Global Human Resources (2009), and EVP of Global Procurement Development (2011), which later encompassed Global Purchasing and Supply Chain (2013). Such rotations do not aim to make the officeholder an expert in each field; rather, it is a kind of cross-training that is meant to expose the individual to several aspects of the business. As Robert Dailey put it, the pursuit of cross-training must be an essential feature of work systems that are based on teams.[8] The proof is in the pudding: companies that believe in the competitive edge conveyed by their workforces will not blink at the cost of employee retention or concern themselves with short-term cost increases in incentive programs. They know that these costs are not expenses but investments into their future profits. The same principle applies to project organizations. One seeks to maximize the exposure of a maximum number of employees to a maximum number of functional roles and skill sets. This implies, among other things, the prevention of pigeonholing people into excruciatingly specific fields of expertise for years on end. Nevertheless, a couple of caveats are needed. First, people should not be forced to accept an opportunity to spread their wings. Some people will be happier and more productive in pigeonhole roles and should be nurtured to thrive in those circumstances. Second, exposure does not mean retraining. One does not, for example, take a mechanical engineer and force him into an accountant's job; or make an accountant into a public relations specialist.

Exposure opportunities need to be tailored to the capabilities of everyone in such a way that the individual is more likely to succeed than fail in the new role. The benefits to the organization will be long lasting:

- First and foremost, the propagation policy limits the dangerous dependency on scarce but specific individuals imbued with broad knowledge held solely in people's heads.
- It fosters labor stability within the team and within the organization. When given the freedom to stay or leave in order to grow professionally, people will usually choose to stay.[9]
- Horizontal opportunities nurture an employee's loyalty toward the employer along with the employer's valuation of the employee.
- In crunch times, shared expertise acts as a backup within a team when one individual leaves.
- It sends the signal to the team that the organization genuinely cares about people.

Radial Tactic

This tactic takes its name from the concept of nodes associated with the lattice network. Management is the art of communication. Information originates at a node and moves radially outward, toward other nodes. The *movement* of information is physically limited by distance, time, and potential content distortion. One can measure a radial *distance* between sender and receiver as measured in *delays. Each delay requires a staff position to manage the flow of the information.* The position is required to manage the message traffic. If one person in the communication flow is absent, the message risks degradation. As George Bernard Shaw remarked:

> "The single biggest problem in communication is the illusion that it has taken place."

The most effective and reliable pathway between a sender and a receiver (i.e., the *node*) is the direct link. That is, two nodes dealing in person in the same language, in the same environment and time zone, and with a common basis of understanding of the information transacted. From an accountability standpoint, this reflects interactions between direct reports (worker to lead, group lead to lead). Moving radially out to the next level of the hierarchy creates a potential for message degradation. For example, a group lead who wishes to bypass a lead and task a worker directly is unlikely to be aware of the exact workload, staff availability, and work assignment within the lead's crew. That is why the lead is *in the middle* so to speak—to properly translate the requirements of the group leader. Picture now the case of outsourcing a piece of work to a design team in Nanjing, China. Fifteen time zones separate the two nodes. The Nanjing lead may not appreciate the pressures at play upon the lead. Finally, major cultural differences permeate each person's interactions with power. The probability of message degradation will be very high.

These examples illustrate the concept of distance *delays*. They are, in increasing severity:

- Presence (in person, via teleconference, via phone, via text, via letter, via intermediary);
- Language (shared spoken, shared written, verbally translated, formally translated);
- Environment (same team, same organization, same location, same business culture, same time zone); and
- Knowledge (topic, mandate, workload, project history, business imperatives).

Each source of delay creates a need for a new staff to counter their deleterious effects—to lubricate, if you will, the flow of information. Evidently, one person can handle two or more delays, given the right skill sets. Matters of language and environment could be the purview of translators, for example. Additional probate resources could be assigned specifically to the outputs of the outsourced party. Information flow between the SPT and the SCP definitely entail document control counterparts that are aligned holistically to the project's M&M of document management. The outcome is always the same: delay sources add up to staff increases.

QUALITY IS NOT A FUNCTION

Out of the Noumenon[10]

The reader may have noticed the absence of a dedicated quality function in Figure 13.3, while it appears in the TPM structure of Figure 13.1. In most management circles, quality is something that is inspected after the fact, and affirmed through squad checks and checklists that are signed off by several checkers from within and without the project team. This *postmortem* quality assurance says nothing about the quality of the execution mechanics involved; a deliverable is either acceptable or not, without any insight into the *why*. True quality however is an *emergent feature* of the mechanics. The quality of a deliverable is inherent to it, rather than inspected *into* it. This viewpoint is derived from the seminal works of W. Edwards Deming. While Deming's philosophy had its heyday in the 1980s and 1990s, its applicability to project execution has never been more pertinent.

The Deming Quality Paradigm

A short bifurcation is in order. William Edwards Deming (1900–1993) was an American statistician and engineer. In the aftermath of the Second World War, he became instrumental in Japan's transformation into the manufacturing powerhouse that it is today. Older readers may recall a time when *made in Japan* was synonymous with poor quality. General Electric's Six Sigma program and Toyota's quality management system are descendants of Deming's fourteen management principles:[11]

1. Create constancy of purpose toward improvement of product and service to become competitive, stay in business, and provide jobs.
2. Adopt the new philosophy. We are in a new economic age. Western management must awaken to the challenge, must learn their responsibilities, and take on leadership for change.
3. Cease dependence on inspection to achieve quality. Eliminate the need for inspection on a mass basis by building quality into the product in the first place.
4. End the practice of awarding business on the basis of price tag. Instead, minimize total cost. Move toward a single supplier for any one item, on a long-term relationship of loyalty and trust.
5. Improve constantly and forever the system of production and service, to improve quality and productivity, and thus constantly decrease costs.
6. Institute training on the job.
7. Institute leadership. The aim of supervision should be to help people and machines and gadgets do a better job. Supervision of management is in need of an overhaul, as well as supervision of production workers.
8. Drive out fear, so that everyone may work effectively for the company.
9. Break down barriers between departments. People in research, design, sales, and production must work as a team, to foresee problems of production and in use that may be encountered with the product or service.
10. Eliminate slogans, exhortations, and targets for the workforce asking for zero defects and new levels of productivity.[12] Such exhortations only create adversarial relationships, as the bulk of the causes of low quality and low productivity belong to the system and thus lie beyond the power of the workforce. Eliminate work standards (quotas) on the factory floor. Substitute leadership. Eliminate management by objective. Eliminate management by numbers, numerical goals. Substitute leadership.

11. Remove barriers that rob the hourly worker of her right to pride of workmanship. The responsibility of supervisors must be changed from sheer numbers to quality.
12. Remove barriers that rob people in management and in engineering of their right to pride of workmanship. This means, among other things, the abolishment of the annual or merit rating and of management by objective.
13. Institute a vigorous program of education and self-improvement.
14. Put everybody to work to accomplish the transformation. The transformation is everybody's job.

Staffing for Quality, Not Quality Staffing

Accordingly, the PPA approach eliminates the quality manager position. Since quality is an emergent feature of the creation process, it becomes a design variable on par with all others. Quality is *designed* into the deliverable from the outset. This implies that:

- The accountable individual owns the mandate of enforcing the use of M&M that have been previously validated for use on the project;
- The accountable individual must incorporate into the work sequence the required set of work performance checks called out by the pertinent M&M;
- The responsible individual must train the workers on the proper use of M&M; and
- The probate individual must be an expert in the application of those mechanics, mechanisms, and checks to validate a proposed output against its complete set of checks.

The reader should note that the elimination of the separate quality manager role does not preclude the adjunct role of quality audits. They are necessary elements of any execution strategy to periodically verify the verification process of each team.

Convergence of Execution

Since the quality of the work is measured intrinsically, without having recourse to a *postmortem* quality check, we may wonder if the same goes for the quality of the interactions between the project participants. In this instance, we speak of convergence rather than assurance, since the objective is smoothness of transactions between people. Convergence in this context occurs at two levels: at the interfaces (between outputs and inputs) and at the transaction (between the people accountable for the outputs and inputs). The interface convergence falls under the purview of *interface management*, which is explored in Chapter 15. The transaction convergence is a responsible function assigned to the project analyst, reporting to the Execution Chief in Figure 13.3.

Project Analyst

Whereas the interface manager focuses on the integrity of the data transacted between activities, the project analyst focuses on the integrity of the exchanges between the individuals and groups involved in those transactions. The *project analyst* is, in fact, the eyes of the PM in matters of relationship nexus (see Chapter 2). In this role, the *project analyst* is both observer and mentor. His objectives are:

- Assess the smoothness and efficacy of the exchanges;
- Uncover sources of divergence, information shortcomings, and deleterious transaction delays, then develop and implement remedial actions;
- Verify that the exchanges that are carried out align with what is right for the project;
- Step in when egos and conflicts threaten to usurp the primacy of the project's health; and
- Advise the PM and his deputy on the overall integrity of the execution.

The role is structured either as a direct report to the Execution Chief, or folded into the latter's mandate directly. With the former, the position is more as an observer rather than a mentor; in the latter, more mentor than observer. In both instances, the individual must be neutral to the mediation process. His guidance is always embodied by the imperative to do what's right by the project.

COST SAVINGS

Optimized Head Counts

Some readers may be left with the impression that the staffing strategies and tactics would lead to excessive head counts. The opposite occurs in reality. The rule of seven, for example, *does not apply* to the division of work within a team. It is perfectly acceptable to have a team of three, two, or even one individual assigned to a specific task. The rule comes into play when deciding who reports to whom. The cumulative impact of the rules is illustrated in Table 13.1 regarding a hierarchy of workers, leads, group leads, division leads, sector leads, and PM (five

Table 13.1 Normative staffing distribution

Level	Workers	Leads	Group Leads	Division Leads	Sector Leads	PM	Total	Percent
1	7	1				1	9	77.8
2	49	7	1			1	58	84.5
3	343	49	7	1		1	401	85.5
4	2,401	343	49	7	1	1	2,802	85.7
5	16,807	2,401	343	49	7	1	19,608	85.7

levels in total). The ratio of workers to the top management level is shown in the percentage column. For example, if the entire team is only made up of the first reporting level (lead) and a PM, the workers make up 78% of the head count (9). If the team includes all levels, workers represent 86% of the head count (nearly 20,000). Notice the constancy of this figure across the various head counts. In a rationally managed team, managers should make up between 14 and 16% of the head count.

Similar ratios apply to labor costs. The clear majority of the costs are tied to the workers. In other words, adding more management positions to a team is financially inconsequential, but productively determinant. That is the fundamental justification for advocating a staffing strategy based on hiring the best individuals with the most expertise.

Shopping for Giffen

We have made the case for assembling a performing team whose expertise and capabilities will survive beyond the project. The team's hierarchy is designed to mirror the plant configuration, which is a necessary condition for managing at the interfaces. The business manager is now able to create a highly performing organization that can generate "A" teams at will, in real time. The question of where to find performing personnel is the next subject to be explored. Performing personnel and teams belong to a class of economic goods called *Giffen goods*. Giffen goods are unique in that a rise in price causes a rise in demand. *Paying the most for the most expertise, diffused across the broadest functions, is the best policy for achieving the most PPA possible.* What labor pools should be tapped? Should recruitment be industry-focused or expertise-based? What is the true price of low-cost outsourcing? These questions are answered in the next chapter.

NOTES

1. The interested reader is invited to consult Phillip Foley's intriguing book *Span of Control—29 Success Secrets*.
2. Characterizing the tendency of a system, especially the physiological system of higher animals, to maintain internal stability.
3. See Watson, D. and Baumol, E. (1967). "Effects of locus of control and expectation of future control upon present performance," *Journal of Personality and Social Psychology*, 6, 212–215.
4. See Fagan, Garret G. (2005). *Great Battles of the Ancient World*—lecture transcript book. The Great Courses Publishers, Chantilly, Virginia, USA.
5. See Foley's *Span of Control—29 Success Secrets* and Ouchi and Dowling's *Defining Span of Control* for more information.
6. This conclusion is amply supported in the literature on organizational behavior. See Robert Dailey's MBA course *Organizational Behaviour* and Organ and Hammer's *Organizational Behavior, 2nd Edition*.
7. See Hackman's *Leading Teams*, Harnish's *Scaling Up*, Latham and Pinder's *Work Motivation Theory and Research at the Dawn of the 21st Century*, and Pfeffer's *Competitive Advantage through People* in the Bibliography for more information.
8. See Robert Dailey's *Organizational Behaviour* course material, Edingburgh Business School, Heriot-Watt University, Edingburgh, U.K., 2011.
9. In general, when people are given the freedom to choose, they choose to be like everyone else.
10. That which is apprehended by thought; a posited object or event as it appears independent of perception by the senses.
11. See Deming's *Out of the Crisis* and *The New Economics for Industry, Government, and Education, 2nd Edition* for more details.
12. The author coined the neologism *diarrethic* to describe slogans bereft of substance. Classic examples include "work smarter, not harder," and "quality is job one."

14

PERSONNEL

Expertise dispels the comforting fallacies of experience.

SUCCESSFUL PEOPLE SUCCEED

The Ideal Team

Once the team structures are defined, the next step is to fill them up—the subject of this chapter. Ideally, we wish to assemble the ideal team, which is the one that realizes the profitably performing asset (PPA) with the least risks and liabilities for its owner. Chapter 12 suggested what this team would Look like: a small cadre of high-priced experts who are cognizant of the project's industry idiosyncrasies and are operating autonomously with minimum supervision. Such a makeup offers the highest valunomy to the owner: lowest head count, lowest labor budget. These metrics follow from the fact that the genuine expert's output requires the least amount of time and supervision, but with the highest degree of correctness. That is why one expert at $150 per hour is better than two practitioners at $60 per hour each, or three juniors at $45 per hour each. The divergence in valunomy increases with increasing divergence between hourly rates.

The opposite metrics ensue when staffing is viewed as *throwing bodies* at a scope of work. Such labor is commoditized and valued in terms of unit costs. The jump from there to lowest labor costs is but a hiccup to the accounting mindset. This stream of thought underlines the drive to embrace *offshoring* in the pursuit of cost containment. As we will see later in the chapter, commoditization requires a critical assumption about dollar equivalency that turns out to be wrong. It assumes that a dollar's worth of labor is the same for any jurisdiction in which the work is carried. In reality, once you factor in the extra costs occasioned by additional supervision, rework, quality checks, recurring trips by the design leadership, lost productivity across wide time zones, the office over-time to connect across continents, and the material execution risks that ensue, the lowest labor cost option will always cost the most in the end.

Twenty offshore workers at $5 per hour each are valunomically inferior to two proficient domestic workers at $60 per hour each.

Many readers will relate to the observation that with so many projects, they never seem to have the time to do things right the first time, but always find time to do things over again to make them right. Rework is the hallmark of low cost labor and a major cause of schedule conflicts. Yet, low cost labor always seems to win out at the outset.

Sources of Labor

Needless to say, the ideal team is a difficult challenge. In rare cases, projects have the luxury of an embarrassment of riches; say, assembling the scientific team for the Manhattan project—which developed the atomic bomb during WW II—or putting together your country's hockey team for the Winter Olympics. For everybody else, scarcity and availability are the twin obstacles. In everyday situations, the demand for expert labor far outstrips the offer. The scarcity is exacerbated when everyone recruits from the same labor pool. Things really go off the rails when those labor pools become oversubscribed, stagnant, or inclined toward sclerotic in-breeding—steep wage inflation sets in; poaching follows; and team instabilities ensue.

Labor pools are children of their industries, which are like countries—they have their own vernacular, values, rules, culture, aspirations, and pasts. They are the product of evolutionary pressures upon their people who *live by intervals of reason under the sovereignty of caprice and reason.*[1] Players in any given sector cherish the comfort of their neighborhood where they first recruit, buy, sell, and exert influence. This is the overriding reason why labor pools become over-stretched. By the same token, recruiters constantly miss out on opportunities to improve their corporate skill gene pools. As the sociologist Seymour Martin Lipset put it, if a person only knows his own country, he actually knows nothing since he lacks the ability to compare a practice, a process, or a behavior against what exists elsewhere.

Neighborhood in our context means more than a domestic, physical location; it relates to an organization's established supply chain inclusive of labor pools. A labor supplier can be domestic despite being half-a-world away. For example, to a smartphone maker based in Eritrea, the preferred domestic supplier of batteries could be in Shenzhen, China. Recruiting domestically is just so much easier than going beyond the mercurial horizon (better the devil you know, as the saying goes). This parochial proclivity is a hard habit to break. Companies, like projects, wallow in their comfort zones. Meanwhile, global forces wrought by international investors heave upon them expectations of speed to market, cost and risk containment, security of supply, and certainty of quality. Domestic labor pools are ill-equipped to answer the challenges. Faced with chronic skill and labor shortages locally, project proponents reluctantly look elsewhere, and fall prey to the promise of cheap foreign labor. This is a costlier strategy than endeavoring to extract greater valunomy from their backyard sources.

Recruitment Techniques

Project recruitment strategies are colored by three widely held tenets: (1) their industry is uniquely complex; (2) experience trumps expertise; and (3) specialization bests cross-training. In the first instance, insiders view their industry as fraught with idiosyncratic complexities. They deem them so patently unique that no foreign insight could possibly be meaningful. In the second instance, players cling to the belief that specific hands-on industry experience (i.e., years spent in it) is absolutely necessary for every conceivable hire, save new graduates. The third instance favors narrowly focused experience over heterogeneous backgrounds. This leads to a segregation of people by domains of expertise; shutting out generalists. In other words, industry experience is allowed to beat subject matter expertise. Together, these tenets conspire to maintain a *modus operandi* that cements the *status quo* and foment the very labor shortages that they purport to overcome. Project and company bosses respond to these shortages by embracing offshoring as a solution. The trouble is, it isn't.

MISCEGENATION

Experience Is Not Expertise

Miscegenation is a wonderful word. Literally meaning the marriage and child bearing between different races, it is also one of evolution's most potent weapons against gene degradation (characteristic of inbreeding). It aids heterosis within the species (whereby the biological quality of a hybrid is improved or increased). What works for genes works for companies as well. Miscegenation is not only viable but *essential* to the long-term survival of an organization. Assuredly, any industry is unique in some ways. Even the knitting industry will boast features that may be unfathomable to the uninitiated. In engineering, for example, the need for expertise (i.e., subject matter acumen) is highest when dealing with the physics at play. In the environmental field, it is about ecosystem knowhow. In regulatory matters, it is driven by intimate knowledge of the idiosyncrasies at play. But these islands of specializations should not be allowed to dominate a given labor pool. Great swaths of project tasks do not require such depth. For example, accounting methods are never so unique to an industry that they cannot be migrated to another. An engineer does not require twenty years of acid gas compression experience to select a 1,000 kW electric motor to drive that compressor. Any competent electrical engineer versed in the technicalities of motors can do the job. The secret to any recruitment strategy is to differentiate between *industry experience* and *applied expertise*.

Here is a simple test to drive the point home: what do John Furlong, Samuel C. Phillips, Werner von Braun, and Elon Musk have in common? Furlong ran in the 2010 Vancouver Olympics; Phillips was the Apollo program director for the moon shot; von Braun was Director of Marshall Space Center; and Musk is the brain trust behind Paypal, Space X, and Tesla motors. Their common trait? None of them would be given any consideration for a project manager (PM) position over a pipeline project. Never mind that the job is really about control of scope, budget, schedule, and changes—topics that could be thought at the Ph.D. level by all four candidates. The mere absence of pipeline-specific experience disqualifies them right from the get-go.

Look Outside for Expertise

Eventually, project-driven industries shoot themselves in the proverbial foot by denying themselves access to labor pools outside of their well-worn recruitment grounds. Opening those doors unleashes skill migration that, in turn, helps incumbents flush out the old ways, question the bad habits, and cripple the stifling *status quo*. Skill migration brings in new ideas, new perspectives, and new ways of solving problems. In this context, industry experience encompasses the knowledge of the ways and means of an industry. It is a function of time in and of exposure to a variety of situations. Applied expertise, on the one hand, is a deep knowledge of problems, acquired from direct involvement with their solutions. This is the distinction between experience and expertise.

> *Decades of experience do not implicitly equate to expertise but merely a condition of not having died. From the standpoints of execution, productivity, and cost, what matters is expertise.*

Proven applied skills are far more important than mere cognizance and familiarity with the industry.

Experience does matter when the idiosyncrasies of the industry demand it. Regulatory regimes are examples in the forestry and fishing industries. The complexity of the permitting process demands people with direct experience and knowledge about successfully navigating it. When constructing a skyscraper, one needs a group of civil engineers who are specialists in modeling seismic and wind loads—a skill that is acquired through years of practice. That kind of experience matters. Otherwise, it is much better for a project to be endowed with widely-deployable expertise through its personnel.

Breaking Down Skill Barriers

Expertise should further be nurtured in breadth, rather than depth in individuals. Take the example of an army. Its effectiveness is a function of the flexibility of its troops. A single soldier capable of a multitude of tasks is more deployable than a platoon of uber-specialists unable to break out of their narrow field of expertise. The same goes for project teams. Projects will be plagued when they are designed along narrow divisions of functional roles. Project teams need to switch to a flexible, multipurpose labor pool that can be tapped and deployed rapidly. The same argument applies at the business level. Pre-approved vendors create a barrier to owners to go beyond the status quo. Projects will prefer a pre-approved vendor on the other side of the globe rather than develop a local supplier who possesses the expertise but not the industry experience. By daring to break down historical barriers that are tied to experience, project owners immediately expand their access to greater competitive forces. They will gain an advantage in terms of cost certainty, speed to market, and schedule compliance. Yes, patience and tolerance by the owner will be needed at the front end. They are but transient inefficiency blimps on the road to long-term profitability.

OFFSHORING CONSIDERATIONS

Success Conditions for Offshoring

Back in the year 6 CE, Roman legions led by the general Varus were defeated at the battle of Teutoburg forest—northern Germany today. The enemy was a tribal alliance of Germanic warriors led by chieftains who had been trained by these same Romans in preceding campaigns. The example illustrates the dangers of relying too much on an offshoring strategy (having trained the very people who would one day defeat them).

The default position for any project should be the domestic supply chain, as we saw previously. Going offshore can be a sound strategy when one or more of the following conditions are met:

1. The owner wishes to deliver a jolt to the system to shake the domestic supply chain's complacency;

2. The valunomy of the offshoring option is higher than the domestic approach;
3. The expertise required by the work does not exist in the domestic supply chain;
4. The development of the expertise domestically cannot be completed within the schedule requirements of the project; or
5. Political or regulatory exigencies demand the offshoring option.

The first condition exists when a domestic supply chain exhibits monopolistic tendencies derived from a lack of competition. These tendencies strengthen over time when an industry limits its recruitment to familiar domestic labor pools. The clearest sign of this condition is unending inflation in wages, when labor costs go up without productivity increases. The valunomy of the labor *decreases*. It's time for a kick in the complacency pants.

The second condition is a corollary of the first. Given enough time, a monopolistic domestic labor pool will price itself out of the market. Looking offshore begins to appeal to the senses. But there is no greater risk to a project than to award work primarily on unit labor costs. One can always find a vendor who will be willing to buy the job. Or find a vendor in a jurisdiction where people earn dimes on the dollar, compared to their Western counterparts. *The costs of low unit costs are inflated financial risks to the project.* The decision must be anchored to the valunomy of the proposition and established in terms of dollar equivalency. The argument boils down to a simple question: is the valunomy of a dollar of labor in an offshore jurisdiction comparable to the domestic proposition? Unit labor costs play a minor role in this consideration. Of greater concerns are bigger issues such as productivity, competencies, supervisory overhead, number of distance delays (see Chapter 12), and frequency of travel for reviews and approvals. Factoring in these variables may qualify the offshore option as non-valunomic.

Conditions three and four go hand in hand. The third condition is self-evident. The fourth one is tied to the preference for the domestic option. When the expertise is expected to be required frequently by projects, it is in the long-term interests of the project ecosystem (PECO) to acquire it. However, the timeline of a given project may not be compatible with the deployment of this expertise locally. In such instances, the fourth condition is akin to the third.

The last condition is equally self-evident. Project approval may be contingent upon meeting local content conditions. Or foreign investors may insist upon utilizing resources from their home country, for a project executed in another jurisdiction. Whatever the case, offshoring becomes an obligation.

The Advantage of Local Workforces

Let us emphasize once again the superiority of domestic labor pools when valunomically justified. They are less complex, less risky, and easier to manage than those further afield. Valunomic salvation cannot come merely from a relentless pursuit of putative cheap indigenous infrastructures. Higher cost regions cannot compete on unit costs; they can, however, do so on the basis of productivity. Higher unit rates that lead to productivity gains, shorter completion times, and higher first-pass quality outcomes will always be more valunomic than cheap labor options. What's more, many owners will willingly pay a premium to shorten execution timelines.

Western labor pools are especially advantaged in this respect. They represent an enormous reserve of untapped efficiency gains to project execution. The similarities with the untapped world of nanotechnology are inspiring. The latter was given form in a 1959 speech by Richard Feynman to the American Physical Society (see Richard Feynman's *The Pleasure of Finding Things Out*). The same goes for project labor: there is lots of room at the bottom, thanks to investment in software. These applications offer stupendous opportunities to reduce labor through productivity and throughput gains, lower error-free rates, and the use of intelligent-design systems. The key is to coalesce people and technology to work harmoniously. Such symbiosis is already embedded in the DNA of certain industries. Look at Apple, Samsung, Toyota, and Dow chemicals—all of them constantly face competitive pressures to do more with less, to produce better with more bang for the buck. Surely the project execution industry can learn a thing or two from them?

Investing Locally

Blindly going offshore in the pursuit of apparent labor cost savings does nothing to help the productivity agenda. Going far afield is fraught with risks, control losses, quality degeneration, and seeding of future competitors. All participants in PECOs must take a step back and embrace a policy to strengthen domestic supply chains:

- Broaden the expanse of the domestic labor pools;
- Embrace functional expertise at the expense of industry experience;
- Aid the diffusion of that expertise in the labor pools through cross-pollination of skill sets;
- Pursue an aggressive agenda of valunomic allaying of people and software to deliver efficacy, productivity, and throughput quality;

- Throw open the doors of the supply chain ecosystem to embrace suppliers of all ilk who are willing to get qualified into approved vendors; and
- Execute within the project management office's immediate reach.

FIT-FOR-PURPOSE EDUCATION

The Diploma Arms Race

In his fascinating book, *Talent Is Overrated*, Geoff Colvin noted that labor has undergone a fundamental change over the past century; one that has made financial capital plentiful and human capital, scarce. The statement is true at face value but warrants one caveat. With a planetary population approaching nine billion, it's hard to make the case for scarce human capital. What is lacking, really, is *competent, valunomic* human capital. After all, never in history has so much education earned by so many yielded so little employability. The fashion is not new, surprisingly enough. Back in 1949, in the play *All My Sons*, the famous playwright Arthur Miller had his character Keller decry how:

> *"everybody's gettin' so goddamn educated in this country there'll be nobody to take away the garbage... You stand on the street today and spit, and you're gonna hit a college man."*

For decades, we've witnessed an education arms race spurred on by an explosion of academic credentials in all matters of job descriptions. It is assumed that any college degree enhances hiring prospects. In countries like South Korea, the entire adult population is just about saturated with university graduates. China already graduates more university students than America and India combined. But, quantity is not the same thing as quality; degrees are not guarantors of employability; and volume is not a measure of skill sets. Study fields are not created equal. Skills must produce economic performance, and must do so within an information technology (IT) framework. The key to this statement is *great performance*. Skill sets must be revenue-generating and profitably productive. Then—and only then—will deeper knowledge and academic credentials prove worthy of pursuit. Knowledge of this kind implies dedication over time. A great performer seeks excellence for the task at hand *regardless of its merit relative to the performer's educational baggage.* Imagine a situation where you, as PM, are asked to train new hires from scratch. Having defined the nature of each position, you set out to define the skill sets required. How many of these positions would genuinely require a bachelor degree? A Masters or Ph.D.? Some are obvious: engineers, accountants, lawyers, and architects—others, not so much. Document management, for example, is bereft of glamour and power within any organization. It takes a special attitude to execute the repetitively mundane, the invariant routine, the process-bound mechanics. And yet, in my experience, document management is one of the unheralded heroic processes of successful projects. A top-performing document management specialist is worth more than any passably competent engineer. Academic credentials are nearly irrelevant to the function. In the extreme, they can even become *hindrances* to the execution of the work. Attitude, mental stamina, and attention to minutia—those attributes separate the performer from the mediocre.

Elements of Performance

The true guarantor of sustained performance is the right fit between the nature of a function and the person's disposition. Willingness to learn on the job is no small matter as well. Yes, the ramp-up time will be longer, but, under proper supervision, the process will not be as burdensome. For starters, the upside of this approach[2] is an ability to recruit much farther and wider within the labor pool. Second, it creates an opportunity to nurture loyalty and retention from these new hires. Third, it leads to higher individual valunomy. In shifting the interview premise from academic credentials to experience and commitment, you stand a greater probability of matching the person to the job *for the long term*. Note that this statement must not be interpreted as a wholesale rejection of academic credentials. They still matter in subject matter expertise. But the case against diploma recruitment was best made by the head of hiring at Google, Laszlo Bock, in his book *Work Rules! Insights from Inside Google that Will Transform How You Live and Lead*. Google will acknowledge the experience gained by a person during college, but posit that a degree doesn't say much about talent or grit. In Google's eyes, a college degree simply reflects a person's suitability to the academic mold. Google is far more interested in people who succeeded in the world in spite of lacking a college education. To Google, these are the exceptional people that they seek above all others. And lest the reader dismiss the argument because Google is, well, *Google*, this is how Eric Stille, CEO of Nugget Markets, describes the company's philosophy[3] of recruitment: they hire on the basis of attitude, knowing that the people can be taught the business of grocery.

The Military Connection

Military veterans honorably discharged. Those four words describe what is perhaps the richest vein of motivation, skills, leadership, and drive to perform. It is, unfortunately, all too often overlooked by organizations large and small who wish to mine for talent far and wide. This is one pot-of-gold at the end of the recruitment rainbow that a project team simply cannot afford to dismiss.

LESSONS LEARNED

Many lines of arguments in this chapter run counter to orthodoxy and warrant further emphasis. The case favoring domestic labor pools was made. These pools will be the superior option when:

- They are endowed with intrinsic valunomy and are superior recruiting grounds; and
- Their valunomy is best achieved from cross-pollination and imports from outside sources.

By contrast, offshoring must not be justified on the basis of unit labor costs. To be proficient and valunomic, labor supply chains cannot be left to their own device. They must not be permitted to uphold specialized expertise as the barrier of entry into an industry. To do so is to set in motion the mechanics of self-preservation that lead to labor shortages, skill stagnation, and cost inflation. Owners must be willing to abandon their hidebound tendencies and broaden their exposure to market capabilities far and wide.

The final point: recruit on the basis of talent, determination, loyalty, and the match between a job's genuine requirements and the attitude of the individual considered for the position. Once on the inside, nurture your people to deepen their knowledge of the job; force them out of their comfort zones through cross-pollination; never take them for granted, especially in business downturns; and reward performance blatantly and unabashedly.

NOTES

1. Thomas Browne (1605–1682). English polymath and author of various works across several scientific fields.
2. This argument is sublimely presented in Eric Schmidt's *How Google Works*.
3. *Fortune* magazine, August 1, 2015, page 38. Nugget Markets is a U.S. company headquartered in Woodland, CA, with $275M in revenue for FY 2014.

PART 5—WHEN

A play, in two acts, on the application of project management to the conflict between Plan and Reality.

15

3:2:1 MANAGE!

Truth before process; facts before whims.

FROM PLANNING TO EXECUTION

Getting the Show on the Road

It has taken us fourteen chapters to lay down the foundation of an execution strategy for a project. The mobilization of the framework and project teams was necessary to perform some of the execution work proper, as we saw in Chapters 10, 11, and 12. The reader should realize at this point that the entirety of the work done so far on the project has been on its planning. On the *development* timeline, we are at the beginning of the first life-cycle phase, *asset mitosis*. A handful of people have been involved in the framework and project management office (PMO) teams. The rest of the work for Phase 1 can commence once the baseline asset execution framework (BAEF) and phase execution plan (PEP) are published, the team's key personnel are mobilized, and the owner has given the go-ahead. The project finally transitions from planning to operational.

Initial Caution

To execute is to manage the dynamics of the project. Once a project's momentum is in play, its inertia will resist all changes to its pace or direction. The role of the project manager (PM) is to maintain the upper hand over that inertia at all times. Thermodynamics' second law is pertinent here: when left to its own device, the project will tend toward a state of increasing disorder. Getting through the planning work is linked, in one form or another, to the first two components of the definition of project management appearing in Chapter 2 as *organization* and *business*. At the operational stage, the third component—*relationship nexus*—takes over. The mechanics and mechanisms (M&M) of the execution continue to matter but are secondary to the human element. On the whole, project management is personal in practice, local in nature, and idiosyncratic in execution. Even the corralling of physics unto an economical path (your author's definition of *engineering*) varies from place to place. What passes as acceptable construction practices in Krasnoyarsk (Russia), in Oyo (Nigeria), or in Texas (USA) would not pass muster in Alberta (Canada), in Hesse (Germany), or Loire (France). Project management, like politics, is local. For this reason, there is no universal approach that will fit all projects in all circumstances. There are, on the other hand, certain practices that are common to the execution of all projects, falling under the heading of *routine practice*—the subject of this chapter. Troubled projects are discussed in the next chapter.

COLLECTION SUBSTRATE

Project Control in Real Time

We begin with an exploration of the *collection substrate*, which is the mechanics of project information. Execution implies control. *Effective* control is only possible through progress metrics captured and compiled *in real time*. *Postmortem* reports serve a journalistic purpose but offer little in the way of proactive mitigation. Real-time reports are therefore essential to the efficacy of control.

The set of mechanisms involved in this integrated datum management is called the *collection substrate*, illustrated in Figure 15.1. The foundation of the substrate is the work breakdown structure (WBS). On top of it sit the master schedule and the project's organizational chart. Then comes the labor layer, made up of the codes of accounts (CoA) and the time sheet system. Further up sits the project directory, which supports the estimating database. The reader will notice that these elements are common to both the profitably performing asset (PPA) and traditional project management (TPM), but do not exist in an integrated manner in the latter. Indeed, each component usually possesses a datum structure that is independent of the others, preventing unhindered datum movement between them. As an example of this heterogeneity, consider the WBS, project file structure, and time sheet codes of an actual project. A portion of the WBS is shown in Appendix 5 (truncated down from an original total of 32 pages). The structure of the file directory appears in Appendix 6. The CoA were, in turn, uncorrelated to either one. The organizational chart emulated Figure 13.1. The WBS mirrored the hierarchy of the schedule, while neither one tied back to the asset's physical configuration. The reader can imagine the

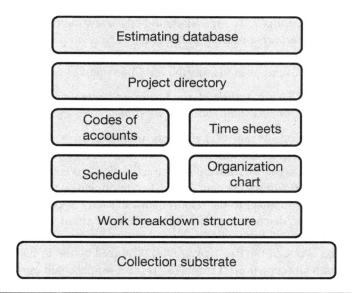

Figure 15.1   Elements of the collection substrate

difficulty of finding out how many hours were recorded by a given individual working on a set of calculations for a specific system, and then locating that set of calculations in the project's file directory.

Channels of Information

The *collection substrate* creates the channels through which the metrics of the execution's progress are recorded. The seven components share the same structure inherited from the physical configuration of the asset (see Figure 12.11). The reasons for the unifying structure echo Chapter 13: to achieve uniformity of control across all phases, all project participants, and all scopes of work.

Channel 1: The WBS

To most project management professionals, the WBS is a scheme to dissect a project into manageable work pieces. This definition applies to both TPM and PPA approaches but differs in its implementation, as we will see shortly. The WBS results from the atomization of the physical configuration of the asset down to the component level. It is subject to the second staffing strategy of Chapter 13: labor or physical basis. Traditionally, the pre-shovel works tend to adopt the labor basis; and the post-shovel works, the physical (basis) labor. In the PPA model, the physical basis governs. The resulting WBS structure is illustrated in Appendix 7. The reader should take a few moments to compare it to its TPM counterpart appearing in Appendix 5. Note, in particular, that labor functions such as engineering, design, and construction do not feature as elements of the WBS, except in the fourth section on management.

> *Once the WBS is set, its skeletal structure should be mapped identically to all other components of the collection substrate.*

Further subdivisions of the WBS elements are added as required by each life-cycle phase, in terms of the unit transformation process (UTP) pairings (input-output, constraints-enablers, attributes-characteristics, and targets-metrics). One instance of it is shown for element 1.1.1.1.1 (components). Some elements will change over time to adapt to the requirements of each life-cycle phase. Tweaks will be justified in discrete numbers, but never to an extent where the skeleton as a whole is materially altered.

The WBS is one of the first deliverables produced by the PMO. Once set, it flows through all scope project teams (SPTs) and supply chain partners (SCPs) involved with the project. Finally, to promote consistency of communication, the WBS must be accompanied by a *lexicon* document that will encompass all abbreviations, acronyms, and idiosyncratic expressions germane to the project.

Channel 2: The Schedule

The master schedule follows the publication of the WBS—but *never precedes it*. Both the WBS and schedule form the primary management toolkit to the PM. They are owned by the PMO, but can be developed jointly with the SPT and SCP. The schedule must not be a regurgitation of the WBS, nor act as a detailed checklist of the entirety of the tasks, activities, and deliverables to be produced. A schedule that includes thousands of elements spanning 30 sheets of $11'' \times 17''$ paper is useless for effective management. The structure of the schedule emulates the physical configuration of the plant (embodied in the high-level WBS). Details of each group of tasks should be limited to the requirements of *managing at the interfaces*. That is, a task, activity or deliverable belongs on the schedule when it must be so managed, at the interface between sequential dependents *external* to the pertaining *accountable party*. Internal squad checks, for example, do not belong on the master schedule.

There must be only one master schedule—owned and enforced by the PMO. All other project partners must operate from that single schedule. Specific scopes of work assigned to an SCP can be detailed further in the SCP-managed schedule. What must not happen is the situation where each partner maintains a separate schedule that is incompatible with the structure of the master schedule—updates will never be seamless. By keeping the master schedule within the PMO, the project inherits a single, unifying picture of the execution timeline. At once, that timeline is imbued with complete transparency. All project participants (SPT and SCP) are forced to operate in full view and are denied the luxury of hiding slippages that would otherwise remain invisible in the multi-schedule scenario.

The management of the schedule is carried out in accordance with the accountability assignments registered in the WBS:

- The PMO is accountable for Level 1 and probates all others.
- The SPT is accountable for Level 2 and/or 3 activities.
- The SCP is accountable for Level 3 or 4 activities.

Vendors are free to maintain their own internal schedule to ensure that the timelines of their consequent managed interfaces are satisfied. The owner, however, should not be required to pay for these internal schedules when they are not deemed managed interface deliverables:

- *Schedule reviews*—The schedule should be reviewed jointly by all parties regularly (weekly or biweekly) to capture changes and trends *proactively*. *Postmortem* notifications of slippages and missed dates are not acceptable and represent a failure of work management. Analyzing the schedule frequently helps to anticipate changes that are essential to the effective management of the work progress by the pertinent manager (PMO, SPT, or SCP). This recurring review mechanics is an integral part of the interface management carried out by the PMO and its partners, as discussed later in the chapter.
- *Control curves*—Reviews are opportunities to complement the schedule's health check with ancillary tracking reports on cash flow outlays, labor histograms, deliverables status and cost time resources (CTR), and datasheets. These ancillary reports provide the PM with immediate feedback on the overall state of the execution. Issues can be detected before they become malignant, and remediation schemes put in place to keep the project train on the rails.
- *Crashing the schedule*—Some organizations exhibit a proclivity for pursuing schedule acceleration in the pursuit of saving time. The reflex is especially dominant at the start of a project when the parties involved are eager to get going in order to get billing. That is a mistake. The axiom *no time can be meaningfully saved by saving time during execution* remains an essential condition of the success of a project. Not only is it important to execute the eleven life-cycle phases, the work must proceed

sequentially between phases. Overlaps, parallel execution, and out-of-sequence jumps may compress a schedule, but at the high costs of re-work, errors, gaps, holds, fabrication overruns, construction delays, and widening risk percolation.

Channel 3: Organizational Chart

Refer back to Chapters 12 and 13.

Channel 4: Codes of Accounts

These codes link a specific task or activity to an element of the WBS. The codes are usually derived from a company's accounting framework and will therefore not be explored further herein. On the other hand, the basis of these CoA must be emphasized once again: it must be forged from the physical configuration of the asset. All records captured by the basis must be traceable uniquely to that configuration.

Channel 5: Time Sheet System

This system is explored in detail in Chapter 17. The admonitions offered for the basis of the CoA apply verbatim.

Channel 6: Project Directory

The project directory must have a folder structure that replicates the WBS structure.

Channel 7: Estimating Database

The datum structure of the estimating database must replicate the WBS structure as well. Additional requirements will be discussed in Chapter 17.

INFORMATION EXCHANGES

Kick-Off Meeting

Kick-off meetings must occur after the contract award. In the PPA framework, the kick-off meeting is not a single event but a session spanning several days.

It will involve all functional groups from each project partner. Topics of review will include, at a minimum:

- The contract review conference: the leadership team of each project partner reviews, page by page, the contract and the scope of work.
- A gap analysis by each partner between the contract's contents and the partner's original proposal. Partners tied contractually will develop a strategy and timeline to resolve these gaps, possibly through contract amendments or scope adjustments.
- An invoice dress rehearsal: preparation of fictitious invoice and submission to the owner to work out the bugs and disconnects.
- The finalization of the partner hierarchies.
- The finalization of construction and procurement strategies.
- The final review of the master schedule and associated deliverables.
- Review of scope tasks and activities by their designated probate leads.
- Review of administrative and commercial procedures.
- The finalization of the change management process.
- Review of past lessons and adoption of pertinent ones for inclusion in the PEP.
- Roll out of project web site and project systems.
- The finalization of the interface management plan.
- Review of the commitments made by the owner to project ecosystem (PECO) stakeholders.
- Review of the owner's standard operating landscape (SOL) and standard operating environment (SOE).

Once the kick-off session is completed, evidenced by sign off of each partner's PM, the actual execution work for the project can be initiated. Each partner initiates her project scope in the following sequence, over a period of three to six weeks:

- Team mobilization
- Finalization of Level 3 or 4 schedule along with deliverable lists
- Finalization of baselines for budgets, schedule, cash flow predictions, manpower loading
- Finalization of phase execution plans specific to the partner
- Activation of tele-presence framework
- Activation of all information technology (IT) platforms, systems, and cloud applications
- Training of functional leads
- Implementation of the SOE/SOL
- Start the contracted scope of work

Communications

The reader will be familiar with the generic requirements of *effective written and verbal communication skills* and *a superior public speaker*. Every job posting has them, and every applicant will claim to possess them. Yet, few people actually prove themselves worthy of the praise. Communication goes beyond copacetic-worded sentences; it is a vital mechanics of control to the PM, serving four purposes:

- To inform and rally people around the needs of the project;
- To aid the efficient flow of information across the PECO (within and without);
- To structure and materialize decision making; and
- To control the message.

The last item sums up the existence of communications. Controlling the message is a quintessential skill of a performing PM. The term is not pejorative: messages must be controlled to protect projects against false interpretations, negative spin, or rampaging rumors based on ignorance or misunderstanding. It is only when nefarious intents require concealment that the idea of message control takes on an ominous connotation. In this age of social media, *any* form of digital message is a potential crisis waiting to explode. Perfectly innocent e-mails exchanged between the parties privy to a mutually understood context can be blighted by negative interpretations of dabblers once removed from the context.

Digital communications within a project context require a few rules of engagement to protect the writers, the readers, and the project itself:

- The first rule pertains to privacy. No digital exchange is private. *Always* assume that it will eventually end up in the public domain, and write accordingly.
- The second rule governs contents:
  - E-mails suffice for routine, mundane matters
  - Deal with delicate matters in person or by phone
  - Deal with critical matters in person or by phone
  - Never rant by e-mail; when upset, wait a day to write
  - E-mails are not adequate mechanics to communicate a formal decision
- The third rule deals with delivery media:
  - E-mails are adequate communication means within a project
  - Never text (via twitter and the like)
  - Never publish on social media (like Facebook)

   ◻ Personal media contributions can still be tied back to the project; the line between personal and professional persona is rapidly vanishing—don't mix
- The fourth rule applies to external control:
   ◻ *All* exchanges with the public must be handled by a dedicated communications or public relations group that reports to the framework team
   ◻ Never fester—when an issue comes up on the outside, resolve it now, when it is small: issues, contrary to wishful project management thinking, never go away; at most, they hibernate until they burst forth in a flurry of seeds of discontent
   ◻ In project matters, you may know best, but outside concerns don't care; humility is your guide; their care is your priority

Meetings

Meetings are an enduring legacy of the birth of the modern enterprise (sublimely studied by Ronald Coase, 1991 Nobel laureate in Economics[1]). Meetings can be summed up as a *bunch of people sitting around a table* (bopsaat), with dabblers dawdling away in serene unproductive contentment. Meetings can be potent communication mechanisms *when properly conducted*. The trick is to know how to conduct them:

- One-on-one meetings are best.
- Three people are next best. Then four, then more. Effectiveness decreases with increasing attendance.
- Always publish an agenda early enough for attendees to prepare.
- Upon the first instance of a meeting (recurring or not), set up a utility whereby the business card of every participant is scanned before the start of the meeting and e-mailed to every other participant automatically.
- Publish meeting minutes within 24 hours of ending the meeting.
- Publish decisions made during a meeting via the *project directive* mechanism discussed later. Do *not* rely on minutes as the formal issuance mechanism.
- When presenting slides, keep them clean and uncluttered, *and do not read off them.*[2]
- Batch all recurring weekly meetings on the same day. This way, people will be free to be productive the rest of the week.

Of course, in this day and age, no meeting is complete without someone joining remotely. Reliable software solutions abound to connect disparate offices efficiently. In the absence of alternatives, one must make due with conference calls. Once again, the *status quo* is often justified but rarely justifiable. If conference calls with out-of-office locations are to be the norm on a project (a project that will spend millions or billions of dollars), it behooves each party associated with the project to secure access to a genuine, realistic video conference facility. The benefits to the efficiency of the communication thus imparted are orders of magnitude greater than the cost of the access. Remember that 100% of a spoken message is interpreted through nonverbal body language perceived through visual cues.

Cultural Cluefulness

A corollary to the issue of remote participation deals with cultural diversities, which is code for *sensitivity*. Projects that rely on contributions from across the globe inevitably face the risk of miscommunication, misunderstanding, or worse—unintended social slights. People cultures are profoundly influential to behavior (notwithstanding the corporate cultures at play). When discussing matters in a networked meeting, each speaker should:

- Not assume that everyone understands the acronyms and idiosyncratic expressions specific to a project—distribute the WBS lexicon *before the meeting*;
- *Translate* the lexicon if two or more native languages are at play;
- Bring a translator if key participants are not fluent in the majority language for the meeting;
- Avoid figures of speech—for example, referring to "XXX" could be interpreted differently by some people beyond the Roman numeral 30, especially if doubt leads to a Google search;
- Speak slowly and clearly—this rule is golden in any venue, but is particularly pertinent to a multi-language setting; and
- Finally, if a speaker is possessed of a strong accent, speak slower still.

Speaking Abilities

Good communication begins and ends with the communicator. Imagine Clark Gable attempting to tell Vivian Leigh that he frankly, didn't give a damn—in Chakhar, a dialect spoken in Mongolia. The emotional charge of that scene would be altered, to say the least. The same effect goes for the more mundane case of team exchanges. A global project setting guarantees that teams will be assembled from a diverse cast of individuals with a variety of cultural backgrounds. Leads, managers, chiefs, directors, and the like will see a fair share of eminently qualified personnel whose skills in the dominant language of the project team will be underwhelming. Thick accents, grammatical delinquencies, and stunted vocabularies can plague the communication abilities of a person. This is not to disparage such individuals, but simply to acknowledge that some people can be difficult to understand. All that we can do is to commiserate with the person who struggles with the challenge, whose excellent technical skill sets may be doubted on account of language. From a performance standpoint, should such a person be nominated into a leadership role, whatever the hierarchy level? The answer is not about fairness but about project imperatives. Can the individual communicate effectively with people? If not, the project is ill-served by giving that person a chance to learn on the fly. Of course, all is degrees in this discussion. It becomes a judgment call by the PM. Such a person can still deliver valunomy from an expertise standpoint. But valunomy to the project cannot be sacrificed at the altar of fairness. Fairness begins with the individual. If the latter is not prepared to admit the shortcomings and take steps to remedy them, why should the project be expected to take on the risk?

FORMALIZING DECISIONS

We have already postulated a prohibition against the use of e-mails to publish formal decisions. If not e-mails or texts, what then? The method depends on the intent.

Formal Letters

A formal letter is the preferred medium for management or business relationship issues between project partners. Letters are also suited to commercial and legal matters between partners and external entities.

Memoranda

Memoranda are the equivalent of letters for internal matters communicated within a partner's organization or project team. They are the default medium for publishing decisions that were made during meetings (and noted in the meeting minutes) to the participants of that meeting.

Project Directives

Project directives are suitable for decisions arising out of the execution of the work by any functional discipline or partner's scope of work. The PMO, for example, would issue a directive to instruct an SPT to stop work on a specific task; issue a revision to a technical specification; authorize a vendor to deviate from a contractually-imposed standard; establish new document control mechanics, along with its attendant mechanisms; or publish a decision on an interface management issue. The reader should note that some organizations prefer to divide project directives by function. Engineering notifications, for example, would be published under an engineering change order. Vendor inspection frequencies could be issued under a procurement notice. Whether the mechanics chosen by the project dictates one form or many is up to the PMO's PM. The mechanics and template forms are then flowed throughout the project partners, for purposes of uniformity and traceability (which implies, among other things, the requirement to control the numbering system for the entire project, via the interface manager).

Change Orders

Change orders are utilized to communicate a decision that affects asset compliance or asset performance. The change order, like the project directive, may include cost and schedule impacts to the project. The main difference between the two is the nature of the decision. The default mechanics is the *project directive*. If the decision contains specific instructions on the execution of the change, the change order is preferred. Consider the example of a pressure vessel subjected to stringent welding requirements. If the decision involves the approval, by the owner, of a welding method that is prohibited by that owner's own welding specifications, a project directive would be issued (likely in the form of a formal letter to the vendor). If the allowed welding method is to be implemented in accordance with specific instructions provided by the owner, a change order would be issued (again, in the form of a formal letter).

Unacceptable Formats

Spreadsheets and database-generated reports are not acceptable means of publication. A project will generate a multitude of spreadsheets and tabular records to track, compile, define, and measure the stream of inputs and outputs. The risk register is one example of such a record. Any decision that arises out of the mitigation decision on a given task must be published via letter, memo, directive, or change order, as the case dictates. Inserting someone's name under the *action* column doesn't cut it.

Event Chronology

There will be times during a project when it is necessary to track down a sequence of events that led to the making of a particular decision. This can be a time-consuming endeavor often plagued by findings bereft of documentation. Sorting through the mass of e-mails, meeting minutes, and people's recollections can be daunting. The sequence of events leading up to a decision is essential when it comes to understanding the minutia of execution from which the *post-mortem* review is conducted. The master schedule is not suitable for this task. What is proposed instead is an *event catalog*—an example of which is presented in Appendix 8. The *event catalog* is constructed from the master schedule, with the activities from the schedule tagged by the shaded circles in the left pane of the page, under the *Plan* column. The shaded bars shown in the *Work* column would bear the name of the work breakdown element appearing in the schedule. Finally, the unplanned events, occurring in relation to the scheduled activities, appear in the *Event* column on the left pane. An event can be a published record (a project decision, change order), an impromptu meeting, an e-mail, or any other instance that triggers the publication of the record. The right pane captures succinctly the essence of an issue raised during an event, and links it to the published records on the issue raised. The event catalog is especially useful during construction, when field problems occur and get resolved on the spot, without necessarily flowing through the formal project management channels because of time constraints.

The example in Appendix 8 can be modified as needed. If the number of planned activities is high, it may be better to show only one discipline, rather than the several involved with the same issue. Each cataloged event is sorted by logical attribution (in the case of Appendix 8, it is done by the installation xx). Long timelines are captured by multiple pages that are simply appended when required. The actual decision records are not issued via the event catalog. The latter is only used to document the chronology of events. Finally, and in keeping with the database arguments posited in Chapter 17, the *event catalog* should ideally be implemented as a database.

INTERFACE MANAGEMENT

How to Converge Multi-Party Execution

If control is the first objective of project management, convergence of execution is the second. Convergence manifests the principle of managing at the interfaces, which was discussed in Chapter 4. The mechanics of convergence is called *interface management*, and is a *responsible function* that operates one step removed from the probate action illustrated in Figure 4.1. From this figure, we see that the probate party certifies the seamless junction between an output and its successor input. When both are correctly defined at the outset, they must mate identically. The responsible interface function enters the picture when, whatever the reason, the nature of the output, the input, or of both, cannot achieve the fitted match. The difference can be subtle, but never immaterial. A badly designed output meant to mate with the successor input belongs to the *probate party* to resolve. A perfectly designed output that cannot mate correctly to the successor input is an interface management issue. In the former case, the *impact* of the resolution does not spread beyond the paired processes shown in Figure 4.1; in the latter case, it does.

An Example

Consider the example of an industrial centrifuge equipped with a drain plug meant to be connected to a self-contained, gravity-fed tank that was remotely installed from the centrifuge. The output in this instance is a pipe that is connected to an intake port on the tank. The design of this output-input pair is approved by the probate party. Assume now that, in the course of the project, the tank could only be installed at a different location with a higher elevation than the centrifuge. The output-input pair cannot work, as it now requires a pump to overcome gravity. This change belongs to the interface manager to coordinate its resolution, which may affect other design centers as well (the foundation, for example, could require modifications). That is what is meant by the impact of change extending beyond the output-input pair.

Interactions with the PECO

All projects require interface management by virtue of their relationship with the PECO, mediated by the framework. Note, however, that interface management belongs to the *project* rather than the *framework*. The extents of the mandate will expand with additional contributions from engineering, procurement, construction, and SCPs.

Convergence Mechanics

The importance of interface management is such that a project will fail from interface management's deficiencies. Interface management premises that errors will happen and changes will be incurred. It has nothing to do with error prevention and change mitigation. Instead, its purpose is to control the impact of a convergence issue, in order to obviate surprises and unintended consequences. *Interface management shuns the blame game in favor of full disclosure.* Its framework is molded accordingly on the basis of six tactical ideas:

(1) capture, (2) resolution, (3) escalation, (4) management of change (MOC), (5) dissemination, and (6) transparency:

1. *Capture*—As the name indicates, capture seeks to flag an issue as soon as it comes to light, and document it in a controlled fashion. No issue is too small or too benign to be allowed to fly under the radar. *All* issues are therefore subject to *interface oversight*. They are so governed for reasons of state: the state of a nonconvergence must be understood in terms of its impact on the project. The capture process proceeds throughout the life of an instance until it is resolved and closed. It also encompasses the means of notification, the documentation generated, the trail of inputs and exchanges leading to the resolution, and the quantified impact to the project as a whole.

2. *Resolution*—This is the mechanic for addressing an interface issue. It is more process than paperwork, more people than procedures. The resolution stage ultimately leads to the decision made by the project team to deny, fix, alter, or expand the initial issue. The process is in fact a micro-scale project unto itself, which consumes time, labor, and possibly materiel to reach a satisfactory conclusion. Its output could include such deliverables as calculations, drawings, analyses, procurement paperwork, change orders, project directives, and project baseline adjustments.

3. *Escalation*—Interface issues are resolved on the principle of *proximity*: in other words, *those closest to the issue are the best to solve it*. Resolution mechanics are fundamentally a *bottom-up* methodology. Issues that crop up at the lead level should be resolved at that level, even when leads from different SPTs or SCPs are involved. When they cannot be solved from within, they must be elevated to the next level, according to the project's accountability matrix. At each step, the interface team acts as the responsible party for the process by coordinating and enabling the resolution mechanics until closure is achieved. Within the project, the escalation buck stops with the PMO manager, who must then validate the resolution with the framework lead. In a joint venture or corporate partnership scenario, the framework lead assumes the final say on all interface management issues.

4. *Management of change*—The MOC process will be familiar to the reader who is already experienced with the management of projects. It is the same in TPM and PPA. Once an interface issue is satisfactorily resolved, its solution must be implemented and its cost/schedule impact assigned against the project's baseline allocations. At a minimum, the solution implementation will be authorized via a *project directive* or

a *change order*, as discussed earlier in the chapter. Significant changes affecting the contract or the scope of the project would be handled via formal letters issued by the PMO. *At no time should the authorization be communicated via e-mail, voice mail, or social media.*

5. *Dissemination*—This process occurs once the MOC process yielded an authorization to implement a solution. The dissemination process aims at keeping *all project partners apprised of the decision rendered on a specific interface issue,* regardless of any partner's distance from it. It bears repeating that interface management is not a witch hunt to burn a partner at the bad design stake. The blame game, when required, must be pursued by the PMO on the basis of confidentiality and respect for the presumed guilty party (lest circumstances lead to bad blood and pervasive distrust). The dissemination process must limit itself to documentation that focuses on the nature of the decision taken. It can, however, reveal valuable lessons about the origins of the issue, which become part of the project's *lessons learned.*

6. *Transparency*—Transparency exists in tandem with dissemination. All project partners should have full awareness, in real time, of all interface issues from capture to dissemination. At the outset, an issue unsuspected of certain ramifications may be deemed applicable to a partner who was not initially involved with its discovery. In this fashion, any number of partners may choose to participate in the resolution after notifying the interface manager. Reviewing all interface issues upon capture is therefore a mandatory requirement that is imposed on all SPT partners (SCP partners are excluded from this obligation). Finally, transparency cannot function without rigid controls. Access cannot be a free-for-all for readers and writers. Wider transparency dictates tighter central control. The interface management software is the operating system of the entire operation. To work, one needs protocols, mechanics, and mechanisms to achieve uniformity of usage and consistency of execution. These must be defined by the PMO in a project-wide interface management plan.

Software

Transparency implies real-time access, which, in turn, implies software. A key element of a performing interface management framework is the deployment of a web-based document management system, operated by the interface management team. Passive folder drives, spreadsheets, and collaboration software *do not meet this requirement.* Interface management must run on the back of powerful document management systems that are essential to managing metadata and metafiles; advanced searches; version control; distribution control; and limitless data transmissions.

Accountability

We have already stated that the interface manager is the responsible party in this realm. We now define who is accountable and who probates an interface issue. The interface issue materializes at the output-input junction. By default, the probate individual (within the context of Figure 5.1) is in closest proximity to the issue. In terms of interface management, that individual is *accountable* for its resolution. The probate function of the resolution flows to the direct supervisor of that individual. It is perfectly admissible on the other hand to de-rate hierarchically these two assignments. That is, the probate individual retains the probate role for the interface issue, leaving the individuals respectively accountable for the output and the input in those same roles from an *interface* perspective. In this scenario, one must assume that the interface issue is resolved between the three individuals, and that the issue *does not propagate beyond the junction*. The escalation of an issue follows a fractal pattern. That is, the individual probating the junction becomes accountable for the resolution of the issue, under the probate authority of the next hierarchical lead (lead to group lead, group lead to director lead):

- *Resolution ownership*—We discover herein a review process that goes beyond interface issues, one that is intimately related to dabbling concerns and squad checks. The accountability for an output, be it a deliverable or an interface issue, includes the accountability for the review process for that output. This *owner* is given the freedom to call up pertinent subject matter experts (SMEs) to collect professional assessments and viewpoints. These *reviewers* participate in accord with the expressed needs of the *owner* and cannot veto his final decision. Once the decision is published, it is made available to the group of reviewers and to a second group called the *readers*. Readers come into play as passive observers of the *fait accompli*. They are given the opportunity to consult the published information for their own benefits, but have no recourse to critique or reject the published information. Readers, from an interface standpoint, are solicited at the outset when an issue is raised and included in the closure process once dissemination has occurred.
- *Resolution closure*—The dissemination of a resolved interface issue implies completion. We now state the requirement explicitly: when disseminating the resolution of an issue, the interface manager must declare the matter closed. If more work is needed to complete the resolution, he can still disseminate the solution with the caveat that it is provisional. It is up

to him to elaborate a strategy to follow up on all the loose ends associated with an issue. An issue is explicitly unfinished until closure has been declared. It goes without saying that a project cannot be completed with interface issues still outstanding.

CHANGE MANAGEMENT

Prime Directive

Dealing with changes is the third vector of a PM's willful obsession. The M&M of change management are an intrinsic feature of all project organizations. What they are, in detail, is their business. Our interest with the topic is summed up as follows:

Whatever your change management process is, enforce it unconditionally.

Change Life Cycle

The details of the mechanics should follow a logical sequence. First, receive the change request. Then, analyze it, figure out its merits, and assess its impact to the project's allocations. Finally, either approve or reject it. If the change is justified (pursuant to the discussion of Chapter 6), the PM should sign off without delay. Under no circumstance should you agree to implement the change ahead of approval. You will save neither time nor money and could possibly raise your risk potential. The emphasis warrants repeating: no time can be meaningfully saved by saving execution time. Whatever the change request, don't dally, don't waste time, don't dabble: get on with the consideration and decide one way or another, but decide! If the urgency of the situation does not suffice to stir you out of your management stupor, the urgency is obviously not so urgent after all. Decide, then move on. The only outcome that you get out of delaying a decision are more costs, more risks, and missed deadlines.

RISK TRACKING

The Register

Most organizations possess a policy on project *risk management*. Most will require the regular compilation of a *risk register*. Some will mandate conducting quantified risk analyses to derive the statistical probability of meeting budgets and schedules. In most cases, the emphasis is on *tracking* and periodic reviews. In TPM circles, a risk is usually defined in terms of an unplanned event that may occasion either a positive or negative impact on the project.[3] In the trenches of project execution, a risk is never positive. Positive risks are called opportunities. To paraphrase Churchill, a risk is a threat inside an uncertainty wrapped in a danger.

Often, risk management is carried out for the sake of going through the motions. Much like its motion-brethren (such as monthly senior management reviews, yearly personnel performance evaluations, postmortem change approvals, and after-the-fact schedule rebaselining), risk management is regarded as a task that must be checked off a checklist to create the illusion of active oversight. In reality, it fosters the misleading impression of control, whereas none actually occurs.

Ingredients

Management, in a big picture PPA sense, was discussed in Chapter 3. Down into the weeds of daily execution, management is first and foremost *anticipatory* in nature. This nature is the quintessential imperative of genuine risk management. As long as the execution work unfolds according to plan, the PM really has little to do other than cruise along at a leisurely pace. The PM earns her keep in the act of *anticipating* potential problems before they erupt into wrecking balls. It is the same exact story with managing risks. *Risk, like quality, is an emergent feature of the work.* Projects must be managed by their risks. Compiling a risk register and reviewing every month isn't risk management; it's postmortem journalism.

To manage a project against a risk is to engineer the pertinent element of the execution strategy to account for the risk from the outset. We have already explored what this means in Chapter 8, through the concepts of intrinsic, gambler, and resilience risks. Imagine now that a project is in full swing and is confronted with staff shortages prone to wage inflation. The risk is threefold: (1) poaching of team personnel by outside competitors; (2) unavailability of certain skill sets in sufficient numbers; and (3) upward pressures on hourly rates leading to high turnover rates. This triple-face risk must be proactively managed before people are hired.

The PM could consider any number of tactics to counter each aspect of the risk, such as:

- Implementing a potent reward program to help retention (quarterly bonuses, for example, or signing bonuses)—whatever the costs, they are likely to be lower than the expense associated with ongoing recruitment and inflationary salary pressures;
- Offering to award loyal personnel with wider horizontal opportunities and training;

- Negotiating sleeper subcontract agreements with competitors as backup teams;
- Pursuing a recruitment strategy outside of the box, as advocated in Chapter 13; or
- Establishing a generous quarterly rate increase policy across the board.

Obviously, all of those options would add costs to the project; but consider, however, that doing nothing will cost *more*. In this case, spending money on the people you already have is a more valunomic investment than merely paying up more to grab whatever talent can be reeled in. Whatever the tactics selected, what matters next is to implement them now, rather than wait for the risk to materialize.

Which risks should be tracked? A risk register will be useful when it serves to anticipate an issue from which proactive management occurs. To be necessary, the risk register must not be a free-for-all record of anything that threatens the project. It must record only those risks that are risks. If you, the reader, are sitting in an office with a large window behind you, you are exposed to the remote risk of getting killed by a meteorite crashing through that window. The odds are admittedly less than slim, but they are not zero. Should you take measures to counter such an eventuality? The answer is, of course, no. This risk does not belong on the risk register.

Tracked Risks

The example is facetious, but the underlying message is not. What risks warrant tracking? Remember that *to track* implies *to proactively manage* (as in monitor, quantify, counter). Force majeure, acts of Gods, random politics, and natural disasters are all potentially destructive to a project, but cannot be managed proactively. We categorize *tracked risks* as follows:

- A risk warrants tracking when it will manifest itself as a result of a predictable set of circumstances. This first criterion excludes force majeure, acts of gods, natural disasters, conflicts and wars, wholly random events, and political upheavals—to name but a few. If a team member is befallen by severe sickness, a long absence may be anticipated, and thus mitigated by appropriate plans. If a region is tending toward labor shortages, the financial risk associated with it can be mitigated with alternate recruitment tactics.
- A risk warrants tracking if, upon occurrence of it, there can be applied an equal but opposite deterrence. For example, if the project is in a region prone to forest fires, devise countermeasures before the fire erupts. On the other hand, if the project is in an area exposed to severe tsunamis that are too strong to be contained by levies and walls, the risk

is uncontainable and is therefore not tracked (which begs the question: why build there in the first place?).

- A risk that does not satisfy either is best managed within the project or company's emergency preparedness strategy.

Risk Ranking

The risk register is compiled from opinions. That is why it is called *qualitative* risk management. It will serve the anticipatory mandate when its assessment is quantified. Quantified outcomes drive the *contingency* and *reserve* budgets (discussed in Chapter 8). The mechanics of quantification generate the ranking of risks based on the product of a risk's likelihood of occurrence (probability) and its impact to the project (consequence), each one based on a five-degree scale shown in Table 15.1.

There can be 25 rankings for a given risk, as shown in Table 15.2. These 25 rankings are, in turn, grouped into four risk levels: Level 1 (ranking < than 4); Level 2 (3 < ranking < 7); Level 3 (6 < ranking < 13), and Level 4 (ranking >12).

The four risk levels will be defined in terms of mitigation control:

- Level 1: No action required to enhance controls over the risk.
- Level 2: PMO manager must be notified. A mitigation action must be implemented.

Table 15.1 Risk scaling table

Degree	Probability	Consequence
1	Near certainty	Insignificant
2	Likely	Minor
3	Possible	Moderate
4	Unlikely	Major
5	Rare	Catastrophic

Table 15.2 Risk ranking matrix

		Consequence				
		1	2	3	4	5
	1	1	2	3	4	5
	2	2	4	6	8	10
Probability	3	3	6	9	12	15
	4	4	8	12	16	20
	5	5	10	15	20	25

- Level 3: Framework lead must be notified. A detailed risk mitigation plan must be implemented that includes (a) estimated cost and impact of risk; (b) estimated cost and impact of mitigation; (c) estimated cost and impact benefit of mitigation.
- Level 4: Owner must be notified. Immediate action is required. A detailed risk mitigation plan must be implemented that includes (a) estimated cost and impact of risk; (b) estimated cost and impact of mitigation; (c) estimated cost and impact benefit of mitigation.

The last step is to associate the risk levels to the schedule, cost, and asset performance impacts. The mechanism is the same in all three cases:

- Select the limit corresponding to the highest degree:
    - The schedule limit should be the contingency (longest acceptable time overrun measured from target).
    - The cost limit should be the *risk budget.*
    - The performance limit should be the difference between the nameplate target and the lowest acceptable nameplate minimum.
    - Each of these limits is termed the *time, cost, and performance basis,* respectively.
- Create a table of scaling factors matching the degrees. These factors are based on the rate of increase of impact between successive degrees. The rate can be any number, but two is suggested. The scaling factor is given by Equation 15.1:

$$Factor = \frac{100\%}{Rate^{(5-degree)}}$$

15.1

The corresponding scaling factor matrix is shown in Table 15.3.

From the scaling factors, calculate the impact, by degree, for the cost, schedule, and performance. For example, assume that the cost basis is $1M, the time basis is 10 weeks, the performance basis is 700 kg/s (a flow rate), with a degree rate of 2. The results are shown in Table 15.4.

Finally, assess the driving risk. For each one (cost, time, performance), calculate the *severity* and choose the highest value as driving risk. For example, assume that the probability of occurrence of the risk degree 3; that the cost impact of the risk would be $100,000; that the time impact would be 3 weeks; and that the performance impact would be 425 kg/s. From Table 15.4, we extract the following consequence degrees:

- For cost: $100,000 is between $60,000 (degree 1) and $130,000 (degree 2). Degree = 2.
- For time: 3 weeks is between 2.5 (degree 3) and 5 (degree 4). Degree = 4.

Table 15.3 Scaling factors

Scaling factors (%)			
Degree	Rate		
	2	3	4
1	6	1	0
2	13	4	2
3	25	11	6
4	50	33	25
5	100	100	100

Table 15.4 Sample calculations of risk impact

Degree	Factor	Basis		
		Cost (× $M)	Time (wks)	Performance (kg/s)
	2	1	10	700
1	6	0.06	0.63	43.75
2	13	0.13	1.25	87.50
3	25	0.25	2.50	175.00
4	50	0.50	5.00	350.00
5	100	1.00	10.00	700.00

- For performance: 425 kg/s is between 350 (degree 4) and 700 (degree 5). Degree = 5.

therefore:

- Cost severity = 3 (probability) × 2 (consequence) = 6: Level 2 from Table 15.2.
- Time severity = 3 × 4 (consequence) = 8: Level 3 from Table 15.2.
- Performance severity = 3 × 5 (consequence) = 15: Level 4 from Table 15.2.
- The performance risk is the greatest of the three. It governs.

The logic of selecting the cost, time, and performance bases follows from the following considerations:

- A risk that threatens to consume the entirety of the project's *risk budget* is deemed catastrophic (degree 5), and therefore assigned a scaling factor of 1.0
- The scaling factor for degree 4 is 1/rate
- The scaling factor for degree 3 is (1/rate)/rate, or $1/\text{rate}^2$
- The scaling factor for degree 2 is $1/\text{rate}^3$
- The scaling factor for degree 1 is $1/\text{rate}^4$

The scaling can differ from 5 and be just as well based on 4 or 8. A more conservative approach could just as easily assign the catastrophic categorization to a risk valued at, say, 60% of the *risk budget* and likewise for a more liberal approach, pegging it at 140% of the *risk budget*, for instance. The choice belongs to the PMO manager and framework leader.

RISK ANALYSIS

From Qualitative to Quantitative

The risk register is well suited to capturing the exogenous risks that prey upon the project. But risks arising from the execution proper (the emergent risks) are more difficult to discern. These endogenous risks may coalesce into vectors of cost and schedule overruns. Complexity springs to life once again. In this instance, the better mechanic is statistical analysis. The technique allays a multitude of variables and their variations into a probability distribution for the likelihood of achieving a target. The results help the project management team maximize the likelihood of achieving the project's allocation targets within a minimum confidence level (typically, 85% or more). There exist a number of commercial software applications for this purpose, relying principally on the mathematical model known as *Monte Carlo*. The model is created from a set of input variables (such as a target date or a work package budget) that are numerically quantified over a range (minimum, target, maximum). The technique performs a large number of simulations across the total number of possible scenarios represented from the variations of each variable (in this case, the number of simulations is a function of the number of variables to the cubic power). The results form a probability distribution for achieving all targets, typically ranging from 5 to 95% in confidence levels.

Confidence Levels

Monte Carlo results are statistical in nature. For example, a project can be shown to be on track to be completed on schedule with a 90% confidence level. That is, there is a 90% probability of hitting the completion milestone. The individual impact of interdependent tasks is automatically generated. The results thus enable the project management team to plan and implement remedial actions where required. Note that the 100% confidence level is unrealistic (mathematically, an asymptotic function implying infinite resources). Practically, the PM should target a level that is actually manageable (in the anticipatory sense); common practice pegs it between 80 and 90%. This is the target confidence level, which is expressed as a *P-value*:

- P10 represents a 10% probability of success. It is normally associated with the ideal case where all variables align in perfect synchronicity. It is the most optimistic case, and also the least likely to materialize. *It implies a 90% probability of failure.*
- P50 represents a 50% probability of success. It is a more realistic interpretation of the likelihood of success with built-in variability across several variables.
- P85 represents an 85% probability of success. It is a more conservative scenario in which materially significant variations in several variables are allowed to occur.

Managing to a P-Level

Evidently, higher P-values imply greater probabilities of success. But higher P-values also imply larger resources and longer execution timelines. The relationship between *allocation* and P-levels is exponential rather than linear. To wit, the 15-point difference between P80 and P95 could require a 100% increase in cost and time. The choice of a P-level is one that is made at the start of a life-cycle phase and prescribed in the *phase execution plan*. The risk analyst peruses the results to identify the significant risk drivers that are materially significant to the target P-level. The PM and risk analyst assess the impact of each risk driver and elaborate possible scenarios to avoid, transfer, mitigate, or absorb it. The exercise is meant to *anticipate* the effects of the risk if nothing is done to corral it.

Analytical Imperative

Any time circumstances change materially, the project should be analyzed statistically. The analysis should also take place periodically, preferably ahead of major milestones. At the very least, an analysis should occur ahead of the planned 30, 60, and 90% completion milestones of each phase. The timing is critical: the results of an analysis must be available with sufficient time ahead of a milestone to enable the implementation of a meaningful risk mitigation plan. Once again, merely going through the motions without any ability to act upon the results is a waste of project time and money.

Go for Schedules, No for Costs

Edward Merrow has remarked that schedule analyses yield highly useful results to the project management team. This is a consequence of the mathematical linearity of schedules (embedded in the series Equation 16.1 in the next chapter). The variation to a given schedule element propagates linearly across the *schedule* network) but rarely lead to exponential or chaotic behavior. The same cannot be said about costs. A single schedule change may reverberate over time across a multitude of cost changes. The propagation of those cost changes is nonlinear, owing to inherent mathematical couplings. For this reason, the Monte Carlo analysis of project cost does not correlate with improved cost control. In *Industrial Megaprojects*, Merrow goes so far as to declare that cost simulations using the Monte Carlo technique are not only worthless, but detrimental to a project. Notwithstanding that statement, organizations still cling to going through the Monte Carlo motions in the belief that any mathematical analysis is better than none. Monte Carlo results are, after all, graphically impressive and prone to create the illusion of proactive control. The illusion is fostered by the sense of *plausibility* of the results, which creates a comfort zone around the uncertainty. What is mathematically derived is often accepted unconditionally. Therein lies the fallacy. Mathematically, the Monte Carlo technique assumes that variations of a given control element occur independently of other elements. Merrow remarks correctly that this assumption is overwhelmingly debunked in real-world projects. Whatever can go wrong, will go wrong—in groups, not individually—leading to a cascade of problems propagating throughout the project's activities. Whereas some proselytizers of the Monte Carlo technique will lay claim to their capability to model these interdependencies, the reality in the trenches of project management shows that this belief is pure fantasy.

Therefore, a project will be better served by not performing Monte Carlo analyses on costs and budgets.

Postmortem Reviews

The transition between successive life-cycle phases presents a different set of risks that must be assessed. The preferred method in this instance is the *benchmarking session*, which will generate the data required by the *close-out group* of documentation (described in Chapter 18). The benchmarking session should be structured in five parts, each requiring prior investigation by the project team:[4]

- Part 1. Benchmark metrics—These metrics encompass the entirety of the quantities, performances, ratios, productivity rates, quality rates, and other measures derived from the execution of the work. Drawing counts, equipment counts, man-hours per system, and man-hours per the WBS element are examples (associated with the *attributes, characteristics, targets,* and *metrics*).
- Part 2. Root-cause analysis: success—Identify the elements of the execution strategy that were especially successful and determine the root

causes of their success. Extend the scope of the consideration to the principal SPT and SCP involved. Tie these success stories back to the specific sections of the execution strategy documentation to carry forward to the next phase.

- Part 3. Root-cause analysis: failure—Same as Part 2, but for those elements that were deemed deficient or failed.
- Part 4. Go-forward constraints—Identify which elements of the scope of work are not ready for transmission as inputs to the next phase. Identify the remediation plan to complete them.
- Part 5. Lessons review—Go over the lessons learned in the course of the execution, in accordance with the mechanics presented in Chapter 17. Identify which lessons have been correspondingly implemented and published, and which ones are pending. Develop a plan for the completion of the process for the latter.

Antifragile

We conclude the topic of risk management by opening a vista into an execution schema that skips risk tracking altogether (lest it leads to the illusion of proactive control). The act of *anticipation* eliminates the element of surprise carried by a latent risk, leaving the alert PM in a stronger position to devise a mitigating strategy before the risk strikes. The risk register will be an essential tool of project management as long as it is used in an anticipatory manner and it leads to immediate remedial actions or plans. However, there will always be unpredictable events that come out of nowhere to threaten the execution of the work. It is neither desirable nor possible to anticipate all risk potentials, especially from the *black swan category.* This fact of statistical life must be emphasized again. Black swan events are random and therefore intractable. They are nonmeasurable and nonpredictable, which implies that they will continue to be so, regardless of the number of Ph.D.s you can throw at them.[5]

The question naturally arises as to what can be done to manage risks if they cannot be anticipated. Taleb answers this question convincingly with one word: *antifragility.* The reader is encouraged to consult Taleb's *Antifragile* to delve into the subtleties of the thesis. Taleb defines antifragility as the ability of a system to strengthen when acted upon by stressors. *Antifragility* thus stands in as antonym to *fragility,* which is degraded or weakened by stressors. That which is *resilient* remains permanently unaffected by stressors. A wine glass, for example, is fragile to a physical load. A steel rod is resilient, within its elastic domain. A bicep muscle is *antifragile*: it will strengthen, over time, when subjected to increasingly higher loads. Consequently, a project that is endowed with an *antifragile* quality will be able to respond to the randomness of risk potentials. The project management team, when engineered in accordance with Chapters 13 and 14, will be antifragile. An execution strategy elaborated on the principles of Chapters 10, 11, and 12 is inherently antifragile. A master schedule constructed on the basis of facts and embedded variability, as discussed in this chapter, will be antifragile in the face of unforeseen slippages, delivery delays, and regulatory failures. You can test the fragility of your project with a simple thought experiment: if your high-performance PM becomes unavailable for an extended period of time (a severe ailment, for example), what will be the ramifications on the project as a whole?

CONTRACTS

The Illusion of Control

The exacting, invariant nature of a contract makes it a double-edged sword to a project's execution. Their minutia creates a precise and uniform framework within which expectations are clear. The same minutia freezes the relationship between the parties in a way that can be inflexible. Contracts carry a salient risk when they turn out to be ill-suited to the *nature of the work to be performed.* The legalistic rigidity of contracts fosters the illusion of certainty, and of control, sometimes at the expense of the future performance of an asset.

The risks to a project start with the mechanics surrounding the preparation and award of a contract. Why go through a bidding process as a prerequisite for contract award? After all, the most efficient way to go about this business is to go sole-source. Owners with plenty of vendor histories will already know whom they will like, prefer, doubt, and shun. Nevertheless, most owners opt instead to go through the tedious, onerous, and labor-intensive motions of competitive bidding. In North America, the Sarbane-Oxley Act passed by the U.S. Congress in 2002 is the ominous force behind this motivation.[6] Competitive bids create an impression of procedural righteousness and offers legalistic cover to business managers who choose losers and winners.

Traditional Bidding Process

Going through these motions is the *modus operandi* of the contract award mechanics in general. Bid packages and *invitations to tender* (ITT) will tally hundreds of pages as protection against tort liability. Mountainous piles of documents are compounded by equally numerous evaluation criteria that spread like a plague of locusts over the fertile competitive land. Bidders will respond in kind, through a deluge of proposal documentation that can overwhelm the mental wherewithal of the bid evaluation team. One example drawn from the author's experience is telling. The owner's bid package included nearly a hundred documents ranging from technical standards to management procedures, control templates, scope definitions, and general policies and procedures. All told, the bid package contained more than 3,300 pages. The winner (an international consortium) had submitted a proposal comprising nearly 1,800 pages of plans, execution strategies, sample drawings, reporting procedures, proposed IT infrastructure and corporate policies on everything from safety, to human resources, to overtime, to office stationaries control. The bid preparation alone required almost a year of work; and the bidding process, another year.

From the start, the ITT required the vendor to engineer a complete project execution and mobilization framework ready to go on the first day after award. The winner duly obliged, on day two. Two weeks after the project award, the inadequacy of those preemptive plans surfaced. Three months later, the invoicing process among the consortium partners was still being worked out. One month after that, the division of the scope of work among them was grudgingly acknowledged as flawed. Twelve months or so later, the owner pulled the plug and awarded the work to a new firm. In hindsight, that outcome was foreseeable. None of the framework planning activities explored in Chapter 9 had taken place. The bidding strategy embraced by the owner was, in the end, so far off the mark as to not even be wrong.

Hard Lessons

The example is representative of common practice in the project world. From it, we are nevertheless able to extract several key insights:

- *Proposals are always created in a vacuum*—Unless the owner has figured out in detail the execution strategy (released via the BAEF), the bidders can only guess at how the work will be executed. Their proposals will be a measure of their understanding of the scope of work and the owner's putative expectations. Owners who fall into the trap of requesting execution plans from those bidders during the proposal stage are creating an illusion of control that is nonexistent. And the trap is twice burrowed: such plans can only come to fruition when developed jointly with the owner.
- *Boiler plate contracts and proposals are rampant*—Whether a proposal contains a hundred pages or a thousand, the contents of those pages will come overwhelmingly from boiler plate text imported by cut-and-paste lifted from previous bids. When a bid package creates the expectation of acres of felled trees to build up paper volumes, the bidders

will be instinctively verbose with their contents which inevitably lead to filler fluff.

- *Mental midgets*—People are incapable of holding a mental picture of a bid package containing hundreds of pages, let alone a thousand. Consequently, neither the owner nor the bidder can realistically aspire to grasp in its entirety the true merits of a bidder's proposal. For the owner, this difficulty is magnified manifold by the number of bid proposals received.
- *Slick book covers*—Proposals are akin to job interviews and likewise detached from the nature of the position. Some people are sublimely competent in interviews but utterly useless in their jobs. The same goes for proposals. Some companies have mastered the art of the proposal— Olympic biddings are marquee illustrations—others, less so (without implying that they cannot do the job). The true art of the bid evaluation process lies in being able to go beyond the book cover to uncover what is substantively pertinent to the project.
- *Bid equalization is fiction*—Competitive bids are typically assessed on a comparative basis with others through the so-called mechanism of bid spreads (a.k.a. bid equalization). Genuine equalization is only possible when the work description is conceptually bounded. Take the example of a custom house. It is *impossible* to assess even one proposal from a single architect if the work description is limited to building specifications, space allocations, number of levels, surface finish prescriptions, and the like. It is possible if you first develop the outline, footprint, and floor plans (i.e., drawings). The same logic applies to equipment and plant projects as well. For an installation or a single piece of equipment, this means functional schematics. For an entire plant, you need at least the functional schematics and a preliminary overall layout. Asking bidders to quote on such work on the sole basis of specifications and standards is an exercise in futility.

PPA BID MECHANICS

What Bidding Should Look Like

The last point is the perfect segue to our next question: what *are* powerful bid mechanics? We will infer the answer from an instructive sports analogy. Every year in June, the National Hockey League (a.k.a. the NHL) holds its draft of junior players (drawn from across the globe). From a management standpoint, the draft is a pure incarnation of an efficient competitive bid process:

- Invited players have already been vetted and prequalified. Proofs of skills and experience are not solicited.

- Inversely, no player from another sport, regardless of his athletic magnificence, will be considered.
- Performance trumps contract price. No player gets chosen on the basis of being cheaper than a superior alternative. Skills, attitude, learning abilities, and potential contribution to a team are what matter.
- The risk to a team owner lies elsewhere than with proficiency. Can the player make the transition to the big league (i.e., can he succeed with this new scope of work)? Can the player fit in with the organization and the media glare that comes with it (i.e., can he handle the PECO)? Can he manage the sudden wealth showered upon him (i.e., can he control costs and schedule)? And can the player handle the coaching requirements and expectations (i.e., can he manage changes)? Here, the idea of acceptance maturity rating percolates to the surface.

The Four Stages

The mechanics are broken into a four-stage sequential process: Stage 1 (prequalifications), Stage 2 (specifications), Stage 3 (selection), and Stage 4 (award):

The four-stage procurement mechanics are the sole method for meaningfully equalize bids:

- Stage 1 identifies which organizations (internal or external) are qualified in terms of skills, expertise, experience, project mechanics, and mechanisms to execute the anticipated work in full compliance with the owner's SOE. Stage 1 occurs *before* any contract work is considered.
- Stage 2 defines the conceptual baseline which will set the bounds of the work to be quoted by bidders. This baseline would include things like drawing schematics, equipment outlines, allowable footprints, physical restrictions, and all pertinent engineering/regulatory specifications (governing codes, owner standards, equipment datasheets, performance calculations).
- Stage 3 invites prequalified bidders (pursuant to Stage 1) to submit their proposals for a detail designed and/or fabrication of the equipment so specified in Stage 2. Stage 3 also includes the *comparative equalization of the proposals* from which the bid issuer determines which bidder offers the highest probability of fulfilling the supposed contract in a manner that helps the realization of the PPA.
- Stage 4 awards the contract, finalizes the terms and conditions, and authorizes the winning bidder to commence the work in accordance with the execution strategy designed by the framework team.

Stage 1

Stage 1 is divided into two parts. Part 1 quantifies what a vendor can and cannot do, along with his experience with previous pertinent works. Technical audits may be performed to validate an aspiring vendor's statement and ultimately award the vendor an acceptance maturity rating in accordance with Chapter 6. The discovery process extends to staff qualifications, personnel retention strategies, legal concerns, financial strength, and levels of PECO exposure, to name but a few. Part 2 assesses the responsiveness of a vendor to execute a contract within the strictures of the owner's mechanics, mechanisms, SOE, management plans, and metric expectations. Such requirements could include quality management; health, safety, social, and environmental (HSSE) policy and management; engineering data management; document control systems; change management; and project reporting—to name but a few. Vendors must be willing to commit themselves to abide by these requirements when a contract is awarded. The details of that contract will only appear at the end of Stage 3 or the start of Stage 4, leading to immense simplifications in the bidders' proposals.

Stage 2

In Stage 2, we create the minimum set of work scope and definition from which a bidder can accurately quantify the corresponding costs and timelines to realize the intended object of the contract. This definition work is ideally suited to a contractor who possesses the knowhow—thus, Stage 2 is itself open to be contracted out. In our custom house example, one architect could be hired to develop the preliminary plans.

Stage 3

Here is the bid process proper. The bid package is developed by the owner from the conceptual baseline of Stage 2. It is issued only to the vendors selected in Stage 1, and excludes *all* information requirements already defined and obtained in Stage 1. The bid package must be limited to what is to be done by the vendor and over what time frame in order to produce the contract deliverables specified by the owner. A bid package requirement (or question) is valid when it meets at least one of these characteristics:

- Confirmation questions to obtain from the vendor a statement of compliance as to the prequalifying terms and conditions; statements of understanding of the scope described; and statements of acknowledgment of the various SOE elements to be implemented by the owner to govern the execution of the work under the contract.

- Content questions to obtain from the vendor information on his proposed team, key personnel, resources, project-specific capabilities, requirement-specific software applications, and subcontractor strategies to be adopted as part of the contract execution strategy.
- Capability questions specific to the bidder's ability to undertake the work upon contract award, evidenced by pertinent financial proofs and labor availability.
- Allocation questions regarding pricing, scheduling, and cost structures.

Alternatively, a more daring approach by the owner would be to employ an open-ended approach to the bid questions, based on two—and only two—requests:

- Explain your proposed strategy to execute the scope of work in accordance with the terms and conditions of the contract; and
- List the cost and schedule targets associated with your strategy.

Such an approach places a much higher burden on the bid evaluation team. In return, the pith and substance of each proposal can be rapidly gauged in terms of scope understanding, substance versus fluff, and the inherent capacity of the bidder to orchestrate a project execution strategy. Ultimately, the outcome of Stage 3 is the recommendation for award. The recommendation will have avoided the nine deadly sins that will be discussed in the next chapter so that whoever wins the job offers the best prospects of success to the project.

Stage 3 serves to select the winning contractor. It is not to negotiate the contract terms.

Stage 4

This last stage initiates the work. It is driven by three objectives: nominate the winning bidder, negotiate the contract, and initiate the work. Note that the initial activities of the work will focus on the *defining the execution* strategy—jointly by the PMO and the vendor's PM team. Mobilization and implementation follow in accordance with Chapter 11.

TIGHT BIBS

At this point, we turn our attention to the day-to-day issues that affect a project over which the PM and his team hold great sway.

The Irritants

PMs earn their medium-high bucks for their ability to execute in the big-picture realm. They also make their mark at an entirely different level, in the mundane world of petty annoyances. Every team and every organization is prone to little irritants that don't stop the work, but sap the goodwill of the people. Things like mosquito bites; a thermostat set too high or too low; a missing procedure for transmitting documents between third parties; a cantankerous reception-ist; or parking shortages. Stuff that bugs people won't necessarily make them quit, but they won't stop complaining about them either. It's hard to complete a marathon with a pebble in one shoe. The effective PM can have an immediate impact on the team by fixing these bugs, eliminating the irritants, and settling the unsettled. At most, these actions require a few hours to consider, several minutes to decide, and seconds to roll out. Kill the mosquitos! Loosen the tight bibs! Make your immediate world a better place! These little things may be beneath a PM's pay scale. But they are opportunities for the leader to do some-thing immediately tangible for the team, without fanfare or commotion, which will yield good will, trust, and loyalty in the long run—and cost nothing to the budget, in relative terms.

Managing Changes by Anticipation

Let us return to the idea of management by anticipation. The PM will exert great influence over the success of the project by taking care of the small trem-ors shaking the orderly conduct of the *planned* work. *Planned* is the key word here. As long as the work of the team unfolds according to the baseline execu-tion strategy, the PM is effectively cruising along at a leisurely pace (not quite kicking sand up at the beach, but close). As soon as a change to the baseline is contemplated, the PM must kick into anticipatory high gear:

1. *Assess* the merit of the potential change. If specious, squash it immedi-ately; if meritorious, move to *consider*.
2. *Consider* the impact. Evaluate at a high level what the ramifications of the change will be in terms of costs, schedule delays, performance vari-ations, and potential reasons for approving the change. Then, *advise* the client.
3. *Advise* the client. This is a heads-up notice that the PM offers the client. The intent is to give the client an opportunity to ascertain the merits of the change before engaging the full change notification process. At this time, the client either kills the proposal or requests a formal *change notice* from the PM.

4. *Change notice*. The PM prepares the detailed change notice in accordance with the requirements of the contract and highlights the time constraints that must be understood by the client to complete the approval process. The change notice is formally transmitted to the client for *approval*.
5. *Client approval*. As the name implies, this is the interim period during which the client either approves or rejects the change notice. If rejected, the deal is closed. If approved, the *baseline update* is undertaken.
6. *Baseline update*. The PM updates the execution strategy commensurate with the impact of the change notice. The new baseline is released to the client for *approval*.
7. *Baseline approval*. The client either rejects or approves the revised baseline. Rejection triggers a back-and-forth exchange with the PM until consensus is achieved. Once approved, the PM publishes the new baseline and directs the team to execute the work subtending the change notice.

Protecting the Owner

The PM is required to protect the client against himself. Oftentimes, what the client wants and what is needed are not the same. It behooves the PM to engage the client diplomatically to change the discussion from *want* to *need*, and then offer a path forward to meet that need. The PM is, in effect, protecting the project against the whims of a client who may not possess all the information necessary to support the request. The client will always be the final arbiter of any decision. It is the duty of the PM toward the client to protect the integrity of the PPA within the bounds of his professional judgment. If overruled, so be it, but at least it's with a clear conscience.

Grenades

The last mundane point is the personal conflict. Given enough time and enough people, conflicts will inevitably flare up. Professional judgments may disagree, egos may clash, personalities may not mesh, or cultural idioms taint perceptions. Whatever the case, these conflicts must be resolved as soon as they are noticed. Letting them fester in the hope that the problem will eventually go away never works in any way. Festering leads to intensification, or propagation, or both. To a project, a conflict is a hand grenade with the pin removed: if it has not blown up yet, it will soon enough. The job of the PM in this case is straightforward: remain alert to detect nascent conflicts, and then take appropriate action to nip them in the bud (more on this in the next chapter). Problems never go away—deal with them now.

ONWARD TOWARD OFF THE RAILS

Facing Reality

One of the true measures of an effective PM is the ability to manage the risks around the project. Proper execution is a matter of organizational delegation, proper sequencing, and skillful application of knowledge. In the limit, a project devoid of risks equates to a PM without justified existence. The valunomy of a PM begins with outstanding people skills, buttressed by organizational acumen, and crowned with poise under the pressure of swarms of risks pounding the gates of execution. The successful PM manages to the risk and continually assesses the project's trajectory via the tools of risk profiling and risk analysis, among others. Several other techniques and analytical approaches are available for this purpose, but they all boil down to the same two things: face reality and quantify it. The secretive Pythagoreans of classical Greece used to say that *all is number.* So it is with project management. The manager cannot hope to succeed without understanding the dynamic statistics that are constantly generated during execution. These numbers need a common basis of reference to correlate each other symbiotically; the emphasis on the foundational WBS. Numbers will clash from different sources, indicative of convergence issues.

What Lies Beneath, Lies Hidden

Finally, numbers conceal the true health of an execution strategy, spawning the prioritization of risks in the PM's mind. Numbers are a manager's best defense against the vagaries of a project's life. But they will become enemies if numbers are all that the manager bothers to be concerned with. Too little or too much focus on them leads to the same path of derailment. Like any good golfer who must accept the occasional shot from a sand trap, the PM must be able to deal with things going off the rails, if only to recognize when it is about to happen, and what to do about it. Adversity is a fact of project life—and the focus of our next chapter. Once again, facing reality is the prime directive. In the immortal words of Oscar Wilde:

> "A cynic is a man who knows the price of everything, and the value of nothing."

NOTES

1. See Coase's *The Nature of the Firm* for the original 1937 paper on the subject, which led to an entire subset of economic science.
2. See Verne Harnish's *Scaling Up* for more wonderful tricks of this kind. A great read for any student of the art of management.
3. See Colin Pask's *Magnificent Principia* for more details.
4. Depending on the extent of the findings, the session could be held in multiple instances to cover each of the parts.
5. See Nassim Taleb's wonderful book, *Antifragile—Things That Gain from Disorder*, for more
6. The act was passed to protect shareholders and the general public from accounting errors and fraudulent practices of businesses in the wake of the infamous Enron accounting scandal. Several Western countries have since ratified like-minded legislation.

16

4:5:6:7:8 FIX IT!

---

*Corporate boards too often continue to throw money at bad
projects because nobody is willing to step up to the plate,
admit the failure, take the blame, and change directions.*

SUCCESS IS ALSO A FAILURE TURNED
INTO KNOWLEDGE

Most project managers (PMs) will, at some point, confront a project gone rogue
that they will restore and get back on track. Some, however, will have gone seriously wrong; these are the subject of this chapter. We assume that the project has
gone off the rails and look at ways to salvage the situation. Barring a black swan,
the seeds of failure are usually backed into the plan from the outset and allowed
to mature during execution. The two main causes of this open our discussion:
estimating and contracting.

BUDGET BUSTING

Wishful Thinking

Imagine yourself as PM. You have just completed your first total installed cost
(TIC) estimates for an industrial plant, which came in between $25M and $100M,
with a nominal target of $50M. The resilience analysis concluded that the owner is
financially able to withstand the upper limit in the worst-case scenario. The owner
approves the project and hands you your marching orders and your *appropriation*
(see PM budget in Chapter 8): get this project done for $40M. Right out of the
gate, your probability of success far subceeds your failure prospects.

The experienced reader will surely relate to this example. The owner has committed three vital errors: (1) he assumes that the $40M TIC is the correct number (without any inkling of the intrinsic cost of this plant); (2) he assumes that the correct number will remain unchanged throughout development; and (3) he creates the false equivalence between target budget and spending limit.

The savvy PM understands that having a budget does not mean that it should be spent. As we stated before, everything should be done to try spending less than authorized, as long as it is never less than is necessary. This line of reasoning underscores the influence exerted by the estimates upon project execution strategies. The temptation to tamper with them is greatest when they diverge from the owner's wishful expectations. Make believe and faith are not strategies. Prayers are not enough. Facing reality must prevail.

The Dynamics of Estimates

What is an estimate? It is a best guess, educated or otherwise, within a given uncertainty range. The uncertainty is a direct function of ignorance: the less you know, the greater the uncertainty. The Institute of Certified Professional Managers methodology relies on the American Association of Cost Engineers (AACE) classification and is illustrated in Figure 16.1. We discern two salient features. First, the uncertainty range is widest at the start of a project (Class 5) and tightest at the end (Class 1). This makes sense: at the outset, the project is an undeveloped concept while at the end, it is fully detailed. Second, the *appropriation* budget changes over time asymptotically toward the asset's true intrinsic cost in the ideal scenario. The reason for the convexity of the increase is equally logical: more information means firmer details, and firm details means more materials.

> Under ideal circumstances, the final value of the Class 1 appropriation budget will equal the initial target budget (see Chapter 8).

Degrees of Execution Risks

The question that we must ask ourselves now is quintessential to the success of the project. What should govern the selection of the *appropriation* budget as work progresses over time? The answer is two words: execution risks. The preservation of the owner's financial interests dictates a management course that minimizes them above all other considerations.

The weakest risks lie in the region sitting above the *safe* curve shown in Figure 16.2. This curve is the *allocation* budget, which sits above the TIC curve (representing the asset's intrinsic cost). The highest risks are found below the *danger* line, corresponding to the high risk in Figure 8.1. The extreme risk is the

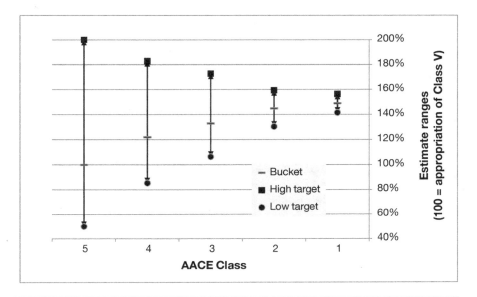

Figure 16.1   Evolution of an estimate's uncertainty range over time: the progression of the work increases knowledge of the asset, which helps reduce uncertainty and increases the accuracy range of the estimate

curve defined by the bottom limit of the TIC's accuracy range (extreme risk in Figure 8.1). Do not interpret Figure 16.2 literally. It is statistically representative of a typical investment project. It is *statistically possible* to succeed in the danger zone if the stars and the fates align perfectly. Realistically, however, such an execution strategy amounts to playing the lottery with zero margin of error: either you win every single roll of the dice, or face immediate ruin.

Facing Reality

Figure 16.2 is divided into four *execution zones* as a function of management risks:

- Zone 1 is the safe region
- Zone 2 is the delicate region, bounded by the TIC (intrinsic) and safe curves
- Zone 3 is the risky region, bounded by the TIC (intrinsic) and danger curves
- Zone 4 is the danger region, beneath the danger curve

Picking a zone is where facing reality meets reality. If the economics can't be made to work economically, one can either abandon the project now or get into the spin cycle discussed in Chapter 8. Arbitrarily picking Zone 3 or 4 just

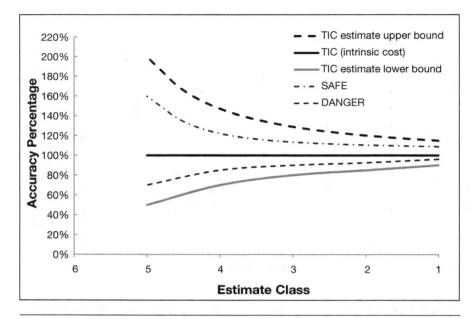

Figure 16.2   Map of the risk regions overlapping budget option lines: the safest execution strategy lies between the *high* target line and the *safe* line; the riskiest strategy, and the most likely to fail, is to choose an *appropriation* level below the *danger* line

because the numbers are easier to sell is symptomatic of the *Einstein Cross syndrome*.[1] Despite the formalization of the mechanics used to derive the estimates, one should never lose sight of the fact that *estimates are nothing but guesses.*

The Einstein Cross

The Einstein Cross is an extraordinary manifestation of the theory of general relativity. According to Wikipedia:

> "The Einstein Cross or Q2237+030 or QSO 2237+0305 is a gravitationally lensed quasar that sits directly behind ZW 2237+030, Huchra's Lens. Four images of the same distant quasar appear around a foreground galaxy due to strong gravitational lensing. According to current interpretations of redshift, the quasar is located about 8 billion light years from Earth, while the lensing galaxy is located at a distance of 400 million light years. The Einstein Cross can be found in Pegasus at 22h40m30.3s, +3° 21′ 31″."

In essence, the four quasar images forming the cross around the Pegasus galaxy are actually four images of a single quasar sitting behind the galaxy. The enormous gravitational heft of the galaxy deforms local space-time to such an extent that it bends and diffracts the light emanating from the quasar into the illusion of the Einstein Cross. The math is horrendously complicated, but the imagery is sublime.

DECISION-MAKING GATES FOR IMPENDING BUDGET BUST

What should a PM do when faced with a forecast that threatens to blow the cover off the chosen *appropriation*? This off-the-rail situation is common enough to warrant scrutiny. The action plan in such an instance involves a series of decision gates considered by the project management office (PMO) PM, the framework lead, and possibly the owner.

Gate 1: Immutable Budget

If the *target budget* cannot be reconciled with reality in the here and now, the project is presented with a simple yet startling choice: abandon the project or proceed to Gate 2.

Gate 2: Validate the Actual Forecast

Verify the sources of data from which the forecast was compiled (discussed briefly in Chapter 17 in the *Estimating* section). If the forecast remains valid as presented, either abandon the project or revisit the scope in Gate 3.

Gate 3: Scope Justification

Perform a high-level engineering review of the entire scope of the project to determine what functions, systems, and installations can be scaled back, simplified, modified, or eliminated now, with the option of reintroducing them in the future once the asset has generated the necessary profits to restore the original configuration. *This review will add costs to the project.* The impact of each change must be quantified in terms of the profitable performance of the future asset. If done on the cheap now, it will be redone later for certain—and it will not be cheap. If the holistic impact is acceptable to the owner, proceed to Gate 4. Otherwise, go to Gate 5.

Gate 4: Rescale

The configuration changes arising out of Gate 3 must be engineered anew into the new plant configuration. The work on the project, either in part or in whole, must regress to a previous life-cycle phase; far enough into the project sequencing to redevelop the offending cost estimate. Consider also a parallel exercise at a senior management level to revisit and redefine the decision-making mechanics that govern the selection of the estimate zone. The lesson? Pick Zone 1 by default, or Zone 2 by debate (commensurate with a higher contingency budget). *This rework will add significant engineering costs to the project and must not be performed perfunctorily by cutting corners to speed things up.* At the end of this cycle, return to Gate 1.

Gate 5: Clutch Decision

At this stage, it is reality that confronts the owner head on. The original *target budget* was clearly inadequate. Either the project is abandoned or gets adequately funded (through partnerships, joint ventures, or other means). The extra funding will likely excoriate the original execution strategy and impose on the new project ownership a broad recasting of the framework, execution strategy, project team structure, and scope of work for the project. Such is the consequence of not facing reality up front in the selection of a proper estimate zone against which the project will be managed.

RELIABILITY OF ESTIMATES

Trusting the Sources

Chapter 17 discusses the mechanics of generating the sources of cost data from which estimates are compiled. Our concern at this juncture is the trustworthiness of those sources. Not all cost data are created equal; in fact, some are very much more equal than others, depending on their shepherds. Trustworthiness is a function of three characteristics of the *estimator*: inoculation, competence, and independence.

Inoculation of the Estimator

Inoculation refers to the estimator's first-hand exposure to the effects of incurred costs. Having been directly exposed to a genuine cost in the past, the estimator is *de facto* cognizant of its origins and variability. The estimator is said to be inoculated against the uncertainties of a cost (from first-hand ignorance). An inoculated estimator operates from experience instead of theoretical musings that are untested in a real setting. A seasoned air traveler, for example, will know better than to trust the price quoted by a travel web site than a novice flyer who may not suspect that luggage fees, airport improvement fees, and fuel surcharges can easily double the quoted airfare price.

Competence

Competence speaks to the estimator's qualification to properly assess a cost. Competence is the counterweight against unshackled cost drivers. For example, a car mechanic has a much higher sense of the anticipated cost of a repair (say, changing a timing belt) than a novice car owner ignorant of the belt's existence. The former will scrutinize the repair shop estimate far more proficiently than the latter ever could.

Independence

Independence, finally, pertains to the estimator's absence of ulterior motive with the presentation of the estimated cost. Take the example of a consultant who is hired to develop a Class 3 construction cost estimate. The project has yet to receive its final investment decision. If the consultant intends to bid for the construction work, he will be tempted to minimize the final numbers in the hope of enhancing the probability of project approval (such behavior is, in fact, hard to resist, especially with construction initiatives). Without the bid motive, the consultant will feel freer to deal with the reality of the cost sources, rather than the fate of the project.

Biases

The reader should note that these characteristics are pertinent to owner and partners alike. Owner teams are especially prone the perverse effects of the independence character. Construction firms often exhibit competence weaknesses when pursuing new market opportunities beyond their core business. Engineering consulting firms exhibit a proclivity toward inoculation deficiencies when estimating construction costs associated with designs that they have never built.

The issue of trustworthiness comes to the fore when a PM receives a cost estimate that seems out of whack with reality (too high or too low). The determination of the reliability of a set of estimates should be vetted through a four-step process:

- Gate 1: *Gut check*—Regardless of the estimates' perceived correctness, or lack thereof, the first step is to perform a reality check against historical data. In the vast majority of the cases, the project management team will have access to cost data from past projects, which should provide at least a basis of reference to gauge the reasonability of the estimate.

- Gate 2: *Low ball*—If the estimates seem low, the PM should perform an assessment of the inoculation, competence, and independent features of the estimator's character. Ideally, this assessment will have been done *before* the work is awarded. If not, and the estimator is found lacking in any one of the three, the best course of action for the PM is to validate the estimates independently through a second, vetted estimator. *This will add some costs to the project.* Alternatively, in the spirit of managing against the resilience risk, the PM could simply double the estimates and go with those.

- Gate 3: *High ball*—In this instance, the PM should focus on four areas:
  - Is the scope of work specifically understood by the estimator?
  - Does the estimator possess first-hand experience of the project ecosystem (PECO) specific to the project?
  - Is the estimator privy to unique information of historical perspective that is applied integrally to the estimates to be conservative?
  - Is the competence of the estimator, as defined before, matching the nature of what is being quoted?

The answers will inform the PM as to what steps to take. In most cases, the estimates must be redone based on clarifications provided by the PM, or validated by a triple-vetted alternate estimator.

- Gate 4: *Strike*—In this case, the cost estimates are deemed essentially correct by the PM. In keeping with the mantra of managing against the resilience risk, the PM should proceed with the upper bound of the estimate range as a go-forward baseline (Zone 1).

SCHEDULE BUSTING

The Project Manager's Hammer

Costs are to an owner what the schedule is to a PM. They form both sides of the proverbial project coin (with performance circumscribing its periphery). Costs follow performance, which follows schedule. The schedule, more than the costs, reflects the acumen of the PM and the capabilities of the project team. It therefore follows that a misbehaving schedule may be indicative of oversight delinquencies. We say *may* rather than *is* because slippages can be externally driven by factors outside of a manager's control. Nevertheless, since the schedule is an artifact of a team's execution strategy (in opposition to costs, which are consequences of the execution), there is no escaping the conclusion that schedule delays may reveal a deficiency with the plan. To fix a schedule problem, the PM must get a handle on its roots. Some are seeded within the PMO's physiognomy; others are buried in the essence of a vendor. Mathematically, a schedule is described by Equation 16.1:

$$\sum_{j=1}^{m} \sum_{i=1}^{n_j} \left\{ \frac{Scope_i}{Productivity_i} + Lag_i \right\} = Timeline \qquad 16.1$$

where:

- m is the number of functional disciplines involved in the generation of outputs;
- n_j is the total number of "i" scope elements executed by each "j" functional discipline;
- $Scope_i$ is a work element, measured in number of outputs;
- $Productivity_i$ is the rate of outputs generated per unit of time;
- Lag_i, as defined in schedule parlance, is the time between the end of a scope and the start of its successor; and
- $Timeline$ is the duration required to complete the project.

Problem Drivers

Equation 16.1 underlines the origins of schedule problems, as they can all be traced back to one or more variables, especially the *scope* and *productivity* parameters.

Scope Drivers

Scope mirrors one's comprehension, or lack thereof, of what work must be done, in what quantity, according to what sequence, and to what standard operating environment (SOE) requirements. Work, quantity, sequence, and SOE altogether, and together only, enable a PM to quantify the resources, tools, and allocations to be marshaled into a cohesive execution strategy for a given scope. Sequencing also factors into the quantification of the scope, since the work could be done either in series or in parallel. Work in series is the approach favored by the life-cycle phases. There will always be an opportunity to run things in parallel; however, this approach is inherently riskier, as it places various inputs and outputs simultaneously in time, from which execution divergence may arise.

Productivity Drivers

Productivity determines the staffing count necessary to get the work done in accordance with the schedule. It is important to employ the staffing strategies advocated in Chapters 14 and 15, especially the pursuit of cross-training and skill pyramids within a team. Those requirements come first; the milestones and deadlines flow their inclusion into the productivity calculations.

Types of Schedule Slippages

With these precepts in hand, we turn our attention to fixing busted schedules. Keep in mind that any fix to a schedule will add more time to the project, at an extra cost to the established baseline budget. The types of schedule slippages include several types of delay sources: indecision, change rain, low bids, diffidence, ignorance, fabricator, and politics:

- *Delay from indecision*—Indecision and its corollary, *change rain*, are the primary mechanisms through which schedules get stressed. Whatever the change considered, what matters to the schedule is to make the decision: approve, reject, or modify, but make the decision. Recurrence of this mechanism is indicative of a probating hierarchy that is either wrongly assigned or not uniquely prescribed. The fix:

    - Assign a probate individual who is qualified to assess the proposed change;
    - Impose (or enforce, more correctly) a strict approval timeline uniformly across the project team; and
    - Remove probate individuals who are unwilling to make decisions under those terms.

- *Delay from change rain*—This scenario plays out when a project team tends to request constant changes and modifications. This stream of changes utterly wrecks the efficient unfolding of an execution. It is symptomatic of review and probating mechanics plagued by dabblers. It is usually compounded by a scope of work ill-defined by the PMO; and is aggravated by internal circular debates spawned by divergent objectives. The fix:

    - Stop all work until the scope of work is arrantly defined, the SOE firmly imposed, and the understanding of their combined ramifications understood within and without the PMO team; and
    - Assign a single probate individual (not team or group) with full powers to resolve all outstanding changes holistically.

- *Delay from low bids*—This is the nefarious instance of a contract awarded on the basis of lowest price. The owner is solely to blame for awarding such a contract in the first place, which may have been quoted by the winner to *buy the job*. The fix:
  - Learn this lesson once and for all: cost-cutting costs more in the long run;
  - Learn the lesson that it is better to adopt a schedule with enough time to do things right, rather than finding time later to make it right;
  - Place the contract in abeyance;
  - Convene an extraordinary session with the bid winner to assess the level of divergence between the real effort requirements of the scope and the quoted allocations;
  - Confront the bidder's performance commitment (discussed in the *Contracts* section later in this chapter); and
  - Rebaseline the schedule against the new agreement; or
  - Cancel the contract and start anew with a credible vendor.

- *Delay from diffidence*—When a task never seems to end, despite being 90% or so complete, it is usually a harbinger of hesitation by the party doing the work, arising out of a skill set or knowledge shortcoming *that is known by the party*. For example, a design could be coming against a severe difficulty that exceeds the capability of the design software or is beyond the technical expertise of the designer. The confident PM would immediately flag the issue and fix it. The sheepish manager would allow the work to continue going in circles lest his team's reputation becomes tarnished. Whatever the case, and it is a frequent case for sure, the fix by the PMO manager is straightforward:
  - Convene a meeting to review the issue and identify the means of resolution;
  - Accept, without blame, the deficiency of the working party;
  - Immediately retain the services of a pertinently specialized subject matter expert (SME) firm or consultant;
  - Review the remainder of the working party's scope of work to identify all other applicability of this shortcoming, and reassign the work to the SME; and
  - Issue a contract change order to the working party to reallocate that scope to the SME.

- *Delay from ignorance*—This type of delay is similar to the previous one, with the exception that the working party is genuinely unaware of its deficiency. Most often, this ignorance is driven by a blind belief in software power, without understanding the physics limitations underlying its code. The fix is the same as that for the diffidence delay.

- *Delay from fabricators*—Getting bits, pieces, equipment, and complex systems fabricated by vendors is fraught with schedule risks. A myriad of schedule problems can be encountered on account of materials, quality, productivity, and logistics. The larger the order, the greater the risk to the project, principally on account of the effective monopoly granted to the fabricator by the purchase order—once that order is in, the owner is at the mercy of the fabricator *for this order*. The fix in this case includes:

  ◻ Separate the design from the fabrication, by getting the design done independently first, in the first five life-cycle phases;

  ◻ For large orders, get at least two vendors to fabricate the same design;

  ◻ For an existing order that is already behind schedule, reallocate to another fabricator those items that are not yet started; and

  ◻ For very large orders, retain a third fabricator to reduce the monopoly risk further.

- *Delay from politics*—There is nothing to be done in most cases, other than wait patiently. Some jurisdictions may be prone to *rail greasing* and graft, but the PM is warned: enter the fray at your peril, and certainly never out of your own volition.

Delays Always Add Costs

Schedule slippages are the bane of project management. They are both cause and effect of a project's management, borne on the wings of its execution strategy. *Delays will always add costs to a project* (and sometimes to the benefit of the asset or its valunomy); however, the larger the scope, the higher the schedule risk. The greatest contribution by project management is to tightly and obsessively control the evolution of the work against the established schedule baseline. Speeding things up by *crashing the schedule* is an open invitation to blow that schedule *and* blow the budget in one fell swoop. Just like the fact that no real cost savings can be had from cutting costs, no schedule can be preserved by cuts and shortcuts if the ultimate objective is a profitably performing asset (PPA). No time can be saved by arbitrarily saving time along the way.

CONTRACT BUSTING MOVES

The Need to See Blinds the Sight

To an owner, the contract is a security derived from the rule of law. To a PM, it isn't so much the contract, but the contract performance commitments that are affirmed. The contract is the ultimate tool of the PM to get the work done by others. But it can also be a harbinger of execution off-railing depending on its structure. The reader should remember that contracts are like marriages: they end either in death, divorce, or senility. Know what you are getting into before you make it official.

The Illusion of Certainty

Because of the legal complexity of negotiating, issuing, and enforcing a contract, project management teams are immensely reluctant to cancel one, even in the face of sustained performance failure. Managers prefer to pin their hopes on the possibility of a turnaround. The fear of admitting failure can overwhelm senior managers. Fear must be overcome, nevertheless, if the project is to succeed. Contracts are about *performance*. Performance earns payment. The gray areas between the shades of gray are few and far between. Uncharacteristically, performance is not difficult to enforce: one must first set the expectations and hold accountable those who were hired to execute against these expectations. The binary nature is inhered from the choice between *performance* and *justification*. Either a piece of work is managed on the basis of performance or on the basis of justifying excuses. By the latter, any failure can be rationalized, excused, justified, or explained away, often to preserve the *status quo*. The *status quo* is often justified, but rarely justifiable. Contract performance goes off the rails when one justifies the justification. This deathly hallow is the unfortunate default stance of PMs who are fearful of laying down the law, lest they confront and be forced to adjudicate confrontations (reminiscent of a *getting-to-yes* mindset perused in Chapter 6). The corollary of a PM who prefers to deal with sycophants and invertebrate consultants creates the same outcome: a contract derailed from the righteous path.

> *Contracts managed for performance can succeed; those managed by justification cannot.*

Consequences Front and Center

Notwithstanding, it is not enough to declare one's intent to manage for performance. To be effective, the policy must be complemented with a consequence table that spells out what happens to a party found delinquent in a specific performance measure. A consequence can be positive (financial reward for superior metrics, for example) or negative (financial penalty). Without this table, any judgment of a probate party regarding an accountable party is liable to arbitrary tendencies and inconsistent outcomes. Consequences were already identified as the fifth condition of an effective key performance indicator program, in Chapter 10. The same logic applies to this consequence table—no table, no enforceable performance, only justifications. As an outcome, performance is binary. As mechanics, it is analog. The mechanics of performance rests on a foundation of continuous improvement in which step failures are expected and encountered, and from which learnings and innovations sprout. Performance is first and foremost about people, in lockstep with the arguments postulated in Chapters 14 and 15. Performance is also about the mechanics and mechanisms of execution, to discover what works and what doesn't; what's optimal and what's not; what helps and what hurts; what to keep and what to drop. Performance, finally, is about understanding the synergies underlying them all, and about deciding on the basis of rational fact, not ethereal whims of harmony.

The Contract as a Source of Failure

Contracts that are bad, ill-suited, wrongly awarded, or incorrectly motivated are instances of execution derailment from the outset. This situation follows from the fact that the contract locks the parties into a legal straightjacket that suffers no ease of alteration. When a conflict erupts between the parties, tempers can flare up and acrimonious accusations can fly in every direction. In the case of the owner, who always ends up paying in the end, frustration can lead to a hardened monopsony mindset that is tainted by ego impulses. The owner is left with two choices: (1) to be right or (2) to do right by the project. Unfortunately, the former is enshrined by the rule of law. We say *unfortunately* because it works in favor of the ego rather than the project. By law, either party to a signed contract is equal owner of the contract and has therefore the legal right to demand of the other party a complete and unconditional performance in accordance with the terms of that contract. Lawsuits are one option to pursue one's validation of righteous entitlement. But it is a nuclear option leading to a Pyrrhic victory: a zero-sum game in which one side's gain is at the expense of the other's loss. You may have been found in the right; congratulations! Too bad about the project, though.

Above All, Do Right by the Project

Contracts notwithstanding, no party to a contract will willingly meet its obligations under the threat of financial ruin, no matter how "right" the other party may be. What the payer gets out of such a situation will be shoddy work, corners cut, designs banged together and bridges burnt. Worse still, the asset is likely to be plagued by a performance shorn of profitability. The law may be on the payer's side, but at the expense of the PPA. Doing what's right for the project requires much more of a PM than the pursuit of righteousness. It may require him to trample upon his own ego. Need we say more? This is excruciatingly difficult for people who are accustomed to running the show. What's right for the project also depends on the success of those contracted to realize it. Sometimes, this will mean that the owner (or the payer, more precisely) must help the contractor along the way. History is our witness; even mortal enemies in war understand this lesson. To wit, consider the example of the anti-French coalition that stood in opposition to Napoleon. After his defeat, the coalition's leader, Pierre Metternich, resisted all calls for disbanding his group on the grounds that France would still be the ultimate counterweight to any threats arising from unknown quarters to the peace of Europe (see Francis Fukuyama's *The Origins of Political Order* for more details). Sometimes, it can be onerous or time-consuming. If the contractor is worth the effort, the effort is worth the expense. If it is not, cut your losses now and cut him loose: there is no point in throwing good money at a hopeless cause.

NINE DEADLY CONTRACT SINS

Whatever failing is embedded into a contract will remain throughout its enforcement life. We can identify nine such deadly sins—and test the owner's resolve in the face of being right for himself or for the project. In all instances, the proper basis of assessment for a set of competitive bids is to quantify the valunomy.

1. Lowest Bids

As procurement practice goes, this one takes the Oscar for best performance in a leading actor category. The theory goes something like this: after equalizing all bids and ranking them in terms of technical compliance, the lowest price wins. The mistake is in the compliance part—there are no such things as multiple bids with equal technical compliance. Some are technically superior to others, and vice versa. Yet, even when a bidder is not as compliant as others, its low price may be sufficient to earn the job. This is the purest incarnation of the distinction between *cost effectiveness* and *valunomy*. Low bids save project money *now*, most likely at the expense of the PPA *later*. This effect underscores the importance that the cost factor, e_c, in Eq. (2.1) is greatest when dealing with low bids.

What is rarely done during a bid analysis but should be is to assess what valunomy accrues to the owner from the higher costs exhibited by the other bids. For example, imagine two bidders invited to verify the stresses in a buried pipeline. One proposes using a canned, code-checking software; the other, a full-field simulation of the material behavior via nonlinear finite element analysis (FEA). The former will be cheaper than the latter, but the latter is the only one that can genuinely achieve credibility of results during the nucleation life-cycle Phase 6. In this case, the extra cost associated with the FEA approach is the only one that furthers the PPA agenda. The entire premise of this book has time and again argued in favor of pursuing the highest valunomy possible for the PPA, which implies doing the most to get there, not the least.

The cheapest option always costs the most in the long run.

2. Lowest Capital Costs

What goes for competitive proposals goes for equipment as well. Case in point: an industrial chemical plant requires 3,000 kW of new compression as part of a capacity expansion. One option is a natural gas powered engine coupled to a six-throw reciprocating compressor, with an $18M TIC hit; the other, a 3,300 kW gas turbine driving a centrifugal compressor with a $24M TIC. From an accountant's standpoint, there is no option: the engine drive is the only game in town. For the operator, who will be running and maintaining this equipment for 30+ years, life-cycle costs are the true concern (things like uptime—91% for the engine, 99.6% for the turbine, and planned downtime/loss of production revenues—32 days a year for the engine, 12 days for the turbine). One can show, however, that the turbine is by far the lowest option in terms of cost of ownership. From the perspective of maximizing the PPA, the turbine option is, hands down, the winner.

3. Utopian Bids

This is the scenario that comes up when most of the technically acceptable bids cluster around a median price, except for one that is noticeably cheaper. This is also the case when a supplier who is new to the business is invited by the owner to inject additional competing pressures. This new supplier accepts all terms and conditions of the owner, whereas the other bids are accompanied by lengthy (and historically expected) exceptions. The reflex by the owner is likely to pick the newbie. After all, what could possibly go wrong with contract law on your side? The pretender's bid wins out through a belief that the contractual obligations will guarantee the delivery of the specified quality—except that exceptions start flying off the e-mails as soon as the order is placed. In the heat of schedule pressures, you can forget the law; even if the owner is in the right, it does not solve, in any way, the actual problem of having placed an order that was never going to be satisfied in its original presentation. The lesson: experience tells us, time and time again, that there is a minimum price that must be paid for a given good or service. If the owner is naive enough to believe in the enforceability of such a deal at the expense of the vendor, the owner deserves the relationship and all the woes that come with it. You can no more buy a brand-new McLaren Veyron for 60 cents on the dollar than you can maximize the long-term return on investment from a plant bought on the cheap.

4. Dabbled Bids

Some readers will know this drill, which goes something like this: the owner reserves the right to veto any proposed team member offered by the bidder; or, he decides to alter the bidder's execution strategy advocated in the bid; or, he dictates what software to use for specialized tasks (previously absent from the bidders' instructions) after noticing a preference from one of the bidders; or, any other dabbling act that contravenes the principle of accountability that lies at the heart of any contractual intent to commit. To dabble is to cripple accountability. Even in the case where a bidder proposes a PM that the owner deems dubious, that choice is for the bidder to make and to assume the consequences (the owner is highly unlikely to know the background story that went into the decision to select that individual in the first place; someone with a previous bad history may have learned from it and be in the position now to offer a much better prospect). The lesson? Don't dabble with a bidder's proposal. If you break it, you own it—not the bidder. Accept bids as presented and judge them accordingly.

5. Hubris Contracts

Chapter 9 discussed at length the monopsony tendency of owners. The behavior is especially noticeable in large, wealthy organizations accustomed to getting their way with projects. Hubris, a sense of technical superiority, or a broad portfolio of past projects all contribute to the owner's own sense of prowess. The effect on the project, however, is to foster a confrontational environment whereby differing professional judgments of contractors are frowned upon by the owner. Contractors will respond in one or two ways: continue to butt heads to uphold their integrity, or transform themselves into invertebrate contractors who are willing to twist themselves into any shape to satisfy the owner's volitions. This is a variant of the zero-sum game in which the objective is to be right, rather than do right by the project. The owner will most likely win the day. But the victory will come at the expense of the project. There are no economic benefits to this. If an owner has gone through several contractors recently and found them all lacking, the common denominator is the owner, not the marketplace. If you don't trust the competence of the contractor, why hire him in the first place?

6. Harmony Contracts

Battle fatigue characterizes this sort of contract, which happens when one contractor is hired for two or more phases of the work. The contractor's performance initially subceeds expectations. Recurring shortcomings raise red flags. The solution would be to switch contractors for the next phase, except that the PMO prefers to deal with the devil it knows. Alternatively, the owner could award a job to a disgruntled vendor who has been passed over many times in the past to keep this vendor interested in future bids (to act as a price check upon the competition, for example). Both cases end up in the harmony bin because the owner has effectively given up on the arduous task of expecting performance to favor the price of institutionalized justification. The end result is unlikely to improve. To choose justification over performance is to choose the outcome.

7. Blind Contracts

The seventh sin is a variant of the first two. Owners go global with their supply chain strategies in the pursuit of cost savings and certainty of delivery (not to mention leaps of faith for the quality that will ensue). It is always possible to find a supplier who will be willing to promise the world without really intending to pay for it. Inevitably, the reality of reality will soon set in, usually in the form of PECO constraints that were never fathomed by the vendor.

8. Poaching

The owner who hires the best people from his contractor's team commits a grave mistake. The action cripples the contractor. These people achieved success within the strictures of the contractor's operational framework. There is no guarantee that this success will follow when migrated to the owner's environment. An engineering firm, for example, employs people to dwell in the technical weeds, where they are competent, comfortable, and confident. There is little correspondence between the nature of this work and that of an owner's PMO environment. Working at the execution level is entirely different than working in the realm of oversight. The performing design engineer, the stalwart PM, or the savvy construction superintendent may struggle with the execution-to-oversight transition. By poaching, the owner degrades the very team it hired to succeed. The contractor is forced to scramble to fill the position with someone new (thus running the risk of further degrading the team's performance if the individual is a tight bib). And that is to say nothing of the corrupting influence that such a move will have on the rest of the contractor's team and the strain on the business relationship. The owner would be better advised to offer the contractor additional monies to be showered on prized individuals to keep them happily employed.

9. Global Gobble

Some organizations embrace globalization through supply chain management (SCM). Strategic sourcing, global procurement, and enterprise service agreements are three examples of endeavors pursued by SCM teams in the name of economies of scale, cost efficiency, and long-term performance guarantees. Engineering practices and project execution methods usually follow suit. What these strategies tend to forget is that projects are local affairs that are entirely constrained by their PECO. The result is sets of cumbersome procedural frameworks that add costs, managerial complexity, uncertainty, and local exclusions to the detriment of a project's success. Things go off the rails as soon as the global framework is imposed. Local suppliers who may have enjoyed a hitherto long relationship with an owner find themselves crushed by new prequalification demands that are devoid of relevance to the PECO's local character. The demands are then used to disqualify them, despite being the only feasible game in town for the project. Burdensome vendor evaluation scoresheets are used, replete with dubious questions that create the impression of thoroughness at the expense of usefulness. Engineering standards created for one region of the globe are unilaterally imposed on another where their applicability is tenuous at best. Construction methods that were developed in response to past failures by incompetence fail to account for the skills of the local labor pools. The bottom line: projects are local affairs and rarely global affairs.

CHOOSING THE RIGHT CONTRACT

Avoiding Square Pegs in Round Holes

The nine deadly sins can wreak havoc on just about any type of contract. One will usually suffice to create problems for the project; two or more are sure to derail anybody's best intentions to do right by it. Compounding the difficulty is the greater evil of discordant contract types. It is not enough to define the scope of work, the expectations, the deliverables, and the mechanics of a contractual relationship. It is equally important to choose the most suitable type of contract for that relationship. Picking the wrong one further exacerbates the derailment prospects down the road.

Contracts come in a variety of forms. The Project Management Institute, for example, identifies three primary types in the *PMBOK® Guide—Fifth Edition*, each with variants:

- Fixed-price contracts: variants include a firm fixed price, a fixed-price incentive fee, a fixed price with an economic price adjustment, and design-build arrangements.
- Unit rate contracts: variants include cost plus a fixed fee, cost plus an incentive fee, and cost plus an award fee.
- Time and material contracts.

How to choose the right contract type? We readily recognize the legal enforceability of a contract as the ultimate mechanism, albeit a nuclear one, available to a party signatory to it. Legalities notwithstanding, such recourse represents one of the worst scenarios to a PM who is bound by budgets, schedules, and performance expectations. To launch a court action is to abort a project for all intents and purposes. Our objective is to eliminate the risk of a lawsuit to secure the delivery of the PPA.

Fixed-Price Contracts

- *The appeal*: implies a promise of cost certainty and is suitable for any project scale and manpower requirements.
- *Excellent for*: service, material, or fabrication/construction contracts characterized by a defined scope, expectations, timelines, and budget, without any anticipation of changes or modifications.
- *Good for*: a well-defined scope with expectations and outcomes that rely explicitly on the expertise of the contractor to work out the grey areas with minimal interventions by the owner. A minimum number of changes can be expected to arise during execution at the fringes of the work but not to its core. Also, these are good for work performed by unionized labor.
- *Bad for*: owners insisting on first-hand involvement during the execution and the approval of the progress. The ill-defined scope is incapable of affirming the final configuration of the expected outcome (deliverables, timeline, budget). Heterogeneous labor pools prone to variability and low skill set levels.

- *The reality*: fixed-price contracts are ideal when the scope is perfectly defined, the SOE is understood and implemented, and the deliverables are enumerated. On the other hand, these contracts struggle to control costs when owner-guided development work is required—whether at the design, engineering, procurement, or construction stages—resulting in costly change requests. Fixed-price contracts put contractors firmly in the driver's seat when changes are contemplated. Contractors are motivated by productivity and cost cutting, sometimes at the expense of quality. These contracts guarantee that the owner will never pay less than the contract price, but likely more than planned. Quality of outcome requires sedulous vigilance on the part of the buyer.

Unit Rate Contracts

- *The appeal*: these contracts are similar in appeal to fixed price arrangements in cases where the number of deliverables cannot be known ahead of time. They are the preferred structure in field services and construction. They are also best when billing occurs on the basis of physical work progress. They minimize the administrative burden on the owner for invoice validation and paperwork accretion. Vendor exhibits high tolerance to changes through cost recovery terms but will be intolerant otherwise.
- *Excellent for*: construction and fieldwork; mass production; engineering, design, and procurement activities with itemized scope bereft of exact deliverable quantities (for example, a fixed price for a specific type of drawing); specialized tasks performed by expert firms; life-cycle Phases 5 through 10; minimum changes.
- *Good for*: life-cycle Phases 3 and 4; R&D (research and development) initiatives based on itemized tasks; weather-dependent work; and design and fabrication of standardized equipment (low customization).
- *Bad for*: life-cycle Phases 1 and 2; variable scope of work with undefined deliverable sets; high customization of designs and fabricated parts; extensive involvement of the owner in the design/fabrication processes; and a high number of changes.
- *The reality*: unit rates are often the only option available in the field for such cost drivers as equipment rental, consumables, civil works, the construction of linear assets, and the fabrication of standardized parts. They are superior to reimbursable contracts for controlling engineering and design work once the concept is established. These contracts also guarantee that the owner will never pay less than the contract price, but will pay more if changes or weather delays are incurred. Quality of outcome requires vigilance on the part of the buyer.

Design-Build Contracts

- *The appeal*: best structure to offload the risk from the owner to the contractor; the allure of cost and schedule certainty based on acknowledged expertise of the contractor; they permit hybrid contract types from design to fabrication, with changes permissible during the design stages only; they are similar in drawbacks to fixed price and unit price contracts.
- *Excellent for*: procurement of complex installations and systems from a single supplier within his sphere of expertise; construction of large-scale plants based on modular design; and access to international suppliers with established reputations.
- *Good for*: engineering and design development of standard design technologies that are intended to be supplied by the same organization that did the design; vendor-supplied equipment designed in-house, with some design interventions by the owner; and the expertise of the vendor is acknowledged by the owner.
- *Bad for*: changes in contractors between successive life-cycle phases; highly customized equipment based on the owner's inputs; modifications to off-the-shelf systems for customized applications; a high degree of involvement of the owner's inspection crew during fabrication; and unionized shops; projects requiring in situ construction using local labor.
- *The reality*: design-build contracts are common to large equipment manufacturers who consider the cost of the design as a loss leader to get the fabrication/construction component of the contract (where the real money lies); design-build contractors rely on in-house designs and methods that translate into engineering drawings with just enough information to enable fabrication/construction; design changes, extensive SOE requirements, and the owner's insistence on participating in and approving all stages of the work destroy all cost/schedule control benefits. These contracts should be reserved for well-established vendors who know what they are doing and are left alone to build what they signed up to deliver; the quality of drawings and specifications will subceed that expected from a reimbursable schema; and the quality of outcome requires extreme vigilance on the part of the buyer.

Time and Materials Contracts

- *The appeal*: perceived superiority for controlling costs and schedule of an undeveloped configuration of outcome; preferred structure for services and development work during the early life-cycle phases of a project; and high tolerance to changes and work offshoring.

- *Excellent for*: limited scope of work associated with the first three life-cycle phases (asset definition, asset requirements, and installation requirements); R&D initiatives that can be divided into a finite number of stages; and work requiring only small teams (up to 20 or so) with minimal overhead.
- *Good for*: evolving project configuration that can be tightly controlled by functional discipline, despite extensive owner involvement; medium to high number of changes expected; very small fabrication and construction initiatives independent of weather and politics.
- *Bad for*: large scope of work or scope requiring large execution teams; projects requiring unionized labor, inexperienced, incompetent, or graft-prone contractors.
- *The reality*: typically used for services, the reimbursable contract requires a high level of oversight and daily management by both the owner and contractor. It is well suited to the initial stages of a project's life cycle, when scope, outcome, budgets, and schedules are dependent on the progress of the work. These contracts work against the interests of the owner and the service contractor simultaneously. The built-in incentive of the contractor to maximize billable hours guarantees that the owner will see zero benefits from continual improvement, past experience, innovations, or productivity enhancements stemming from the work. The contractors exhibit a proclivity for labor accretion, overhead resources, and the tacit capture of labor inefficiencies against weakly controlled work breakdown structure elements. Simultaneously, contractors are locked in from the outset in terms of theoretical profitability. Reimbursable contracts will not lead to cost savings. The drawback is felt mainly by the contractor, whose target earnings before interest, tax, depreciation, and amortization represents a theoretical maximum that is unlikely to be achieved in reality.

Silver Bullets and Red Bottom Lines

There is no single contract type that will fit all situations. To each type's weaknesses correspond a variety of measures to counter their effects. For example, the obsession with maximization of billable hours in a reimbursable contract can be mollified by reward fees for uncovering potential cost saving opportunities. It behooves both parties who are involved in a contract to understand their respective motivations to select the most appropriate contract type. To wit:

- The owner seeks speed to market, cost and schedule certainty, security of supply and assurances of quality—with their associated risks carried by the contractor.

- The contractor targets certainty of revenues, maximization of profits, guarantee of success, and assurance of repeat business from the owner— with all risks borne by the latter.

We also need to emphasize the necessity for the owner to be a genuine advocate of the contractor's success in the person of the framework lead. Almost by definition, contracts are zero-sum games in legal terms, subject to the threat of litigation and project derailment when conflicts arise. The onus is on the owner to go beyond the terms in order to empower the contractor to achieve the objectives of the contract. The contractor, in turn, must acknowledge the owner's active role in helping his own success, and perform in a way that will justify the owner's efforts. None of this is possible, however, if the contract type is not matched to the circumstances that should promote its benefits.

PERFORM OR JUSTIFY

Divergence of Expectations

Misunderstood expectations are by far the most common source of off-the-rail situations. Expectations are uniquely personal in the realm of project management. The people vector is also the most difficult variable to control. This underlines the importance of alignment between people and project objectives, and between objectives and execution strategies. Whatever is expected, imposed, or directed at whatever organizational level, must flow through the hierarchy right down to the front lines where the heavy lifting of the execution takes place. Derailment will occur when that flow simply does not flow. Earlier in the chapter appeared the statement: "either a piece of work is managed based on the basis of performance or on the basis of justifying excuses."

Contract performance goes off the rails when one justifies the justification.

This proposition forces the owner, the framework lead, and the PMO to make a choice when facing adversity. It is much easier, at the personal level, to manage by justification rather than performance. The approach offers wiggle room to defer hard decisions to later or never; and to avoid making the tough calls that could lead to zero-sum gains. Confrontations are mollified and egos can be protected while colleagues and acquaintances are spared the ax. But managing this way comes at the costly price of taking a hit to the probability of realizing the PPA. By contrast, managing by performance always carries the potential for direct, uncomfortable confrontations that could lead to zero-sum gains. Performance must be rewarded well; nonperformance should get the boot. One is forced to operate within an execution schema intolerant of repeat failures, under the harsh glare of highly visible expectations. It is an environment akin to professional athletes who succeed or fail in the full view of everyone.

Decisions Are a Form of Performance

The game is not for the faint of heart. At the same time, managing under such a paradigm is far simpler: clear expectations create a climate of certainty. Decisions are less prone to dilly-dallying and waffling since they are based on unequivocal criteria defined ahead of time. Decisions derive from quantifiable facts, rather than meaningless equivocations and sentiments. The organization is free to decide what performance means and how it will be measured. The crux of the matter is to devise the rules for reaching a decision. Once again, in matters of performance, we are aided by simplicity. I, for one, favor the strike zone approach: three strikes and you're out. The first strike warrants a warning. The second strike warrants a notice. The third strike automatically results in work stoppage or cancellation.

What can be done when a contractor, selected by the owner by acceptance maturity rating, turns out to be less mature than anticipated? First, the owner must accept a portion of the blame since he made the selection. Second, both owner and contractor should get together to discuss frankly the reality observed, without seeking culprits or guilty verdicts. *Until proven otherwise, it is still in the best interest of the project to see the contractor succeed.* However, if the contractor proves unwilling or unable to succeed, the owner has little choice but to fall back on the performance expectation to salvage the fate of the project. This may very well mean yanking the work, in whole or in part. The other option—doing nothing—leads to a case of the sixth sin, *harmony contracts.*

When Failure Is Self-Inflicted

There may be instances when the framework or the PMO caused a project to go off the rails. Here, the onus is on the owner to hold both teams accountable to their respective performance commitments. It's a much tougher situation for the owner, who is confronted with the perception of having erred in the team choices. The owner must sidestep the clash of egos and remain focused on the ultimate objective—the success of the PPA. He is presented with three options:

- The project itself cannot be realized in accordance with the assumptions, conceptions, and allocations posited at the start. Whatever the adjustments, they will inevitably impact the economics of the endeavor. If the economics don't work, cancel the project. There is no sense in throwing good money at a bad project, no matter what ego pains (individual or corporate) will ensue.

- If the adjustments can be made, make them, modify the charter, and relaunch the project.
- If the project is feasible but plagued by team dysfunctions (framework or PMO), fix the teams, starting at the top and moving downward until the problems are solved. This means, among other things, that the first ones to go will be the framework lead, then the PMO manager.

The Case of a Bad Apple

In a different scenario, the organization is plagued with at least one individual who doesn't fit the culture of the team. This case can arise despite good intentions all around. Some people, through no fault of their own, are not suited to the environment. The decent thing to do is to acknowledge the situation and agree on a parting of ways. Better yet, help the individual land somewhere else; this sends a deeply positive message that will reverberate within the team. The message conveyed to the team will reflect the true values of the organization, relative to its touted principles (talking the talk and walking the walk). When the two diverge, people remember the hypocrisy implied.

How an organization handles the removal of an individual says more about the organization than the individual.

In yet other cases, the clash is more pugnacious. Incompetence, irreverence, misogyny, cultural predispositions, or some other feature of character renders the individual unable to operate harmoniously within the team. This scenario demands an unequivocal response. The individual must not be allowed to fester and poison the environment.[2] Remove the person politely but firmly. *Under no circumstance should you promote that person out.*

MANAGEMENT ISSUES

What about bad managers? The response is anchored to this statement from Chapter 3:

The truth of the matter is that bosses play an out-sized role in the success or failure of their organizations.

It is the same with projects: ultimately, the fate of a project rests in the hands of the boss. Bad managers and project leads, of course, lie somewhere on a continuum of performance reminiscent of the boss archetype scale seen in Chapter 3. Generally, leadership issues come in 500 shades of gray. Nevertheless, once a leader's shortcomings are shown to be detrimental to the project, removal must happen quickly. Some organizations will offer leadership training as a mitigation solution. To suggest such training is a tacit admission of nonleadership; for example, you have the wrong person in that job. Do not waste money on leadership training to fix a deficiency. *Leadership training is valuable to genuine, nascent leaders. It is never valunomic for remedial purposes.*

Externally Stressed

This is a leader who is experiencing chronic stress, fatigue, or burn-out. It is readily identifiable by changes to the person's mood, the more so when the change goes from cheerful to austere, positive to brooding, vivacious to taciturn, or patient to bellicose. *This person needs help, not removal.* Whether the cause is personal (family ties, sickness) or professional (idiot boss, overburdened, unending dark tunnel), pull the individual aside, explore the issues, and alleviate the burdens. In most cases, it's the circumstances that are crushing the individual, not the individual tainting the circumstances. Compassion, understanding, and firmness will help the person get out of the quagmire. Send the person on a paid vacation. Reassign some of the workload. Appoint a deputy. Choose to do those things to help the person succeed in the long run. Remember, once again, that the success of the person is a component of the success of the project.

Internally Lacking

When the mood swings spread to a group or a team, it is almost always because of bad leadership. There will be times when times are tough (layoffs, project cancellation, organizational uncertainty), which will invariably affect workers. That's when the leader matters. The good leader cannot control external circumstances but can help the group maintain cohesion and focus in trying times. The bad leader will exacerbate exponentially the damages to the group's morale. Absent any such external circumstances, the bad leader will in fact be the source of the dilapidation of the group's attitudes. From the project's perspective, it is imperative that such an individual be removed (or demoted or reassigned—but not promoted out). Whoever assigned this individual in the first place may hesitate to take action, lest it reveals a failure on her part. Allowing the individual to stay on and fester can only lead to one outcome: the bad leader should cease being the leader. Oscar Wilde's words are pertinent:

> *"Some cause happiness wherever they go; others, whenever they go."*

Keeping a bad leader in place will lead to team disintegration. The old adage *it's the best ones who leave first* is the telltale sign. Your best workers are the ones who have the least difficulties finding employment elsewhere. Life is too short to put up with this sort of nonsense, but the best ones have a shorter tolerance span yet. If your best people get on the exodus bus, you have very little time left to stem the immigration. The leader has to go.

The Monologist

Another indication that the leader may not be suited to the job is talking too much. Great leaders listen more than they talk and excel at building consensus. Their *talking-to-listening* ratio is inversely proportional to their position in the pecking order. By contrast, the bad leader repeatedly dominates the conversation; rambles on in endless monologues during meetings; and dabbles in everybody's responsibilities. Such people aren't leaders: they are thymotic (i.e., having a desire for recognition) self-promoters. Being unable or unwilling to trust their subordinates, they resort to micromanaging them as a means of control. The solution? Removal—now.

The Obvious

All those telltale signs are rooted in impressions, observations, and opinions. One must, therefore, always be careful with the decision process leading to removal. Violations of an organization's code of ethics are unequivocal no-brainers. Other signs, while not codified in a standard of practice, are still self-evident, even to a casual observer. Among others we note:

- Being prone to differential treatments (respect or contempt of an individual by the leader is a function of the latter's blind spots);
- Proclivity toward nepotism;
- An inability or refusal to make decisions;
- A tendency to make the wrong decisions at the wrong time, all the time; and
- Exhibiting a Napoleon complex through mood swings and monologues.

These kinds of behavior are indicative of a flawed leader for the given circumstances. Coaching may be advised. Cultural awareness may be useful. Self-recognition of one's own precarious standing may suffice to change things. If not, reassignment, demotion, or termination is the remedy. To emphasize the point one last time: either perform for the sake of the project or justify for the sake of the supervising individual.

The Survey Machine

Bad or deficient leadership may not be visible or evident to the PM, the framework leader, or the owner. All that is seen is a palpable tension in the air. Owners may wish to conduct an internal survey (or contract a third party for this purpose) to uncover the truth. Surveys can be very effective tools when they are conducted honestly and courageously—and underwritten by a commitment to act upon the findings, though they may be ugly or threatening. They will, however, be useless and indeed detrimental to the project if they turn out to be an exercise in creating the impression of an owner's concerns with the well-being of his teams. Surveys are useful when they are timely, truth seeking, and immediately followed by pertinent actions. Finding out what is going on will turn from a positive to a negative if nothing comes out of it. The outcome will veer toward morale destroyer if the findings, ugly though they may be, do not result in material changes. Going through the motions is not enough. Setting changes in motion is necessary.

> *It is better to do nothing than conduct a survey merely for the sake of going through the motions to create the illusion of management concern.*

If a survey is deemed needed, the proponents must first define what remedial action will be taken as a function of the nature of the finding. For example, if the survey aims to assess the performance of the PM, a positive finding could be tied to a bonus, a pay increase or a promotion; but in the case of a negative finding, could result in removal of the individual, demotion, or termination. The people surveyed should not know the consequences to be derived from their aggregate answers, but the management group overseeing the survey should be committed to following through on the preordained consequences. If you are not prepared to spell out from the outset the consequence of a finding (good or bad), or follow through on action items, the survey will be a complete waste of time and money—at the cost of morale erosion.

> *To survey or not to survey: If you're afraid of the answer, don't ask the question.*

BUSTED DESPITE GOOD INTENTIONS

There will be times when a project has gone off the budget and schedule rails despite the best of intentions. The best laid plans, created under the best of intentions, and managed with ubiquitous diligence by all parties involved, simply cannot hope to eliminate the temporal variability of budgets and schedules. For example, the initial estimates—vetted and acquiesced by all at the outset—may have been overly optimistic. Productivity rates may have been overestimated. Time lags surrounding vendor information may have been underestimated. Exchange rates, interest rates, or inflation may have spiked unexpectedly. These kinds of factors are quite routine features of large projects spanning several years. Even in the case of fixed-price contracts where the owner has the complete upper legalistic hand, the project will not be served by strict adherence to contractual obligations if, in the process, the accountable party is being financially crippled. The PMO manager may, of course, choose to be *right* and demand unconditional compliance by the vendor. Such a stance may be personally gratifying but unlikely to do *right* by the project. In these and other like circumstances, doing *right* by the project requires flexibility and open mindedness from the project leaders.

Anticipation versus Reaction

A project will generally involve at least three leaders: one from the owner, one from the framework, and one from the PMO. More leaders will appear on the scene when the scope project teams (SPTs) are hired. Each leader, in turn, is part of a triad. For example, the PMO manager, looking forward, stares at her SPT counterpart; looking backward, she withstands the stare of the framework lead. This triple relationship is always implicated when budgets or schedules are threatened. When all three individuals are diligent in anticipating variations to the execution baseline, cost and schedule changes will not come as a shock. Otherwise, systemic shocks will reverberate.

Standing Your Ground

The telltale sign that a PM is reacting instead of anticipating is the dreaded change notice that appears *after the fact*—when any possibility of mitigation is gone. This reactive stance is common among the *justify* set, for whom performance is a curse to accountability. Reasons, justifications, and excuses will be given to explain away the affair. They are but smoke in the mirror. *After-the-fact* reporting is *not* project management, it is journalism. Simply reject the change notice. If the rejection inflicts financial pain on the team that is guilty of the *postmortem* change notice, so be it. If it threatens the survival of the team or the stability of the commercial relation, the oversight manager (framework lead to PMO manager, PMO to SPT, SPT to SCP) has options:

- Work with the offending party to correct the internal process, pay the extra costs, and watch how the behavior changes;
- Request a change of manager if the behavior continues; or,
- Cancel the contract if the behavior continues.

The final bullet is fraught with painful ramifications. However, if the expectation of performance is to mean anything, it must carry the logical consequences of its absence. Otherwise, the entire oversight edifice will change to the *justify* mode, which is injurious to the health of the project.

THE PROJECT IS LORD AND MASTER

Let us emphasize the imperative of an execution strategy: do right by the project. Everyone involved with project decisions must be prepared to resolve problems as they arise, impervious to the fear that they stir. Like a professional golfer who knows that he will one day need to get out of a nasty sand trap, the PM and his team must possess the knowhow, acumen, and decisional wherewithal to address a serious problem head-on, when they occur. Facing reality, no matter how ugly, remains the only strategy to protect the integrity of the project. Facing reality is the first step. Stepping up to the decision is the harder act that follows. Setting egos and contract terms aside in favor of what's right for the project is essential. These are the circumstances that justify the medium-high bucks paid to stalwart PMs, whose valunomy was first forged in the fires of adversity. Managing for performance frames the ground rules against which such decisions can be made. These are the same grounds that nurture the seeds of success for the future PPA.

NOTES

1. The Einstein Cross is a perfect representation of the tendency of PMs to choose to look no further than pleasing cost estimates rather than probing them deeper.
2. Mediocrity is the shortest distance to failure, no matter how many dimensions there are.

PART 6—WHAT

*A brief history of time, spent on the means and ways
of realizing a profitably performing asset.*

17

MECHANICS AND
MECHANISMS (M&M)

Knowledge is not software. Software is not expertise.
Expertise is not experience. Experience is not results.
Results are not answers. But answers are the answer.

TO A HAMMER, ALL IS NAIL

To Innovate, Not Regurgitate

This chapter is about the tools, techniques, and processes of execution. Every business and every organization will already possess the toolsets to do the work. The objective of this chapter is to explore opportunities to innovate these tools, processes, and procedures. The reader interested in the basics of the standard toolkits will be well served by consulting his nearest bookstore. Here, as elsewhere in the book, the *status quo* will be challenged. And the power of software will be front and center to the opportunities advocated herein. In particular, we will suggest avenues for advancing the state of the traditional art beyond spreadsheets, e-mails, and Guttenberg's paper paradigm.

Definitions

Two definitions are posited. The *mechanics* are a process, procedure, methodology, or technique for executing a set of related tasks. The *mechanism* is the tool to execute a task. For example, cost estimating is a mechanic, while the cost database is a mechanism. In terms of what, why, when, where, who, and how (W5H), the *mechanics* address why and what while the *mechanism* informs us on the who, when, where, and how.

Complexity, Corralled

In Chapter 4, the exploration of complexity led to the conclusion that complex projects could only be mastered algorithmically *because complexity is a feral beast that can only be tamed through software, if only from the perspective of sequencing and process flow visualization.* Fortuitously, software is everywhere in the project world. Paradoxically, such profusion is difficult to integrate and often results in heterogeneous digital frameworks that are incapable of achieving algorithmic mastery over the mechanics of project execution. The marketplace is replete with software solutions advertised as complete enterprise solutions that enable collaboration, cloud-based access, and real-time data management. None operate on the *unit transformation process* or integrate the elements of the *collection substrate* (see Chapter 15) into a singular datum architecture. The existing information management paradigm is effectively disconnected from the genuine needs of effective project management. The potential capacity of software to solve this quandary already exists but remains untapped. The *collection substrate* is itself a subset of a wider digital information landscape represented by the *3-D model kernel*.

FOUNDATION—THE 3-D MODEL KERNEL

Digital Framework

The 3-D model paradigm was introduced in the subsection *Information Nucleation* in Chapter 12. The proper perspective starts with the asset in its operational setting: the plant. The plant is an integrated network of processes, equipment, machines, and installations operated in real-time from a central control center. The datum universe gushing from this highly diverse complexity is beyond mental reach. A digital infrastructure is necessary, under the form of the *3-D model kernel*. That is, the entire plant, its installations, its systems and its components are mapped to a corresponding digital 3-D virtualization of those elements. Each 3-D model forms the kernel of each system. All subsequent types of information, documentation, dynamic data, and life-cycle records are tied back to this kernel, supposedly under comprehensive database architecture. The graphical user interface (GUI) is critical to the proficiency of the information management system. Access must be intuitive; displays must be object-based rather than textual; menu drill-down must be fast, traceable, and easily retroacted; searched information must be intuitively retrieved, copied, and transmitted up or down; response lags must be fractional; and access must be impervious to location.

The *3-D model kernel* comes into being during the *development* of the asset. Its datum architecture, on the other hand, must be asset-invariant. That is, the mechanics of *capture* of the development data must be the same, regardless of the nature of the asset. This invariance is essential in the context of future changes. Over time, assets may be expanded, modified, scaled down, repaired, altered, or retired. Data will be generated in each instance, which must be appended to the 3-D model kernel. It stands to reason that one should never be required to reengineer the architecture of the system to merge later projects to the existing asset baseline.

> *The requirements and specifications of the 3-D kernel's datum architecture should be defined through a stand-alone and owner-managed project with a scope of application spanning the owner's entire holding of existing assets.*

Configuration Management

The first subsystem of the 3-D model kernel is the configuration management module. The term *configuration management* is well understood in the realm of reliability and maintainability. Numerous software solutions exist in the marketplace. To be useful, they must be able to operate seamlessly with the datum architecture of the *3-D model kernel*. This interoperability is evidently a function of compatibility of programming languages and universality of datum structures.

Interactive Electronic Technical Manuals (IETM)

IETM form the second subsystem of the kernel. They come to us as offshoots of the military's acumen in operational data management. Their origin predates the advent of the internet, and sought at the time to achieve what we take for granted today in web browser interfaces (SGLM and HTML languages played a large part in the evolution of contents coding now permeating the internet). Their pertinence to the *3-D model kernel* is affirmed by the proliferation of disparate, eccentric documentation generated by a project. They include:

- Manuals (operating, testing, troubleshooting, maintenance, repairs, configuration management records);
- Equipment fact sheets (datasheets, catalogs, application data, brochures, order sheets, specification sheets, exploded parts lists);
- Diagrams (schematics, assembly drawings, installation drawings, troubleshooting trees, control and shutdown keys, alarms and set points); and
- Handbooks (training, testing, qualifications).

Datum Construct

The list of IETM is illustrative of the datum classes that will be created by a project. The sum of these *content elements* forms are what we will call the project's *datum construct*. The relevance of the *datum construct* ties back to the *3-D model kernel* through accessibility. The potency of the kernel is its ability to connect a user to the entire *datum construct* underlying the asset. It is, quite frankly, wasteful to link, say, a live 3-D model of a pump system to a static, passive PDF version of its operating manual. That manual must possess the datum associativity, interoperability, and accessibility that are already woven into the fabric of the 3-D model kernel. Every single content element of the *datum construct* must be implicitly *networked* into every other content element of the construct. The integration of the *datum construct* to the *3-D model kernel* will require a significant level of sustained effort. One simply cannot proceed from paper versions and static PDF files generally encountered in the deliverables set of a completed project. That set is incapable of real-time changes, updates, and maintenance and is effectively outdated the day it is released. Their contents must be transformed into genuine IETM from the get-go. Operational readiness of these elements is the corollary proposition: unfettered, instantaneous access to the information buttressing the existence of the asset. Such access is a critical enabler of the profitable performance of the asset.

Document Management

Populating the *datum construct* falls under the purview of document management. During the *development* phase of the asset, *document management* is the information gateway that transits the content elements of the *3-D model kernel*. Once the asset is operational, document management mutates into a permanent information management engine for the 3-D model kernel, along with the associated *datum construct*. This mutated role places tremendous constraints on the data operability of the software application. Evidently, it must be a database, not a file or directory manager. It cannot be a specialty web browser with FTP capabilities. It must satisfy simultaneously the requirements of the kernel and its subsystems. The software must be able to handle metadata sets and multimedia files. Customization of datum interfaces, datum structures, code translation, and GUI frames is inevitable—no application exists in canned form that would do this out of the box. There will be a definite level of effort required at the front end of the project to develop the architecture and GUI of document management software, in parallel with the design efforts for the 3-D model kernel. The task is neither simple nor fast. It is a thoroughly genuine code creation project that will not suffer fools or improvisation. It should therefore be developed as a stand-alone project by the owner *prior* to initiating the project.

The Writing Department

Projects, obviously, produce an enormous amount of textual contents. Plans, engineering reports, quality reports, legal briefs, presentations, letters, regulatory submissions, permit applications, and what-have-you. The text will be redacted by a multitude of people across a diverse range of expertise and experience, under varying degrees of pressures, expectations, and liability. Projects face the continuous challenge of publishing this armada of written artifacts with uniformity of style and presentation.

Writing is an art that is not easily mastered from occasional sessions. Style, which conveys the imprint of a project, is even more transient than text in matters of consistency. It is simply not possible to achieve consistency and uniformity of presentation through the goodwill of a project's multiple authors. The solution is a *technical writing department*. A pair of proficient writers suffices to support a hundred-person team. The valunomy of their work is extracted from the very precision that they impart upon a text. This precision eliminates the costly, burdensome back-and-forth editing cycle that would otherwise ensue between authors and reviewers. The *technical writing department* is, in fact, the most valunomic strategy for streamlining the publication process and for achieving consistency of presentation over time. The cost of the department is recovered several times over from the labor expenses that would otherwise arise from inter-disciplinary editing cycles.

The efficacy of the *technical writing department* is contingent upon four rules:

- The *technical writing department* develops and owns all document templates, as well as the all-important *style guide* (which includes the rules of visual presentation and formatting, the grammar, the definitions and acronyms, and language accuracy).
- The *author* is accountable for the *contents* of a document, and leads the review and approval mechanics preceding its publication. Accountability extends to correctness of meaning, precision of information, and technical veracity.
- The *technical writer* is accountable for the compliance verification of the contents against the templates and the *style guide*.
- The *author's boss* is the probate party if conflicts arise between the author and technical writer when *consistency changes* proposed by the latter are rejected by the former. The default position is to accept the consistency change if the meaning conveyed by the contents is unaltered.

DIGITAL MISCELLANY

The datum construct, the 3-D kernel, and document management are examples of big-picture, systemic mechanics dealing with information. We turn our attention to more mundane mechanisms that are ubiquitous to the project world but rarely given any consideration, much to the detriment of the project execution's fluidity.

The Date Format

Imagine receiving a $1000 check, dated cryptically as 11/12/10? Can you unequivocally tell whether this date means 11 December 2010, December 10, 2011 or November 12, 2010? If the check was written in French, there would be no confusion: the date would signify 11 December 2010. In English, not so much. Project consistency demands a single, unambiguous format, which should be defined by a convention captured by the standard operating environment (SOE) (and referred henceforth in the baseline asset execution framework [BAEF] and the phase execution plans [PEPs]). For global delivery projects, ISO standard 8601 should be adopted, whereby the date is scripted as year-month-day (with or without hyphens, but with the year being all four digits to avoid confusion), and hour:minute:second for time (with or without colons) (hours counted on a 24-hour cycle). Alternatively, the inverse construct for the date will be equally precise: day-month-year.

Teleconferencing

This matter was discussed previously in Chapter 11. Every project office should have access to a full-fledged video conferencing facility. Embrace this twentieth century technology!

Progress Reporting

Weekly and monthly reports are a permanent feature of the project management landscape. Most organizations will opt for the simple typed report (either PDF or DOCX in most instances). Others will up the ante with a form generator deployed over an intranet. Very few will pursue the form generator as a database implementation, even though it is the better mechanism. The database solution flows from the *3-D model kernel*: adopt a database application to generate, publish, and manage all reports generated by the project. The architecture of this application should as a minimum include:

- Database application equipped with a form generator;
- Access to the form via web browser;

- Automated distribution built in for each report type.
- Between successive reporting periods, automatic insertion in the section, *progress this period*, of the contents of the section, *forecast for next period*, that were published in the previous report; and
- Utilization of the cloud for publishing and distribution.

Cloud Shoveling

The cloud paradigm offers projects a ready-made infrastructure to store and retrieve all information generated by a project. It is a demonstrably potent solution where an owner's expansive assets are distributed widely across geographies, and the preferred default position for profitably performing asset (PPA) data transactions. But the state of the art, at least as of the writing of this book, is still lacking in critical areas.

The first area is security. One can never assume that the infrastructure is inviolate. A prudent strategy is to permanently overestimate the resolve of faceless hackers to breach the bulwarks circumscribing your cloud. Pushing the argument further, the information technology manager should first assume that a breach will occur at some point in time and devise the appropriate measures to counter, mitigate, and recover the upper hand.

Avoid the cloud when dealing with datum sets and operational control systems that are strategically critical.

The second area is engineering design. Concurrent engineering and design are features of any industrial-strength technical application platform. The natural reflex is to assume that this capability can be deployed through the cloud. The assumption is conceptually feasible but realistically unworkable given the state of the art today—the bandwidth is simply not there. A concurrent engineering or design framework places enormous demands on the throughput capacity of the underlying network. Even the simple case of a live-streaming of a 3-D model presentation will utterly strain the fiber optic backbone of most companies. For the time being, and for the foreseeable future, the cloud will not be a suitable environment for a concurrent design schema.

Time Sheets

Every company has a time-sheet system, be it paper or electronic, in which case it is inherited from the owner's enterprise resource planning system. It is unlikely, in such instances, to have a structure compatible with the plant's physical configuration, or to satisfy the compatibility requirements of the *collection substrate*. Furthermore, it may lack the controls to prevent *hours dumping*—whereby individuals with no specific charge codes record some or all of their hours against that project simply because it is there. This problem is surprisingly widespread in the project world and leads to all sorts of *postmortem* activities to detect and redress the charges—which adds unnecessary labor costs. These two shortcomings make it very difficult to *manage by anticipation*.

To be effective, the time-sheet system must satisfy four criteria:

- The datum structure of the time record must abide by the single organizing hierarchy provided by the plant's physical configuration.
- It must include a *lockout* default setting whereby *write* permissions must be controlled individually by time record, and assignable to specific individuals.
- It should have a *tagout* default setting whereby each *write* permission must be granted for a specified length of time, extendable by explicit authorization from the project manager *prior* to the next starting period.
- Tallied hours must be available to the project manager in real time for control and analysis.

The first criterion is a consequence of the single hierarchical principle enunciated in Chapter 15, which mapped the plant configuration identically to the work breakdown structure and the project team's organization chart. The second one provides the essential control as to who charges what hours, when, and to what cost account. The third criterion provides control over the entire team over time. The default setting is expiration after a fixed duration, which should not be longer than two months—batch extensions can be easily automated. The final criterion is essential to the idea of anticipatory management as discussed in Chapter 3. Finally, it goes without saying that the time-sheet system must be available for time entries in real time, from anywhere.

IT'S A SPREADSHEET WORLD AFTER ALL

The Justified Status Quo

It's a tad of an itsy-bitsy bit of a statement of the obvious to point to the hegemony held by Microsoft Excel over the project world. Spreadsheets are created at the speed of staccato fingers to tabulate innumerable numbers, graphs, charts, lists, checklists, action items, risks, registers, and cut-and-paste images. It's hard to think of any other application in Planet Project that so pervades the act of writing. If projects were a democracy, Excel would be Imperator for life.

The problems with spreadsheets begin with their circulation, at will far and wide (by e-mail, of course), then recirculated in newer versions as contents change. Spreadsheets are inherently static documents. It is cumbersome to the nth degree to keep up with the multitude of versions that can float around at any given moment. Multiple authors modify them for their own purposes, sometimes losing embedded logic or links. Other problems rapidly creep in at the speed of errors. Cells may be copied without regard to the underlying equations they contain. Equations are overwritten with typed values by pure happenstance or inattention. Ranges are cut and pasted somewhere else, losing the positional relationships in the process. Hidden rows or columns can be inadvertently deleted by an unsuspecting editor. Number formats are mistakenly changed from currency to percentages, creating 100-fold calculation errors. And on and on and on. The list of visible and hidden mistakes that can propagate throughout a project team is innumerable.

Spreadsheets versus Dynamic Records

Projects are best served by customized databases for creating and updating lists, registers, checklists and all other similar *dynamic* documents. Databases are ideally suited to keeping tabs on changing variables like cost accruals, contract lists, part counts, labor hours, construction field tickets, and risk registers. The benefits are manifold:

- Formatting, equations, and content integrity are protected.
- Changes and versions are automatically tracked.
- A single set of records is available.
- A unique set of records is accessible.
- Information is instantly updated and so accessed by all authorized users.
- Charts, statistics, and metrics exist as built-in menus, and baseline comparisons are enabled.
- Everyone can read the same data in real time.
- Access, editing, and distribution permissions are controlled.

One especially important database to create for any project is the project ecosystem (PECO) database, structured in accordance with the information delineated in Chapter 7.

Spreadsheets versus Math

The versatility of Excel makes it a favorite of calculation templates. However, the problems enumerated before are indigenous to those templates, and one more: complex formulae. It is, of course, possible to create simple what-if conditions as equations embedded into a cell. Visual Basic vastly expands the algorithmic capabilities of an Excel worksheet. But most spreadsheets are created by direct insertion of complicated equations into the cells. Therein lies the danger:

equations that are intelligible symbolically become cryptic or undecipherable as 100 character commands. Two additional concerns compound the danger: distribution control and protection of intellectual property.

The project will again be best served by the use of math-specific software to deal with calculations:

- Adopt a commercially available mathematical application, such as Math-CAD, MathLab, Mathematica, or Maple (to name but a few).
- Deploy the various calculation schemes and templates from a database-centric digital warehouse.
- Protection of intellectual property is strengthened: everyone has Excel but comparatively few are equipped with the specific math applications.
- Validation and verification of new and modified schemes is unequivocal to the pertinent subject matter expert.
- Integrity of contents, logic, and algorithmic sequencing is guaranteed.

Math Morass

The case against spreadsheets for complex calculations is best made by example. Consider the following two equations, appearing in Table 5.21a of API 650 (welded storage tanks) to calculate the uplift force experienced by a vertical tank when exposed to internal pressure and winds, and internal pressure and seismic excitation:

$$Force\ 1 = \left(\left(FpPi + Pwr - 0.08th \right) {}^*D^2 {}^*787 \right) + \frac{4Mwh}{D} - W_1$$

$$Force\ 2 = \left(\left(FpPi - 0.08th \right) {}^*D^2 {}^*787 \right) + \frac{4Mrw}{D} - W_1 \left(1 - 0.4Av \right)$$

both subject to a variable, Ks, expressed by:

$$Ks = \frac{1}{\sqrt{Tanh\left(\dfrac{3.68^*H}{D} \right)}}$$

It is, of course, possible to create these equations in Excel. The units in this case are a killer. Pi is in kPa; W_1 in newtons; th in mm; D and H in meters; M in N-m; and the others are scalars. $Forces$ 1 and 2 are in Newtons. If Pi is given in MPa (as was observed by your author in one case), the whole edifice falls apart.

ENGINEERING SOFTWARE

The Wonders of the Deep End

In the right hands, specialty engineering software can be valunomic to a project. The caveat is to apply the right software to the right problem. Pick either one incorrectly and risk getting results instead of answers. There is subtlety in this axiom: the fact that an application is marketed for a specific kind of problem can be misleading. One must look beyond the claim and stare coldly at the method underlying that claim.

All software applications produce results. Projects require answers.

Physics or Code

Engineering nucleation (see Chapter 12) gives us our first example of a misleading claim. Most, if not all, industries operate within a regulatory framework that dictates the codes, standards, and specifications that will govern. As expected, software vendors offer various suites of specialized applications built to apply the equations, fudge factors, and calculation methodologies inherent to a given code (or standard or specification). By their very nature, governing codes are explicitly limited to specific design cases for which physics formulations are available. In other words, codes are never able, nor do they so claim, to characterize the physics of *any* design under *any* arbitrary conditions. The crux of the matter is this: does the user understand where the limit ends? In an overwhelming majority of cases, the answer is no. As noted in Chapter 12:

> No matter who's running which software, the outcome always produces results. The what you see is not (WYSIN) principle flares up on the basis that results are not answers (results maximize risk; answers minimize it). More often than not, results are not even wrong. Turning results into answers is what makes risk assessment profitable. And getting answers out of results demands a deeply proficient human-software tandem.

The default position for any problem analysis should be to resolve the full-field physics of a problem, rather than rely on canned code software. The PPA will always be better served by a software tool that can quantify the behavior of a design under full-field physics, instead of simplistic closed-form cases. Relying on canned code software always carries the risk that either user or software or both will be operating beyond the intrinsic limitations of the software.

The same argument can be made, of course, for users of full-field physics-based software. Not all simulation applications are created equal. Low cost options may be limited to mathematically linear problems and low nodal counts.

High-end applications will cover nonlinear behavior, but at a higher price. Both are more challenging to master than canned code software. Here, the risk is one of dabbling: not every self-appointed expert in physics-based software is genuinely proficient in the field. Many of them are *menu drivers*—dabblers—without any understanding of the mathematical models and approximations embedded into the solver engines. How is an owner to decide whom to pick? The answer is by retaining the services of a genuine expert who is recognized in the field. This individual will be able to assess the merits of a vendor's claimed expertise and probate the answers inferred from the results so produced.

Red Pens and Markups

All project documents get reviewed. Quite often, multiple reviews will hark back to the age-old pen-on-paper technique. The efficacy of this technique is beyond compare; but its drawback comes up in distribution—scanning, faxing, or courier transmittals complicate the process. Archiving markups is another ordeal: several revisions of the same document make the mere mechanics of storage cumbersome, if not impossible, when operating across several theaters of operation. Existing commercial software solutions address these obstacles elegantly (see for example *Bluebeam)*. These applications make it possible to capture markups by individual authors and preserve them digitally. Access is one mouse-click away. This is the easiest recommendation: abandon the pen and go digital.

Dimensioned Drawings

To fabricate, build, or construct anything, one needs dimensions. Dimensions are bred by engineering drawings. No revelation here. But the presentation of a dimension, on a drawing or other, matters significantly because of the costs derived from it. The rationale starts at the PECO level. An owner tends to procure equipment from vendors familiar with the owner's preferences. Over time, these vendors develop their own preferences for indicating dimensions on drawings. No matter the industry, odds are that even for the simplest of geometries such as a cube, the quantity of dimensioning schemas will equal the number of vendors queried to create the drawing. This unwarranted speciation among vendors *decreases proportionally* the number of possible vendors available to an owner. The situation worsens in global supply chains. On the matter of dimensioning and tolerancing, the gold standards are the ASME standard Y14 series (preferred) and the ISO/TC 213 series (alternatively). The impact to the owner will be the creation of universally recognized dimensioned drawings impervious to localized idiosyncrasies.

Solid Models versus Drawings

Drawings are good. Drawings conforming to ASME Y14 are better. Dimensioned 3-D models are best, as they permit direct interactions with automated fabrication systems without any need for human interpretations of the design intent. The practice of manufacturing parts directly from a 3-D model is common to many industries from automobiles and airplanes to appliances and furniture. There is no need for the intermediate step of creating dimensioned drawings to guide fabrication. Drawings, in this scenario, add no value to the project, but add costs.

ASME Y14.41 establishes the requirements for model-based definition pertinent to 3-D models. Y14.41 is to 3-D models what Y14.5 is to drawings. The existence of Y14.41 is the justification for a second, two-prong recommendation:

- Abandon the practice of producing dimensioned drawings derived from 3-D models.
- Manufacture directly from the dimensioned 3-D models.

COST ESTIMATING

The Killer App to Kill Spreadsheets

The data underlying the estimating mechanics are the ultimate argument in favor of databases over spreadsheets. Estimating tools include historical data on costs, durations, effort levels, location factors, forecasts versus actuals, and performance metrics, to name but a few. The tools incorporate equations, formulae, rules of thumb, and industry practices to calculate the design parameters, quantities, labor hours, and freight. While spreadsheets continue to be rampant in this domain, because of my previous arguments, I tilt in favor of databases.

The mechanics of estimating are a pure instance of a database application.

Critical Feedback Loop

The process of estimating is also the poster child of the principle of *garbage in, garbage out*. As we saw in previous chapters, an estimate is nothing but an educated guess. The feedback loop is essential to the usefulness of estimate data. Note that old records should never be overwritten with the latest data, since they also provide the means to quantify trends (usually inflationary) over time. Estimate data, old and new, must never be deleted.

Performance assessment metrics (PAM) form a subset of the feedback data. For each contractor involved on a project, the PAM datum set should be captured to validate the initial estimated targets set by the owner. These targets can be subjected to a trend analysis to validate their merit; and used to track the performance improvements of the vendor over time. Negative trends from project to project, or even from one life-cycle phase to another, will be indicative of structural problems experienced by the vendor that need to be flagged and corrected, in accordance with the principle of *perform or justify*.

Feeding Back the Vendor

The importance of feedback is especially significant when a vendor is hired by the owner to produce the estimate. Owners are reluctant to release actual construction and operating data back to vendors. Unfortunately, without this feedback, the vendor is unable to validate the original estimate data, which skews the numbers the next time the owner requests an estimate.

> *Vendor-prepared estimates are a waste of the owner's time and money unless the owner is willing to extend the feedback mechanism to the vendor.*

ELECTRONIC TRANSACTIONS

Online Filing

Projects generate an enormous amount of so-called *progress records* throughout their life cycle, from man-hours to inspection results, to daily fuel consumption at the construction site. One example is shown in Appendix 9, representing a daily inspection report for field work during construction. These reports may be prepared by hand from a spreadsheet template, or entered electronically from hand-written inputs (think daily tickets, for example). The entire effort is cumbersome, laborious, prone to errors, and just plain inefficient. Worse, none of the metrics captured by these reports can be tallied, accrued, and analyzed in real time. Projects require real-time analysis, which mandates some form of online record entry. That requirement is best met by browser-enabled, location-independent database applications. Paper reports, daily tracking reports, and inspection reports are just a few of the reports that must be electronically captured rather than transcribed from paper originals. Whatever recurring data are expected from vendors, contractors and consultants should be captured through the same input schema. These include:

- Daily work tickets
- Weekly and monthly consultant progress reports (including labor hours, costs, deliverable status, change register)
- Third-party inspection reports of vendors

- Invoice submissions
- Import and export documentation
- Permits and licenses
- Consumable reports
- Delivery status
- Safety reports
- Mileage records

Signatures

The online form is the perfect segue into the world of signatures. Paper remains popular in the project imagination for its affinity for signatures. An original signature confers upon any kind of document a degree of formality that is essential to managing at the interfaces. The inalterable character of hand signatures is key, but comes at a heavy price. In fact, the cost of ink is astronomical, relative to its evidentiary purpose. The signed document is condemned to live out its existence in a single place. It must be photocopied or scanned. It cannot circulate with ease in the pursuit of several signatures. In other words, it requires a formal handling and tracking infrastructure to be useful within a team setting. Just imagine, for example, the total costs incurred to get approval signatures on an amendment to a partnership agreement involving five partners spread across the planet. The cost of ink is rarely questioned, but highly questionable.

Here is one instance of a no-brainer solution. Go digital. Adopt electronic signatures as the default mechanics and retain ink by exception (where the law demands it). The marketplace is replete with trustworthy applications that have figured out how to address issues of security, datum protection, audit trails, and hacker prevention. Once you have chosen a system, make it an integral and mandatory component of the project's standard operating environment or standard operating landscape. Then, roll with it.

LESSONS LEARNED

Lost Learning

Continual improvement is a quality-driven mechanic. Historically, it was appended to a project's execution plan through the *lessons learned* process. The idea is to write down any lesson derived from a specific situation and apply that lesson to future instances of the same situation. In practical terms, this procedure is based on the guiding principles of continual improvement. To most project organizations, *lessons learned* are managed as a passive database (or spreadsheet, ugh!) that is meant to be consulted later during execution. Its usefulness is dubious at best or irrelevant at worst in this passive state.

Nevertheless, the mechanics of *lessons learned* are meritorious and valunomic when correctly designed. The starting position is to address the organization of the capture information. A captured lesson cannot be of any use to anyone if it can't be found again in its proper context. The organization of the *lessons learned* relies on four *knowledge anchors*: the mechanics, the mechanism, the location, and the PECO:

- *The formal mechanics*—The first *knowledge anchor* is a specific process or procedure that is deployed during execution. Any learned lesson must tie back to at least one such mechanic. The linkage is created when the mechanics are updated and published.
- *The prescribed mechanism*—A lesson learned can apply to the mechanism rather than the mechanics. For example, a procedure may call for a stress intensity calculation on a structural element. The mechanism for performing the calculation may require a change (how to model the element before running it through the stress simulation) as a result of a lesson learned. In this case, the mechanics are untouched but the mechanism is modified in accordance with the lesson.
- *The features of a physical location*—The third anchor is related to location, which is quantified in terms of access, obstacles, limits, or challenges. For example, a communication tower may be located in an area prone to spring flooding. This is a piece of knowledge that characterizes the location and that must be captured.
- *A PECO characteristic*—The fourth anchor is akin to the physical location but at the PECO level. For example, a village near a plant may have become uncooperative. Such knowledge must be captured.

Capture and Application

The implementation of the *lessons learned* mechanic is accomplished in two parts: *capture* and *application*. In Part 1, a separate, central database is maintained by the framework team to capture all new lessons, with built-in linkages to the four knowledge anchors. This stand-alone database serves as the master register to track the progress of the capture and release of the lessons in real time. In Part 2, the lesson is documented as an Annex or Appendix (for anchors 1 or 2), or entered as a new record in the pertinent database (for anchors 3 or 4). The dissemination of the lesson is automated by the revision mechanics associated with the anchor.

Part 2 is the critical step of the implementation process. The learned lesson is no longer considered an opinion to be adopted at the whim of the reader, but a mandatory action imposed on the project's execution strategy. The reader should note, too, that this approach helps the capture of *lessons* in real time as a matter of procedural obligation upon the entire team. *Lessons learned* are no longer viewed as auxiliary steps performed *ad hoc*.

Lessons versus Process

It is possible to misuse the mechanics of *lessons learned*. Some people will submit a lesson suggestion to highlight an instance when a mandatory *mechanic* or *mechanism* was ignored during execution (quite often related to change management…). Those instances *do not* constitute a valid use of the *lessons learned* mechanic. They belong instead to the auditing policy for the project. As the name implies, a *lesson* is a lesson when it sheds light on something new to the project. It could be a deficiency in a mechanism, or a new variable that needs to be added to it. It could be a finding on how to negotiate a deal with a specific stakeholder. Those are valid lessons. Pointing out the fact that the change management process was not followed is not a lesson learned. It is a procedural failing deserving management action.

TRAINING AND DEVELOPMENT

Lip Service

Training and development are ubiquitous themes. Like quality, safety, and workplace equality, they receive an enormous amount of attention and idealized prioritization in public pronouncements. Until, that is, harder times call for cost cutting. Only then are the true feelings of the organization brought to the fore. When times are tough and training budgets are gutted, you know where priorities really stand.

The other reality is that businesses expect their employees to perform from the get-go; nobody is allowed time to *practice* the work. This attitude is anathema to the notions of "A" teams and "A" organizations. It is also harmful to the success of a PPA project.

After-Action Reviews

Amazingly, one of the most potent learning methods available to project teams costs almost nothing. The technique, engineered by the U.S. Navy in the 1960s, is called an *after-action review* (AAR). The technique is ideally suited to the nature of projects and works like this. It considers any event that requires a mobilized solution as a training opportunity. Say a piece of equipment cannot be bolted to its foundation because of misaligned bolts. A solution is found after much finger pointing between the parties involved. The AAR mechanic is triggered *immediately* after the matter is closed. At that moment, and not weeks or months later, the project manager convenes the AAR session with everyone involved in the issue (attendance mandatory). The point of the AAR is *not* to assign blame, but to identify the strengths and weaknesses of the people and information associated with the execution of the work. It is imperative that the project manager keeps the discussion focused on four concerns:

- What was supposed to happen?
- What went wrong?
- What went right?
- Why things went wrong, and why they went right.

The single most important ingredient of the AAR recipe is brutal honesty. Ranks and titles are banned from the room. Comments must be blunt, but respectful. Historically, this rank honesty is the most difficult thing to accept by bosses and managers. But the experience of the U.S. Army has shown time and time again that organizations learned the most and in the fastest time when they subjected themselves to this wholesome naked introspection. The AAR is, in fact, the cornerstone of any development strategy pursued by organizations seeking to operate as "A" organizations and "A" teams.

Top Gun[1]

The U.S. military discovered in the 1960s in the throes of the Vietnam war the atrocious shortcoming of its training philosophy for its F-4 fighter pilots, which did not expose recruits to realistic combat conditions. The reason was eminently pragmatic: in real conditions, training failures could be lethal. The F-4 Phantom was then recognized as the premier air weapons platform in the world. North Vietnamese pilots flew technologically inferior Soviet jets. Despite their dramatic technological advantage, American pilots did not dominate and instead suffered horrendous losses in men and machines (compared to their previous records from World War II). The U.S. Navy ceased all air combats in Vietnam for a year while it established its Fighter Weapon School, better known as the *Top Gun* school from the famous 1986 movie. The school adopted four training principles:

1) Everything that happens during practice, every move, every command, every success, and every error is recorded;
2) The enemy must be as real as possible, only better, with trainers drawn from the best pilots available, emulating MiG flying techniques;

> 3) Each training session is followed by an AAR. Face-saving and self-delusions by trainees, who were defeated 85% of the time, were impossible because of the recorded evidence; and
> 4) After the AAR, trainees go back in the air to do the whole thing all over again, and again, over two weeks.
>
> The program yielded immediate improvements when combat operations resumed over the Vietnamese skies. The success metrics were so staggering that the Air Force and Army set up their own AAR-based training. The impact of the AAR training philosophy was instrumental to the first Gulf War. Operation Desert Storm ended a mere hundred hours after it started with a complete and utter victory over the Iraqi forces.

The effectiveness of the AAR method rests on the realism of the training scenario and on the participation of entire groups, rather than independent individuals. It yields "*order-of-magnitude improvements in performance.*"[2] Realism is the clue to the project application. Every issue, every piecemeal group of tasks is a slice of reality through which learning from experience can be conducted. *Ad hoc* issues are one type of opportunity, but even the conclusion of a set of related tasks by a single group (or interdependent groups) provides an immediate and tangible opportunity to conduct an AAR session. And, need we say it again, at almost no extra cost to the project.

WHEN YOU WISH UPON A STAR

This chapter concludes on a wishful note regarding two giant opportunities for project management innovation. The first is *hazard and operability (HAZOP) automation* associated with process safety analysis. The second, *algorithma*, goes to the heart of the matter of modeling an entire project from the basis of unit transformations.

HAZOP Automation

At some point during the development of the plant, the project must assess the safety of its operations. This assessment in the Oil and Gas industry is done via the mechanics of a *HAZOP study*. The mechanics enable the structured and systematic evaluation of a process in order to qualify and quantify the risks to personnel, equipment, or operation. The work is done in plenary sessions attended by suitably experienced multidisciplinary teams. The HAZOP technique requires participants to image what could go wrong and derive from these considerations the potential HAZOP problems inherent to the process under review. The technique will also employ dedicated software to record the deviations and consequences associated with the uncovered problems.

Two salient points of this definition warrant emphasizing: the analysis is qualitative; and software is used for issue recording and tracking. That is how HAZOP studies are conducted today. The traditional method relies on a large group of reviewers gathered inside a conference room to review the entire set of schematic drawings pertinent to the system, installation, or plant under consideration. The review process focuses typically on the *flow* of a process parameter (a fluid, a granular stream, a signal, electrical power) as it moves throughout a nodal network. The qualitative analysis runs through a set of *upset* conditions for the flow from which the participants deduce effects and consequences, then assess whether the network is equipped with the appropriate safety features to contain the ramifications. The outcome of the analysis is a very large set of issues documented into a table and assigned possible remediation scenarios. Your author once participated in a particularly onerous session that mobilized over 100 participants over three months to review more than one hundred drawings and produced 800 recommendations, each requiring seven signatures to be approved. Imagine the cost to the project.

True Automation

The opportunity to automate this process is fantastic. The qualitative assessment is amenable to a software application where components' behavior is discretized. This enables a single person to perform a comprehensive set of what-if scenarios for all networks in one sitting, and produce the HAZOP issue register in hours, rather than weeks. Remedial solutions can be predefined and tested simultaneously by the software at the same time. The qualitative assessment can then be turned into a quantitative analysis carried out as part of the nucleation life-cycle phase.

Algorithma

Chapter 4 highlighted the fact that complexity is a feral beast that can only be tamed through software, if only from the perspective of sequencing and process flow visualization. There exists no commercial software solution that can codify any phase of a project, let alone the entire project, in accordance with the atomic structure of the unit transformation process. There is, on the other hand, a plethora of so-called project management software that purports to equip organizations with aggregating tools to grasp a project in its entirety. To wit, the reader is invited to peruse the following extracts from several vendor web sites on their respective offerings:

"ABC is an all-in-one project management and collaboration software that brings thousands of teams around the globe closer to project success. Its perfect blend of project management and social collaboration features helps you become more productive and achieve goals faster: keep all your plans and priorities up-to-date, manage all your tasks and files in a central hub, and collaborate in real time with your teammates. ABC makes all your work more organized, manageable, and efficient!"

"BCD is designed for the practical implementation of Kanban and is a highly flexible project management platform that lets you visualize your process, collaborate more effectively, and identify opportunities for improvement."

"A New Way to Manage Enterprise Projects: CDE gives you powerful project management, social collaboration, and real-time visibility for any project or task. More than 2,500 enterprises rely on CDE to eliminate double work and boost productivity and profitability."

"DEF is the leading portfolio and project management solution that manages the full project life cycle from project planning to execution through closure. Key features: MS Project import/export, resource allocation, Outlook integration, issues, intelligent scheduling, and time/expense tracking. DEF is the most customizable software offering Web Services and .NET SDK."

"You're looking for project management software for a reason, right? Something is broken. Either your current tool isn't working or you don't have one and your processes are a mess. The problem is traditional PPM tools only focus on managing projects. You and your teams need more than that. You need one work environment for connecting teams across the entire work life cycle. You need 360° visibility and reporting for execs, project managers, stakeholders, and teams. You need EFG."

"FGH is web-based project management software for teams that makes it easy to plan and coordinate your projects. FGH provides enterprise-level features at an affordable monthly price and is great for managing team members working in different locations."

"GHI is an online project management and task collaboration tool that is redefining how teams work. Its familiar and easy-to-use spreadsheet-like interface, coupled with file sharing, Gantt charts, and work automation features have helped GHI quickly grow into a favorite business app for productivity."

Looking beyond the sales pitch reveals some common threads. First, according to the marketplace, project management is all about collaboration. Second, project management software is a euphemism for *execution reporting*. Third, commercial solutions assume that the WBS and the schedule are sufficient to tie together every other aspect of the execution. Project management is reduced to accessing a variety of reports, charts, graphs, and curves *postmortem*. The implicit assumption shared by these applications is that project management is a function of those reports and the actions that are taken from them. That is not project management; it is postmortem journal reporting.

True PM Software

Genuine PPA management software would start with the *unit transformation process* as the foundational object structure. To this structure would be added the functionality range embodying the accountability principle. With these two elements of the system's architecture, the WBS, the schedule, the manpower curves, and every other traditional project control dataset are produced. Such a system would create visualizations of the complexity of the activity sequencing in 3-D, much like a 3-D CAD package would.

That is your author's hope for a better project management future!

NOTES

1. From Geoff Colvin's *Humans Are Underrated: What High Achievers Know That Machines Never Will.*
2. See Ronald Coase's *The Nature of the Firm* for more details.

18

PROJECT CLOSEOUT

---

*Projects and washrooms: two instances of jobs not
finished until the paperwork is complete.*

IT'S DONE. NOW WHAT?

Closure Requires Closeout

Some projects reach their natural conclusion and others do so prematurely. But all will end, in the end. The subject of project closeout is our concern in this chapter. How does the process look from a project management perspective? Who does what? What records need to be retained, in what format? When is a project actually done? These questions require answers that are often ignored or overlooked in the setting of execution strategy. There is more to ending a project than declaring it done and archiving the files. The scope of the effort is a function of positions within the project hierarchy. The equipment vendor at the bottom will require the least effort to compile the smallest retention set. The scope project team (SPT) will roll up all of the close-out documentation provided by its vendors and subcontractors. The project management office (PMO) will again roll things up for the SPT and supply chain partners (SCPs), as well as its own internal close-out set. At the top sits the framework, whose close-out set will include that of its PMO, the set associated with the project ecosystem, and the set tied to the baseline asset execution framework. Predictably, the volume of documentation increases as you move up the hierarchy. In this chapter, the perspective of the *framework* will underscore the discussion. Lower-level organizations (such as an SCP) can extract their specific requirements accordingly.

The closure of a project is a mandatory element of a PPA execution strategy and must be funded accordingly.

Project Closeout Is Not an Option

A project must be unwound in an orderly manner to make sure that all loose ends are tied, that the final cost picture is completed, that all payments are made and accounted for, and that the remnant records are given the last appropriate rites. Closing a project requires planning, strategy, and patience. The process is carried out along two parallel tracts—*exogenous* and *endogenous*. It applies to every level of the project hierarchy. The *exogenous tract* exists in relation to the contractual relationships between two or more entities (owner-SPT, SPT-SCP, owner-regulator). Closure in this context implies a confirmation that all contractual obligations placed upon the project team have been satisfied and verified through evidentiary documentation bearing signatures. The documentation involved is divided into two groups: *turnover* and *completion*. The *endogenous tract* deals with the information that remains internal to a project team. That information is divided into three groups: *closeout, digital archive,* and *paper archive*. By definition, this information is not intended to be released to parties external to the corporate organization.

Is This All Really Necessary?

Yes, it is. These information sets are required at the end of every contract, life-cycle phase, and development. Closure activities are comprehensive affairs that cost money. Those costs must be factored into the pertinent budgets. The valunomy of this expense stems from the following motivations:

- The contractual scope of work and the associated deliverables are complete, in possession of the owner, and the contract acknowledged as fulfilled by both parties.
- The entirety of the costs, both chargeable and not to the project, have been tallied and invoiced to the owner.
- The project's performance assessment metrics have been gathered and analyzed.
- The management of each party is debriefed on the metrics.
- For the owner, the asset's actual performance and profitability have been quantified through operations.
- All project files and datum sets generated by either party are archived or disposed of in a manner consistent with the requirements of the contract and with each party's archiving plan.

- The 3-D model kernel and its datum construct are implemented and up-and-running.
- Record-keeping compliance to regulatory and legal obligations is met.

An *effective* closeout will begin weeks or months before the scheduled end date of the scope of work. Merely shutting down a job in a few days at the bitter end will only wreak havoc on both owner and contractor and negate any usefulness of the information retained.

THE LAW IS IN PLAY

Obligations

The contract is not the only sheriff in this close-out town. Legislative obligations are the primary drivers behind the retention of records. In Alberta, Canada, for example, the following statutes and regulations have force of law and legal precedence. These legislative codes effectively dictate the minimum retention requirements of the retention of certain documents generated during the execution of a project:

Federal level:

- Canada Evidence Act
- Personal Information Protection and Electronic Documents Act (PIPEDA)
- Employment Standards Code
- Canada Business Corporations Act
- Freedom of Information and Protection of Privacy Regulation

Provincial level:

- Alberta Electronic Transaction Act
- Alberta Evidence Act
- Alberta Limitation Act
- Electronic Transactions Act
- Occupational Health and Safety Act
- Personal Information Protection Act (PIPA)
- The Engineering, Geological, and Geophysical Act
- Alberta Business Corporations Act
- Electronic Transactions Act Designation Regulation
- Electronic Transactions Act General Regulation
- The Engineering, Geological, and Geophysical Professions Act

Future Reliance

The decision to retain a document, notwithstanding the legal statutes, is motivated in part by legal self-protection and expectations of future consultation. The archive in particular is devised to satisfy all three. From a project perspective, the archive becomes the primordial link for the owner to reach back in time. Note that the term *archive* here includes the archives individually created by the project partners and suppliers. To be purposeful, that archive must be structured formally to make access, search, and retrieval efficient. The reader is reminded that digital records are plagued with the issue of file format obsolescence. The archiving system must account for this obsolescence variable. Consider, for example, a spreadsheet created long ago with Lotus Notes, or an engineering report published as a WordPerfect file; unless the archive was equipped accordingly, these files have become inaccessible today.

> *For this reason, archived digital files should not be preserved in their dynamic form, but in read-only scheme. Embedded logic must be extracted and stored in a separate, adjunct document, from which future coding can be effected.*[1]

CLOSE-OUT DELIVERABLES

A Tale of Two Plans

At the project level, the close-out mechanics are owned by the framework. The planning of the close-out mechanic is an integral part of the project execution strategy, resulting in the publication of two governing plans: the *archiving plan* and the *phase completion plan*. The *archiving plan* is owned by the framework. It is written to achieve compliance with the legal obligations governing the work and will apply ubiquitously to all phases of the project. An illustrative example of the plan's table of contents is given in Appendix 10.

The *phase completion plan*, as the name indicates, is specific to a phase of the project. It describes the mechanics and mechanisms pertinent to the *exogenous* and *endogenous* documents. Appendix 11 illustrates the suggested table of contents of the plan. This plan is owned by the PMO.

The Exogenous Tract

The *exogenous* tract encompasses the *turnover completion deliverables*, which are divided into two groups. The *turnover group* includes the documents listed in the contract that must be handed to the client upon completion of the work. The *completion group* defines the set of documents created to support the execution of the close-out activities and requiring the owner's previous approval (evidenced by signature). They form the formal recognition and acceptance by the owner of the completion of the contractual work by the contractor. Examples of completion documents include:

- Demobilization list
- Completion schedule
- Certificate of completion
- Customer feedback
- Approved punch list
- Minutes of owner close-out meeting
- Personnel close-out checklists
- Project assignment authorization forms

Endogenous Tract

The *endogenous* tract encompasses the *close-out group*, the *digital archive*, and the *paper archive*. The *close-out group* encompasses the forms, task checklists, project metrics, and financial documents that are generated by the project team as evidence of closure of all aspects of the project.

Close-out group documents will typically not require a signature from the owner's representative. Examples of documents include:

- Project level
  - Project close-out form
  - Lessons learned register
  - Project close-out report
  - Project information database entry
- Project controls
  - Close-out report
  - Project closeout and benchmark
  - Final total installed cost (TIC) key quantity tracking
- Document management
  - Master folder and file register
  - Digital archive register
  - Archive register
  - Final documentation package checklist
  - Final documentation package release note
  - Archive register
- Project information management
  - Completion checklist

- Accounting and finance
  - ◻ Contracts close-out checklist
  - ◻ Project commercial close-out checklist
- Supply chain management
  - ◻ Purchase order close-out checklist
  - ◻ Surplus materials and equipment reconciliation form
  - ◻ Vendor inspection reports
  - ◻ Confirmation of vendor invoice payments
  - ◻ Import and export permits register
- Construction
  - ◻ Mechanical completion checklist
  - ◻ Absence of lien form
  - ◻ Excess material inventory
  - ◻ Commissioning report
  - ◻ Punch list

The *digital archive* is the set of electronic records, files, and folders preserved for future reference and consultation. The archive is constituted from the cleansed contents of the project's folder. Cleansed contents result from the records maintenance performed by all team personnel (described later). The reader should note that the electronic files associated with engineering, design, and 3-D modeling *do not* belong in the digital archive. These types of files are best maintained within the electronic data management system that is integral to the software applications sustaining these files.

The *paper archive* is assembled from select paper documents deemed essential to the project's long-term knowledge preservation. Such documents meet the definition of *record* provided in the following paragraph.

What Constitutes a Record?

A record is an information element defined as follows:

> *A record is a piece of formatted information (document, digital file, form, drawing) that must be legally or contractually retained as proof of an activity.*

It is important to note that most information generated during a project does not satisfy this definition and will therefore not be subject to project archiving. Records are *proofs of an activity* performed by an organization. A record must have content, context, and structure, and be part of a record-keeping system. Records must be unalterable once they are so designated. Records start out as documents and become official records when they are retained for evidentiary purposes. Accordingly, most project documents do not become records. Examples of a record include: contract negotiation documents, business correspondence, personnel files, financial statements, research, and a history of the business or organization, invoices, drawings, and data sheets.

SEQUENCING OF CLOSURE ACTIVITIES

The sequence of close-out activities begins months ahead of a formal completion date. The sequence is comprised of four stages: *planning, cleansing, completion*, and *wrap*.

Stage 1—Planning

This initial stage establishes the timeline of the close-out activities carried out by team personnel prior to their demobilization from the project. The outcome of this phase is the compilation of the demobilization list and the close-out schedule. The owners of these mechanics are the project manager (PM) and the project engineer/coordinator. Stage 1 should begin at least three months prior to the scheduled end of Stage 2.

The *demobilization list* establishes the expected departure date of all team personnel, as a function of the completion of their respective close-out duties. It forms the basis of the completion schedule. An individual is ready for demobilization when his *personnel close-out checklist* has been signed off.

The *personnel close-out checklist* verifies that each project team member has completed her own individual close-out tasks prior to demobilization. The checklist also verifies that the individual's network connections to the project are severed. The form must be checked by each of the four functional leads from the administration, the project information manager, document control, and engineering design specifications. Once the form is complete, the four individuals sign off on the form. Release from the project is authorized by the project manager via a form preserved in the project directory.

The *close-out schedule* is a subset of the master schedule and presents a Level 2 outline of all close-out activities across all four stages.

Stage 2—Cleansing

Stage 2 prepares the entire set of records required by the group of five previously noted. Stage 2 is carried out by every team member who has generated data, documents, or other pieces of information through his involvement with the project. Such information may be located on the project directory; the project's intranet site; the document management database; and FTP sites. The objective is to cleanse all information holdings of superfluous, erroneous, incomplete, obsolete, and unnecessary data. Another objective of Stage 2 is to determine what records are to be kept in digital or paper format (but not both). The methods of record cleansing are discussed in detail later on in this chapter. Stage 2 is a process owned by the individual team members. It begins at least one month prior to an individual's demobilization date.

The *benchmark and key TIC quantity updates*—In addition to the cleansing activities, team leads compile the metrics generated during the execution, which are then compiled into two deliverables typically owned by project controls. Note that leads can only be demobilized once they have completed their inputs to these two forms. The two deliverables are the:

- Project close-out and benchmarking register, and
- Final TIC key quantity tracking register.

Stage 3—Completion

The third stage encompasses the compilation and transmittal of the *exogenous* deliverables included in the *turnover group* and the *completion group*. Stage 3 is the time to gather all costs incurred during the project, and assign them according to their pertinence as billable to the project or not. Both the owner and the contractor aim at the provision of acceptance certificates, the confirmation/transfer of warranties, the handover of documentation, final inspections, claim resolutions and payment reconciliation, and verification of a final invoice for payment. Several mundane yet critical tasks must be performed to clear up loose ends:

- Expedite the receipt of invoices from contractors and vendors;
- Expedite the submission and approval of personnel expense reports;
- Coordinate the clearing out of offices occupied by owner representatives;
- Reclaim building and parking passes granted to owner representatives; and
- Expedite the submission and approval of quality inspection reports, shop inspection reports, vendor deliverables, and other documents stipulated on the vendor data and documentation requirements sheets.

The *contract close-out meeting*—This meeting should be held in the weeks following the owner's acceptance of the completion group deliverables. The meeting is chaired by the owner. Participants should include the key personnel from each side to review and sign off on the final documentation constituting closure by the owner. The agenda will typically include:

- Owner's evaluation of the contractor's performance on the project;
- Statutory declarations (signed by commissioners of oath or equivalent);
- Final payment release confirmation;
- WCB (Workers Compensation Board in Canada) clearance letter;
- Returns (by owner personnel)—passes, FOBs, tools;
- Liens/Claims/Equitable adjustments;
- Guarantees and warranties;
- Deficiencies and punch list;
- Completion certificate;
- Release of holdback (if applicable); and
- As-built drawings (if applicable).

The process owners of Stage 3 are the project manager, the supply chain manager, and the construction manager. Stage 3 should begin no later than two months before the submission date of each one of the group deliverables.

Stage 4—Wrap

The final stage leads to the physical and financial closure of the project. The close-out group, the digital archive, and the paper archive are prepared. The work begins one month prior to the last close-out deliverable and will typically overlap with Stage 3. It ends in the weeks following the completion acceptance of the project by the owner with the *postmortem review*. The activities associated with this stage are:

- Compilation of the project metrics, benchmarks, and TIC quantities;
- Compilation of the lessons learned;
- Root cause analyses of successes and failures;
- Compilation of go-forward constraints; and
- The postmortem review. This meeting should be held after the contract close-out meeting to review the final metrics achieved by the project.

MANAGEMENT OF RECORDS

The digital archive is the primary repository of project information for future purposes. It includes all digital forms of the records preserved, including native electronic files and folders, and electronic scans of paper records. The archive is effectively created from the folders and files remaining on the *project directory* after its contents have been cleansed in Stage 2.

By default, all contents of the project directory are to be deleted unless shown to be classifiable as a record.

Rules for Project Drive Cleansing

The starting point for the retention of records is the retention matrix, usually appended to the archiving plan and exemplified in Appendix 12. The matrix identifies what information type is to be retained in what file format. The matrix embodies the obligations carried by the applicable legislations. A good default format to start with is the PDF file format. Paper records should be preserved only when required by legislation or when bearing original signatures or substantive hand annotations. Generally speaking:

- Only native files of documents issued to the owner are kept.
- For deliverables to the owner, only the issued revisions are kept. Nonissued versions of the deliverables, whatever the file format, are deleted (variously named *working, deleted, superseded, archive, obsolete, personal*).
- Archived e-mails *only* include those documenting a final decision—specifically related to project deliverables and contract terms. All previous e-mail history strings are deleted. All other e-mails are deleted. E-mail records are to be preserved as Outlook PST folders, identified only by the individual's name, and stored in the subfolder PST in the *Archive Details* folder located under the project directory's root level.
- Owner-supplied templates, standards, specifications, and the like are to be kept in a single project folder. All instances of those documents occurring elsewhere within the project drive are to be deleted, especially from the supply chain management folders.
- PDF scans of signed/stamped documents are to be preserved in the same folder where the corresponding native files are preserved.
- Documents unrelated to the project's contract requirements are to be deleted (party invitations, commercial brochures, working copies of tracking spreadsheets).
- Finally, *all files* and *folders* are governed by the built-in filename limitation of 225 characters (which include folder paths). Originators of any document stored on the project drive are individually responsible for naming files within this limitation.

Rules for Content Cleansing

The digital archive is based upon the original but cleansed project directory structure. The rules for file redundancy, duplication, and transient instances, enunciated before, apply equally to folders. Additional rules for cleansing files and folders are listed in Appendix 13.

Rules for Pictures, Audio, and Video Files

These types of files do not usually qualify as records but may contain valuable information for future references. They can be preserved in the digital archive. For each of the three types, a description list should be created to capture the metadata of the files. The list should include, as a minimum:

- The file name (of the picture, audio file, or video file);
- The subject or nature of the file; and
- The reference to a specific matter kept in the project drive (for example, when a picture presents a defective nozzle weld on a pressure vessel, the reference will be against that pressure vessel name and/or number).

The *Archive Details* Folder

Prior to the creation of the digital archive, a new folder titled *Archive Details* should be appended to the project directory to summarize the contents of the digital archive. The contents of this folder could include, for example:

- Master folder and file register
- Digital archive register
- Electronic data management archive register
- Password list for files that are so protected
- Benchmark metrics spreadsheet
- Final TIC quantity metrics spreadsheet
- Completion documents, including scans of signed originals
- Individual files
- Audio and video files
    - Description list
    - Individual files

Paper Archive

The paper archive is assembled from printed documents that were bestowed *record* status. Like their digital kindred, printed files must be cleansed during Stage 2 before joining the final paper trail in accordance with the following general rules. Keep:

- Documents bearing an original signature from the project's leadership team, the owner's representatives, or a vendor's acknowledgment of acceptance of a purchase order. The exceptions to this rule are documents pertaining to project team personnel, such as project assignment authorization forms. Those are to be deleted.

- All original commercial documents (contracts and purchase orders, for example)
- Audit documents (technical and non-technical).
- Stamped documents—including drawing markups.

Delete or destroy any document that does not satisfy any one of these requirements.

ALEA JACTA EST[2]

With these final words, we have reached the end of exploration of the world of project management. Time to go manage a project!

NOTES

1. Three simple solutions are immediately available: (1) convert all documents in static image files with multiple versions of formats (bmp, jpeg, tif); (2) maintain a couple of computers with the original applications installed; and (3) regularly convert (*save as*) the old files into the current version of the file format.
2. The latin expression *alea jacta est* was made famous by Caesar, upon crossing the river Rubicon; the usual translation gives it the meaning "the die is cast."

19

FINAL WORDS

---

*"One traditional definition of 'management' in older English
dialect was, according to the Oxford English dictionary, 'to spread
manure.' This has not been lost on those of us who have observed,
and misguidedly sometimes employed, managers trained in punditry
who have pursued agendas consistent with that ancient description."*
Brian Day (The Economist, May 23, 2015).

ONE SIDE OF TWO COINS

The story of the linchpin of this book begins not with the dichotomy between
the promises and results of traditional project management (TPM), but with an
echo of this dichotomy heard in an altogether different setting. Back in September 2009, our daughter Gabrielle and son James were embarking on their learning journey in first grade and kindergarten, respectively. Their older brother
Michael was already an old-hand at the game as he entered fifth grade. Soon
afterward, our young ones brought a question home one evening that would
prove seminal to this book. What is the largest number? Their parents answered
that infinity was the largest number. The answer, so self-evident to the conceit
of age, was immediately rebutted by all three children. "What about one million million billion billion (also known as nonillion)?" clamored James. "Or two
million six billion trillion (a.k.a. six *octillion*)?" chimed in Gabrielle. Our explanations could not sway them. To them, there *had* to be a biggest number, and
that we, parents, simply did not want to admit our ignorance of it. The next day,
Michael asked his math teacher, who told him that infinity was not a number.
Aghast at this unexpected attack, your author stepped into the ring with his own
objection to the teacher's objections. But Michael stood his ground (cue in the
parent pride...): the teacher declared infinity a non-number, and that was that.

This is where the idea for this book took form. How could two diametrically-opposed answers be correct? Michael's teacher was right, of course, in that there is no such thing as the number infinity, *per se*, since basic arithmetic rules do not apply to it. On the other hand, infinity is a concept foundational for the entire edifice of mathematics and physics. Without it, differential and integral calculus cannot exist. No calculus means no jet engines, no iPad, no Wii. What goes for infinity goes for project management as well. If the science of project management is correct, why are projects failing by default rather than exception?

THE QUANTUM LEAP

The short answer is that TPM is not complete. Its precepts and principles *are not sufficient to deliver project success consistently.* There is more, much more to project failure than a failure to execute the plans. This book set out to redefine what we mean by a project, and what project management truly is. The new paradigms inform us that the correct perspective must begin and end with the owner. Projects are but a means to an end, to develop profitably performing assets (PPAs). These, in turn, are justified on the sole basis of delivering sustained investment returns to their shareholders over the life of these assets. Nothing else matters. The project is the investment vehicle to realize this asset. This perspective is often lost on owners and contractors alike, who continue to insist on measuring project success in terms of budget and schedule targets. Owners carry an immense reservoir of forgiveness of an arduous development when the asset is found to be more profitable than anticipated.

There will be resistance by some readers to accept this relegation of budget and schedule to second fiddle status. The promise of greater long-term investment returns may not suffice to overcome that resistance, reminding us of Arthur Shopenhauer's pronouncement on the life cycle of a new truth. First, the truth is ridiculed widely by the holders of the *status quo*. Then, it is violently resisted by those who are threatened by it. Finally, it inevitably becomes accepted universally, as if self-evident all along. The persistence of failure statistics reminds us that the *status quo* is often justified but rarely justifiable. Genuine project management is—in practical, *knee-deep-in-the-trenches* terms—about the ultimate asset and its profitable performance. It is a human endeavor, realized through relationships and constrained by people interactions. It is about execution over a landscape in which features must be quantified holistically *before* the work begins. It is carried out by people trained in the mechanics and mechanisms of the work to be done, and it is *managed* proactively on the basis of performance metricized in real time, on the basis of facts, in recognition of the actual reality of the stage upon which progress occurs. Project management is never just the sum of a theoretical construct built upon plans, processes, and procedures. It is about the human element underscoring everything else. Among the multitude of software tools and applications that suffuse the work of project professionals, it is still the human relationship that matters the most to the success of a project. In this hierarchy of project needs, the message is very much in resonance with the idea of human traits anchoring the future of the machine-enabled workplace that Geoff Colvin presents in his book, *Humans Are Underrrated*. In the end, we need only remember that people are led while everything else is managed.

MONEY

No discussion of project management can be taken seriously without addressing the issue of money. Money is a rightful obsession of project people, as it must be. But money is a tool, not a goal, as we saw throughout the text. Money is meant to be spent to acquire the most operating profitability in the future. That is why the concept of valunomy was introduced, in opposition to cost effectiveness. Valunomy views expenditures as investments; cost effectiveness regards them as hits to the bottom line. Choosing valunomy does not intimate greater development costs; cost effectiveness will.

EXPECTATIONS

The budget and schedule expectations are but two of a larger ensemble of expectations spicing up a project's execution. They will be voiced, imposed, and measured; calling forth once more the agency of the human element. Expectations are nothing more than tugs-of-war between people relationships. Expectations have a funny nature that is binary—binary in their *creation* and binary in their *exertion*. Some will be qualitative, others quantitative. Some will be imposed globally, some in highly specific areas. They will be either internal or external. Once named, they are imposed—*exertion*. The act of imposition self-generates its own expectation for the act. To impose implies tracking and assessing; to assess supposes a consequence. An assessment bereft of a consequence is an exercise in futility, a manifestation of the dreaded management style of creating the illusion of management. Incarnated into the idea of assessment is the axiom of execution management—to perform or justify.

To justify is to give leeway. It is to assign primacy of consideration to people ahead of the project. Justifying progress, or lack thereof, is easier at a personal level (and certainly less confrontational in the short term). The diffident manager is thus rewarded for seemingly fostering a more cooperative working environment. To justify is to avoid hard people decisions, thereby protecting the decider's ego. Justification also comes at a high price: the project's own probability of success. The danger of performance is the specter of a manager's guttural need for being right, fostering a zero-sum game. The danger with justification is a manager's fear of doing the right thing for the project. The trick, of course, is to appoint a manager who thrives on performance but is willing to submit his ego to the greater good (i.e., the project).

What's right for the project is what's right.

Within such a decision framework, the performance paradigm is solely able to create a predictable, reliable, and measurable execution landscape in which all players know from the outset what will keep them in or get them out, without any chance to hide. To echo the immortal words of Captain James T. Kirk:

"Sometimes, the needs of the one outweigh the needs of the many."

CHOICES AND DECISIONS

The act of project management can be summed up in two words: *choices* and *decisions*. The project exists in a perpetual state of flux as it evolves from concept to design to construction and finally, operations. Throughout this lengthy and oftentimes complex journey, the project is presented with choices for its leadership to consider. Thus, the owner chooses to initiate or abandon the thing; to set up the framework team or go directly to a project management consultant structure; to hire contractors or get the work done in-house; to scale up or down the configuration of the desired asset; to execute according to either TPM or PPA; or to execute differently, or not at all. These choices will be more than black and white, go/no-go, or yes/no. Many shades of gray will cast a shadow on the chessboard, as instances await a move from the leadership. Owners and managers exert far more influence than they realize on the nature of these choices. A project will succeed or fail, in part, on the judiciousness of the choices formulated by the leadership. It therefore helps to employ a leadership team that has a clue as to how to corral those choices.

Defining the choices is one thing. Deciding on which option to go with is another. In fact, it is the reverse side of the choice formulation, and the one that plays the greater part in making or breaking a project. Deciding on the execution philosophy between TPM and PPA, to give but one example, will have profound repercussions on all aspects of the project. Deciding to manage for performance rather than justification sets up an ensemble of expectations that is wholly different than the other case. Deciding to define a project in terms of a sequence of individual phases, rather than a continuous evolution toward a PPA, also sets in motion a whole set of contractual and financial mechanics that will shape the very nature of the work to be done. Decisions, in other words, are the crucibles in which project managers (PMs) are forged. And project management is cemented into existence through the power pouring out of a chosen PM. You, the reader, choose what choices to consider and what decisions will flow from those choices. You choose to decide, in order to decide what to choose.

The decision, as with most things in life, is yours to make.

****

Postscript: There is an interesting twist to the discussion of the number infinity. By the end of their first school year, Gabrielle and James had successfully derived a Gödel-like, mathematically consistent argument. First, they arrived on their own to the conclusion that there is such a thing as the largest number, one to rule them all. They named it *teddy infinity*. And how might one reach that number, you might ask? By counting to infinity an infinite number of times.

Children are the future, wouldn't you say?

PART 7—MISCELLANY

Appendices, bibliography, lexicon, and index.

APPENDICES

APPENDIX 1—AACE ESTIMATE TAXONOMY

Appendix 1

Estimate Class	Level of Project Definition	Usage	Methodology	Typical Accuracy Ranges		Typical Contingency
Class V	0% to 2%	Feasibility, Concept screening	Capacity factored, Rule of thumb, Expert judgment	L: -20% to -50% H: +30% to +100%		≥25%
Class IV	1% to 15%	Preliminary budget, Feasibility studies, Nonbinding proposals	Equipment factored, Historical/Budget quotes, Parametric models	L: -15% to -30% H: +30% to +50%		15–25%
Class III	10% to 40%	Budget authorization, Control estimate	Preliminary line items, Equipment quotes, Deterministic	L: -10% to -20% H: +10% to +30%		8–15%
Class II	30% to 70%	Forecast to complete, Project change order estimate, Bid tender	Bid cost, Detailed line items with forced take-offs	L: -5% to -15% H: +5% to +20%		5–10%
Class I	50% to 100%	Forecast to complete, Change order check estimate, Lump sum tender	Lump sum, Detailed line items with detailed take-offs	L: -3% to -10% H: +3% to +15%		2–5%

APPENDIX 2—BASELINE ASSET EXECUTION FRAMEWORK

1.	ASSET DEFINITION
1.1.	Capacity
1.2.	Location
1.3.	Plant inputs and outputs
1.3.1.	Feedstock
1.3.2.	Automation levels and controls
1.3.3.	Utility fluid and gas streams
1.3.4.	Emissions and effluent destinations
1.3.5.	Utility sources
1.3.6.	Self-generated
1.3.7.	Externally supplied
1.4.	Targets
1.4.1.	Economic
1.4.2.	Operations
1.4.3.	Reliability and maintainability
1.4.4.	Local and regional
1.4.5.	Corporate commitments
1.5.	Allocations
1.5.1.	Target budget
1.5.2.	Tolerance budget
1.5.3.	Target timelines
1.5.4.	Tolerance timelines
1.5.5.	Investment decision milestones
1.6.	Asset performance assessment metrics
2.	ASSET OWNERSHIP
2.1.	Proponents
2.2.	Name and interest
2.3.	Locations
2.4.	Hierarchy
2.4.1.	Organizational chart
2.4.2.	Executive committee
2.4.3.	Accountability matrix
3.	PROJECT ECOSYSTEM
3.1.	PECO management
3.1.1.	Interaction practices
3.1.2.	Conflict resolution
3.1.3.	PECO performance assessment metrics
3.1.4.	Accountability matrix

APPENDIX 3—PHASE EXECUTION PLAN

APPENDIX 4—TPM DELIVERABLE DEVELOPMENT CYCLE

	Phases		
Deliverable	2	3	4
Architectural drawings			C
Area classification drawing	S	C	
Basis of design	S	P	C
Battery limit tables		S	C
Bill of material for miscellaneous items			C
Block diagrams	S	C	
Building and construction specifications		S	C
Building drawings		S	C
Cable and conduit schedules		S	C
Catalyst and chemicals summary	S	P	C
Cause and effect diagrams	S	C	
Code compliance matrix	S	P	C
Commissioning and start-up procedures			C
Connection and termination diagrams		S	C
Constructability assessment		S	C
Construction scope of work			C
Control schematics		S	C
Control valve data sheet		S	C
Demolition drawings		S	C
Demolition requirements	S	P	C
Drawing list and status		C	
Effluent summary (gas, liquid, and solids)	S	P	C
Electrical design calculations		S	C
Electrical drawing list		S	C
Electrical equipment and material data sheets		S	C
Electrical equipment list	S	C	
Electrical load list and summary		S	C
Electrical site plan	S	P	C
Electrical specifications		S	C
Emergency systems survivability analysis		S	C
Emissions and noise	S	C	
Environmental design philosophy	S	P	C
Environmental impact assessments	S	C	

Equipment specifications and data sheets		S	C
Flushing and cleaning procedure		S	C
Foundation general arrangements	S	P	C
Geotechnical assessment	S	C	
Hazard and operability study (HAZOP)		S	C
Hazard assessment—qualitative	S	P	C
Hazard assessment—quantitative	S	P	C
Hazardous area design	S	C	
Hazardous material notes	S	C	
Heat and material balances	S	C	
Heat trace isometrics		S	C
Human factors analysis/ergonomics		S	C
HVAC equipment	S	P	C
HVAC schematics		S	C
Hydraulic calculations	S	P	C
Hydro test plan			C
Input to TIC estimate	S	P	C
Instrument index		S	C
Level of protection analysis		S	C
Long lead and major equipment list	S	P	C
Loop diagrams		S	C
Materiel identification	S	P	C
Mechanical equipment list	S	C	
One line diagram	S	P	C
Operating and control philosophy	S	C	
P&IDs	S	P	C
Panel board schedules			C
Permitting and approvals	S	P	C
PFDs	S	C	
Pipe stress analysis		S	C
Piping arrangements	S	P	C
Piping isometrics		S	C
Piping specifications	S	P	C
Plot plans	S	P	C
Power requirements	S	P	C
Process description	S	C	
Process simulation	S	P	C
Protective relay coordination and programming			C

Document	Phase 2	Phase 3	Phase 4
P-T diagrams		S	C
Relief and blowdown study	S	C	
Relief load summary		S	C
Relief valve data sheet		S	C
RFQ and RFP		S	C
Roads, paving, and drainage arrangements	S	P	C
Safeguarding drawings		S	C
Safeguarding manual		S	C
Safety case	S	P	C
Safety related instrumentation philosophy	S	P	C
SIL determination		S	C
Single line diagrams	S	C	
Site survey documents	S	P	C
Sizing—ancillary equipment		S	C
Sizing—major equipment	S	P	C
Sizing—process lines	S	C	
Sizing—utility lines		S	C
Smoke and gas ingress analysis		S	C
Specialty item data sheet		S	C
Standard designs and assemblies	S	C	
Structural framing general arrangements	S	P	C
Studies and reports		S	C
Symbol legend	S	C	
Tie-in list		S	C
Transient analysis		S	C
Transportation and lifting assessment	S	P	C
Underground services arrangement	S	P	C
Utility summary for all main operating cases	S	P	C
Weight control reports	S	P	C

Legend
Phase 2 = Initiation
Phase 3 = Baseline
Phase 4 = Planning
S = Start
P = Progress
C = Complete

APPENDIX 5—PARTIAL TPM-BASED WBS EXAMPLE

1.	PROJECT MANAGEMENT
1.1.	PEP
1.2.	Management plans and procedures
1.3.	Project KOM
1.4.	Discipline KOM
1.5.	C&P execution plan
1.6.	Construction management plan
2.	PROJECT ENGINEERING
2.1.	Phase package narratives
2.2.	Company review period
2.3.	Equipment lists
2.4.	Tie-in interface summaries
2.5.	Building list
2.6.	Electrical load list
2.7.	Utility consumption summary
2.8.	Effluent summary
2.9.	Independent technical review
2.10.	Independent technical review report
2.11.	Value engineering workshop
2.12.	Lessons learned review
2.13.	Technical integrity verification plan
3.	PROCESS
3.1.	PFD—plant
3.2.	PFD—utilities
3.2.1.	Interconnects
3.2.2.	WWT
3.2.3.	Flare units
3.2.4.	SSPID
3.2.5.	Lead sheets
3.2.6.	Overall flow schematics
3.2.7.	Storage and loading unit
3.3.	HAZOP
3.3.1.	P&ID Unit A000 fire and fresh water storage and distribution system
3.3.2.	PFD Unit A000 fire fighting system
3.3.3.	MSD Unit A000 fire and fresh water storage and distribution system
3.3.4.	Cause and effect diagram for Unit A000 fire fighting system
3.3.5.	Fireproofing zone MAP's

3.3.6.	Grid layout Unit A000 fire fighting system
3.3.7.	Fire fighting equipment layouts
3.3.8.	Hydraulic calculation sheet for fire water mains
3.3.9.	Typical installation drawings for firefighting system
3.3.10.	Overall scheme for FGS
3.3.11.	Etc.
3.4.	Studies and calculations
3.4.1.	Definition of dynamic simulation study
3.4.2.	Study Report: Start-up Procedure
3.4.3.	Study Report: Study for Future Tie-in
3.4.4.	Study Report: BOG Rate Calculation
3.4.5.	Noise study report
3.4.6.	Study Report: Dynamic Simulation Study for Single Compressors
3.4.7.	Study Report: Dynamic Simulation Study for Integral Compressors
3.4.8.	Etc.
3.5.	Input data to other disciplines
3.5.1.	Process data sheet—flow meters
3.5.2.	Process data sheet—control valves
3.5.3.	Etc.

APPENDIX 6—TPM PROJECT FILE STRUCTURE

1.	PURSUIT DOCUMENTATION
1.1.	Tender docs
1.2.	Correspondence
1.3.	Exec summary
1.4.	Final proposal
1.5.	Proposal appendices
1.6.	Working docs
1.7.	Commercial
1.8.	CVs
1.9.	Project profiles
1.10.	Covers spines CDs
1.11.	Risk assessment
2.	CORRESPONDENCE
2.1.	Incoming
2.1.1.	General
2.1.2.	Customer

11.1.22.2.   Marine
11.1.22.3.   Transport
11.1.22.4.   Geotech
11.1.22.5.   Water—wastewater
11.1.22.6.   Surface water engineering
11.1.22.7.   Contaminated sites
11.1.22.8.   Water resources
11.1.22.9.   Environmental impact assessment
11.1.22.10.   Environmental management
11.1.22.11.   Geophysics—geosciences
11.1.22.12.   Bioaquatics
11.1.22.13.   Risk assessment
11.1.23.   Geomatics
11.1.24.   Regulatory
11.1.25.   EDS
11.2.   Drawings
11.2.1.   Civil
11.2.1.1.   Administration
11.2.1.2.   Civil 3-D
11.2.1.3.   Deliverables
11.2.1.4.   DEPs
11.2.1.5.   InRoads
11.2.1.6.   LiDAR
11.2.1.7.   Models
11.2.1.8.   Outgoing
11.2.1.9.   Received
11.2.1.10.   References
11.2.2.   Drilling
11.2.3.   Electrical
11.2.4.   Mechanical
11.2.5.   HVAC
11.2.6.   Material handling
11.2.7.   Piping
11.2.8.   Pipelines
11.2.9.   Process
11.2.10.   Safety
11.2.11.   Structural
11.2.12.   Subsea
11.2.13.   Telecom
11.2.14.   Architectural
11.2.15.   Environmental planning

APPENDIX 7—PPA WBS EXAMPLE

1.	PLANT
1.1.	Installation 1
1.1.1.	Primary systems
1.1.1.1.	System 1
1.1.1.2.	Components
1.1.1.3.	Inputs—outputs
1.1.1.4.	Constraints—enablers
1.1.1.5.	Attributes—characteristics
1.1.1.6.	Targets—metrics
1.1.1.7.	Structures
1.1.1.8.	Utilities
1.1.1.9.	System ... "N"
1.1.2.	Secondary systems
1.1.2.1.	System 1
1.1.2.2.	System ... "N"
1.1.3.	Buildings
1.1.3.1.	Structures
1.1.3.2.	Foundations
1.1.3.3.	Deep undergrounds
1.1.4.	Communications
1.1.5.	Installation controls
1.1.6.	Effluents and emissions
1.1.7.	Security control
1.2.	Installation ... "N"
1.3.	Installation site-wide
1.3.1.	Circulation
1.3.2.	Distribution
1.4.	3-D model kernel
1.4.1.	Configuration management
1.4.2.	Documentation management
1.4.3.	Cloud database
1.4.4.	Nucleation database
2.	OPERATIONS
2.1.	Control center
2.2.	Emergency preparedness
2.3.	Labor and training
2.4.	Permits
2.5.	Security
2.6.	Shipping and receiving

3.	SERVICES
3.1.	Accounting
3.2.	Customs
3.3.	Legal
3.4.	Regulatory
3.5.	Maintenance
4.	MANAGEMENT
4.1.	Project
4.1.1.	Administration
4.1.2.	Controls and schedule
4.1.3.	Contract management
4.1.4.	Construction management
4.1.5.	Interface management
4.1.6.	Framework liaison
4.2.	Supply chain management
4.2.1.	Procurement
4.2.2.	Contracts
4.2.3.	Material management
4.2.4.	Logistics
4.3.	Project services
4.3.1.	Design systems
4.3.2.	IT systems
4.3.3.	Offices
4.3.4.	Communications

APPENDIX 8—EVENT CATALOG EXAMPLE

INSTALLATION XX			Sheet 1 of 5	PROJECT NAME AND NUMBER Lifecycle Phase 3
Week	Plan	Work	Event	Legend
1				
2				▉ Engineering
3	①			① Discipline action number (Axx) Color-coded to discipline
4				▉ Procurement
5				
6				▉ Contracts ▲① Event from discipline issue (Exx) Color-coded to discipline
7				
8				▉ Construction ✦① Decision (Dxx) Color-coded to discipline
9				
10				
11				ENGINEERING CHRONOLOGY
12	②			A1 Meeting to discuss topic 1. Minutes number MM001-1
13				A2 Drawing issued for issue 1. Drawing number Job123-PID-001 Rev A
14			✦①	A3 Site visit to discuss tope 2. Visit report number VR002-03
15				E1 Change of direction on issue 2, issued by Operations via email xxx
16				D1 Decision on issue 1, published by Project Directive PDE023
17	①			D2 Decision on issue 1, published by Project Directive PDE026
18				
19			▲①	PROCUREMENT CHRONOLOGY
20				A1 Meeting to discuss topic 89. Minutes number MM001-10
21			✦②	
22	③			
23				
24				
25				
26				SAFETY MANAGEMENT CHRONOLOGY
27	①			A1 Meeting to discuss topic 127. Minutes number MM125-2
28				
29				
30				
31				CONSTRUCTION CHRONOLOGY
32				A1 Meeting to discuss topic 127. Minutes number MM125-2
33				
34				
35				
36				
37				
38	①			
39				
40				

APPENDIX 9—EXAMPLE OF A DAILY CONSTRUCTION REPORT

GENERAL INSPECTION REPORT

Page 1 of 2

OWNER _____   **Date** 12-Mar-17

Project name _____   **Contractor** Desert Storm Welding Inc

Project number _____   **Superintendent** Harry Potting

Temp (F) High: 28   **Low:** 13   **Start time** 7:00   End time 20:15

Conditions Sunny   **Report Number** 28

PRODUCTION

ACTIVITY	Station		Feet Complete	Previous Day	Feet Today	ACTIVITY	Station		Feet Complete	Previous Day	Feet Today
	From	To					From	To			
Sandblasting			85%			Access			75%		
Welding			100%			Inspection			20%		
Coating			75%								
Backfill			25%								
Clean up			50%								

SAFETY

Discussed the importance of keeping your mind on the task and ask questions if you are not sure

GENERAL COMMENTS

1. Contractor had sandblasters on-site to continue blasting pipe
2. Inspector and operations representative on-site to perform the x-ray checks
3. Sent crew home for an 8 hour day because sandblasting was interfering with the x-ray checks

POTENTIAL EXTRA WORK

NONE

ENVIRONMENT

No impact

MILEAGE: 88 miles

Print	Date	Print	Date
INSPECTOR		**CHIEF INSPECTOR**	

APPENDIX 10—ARCHIVE PLAN CONTENTS

APPENDIX 11—COMPLETION PLAN CONTENTS

APPENDIX 12—RETENTION MATRIX

Category	Types	Digital (D)	Paper (P)
Signed documents (include all revisions)	Project reports	X	
	Letters	X	
	Minutes of meetings	X	
	Contracts and change authorizations	X	
	Project variation notices	X	
	Project change requests	X	
	Invoices	X	X
	Payment certificates	X	X
	Purchase orders	X	
	Expense reports	X	X
	Close-out forms from clients	X	
	Customer feedback	X	
	Third-party deliverables	X	
	Quality audit reports and peer review reports	X	
Stamped documents (include all versions)	Drawings	X	X
	Drawing squad check comments	X	X
	Project reports	X	
	Calculations	X	
	Inspection reports	X	
	Certificates	X	X
	Data sheets	X	
	Statutory declarations	X	X
	Third-party deliverables (final version)	X	X
Unsigned documents (include all revisions)	Baseline schedule	X	
	Monthly schedule updates	X	
	All project plans	X	
	Third-party deliverables	X	
	Client standards and specifications	X	
	Final key quantity tracking report	X	
	Final TIC key quantity tracking report	X	
	Project deliverables (including revisions)	X	
	Risk register (including revisions)	X	
	Lessons learned register (including revisions)	X	

	Client-supplied templates	X	
	Project presentations to client	X	
	3-D models (final configuration only) and simulations	X	
	Photos and videos	X	
Deleted documents	Administrative forms and weekly progress reports	X	X
	All templates other than client-supplied	X	X
	Copies and exemplars from other projects	X	X
	Copies of codes and standards (not client-specific)	X	X
	E-mails and Outlook PST folders	X	X
	Duplicate, obsolete, superseded, and empty working folders	X	
	Personnel project folders	X	
	Vendor marketing materials and brochures	X	X
	Presentations that are not directly linked to project	X	X
	Audio or video recordings of meetings	X	
	Travel itineraries	X	X
	Meeting agendas		

APPENDIX 13—CLEANSING RULES

Electronic documents. The rules are:

- For the purpose of storing a file in the project folder, the file name must *not* contain the whole document number:
  - GOOD: 04_Calcs\CHD\FINAL 612-PR-CAL\632 Rev A.pdf
  - BAD: 04_Calcs\CHD\FINAL\612-PR-CAL-632 Rev A.pdf
  - Exceptions: drawing files and pdf versions of *wet-signed* documents
- File names must be compact
- If file names are to contain dates, use numerical values instead of spelling out the date (I.E. 11-12-2013 instead of November 12, 2013)
- File names cannot be a long sentence (use key words to identify meaning)
- E-mail file names must be shrunk when the subject is too long
- Delete previous versions of a current file that will no longer be used
- Files must be saved in a single folder and appear *once* in the project drive; delete all other instances
- Delete duplicates of files, usually named "copy of ..."
- Delete multiple commented versions of a file once the final version is issued
- In instances of sorting in a folder, you might have to include a 0 in front of a number to make sense of a logical sequence for a double (or more) digit naming convention, particularly for doc control and references in appendix:
  - Foldername\document 01
  - Foldername\document 02
  - ...
  - Foldername\document "N"
- Instead of
  - Foldername\document 1
  - Foldername\document 2
  - ...

Project drive folders. The rules are:

- Maximum file path name cannot exceed 220 characters (including spaces)
- Folder names must be compact. Always abbreviate.
- Keep folder leveling at a minimum as Microsoft tends to have issues with deeply nested folders. Logically, think through leveling of folders

(e.g., would you create a separate paper file folder for each detail level or would you create a paper file folder that would contain the details?)

- Do not repeat the project number in a subfolder or file names; the project number is already identified
- Sub-folders must not repeat the name of a parent folder:
    - GOOD: Q:\owner\987654-00054\10 Eng\08 Process\04 Calcs\ CHD\ARCHIVE\CHD Liquids\
    - BAD: Q:\Owner\987654-00054\10_Eng\08 Process\04 Calcs\ CHD\ARCHIVE\Archive\
- Use the first part of a document numbering scheme as the folder name:
    - GOOD: Q:\Owner\987654-00054\10 Eng\08 Process\04 Calcs\03-00114-FT-7.7.1-RPT\
    - BAD: Q:\Owner\987654-00054\10_Eng\08_Process\04_Calcs\ 03-00114

For example:

- \03-00114-FT-7.7.1-RPT\2 Rev 1.pdf
- \03-00114-FT-7.7.1-RPT\3 Rev 1.pdf

- In each case, the file name is reduced in length. A bad example is:
    - \03-00114-FT-7.7.1-RPT\03-00114-FT-7.7.1-RPT-2 Rev 1.pdf
- Do not use a single sub-folder. Place all files directly in the parent folder:
    - \04 Calcs\CHD\03-00114-FT-7.7.1-RPT-2 Rev 1.pdf
    - \04 Calcs\CHD\03-00114-FT-7.7.1-RPT-3 Rev 1.pdf
    - \04 Calcs\CHD\03-00114-FT-7.7.1-RPT-4 Rev 1.pdf

    Instead of:

    - \04 Calcs\CHD\Reports\03-00114-FT-7.7.1-RPT-2 Rev 1.pdf
    - \04 Calcs\CHD\Reports\03-00114-FT-7.7.1-RPT-3 Rev 1.pdf
    - \04 Calcs\CHD\Reports\03-00114-FT-7.7.1-RPT-4 Rev 1.pdf
- Delete empty, obsolete, working, and superseded folders
- Do *not* create duplicate folders of an existing folder. Client specifications, standards, and templates, for example, should only appear once in the project directory. This is especially true for the engineering and procurement folders.
- Client-supplied templates and specifications should be stored in a logically named folder at the second level in the project folder hierarchy, and contain an Excel and a word list of the files included in the folder. Those lists will be used for rapid reference to those files when required elsewhere in other project folders.
- At close out, delete all folders and files copied from a previous project

BIBLIOGRAPHY

AACE. Practice 18R-97—*Cost estimate classification system as applied in engineering, procurement, and construction for the process industry.* AACE International publishers.

AACE. Practice 37R-06—*Schedule levels of detail as applied in engineering, procurement, and construction for the process industry.* AACE International publishers.

Al-Harbi, Al-Subhi (2001). *Application of the AHP in Project Management.* Int. J. Project Management, Vol. 19, 19–27.

ANSI-ISA 5.1 2009—*Flow diagrams for process plants—general rules.*

ISO 10628—*Flow diagrams for process plants—general rules.*

Anand, G., Ward, P. T. and Tatikonda, M. V. (2010). *Role of explicit and tacit knowledge in six sigma projects: an empirical examination of differential project success.* J. Operations Management, Vol. 28, 303–315.

Atkinson, Roger (1999). *Project management: cost, time and quality, two best guesses and a phenomenon, its [sic] time to accept other success criteria.* Int. J. Project Management, Vol. 17(6), 337–342.

Baron, Dennis. *Grammar and Gender.* Yale University Press, New Haven, CT, 1986. ISBN 978-0300038835. 260 pages.

Bartusiak, Marcia. *Black Hole: How an Idea Abandoned by Newtonians, Hated by Einstein, and Gambled on by Hawking Became Loved.* Yale University Press, New Haven, CT, 2015. ISBN 978-0-300-21085-9. 237 pages.

Becker, S. A. and Bostelman, M. L. (1999). *Aligning Strategic and Project Measurement Systems.* IEEE software, May/June, 46–51.

Belassi, W. and Tukel, O. I. (1996). *A New Framework for Determining Critical Success/Failure Factors in Projects.* Int. J. of Project Management, Vol. 14(3), 141–151.

Belsky, Scott. *Making Ideas Happen: Overcoming the Obstacles between Vision and Reality.* Penguin Editors, New York, NY, 2010. ISBN 9781101404355. 256 pages.

Bizony, Piers. *The Man Who Ran the Moon.* Thunder's Mouth Press, New York, NY 2006. ISBN 1-56025-751-2. 256 pages.

Bock, Laszlo. *Work Rules! Insights from inside Google That Will Transform How You Live and Lead.* Twelve Editors, New York, NY, 2015. ISBN 978-14555-5479-9. 416 pages.

Bourne, M., Neely, A., Platts, K. and Mills, J. (2002). *The Success and Failure of Performance Measurement Initiatives*. Int. J. Operations and Production Management, Vol. 22 (11), 1288–1310.

Boyer, Carl B. *A History of Mathematics, 2nd Edition*. John Wiley & Sons, Inc., New York, NY, 1991. ISBN 0-471-54397-7. 736 pages.

Briand, L. C., Differding, C. M. and Rombach, H. D. (1997). *Practical Guidelines for Measurement-Based Process Improvement*. ISERN-96-05.

Brynjolsson, Erik and McAffee, Andrew. *Race against the Machine*. Digital Frontier Press, 2012. ISBN 978-0984725113. 98 pages.

Buchtik, Liliana. *Secrets to Mastering the WBS in Real-World Projects*. Project Management Institute Inc., Newton Square, PA, 2013. ISBN 978-1-62825-033-6. 203 pages.

Caron, F., Ruggeri, F. and Merli, A. (2012). *A Bayesian Approach to Improve Estimate at Completion in Earned Value Management*. Project Management Journal, Vol. 44(1), 3–16.

Cartledge, Paul. *Thermopylae—The Battle that Changed the World*. The Overlook Press, New York, NY, 2006. ISBN-10 1-58567-566-0. 313 pages.

Chan, Albert P. C. and Chan, Ada P. L. (2004). *Key Performance Indicators for Measuring Construction Success*. Benchmarking: An International Journal, Vol. 11(2), 203–221.

Chin, Gary. *Agile Project Management: How to Succeed in the Face of Changing Project Requirements*. AMACOM Div. American Mgmt. Assn., New York, NY, 2004. ISBN 978-0814427-361. 224 pages.

Clausewitz, Carl von. *On War*. Wordsworth Editions Limited, Hertfordshire, Great Britain, 1997. ISBN 1-85326-482-2. 373 pages.

Coase, Ronald H. *The Nature of the Firm*. Economica 4(16), 386–405, 1937.

Colvin, Geoff. *Talent Is Overrated*. Portfolio publishers, New York, NY, 2008, ISBN 978-1-59184-294-8. 240 pages.

Colvin, Geoff. *Humans Are Underrated: What High Achievers Know That Machines Never Will*. Penguin Publishing Group, New York, NY, 2015. ISBN 978-1-59184-720-5. 256 pages.

Connors, R., Smith, T. and Hickman, C. *The Oz Principle: Getting Results through Individual and Organizational Accountability*. Penguin Group (USA), New York, NY, 2004. ISBN 978-1-59184-024-4. 232 pages.

Cooke-Davies, Terry. (2002). *The Real Success Factors on Projects*. Int. J. Project Management, Vol. 20, 185–190.

Cropper, William H. *Great Physicists*. Oxford University Press, New York, NY, 2001. ISBN 0-19-517324-4. 512 pages.

Dailey, Robert. *Organisational Behaviour*, course material, Edinburgh Business School, Heriot-Watt University, Edinburgh, U.K., 2011.

Deane, R. H., Clark, T. B. and Young, A. P. (1997). *Creating a Learning Project Environment: Aligning Project Outcomes with Customer Needs.* Information Systems Management, 54–60.

DeLone, W. H. and McLean, E. R. (1992). *Information Systems Success: The Quest for the Dependent Variable.* Information Systems Research Vol. 3(1), 60–95.

Deming, Edwards W. *Out of the Crisis.* MIT Press, Boston, MA, 2000. ISBN 978-0262541152. 507 pages.

Deming, Edwards W. *The New Economics for Industry, Government, and Education, Second Edition.* MIT Press, Boston, MA, 2000. ISBN 978-0262541169. 266 pages.

Dewey, Frederick Holland (translator). *Caesar's Commentaries on the Gallic War.* Translation Publishing Company Inc., New York, NY, 1918.

Dryden, Ken. *The Game, 30th Anniversary Edition.* Triumph Books, LLC., Chicago, IL, 2013. ISBN 978-1600789618. 320 pages.

Dvir, D., Lipovetsky, S., Shenhar, A. and Tishler, A. (1998). *In Search of Project Classification: A Non-Universal Approach to Project Success Factors.* Research Policy 27, 915–935.

Dvir, D., Lipovetsky, S., Shenhar, A. and Tishler, A. (1997). *The Relative Importance of Project Success Dimensions.* R&D Management Vol. 27(2), 97–106.

El-Reedy, Mohamed A. *Construction Management for Industrial Projects.* Wiley and Sons Inc., New York, NY, 2011. ISBN 978-0470878163. 412 pages.

Fagan, Garret G. *Great Battles of the Ancient World—Lecture Transcript Book.* The Great Courses Publishers, Chantilly, Virginia, 2005.

Faraday, Michael. *Experimental Researches in Chemistry and Physics.* Taylor & Francis e-library, London, UK, 2005. ISBN 0-203-21069-7.

Feynman, Richard P. *The Pleasure of Finding Things Out.* Perseus Publishing, Cambridge, MA, 1999. ISBN 978-0465023950. 288 pages.

Feynman, Richard. *The Character of Physical Law.* Random House, Inc., New York, NY, 1994. ISBN 978-0679601272. 192 pages.

Flemming, Q. and Koppelman, J. M. (1998). *Earned Value Project Management—A Powerful Tool for Software Projects.* The Journal of Defense Software Engineering, July, 19–23.

Foley, Phillip. *Span of Control—29 Success Secrets.* Emereo Publishing 2015, ISBN 978-1488857669. 30 pages.

Freeman, M. and Beale, P. (1992). *Measuring Project Success.* Project Management J. Vol. 23(1), 8–17.

Fu, H-S. and Ou, J-R. (2013). *Combining PCA with DEA to Improve the Evaluation of Project Performance Data: A Taiwanese Bureau of Energy Case Study.* Project Management J. Vol. 44(1), 94–106.

Fukuyama, Francis. *The End of History and the Last Man.* Free Press Publishing, New York, NY, 2006. ISBN 978-0-02-910975-5. 433 pages.

Fukuyama, Francis. *The Origins of Political Order.* Farrar, Strauss and Giroux Publishers, New York, NY, 2012. ISBN 978-0-374-53322-9. 608 pages.

Giaglis, G. (2001). *A Taxonomy of Business Process Modeling and Information Systems Modelling Techniques.* Int. J. Flexible Manufacturing Systems, Vol. 13, 209–228.

Griffin, A. and Page, A. L. (1996). *PDMA Success Measurement Project: Recommended Measures for Product Development Success and Failure.* J. Product Innovation Management, Vol. 13, 478–496.

Hackman, J. R. and Oldham, G. (1976). *Motivation through the Design of Work: A Test of a Theory. Organizational Behavior and Human Performance*, 250–279.

Hackman, J. R. (2002). *Leading Teams: Setting the Stage for Great Performances.* Harvard Business Review Press, Boston, MA.

Harnish, Verne. *Scaling Up.* Gazelles, Inc., Ashburn, Virginia, 2014. ISBN 978-0-9860195-5-5. 256 pages.

Hearn, Marcus and Howard, Ron. *The Cinema of George Lucas.* Harry N. Abrams Publishers, New York, NY, 2005. ISBN 978-0810949683. 264 pages.

Kant, Immanuel. *Observations on the Feeling of the Beautiful and Sublime, 2nd Revised Edition.* University of California Press, Oakland, CA, 2004. ISBN 978-0520240780. 124 pages.

Kaplan, R. S. and Norton, D. P. (2001). *Transforming the Balanced Scorecard from Performance Measurement to Strategic Management: Part 2.* Accounting Horizons, Vol. 15(2), 147–160.

Keays, Steven J. *Project Assessment Metrics.* Originally published on www.naiad.ca, 2014.

Kendra, K. and Taplin, L. J. (2004). *Project Success: A Cultural Framework.* Project Management Journal, April, 30–45.

Kerzner, Harold. *Project Management—A Systems Approach to Planning, Scheduling, and Controlling, 9th Edition.* John Wiley & Sons, Inc., Hoboken, NJ, 2006. ISBN 978-0-471-74187-9. 1296 pages.

Kissinger, Henry. *On China.* Penguin Books Publishers, New York, NY, 2012. ISBN 978-0143121312. 612 pages.

Kissinger, Henry. *World Order.* Penguin Press, New York, NY, 2014. ISBN 978-1-59420-614-6. 432 pages.

Ko, C. and Cheng, M. (2007). *Dynamic Prediction of Project Success Using Artificial Intelligence.* J. Construction Engineering and Management, Vol. 133(4), 316–324.

Langhorne, John and William (translators). *Plutarch's Lives.* Harper and Brothers Publishers. New York, NY, 1851. 774 pages.

Latham, G. and Pinder, C. (2005). *Work Motivation Theory and Research at the Dawn of the 21st Century. Annual Review of Psychology*, 56, 485–516.

Mandelbrot, Benoit B. *The Fractal Nature Geometry of Nature*. W.H. Freeman and Company, New York, NY, 1983. ISBN 0-7167-1186-9. 468 pages.

Marsden, Philip. *Rising Ground: A Search for the Spirit of Place*. London, UK, 2014. ISBN: 9781847086280. 352 pages.

Martin, K., Cullen, J., Johnson, J. and Parboteeah, K. (2007). *Deciding to bribe: A cross-level analysis of firm and home country influences on bribery activity. Academy of Management Journal*, 50, 1401–1422.

Martin, Richard. *Brilliant Manoeuvres—How to Use Military Wisdom to Win Business Battles*. Global Professional Publishing, 2012. ISBN 978-1-906-40385-0. 280 pages.

McGregor, D. (1961). *The Human Side of Enterprise*. Van Nostrand, Princeton, NJ.

Menches, C. and Hanna, A. (2005). *Quantitative Measurement of Successful Performance from the Project Manager's Perspective*. J. Construction Engineering and Management, Vol. 132(12), 1284–1293.

Merrow, Edward W. *Industrial Megaprojects*. John Wiley & Sons, Inc., Hoboken, N.J., 2011. ISBN 978-0-470-93882-9. 384 pages.

Milosevic, D. and Patanakul, P. (2005). *Standardized Project Management May Increase Development Project Success*. Int. J. Project Management, Vol. 23, 181–192.

Nasser, Sylvia. *Grand Pursuit: The Story of Economic Genius*. Simon and Schuster Editors, New York, NY, 2011. ISBN 978-0684872995. 376 pages.

NSPE. *Engineering Stages of New Product Development*. National Society of Professional Engineers publisher. Alexandria, VA, 2013.

O'Connell, Fergus. *How to Run Successful Projects III: The Silver Bullet*. Addison Wesley, New York, NY, 2001. ISBN 978-0201748062. 322 pages.

OECD. (2014). OECD *Foreign Bribery Report: An Analysis of the Crime of Bribery of Foreign Public Officials*. OECD Publishing. DOI: 10.1787/978926 4226616-en.

Ojiako, U., Johansen, E. and Greenwood, D. (2008). *A qualitative re-construction of project measurement criteria*. Industrial Management & Data Systems, Vol. 108(3), 405–417.

Olsson, N., Johansen, A., Langlo, J. A. and Torp, O. (2008). *Project ownership: implications on success measurement*. Measuring Business Excellence, Vol. 12(1), 39–46.

Organ, D. and Hammer, J. (1982). *Organizational Behavior 2nd Edition*. Business Publications, Plato, TX.

Orr, Bobby. *Orr: My Story*. G.P. Putnam's Sons, New York, NY, 2013. ISBN 978-0399161759. 304 pages.

Ouchi, W. and Dowling, J. *Defining Span of Control*. Administrative Sciences Quarterly, Vol. 19, 1974.

Pais, Abraham. *Subtle Is the Lord: The Science and Life of Albert Einstein*. Oxford University Press, Oxford, UK, 1982. ISBN 0-19-853907. 576 pages.

Parfitt, M. K. and Sanvido, V. E. (1993). *Checklist of Critical Success Factors for Building Projects*. J. Management in Engineering, Vol. 9(3), 243–249.

Pask, Colin. *Magnificent Principia*. Prometheus Books, Amherst, NY, 2013. ISBN 978-61614-745-7. 528 pages.

Paulson, Boyd and Barrie, Donald. *Professional Construction Management, 3rd Edition*. McGraw Hill Inc., Toronto, 1991. ISBN 978-0070038899. 577 pages.

Pfeffer, J. (1994). *Competitive Advantage through People*. Harvard Business School Press, Cambridge, MA.

Porter, M. (2011). *The Five Competitive Forces That Shape Strategy*. Harvard Business Review Press, Boston, MA.

Project Management Institute. *A Guide to the Project Management Body of Knowledge (PMBOK® Guide)—Fifth Edition*. Project Management Journal 44.3 (2013). ISBN 978-1-935589-67-9. 589 pages.

Reynolds, David West. *Apollo—The Epic Journey to the Moon*. Tehabi Book, Inc., San Diego, CA, 2002. ISBN 0-15-100964-3. 272 pages.

Sawyer, Ralph D. (translator). *The Art of War*. Westview Press, Boulder, CO, 1994. ISBN 0-8133-1951-X. 375 pages.

Schmidt, Eric. *How Google Works*. Grand Central Publishing, New York, NY, 2014. ISBN 987-1-4555-8234-1. 304 pages.

Schmidt, Terry. *Strategic Project Management Made Simple: Practical Tools for Leaders and Teams*. Wiley Editors, New York, NY, 2009. ISBN 978-0470411582. 272 pages.

Schom, Alan. *Napoleon Bonaparte*. HarperCollins Publishers, New York, NY, 1997. ISBN 0-06-092958-8. 944 pages.

Schroeder, Manfred. *Fractals, chaos, power laws*. W.H. Freeman and Company, New York, NY, 1991. ISBN 0-7167-2136-8. 429 pages.

Senior, Bolivar A. and Halpin, Daniel W. *Construction Management, 4th Edition*. Wiley and Sons Inc., New York, NY, 2010. ISBN 978-0-470-44723-9. 460 pages.

Shenhar, A. J., Tishler, A., Dvir, D., Lipovetsky, S. and Lechler, T. (2002). *Refining the Search for Project Success Factors: A Multivariate, Typological Approach*. R&D Management, Vol. 32(2), 111–126.

Stanleigh, M. (2006). *From Crisis to Control: New Standards for Project Management*. Ivey Business Journal, March/April, 1–4.

Stark, John. *Product Lifecycle Management*. Springer-Verlag, London, U.K., 2011. ISBN 978-0-85729-4546-0-1.

Sun, Yong Sun and Ma, Lin and Robinson, Warwick et al. *Engineering Asset Management and Infrastructure Sustainability.* Springer Publishing, London, U.K., 2012. ISBN 978-085729-301-5. pages 885–899.

Taleb, Nassim Nicholas. *The Black Swan.* Random House, New York, NY, 2007. ISBN 978-1-4000-6351-2. 444 pages.

Taleb, Nassim Nicholas. *Fooled by Randomness.* Random House, New York, NY, 2005. ISBN 0-8129-7521-9. 368 pages.

Taleb, Nassim Nicholas. *Antifragile—Things That Gain from Disorder.* Random House, New York, NY, 2014. ISBN 978-0-8129-7968-8. 472 pages.

Tung, R. (1991). *Handshakes across the Sea: Cross-Cultural Negotiating for Business Success. Organizational Dynamics* (Winter), 30–40.

United Nations Convention against Corruption, 2004.

Watson, D. and Baumol, E. (1967). *Effects of locus of control and expectation of future control upon present performance. Journal of Personality and Social Psychology,* 6, 212–215.

Wohlin, C. and Mayrhauser, A. von. (2001). *Assessing Project Success Using Subjective Evaluation Factors.* Software Quality Journal, Vol. 9, 43–70.

LEXICON

ACRONYMS

a.k.a.	Also Known As
AACE	Association for the Advancement of Cost Engineering
AAR	After Action Review
ABSA	Alberta Boiler Safety Authority
AP	Accountable Party
AP/AR	Accounts Payable/Accounts Receivable
APEGA	Association of Professional Engineers and Geoscientists of Alberta
ASME	American Society of Mechanical Engineers
BAEF	Baseline Asset Execution Framework
Bopsaat	Bunch of people sitting around a table
C&P	Contract and Procurement
CAD	Computer Aided Design
CAE	Computer Aided Engineering
CAPEX	Capital Expenditure
CAPP	Canadian Association of Petroleum Producers
CE	Common Era
CoA	Codes of Accounts
COTS	Commercial-off-the-shelf
CPI	Cost Performance Index
CRN	Canadian Registration Number
CTR	Cost-Time Resource
DBM	Design Basis Memorandum/Manual
DD	Detailed Design
DoD	U.S. Department of Defense
DoDoDab	who DOes what, who DOesn't, avoid DABbling
E&P	Engineering and Procurement
EBIDTA	Earnings Before Interest, Tax, Depreciation and Amortization
EDS	Engineering Design Specifications
EP	Engineering and Procurement
EPC	Engineering, Procurement, and Construction

EPCM	Engineering, Procurement, and Construction Management
ERP	Enterprise Resource Planning
FEA	Finite Element Analysis
FEED	Front-End Engineering and Design
FOE	Finance One's Existence
GD&T	Geometric Dimensioning and Tolerancing
GUI	Graphical User Interface
HAZOP	Hazard and Operability
HSSE	Health, Safety, Social, Environmental
IETM	Interactive Electronic Technical Manuals
IFC	Issued for Construction
IP	Intellectual Property
ITT	Invitation to Tender
JCM	Job Characteristic Model
JOE	Justify One's Existence
KPI	Key Performance Indicator
LCC	Life-cycle Costs
LNG	Liquefied Natural Gas
M&M	Mechanics and Mechanisms
MOC	Management of Change
MOE	Maintain One's Existence
MPI	Manpower Performance Index
MTBF	Mean-Time-between-Failure
MTTF	Mean-Time-to-Failure
NCO	Non-Commissioned Officer
NHL	National Hockey League
O&S	Operations and Support
OBaS	On Budget and Schedule
OLE	Object Linking and Embedding
OPEX	Operating Expenditure
P&ID	Process and Instrumentation Diagrams
PAM	Performance Assessment Metrics
PECO	Project Ecosystem
PEP	Project/Phase execution plan
PFD	Process Flow Diagrams
PIM	Project Information Management or Manager
PIPA	Personal Information Protection Act
PIPEDA	Personal Information Protection and Electronic Documents Act
PM	Project Manager
PMC	Project Management Consultant
PMI	Project Management Institute

PMO	Project Management Office
PMP	Project Management Professional
PP	Probate Party
PPA	Profitably Performing Asset
RFP	Request for Proposal
ROI	Return on Investment
RP	Responsible Party
SAGD	Steam-Assisted Gravity Drainage
SCM	Supply Chain Management
SCP	Supply Chain Partner
SME	Subject Matter Expert
SOE	Standard Operating Environment
SOL	Standard Operating Landscape
SPI	Schedule Performance Index
SPT	Scope Project Team
TCO	Total Cost of Ownership
TIC	Total Installed Cost
UTP	Unit Transformation Process
TPM	Traditional Project Management
TRIF	Total Recordable Incident Frequency
VDDR	Vendor Data and Documentation Requirements
WBS	Work Breakdown Structure
WCB	Workers Compensation Board
WMD	Weapon of Meddlesome Destruction
WYSIN	What You See Is Not
W5H	What, Why, When, Where, Who, and How
ZMP	Zero Marginal Product

SYMBOLS

a, b	Generic real number variables
e_c	Additional costs required by extra work to correct/complete the outputs
h	Total of direct reports
i,j,l	Summation indices
m, n	Total number
o	Index indicating operation
p	Index indicating phase number
wd	Duration factor, +1 if maximized, −1 if minimized
wo	Output factor, +1 if maximized, −1 if minimized

A_p	Allocation of a phase
C_p	Completeness factor of a phase
F_j	Functional, grouping several related R_i values together
F_o	Functional, grouping several related R_o values together
FS	Supervisor Factor
Ic	Accrued costs during time interval D to produce the outputs
K_1	Success factor of a set of related F_j
K_o	Success factor of a set of related operational F_o
O	Number of outputs generated at the end of the D interval
Q	Allocation deployment efficiency
R_i	Ratio of actual value to target value
R_o	Ratio of actual value to target value for the operation
SK	Project execution efficiency
TS	Total of salaries of a group of direct reports
V	Valunomy
W	Weighing factor
Y_p	Phase weight factor

INDEX

Page numbers followed by "*f*" and "*t*" indicate figures and tables respectively; and those followed by "n" indicate note.